10/27/09

Dear Dan –

Thanks for ~~your~~ \text{[illegible]} years.

I hope you enjoy my attempt to restore some balance into this debate.

Thanks –

All my best...

[signature]

the Quest for JUSTICE
IN THE MIDDLE EAST

GERALD A. HONIGMAN

A STRANG COMPANY

THE QUEST FOR JUSTICE IN THE MIDDLE EAST by Gerald Honigman
Published by Creation House
A Strang Company
600 Rinehart Road
Lake Mary, Florida 32746
www.strangbookgroup.com

All Internet sources accessed June 16 and 17, 2009.

Illustrations 1, 5, and 6 courtesy of AGS Consulting; 2 and 3 reproduced under
the Creative Commons Attribution 3.0 licensed by users Alexander Z. and
Steerpike, respectively; 4 courtesy CNG coins, www.cngcoins.com.

Publisher's Note: The views expressed in this book are not necessarily the views
held by the publisher.

Design Director: Bill Johnson
Cover design by Justin Evans

Library of Congress Control Number: 2009931063
International Standard Book Number: 1-978-59979-854-7

First Edition

09 10 11 12 13 — 9 8 7 6 5 4 3 2 1
Printed in the United States of America

CONTENTS

FOREWORD

FROM TIME TO time, we hear from world leaders such phrases as "just cause," "freedom and democracy," "human rights and democracy," "peace in the Middle East," "taking the moral high ground," and so forth.

Most people of the region, and in particular minorities (or even oppressed majorities) such as Ahwazi and Palestinian Arabs, Berbers, Assyrians, Kurds, Copts, Jews, black Africans in Darfur and in the south of the Sudan, Druze, and so forth view these world leaders with mistrust. There is a suspicion of all those regional regimes and world leaders when they echo those phrases.

In the not-too-distant past, similar to what happened when Europeans killed and collaborated in the murder of millions of Jews during the Holocaust, Iraqi dictator Saddam Hussein used chemical weapons and launched the Arabs' own Anfal genocide against the Kurds. Arabs likewise have committed similar atrocities against black Africans. Turkey's mass slaughter of Armenians and Kurds, Arab Syria's murder and ethnic cleansing of Kurds, Iran's violence against Ahwazi Arabs, Kurds, Baluchis, and others, are just some of still other examples of this.

All of the above was happening right under the noses of all nations and leaders, yet most either watched it, supported it in one form or another, pretended they did not see or denied it, or funded it. And to this day they, therefore, have helped to maintain those unjust treatments. So, how can the people of the region accept any statements or phrases at face value from those leaders or ever trust them?

In our view, security, stability, and peace cannot be established in the Middle East while dictatorial regimes or tyrants continue to play the role in the region that they have been playing for millennia. In the modern age, such regimes want to keep the boundaries or states that were created according to French and British interests starting more than one hundred years ago and use Islam as a mask to hide personal ambitions, nationalistic agendas, maintenance of power, and so forth. Thus, they use Islam to radicalize people and promote terrorist groups to go after so-called enemies of Islam. In the case of Syria, Iraq, and others, they use religion to fight the state of Israel, maintain a state of emergency in the country, loot all public resources, and punish advocates of democracy in their own countries. They use the Jews, especially, as a scapegoat for all of their own homegrown ills.

In essence, they are looking to defeat democracy and globalization and blame all the problems on the West and Israel. In reality, many Muslims who do not adhere to the pan-Arab agenda recognize, through the Quran itself, the age-old connections of the Jewish people to the land of Israel.

We want justice for all, meaning that all people of the region need to be considered for any peace deals and undoing past sins.

If all the minorities and/or wronged people of the Middle East were to be part of a new Middle East and gain a share of the justice due them, we would have a win-win formula that could be used to help undo the past centuries of dark history. Arabs, Berbers, black Africans, Kurds, Jews, and others all would be part of it. Tens of millions of suppressed, stateless Kurds, for example, would at last have one country, as would Jews, Berbers, and others. And Arabs would have their already existing multiple states as well.

So, the map of the Middle East needs to be redrawn somewhat to undo previous injustices.

Unfortunately, what we actually see from the West is a clear message that they are not interested in human rights, democracy, or freedom and want to continue the status quo, except for the Palestinian Arab issue.

Again, you must deal with the Middle East as whole, including all peoples who were wronged, and be fair to all in order to create that win-win situation to stop radicalization and violence. It is important to allow those earlier artificial boundaries for the states to be redrawn or to develop a new map for the Middle East.

Palestinian Arabs suffered more because of Arab actions and decisions that denied others justice than those of Israel. In fact, if Arab regimes would have left Palestinian Arabs and Jews to eventually make a peace deal between themselves, the Palestinian Arabs would probably have been much better off than they are today. So, again, Arab regimes use Islam, Arabism, and the Palestinian Arab issue to maintain the status quo and blame problems on others.

Finally, promoting true democracy as an alternative; removing legitimacy from murderous, oppressive regimes; and promoting interfaith dialogue, understanding that the Arab-Israeli conflict in particular involves not only Islam vs. Israel, but Pan-Arab nationalism vs. Israel, are all important if these problems are ever to be resolved. Such Arab attitudes must also be addressed by others in the region as well (especially Turks and Iranians) if the suffering of tens of millions of other people throughout the region is to end.

It is important for the United States, Europe, and others to remove their protection from and stop ignoring the actions of such oppressive regimes as that of the Arab nationalist Ba'ath in Syria and support democracy advocates there, in Iran, Turkey, Iraq, Egypt, Morocco, the Sudan, Algeria, and elsewhere.

Mr. Honigman's book argues in detail for just such a solution. It presents a look at justice in the region from a much broader perspective than the view that is so prevalent today, which only addresses the Arab cause.

—Dr. Sherkoh Abbas
Kurdistan National Assembly of Syria

***

It is an honor to endorse Gerald Honigman's book, *The Quest for Justice in the Middle East: The Arab-Israeli Conflict in Greater Perspective.*

Jerry is a friend and a great writer. His book brings out the greater human perspective in the Arab-Israeli conflict, shouting from the heart to a world that has shut its ears to the suffering of the Jewish people and also to others in the region too often ignored as well.

When I speak about peace with Israel, I am often told that I am credible because I am an Arab and not a Jew. But why is that? Who can represent Jewish injustice more than Jews themselves? And is it not time to discuss "justice" in the broader perspective? That is why this book is vital. It is time for the world to listen.

This book will open minds and hearts to the quest for justice for all of the Middle East's peoples—not only Arabs.

The book represents a small voice of only relatively few people in this world. But if minorities such as the Jewish people and others in the region do not get justice, then true justice does not exist. Israel is surrounded by a tribal culture where justice is only given to those related by blood inside the tribe of Dar ul-Islam (sometimes not even there), and no one else.

This book is a cry for justice that will have a sobering effect on a world that is, for convenience, becoming more and more anti-Semitic.

—Nonie Darwish, author
Cruel and Usual Punishment and *Now They Call Me Infidel*

INTRODUCTION

People of the Book! Bear in mind the words of Moses "Enter, my people, the holy land which Allah has assigned for you."

—THE QURAN, SURA 5:20–21, THE TABLE

Then We (Allah) said unto the Israelites: "Dwell in this land. When the promise of the Hereafter comes to be fulfilled, We shall assemble you all together."

—THE QURAN, SURA 17:104, THE NIGHT JOURNEY

I GUESS YOU CAN say that I have been preparing for this book most of my life. My father, twenty-one-year-old Edward Honigman, now of blessed memory, came home from four years in World War II (U.S. Navy Armed Guard), married his seventeen-year-old bride, Sylvia Serota, and a few years later, well, let's just say that their subsequent timing was just about perfect. Lieutenant Edward Honigman would later serve for almost three decades in the Philadelphia Police Department.

I was born on President Harry S. Truman's birthday, May 8, 1948—less than a week before the rebirth of Israel. President Truman would soon fight his own State Department (and others as well) to grant American recognition to the old/new nation of the Jews.

Israel and I both turned sixty on the exact same day on the Western calendar in 2008. Being lunar, the Hebrew calendar differs from year to year.

Prior to returning home from the war, while at port in Alexandria, many years later Dad relayed to me this story, which still sends chills up my spine.

While sitting in a bar in Egypt with some shipmates, he noticed soldiers entering the building wearing Star of David patches on their uniforms. Dad struck up a conversation and learned that they were members of Great Britain's Jewish Brigade. Besides many other Jews serving in the Brits' regular armed forces, these soldiers were mainly from that small part of the original 1920 Mandate of Palestine, which would later become Israel.

Near the end of the conversation, one of the Brigade members told my father, "G_d willing, when this is over, you'll return home and all of this will be a memory. But, for us, it will all be just starting again." He was, of course, referring to the fight Jews would subsequently have with both the Brits themselves—who

1

were backing off from their earlier promises of partition (remember the movie *Exodus*?)—and with the Arabs.

On another stop in Aden, in the southern Arabian Peninsula, one of Dad's shipmates told him to call an Arab who they were doing business with "Yahud." Not knowing what was up, Dad played along with his buddy. The distraught Arab then responded, "Curse me, spit on me, curse my family, but please, please, sir, never call me that." Dad had called him a Jew.

My mother, Sylvia, active since early childhood in Jewish causes (especially the rebirth of the Jewish state), would later become—in addition to an IRS section chief—president of both her local Hadassah chapter and of her synagogue, and active in many other organizations dedicated to helping people of all faiths and ethnicities.

Now, with this as background, let me begin.

A great man once summed up the Arab–Israeli conflict as appetite versus starvation. We will revisit him a bit later. Indeed, the scope of his analogy goes far beyond what he thought at the time, back in 1937, for the same Arab mind-set that allows no room whatsoever for justice for Jews (one-half of whom in Israel were refugees from the so-called "Arab"/Muslim world) also denies justice to scores of millions of other non-Arab peoples in the region as well. Arabs simply call the whole area "purely Arab patrimony"—subjugating and forcibly Arabizing all and frequently slaughtering those who might disagree. There have been millions over the centuries, and the number increases as you read this book.

Perfect justice is a very rare commodity among the realm of man. The most we can usually hope for is the relative variety.

This book does not attempt to be a tour de force regarding Arab–Israeli politics and history, although the author has spent quite a substantial portion of his life studying this conflict in both academic and professional capacities. With the Middle East constantly making the news, there are plenty of the former available.

Rather, this book aims to provide the basics of the conflict to those bombarded daily with news and misinformation coming out of this important region, and to place such topics and issues into a much broader perspective—one too often ignored by those who should certainly know better.

As with all other problems between peoples, there is a case to be made for both sides in this tragic struggle. Nowadays, however, in much of the media, academia, and elsewhere, one is often hard-pressed to discover this. And that is one of the main reasons why this book was written.

The main problem in the Arab–Israeli conflict has always been that one side, the Arabs, has refused to grant that there is any justice due to their adversaries at all.

This has not been the case regarding how Jews have approached this problem.

Somewhere down the road an Israel about the size of New Jersey and its six million Jews (why am I nervous about that number?)—which one needs a magnifying glass to find it on a map of the world—became labeled "Goliath" to the Arabs' alleged "David" in its struggle to survive amid some 170 million Arabs on more than six million square miles of territory.

While the reasons for this are complex, the fleeting sympathy and feelings of guilt some of the Western world felt because of the Holocaust, which helped to allow for the rebirth of the Jewish state, had long since vanished.

The stench of burning and decaying corpses at Auschwitz had subsided. Age-old, ingrained, and often religiously inspired animosities toward Jews again resurfaced, especially after the 1967 Six Day War. Very often they would take on a new disguise, anti-Zionism. This is not to say that to criticize particular Israeli policies is necessarily anti-Semitic, but it is to say that for many, as others have also observed, Israel had simply become the Jew of the Nations—and has been treated accordingly. How else to explain such blatant hypocrisy and double standards as Israel has frequently been subjected to by the non-Arab, Muslim world?

After pulling yet another rabbit out of its hat in thwarting the Arabs' latest attempt on its life in June 1967, Israel sent out a new message to an astounded world: forget about sympathy for dead Jews, à la the Holocaust, if you cannot empathize with live ones.

This book is an attempt to promote justice for all parties in conflict in the Middle East. It will also deal with other key issues too often overlooked.

Ample source notes are included, many from primary sources. But no amount of footnoting will impress academic "justice for Arabs only" extremists and their more subtle, but just as dangerous, variants occupying bully pulpits in their respective ivory towers. My own academic career, unfortunately, was at one point in one of their tenured hands. But instead, they will point an accusatory finger in this book's direction.

So, while I am partially indebted to such folks for inspiring this work—since they avoid the topics presented in this book like the plague—I do not seek the approval of those who suppress and punish free academic discourse in the most extreme of ways.

In the study of Middle Eastern affairs today, some subjects indeed seem to be taboo, while others never seem to leave center stage. Constantly in the spotlight's glare, Israel is frequently picked apart, all in the name of "objective scholarship," of course, while far greater sins of the Arab/Muslim states are usually ignored. Turkey's treatment of Kurds, Arab treatment of Kurds, black Africans, Imazhigen/Berbers, and so forth, are just some of too many examples of this common academic travesty of scholarly objectivity.

In academia, for a variety of reasons, Middle Eastern studies programs frequently have been hijacked by an anti-Israel crew. Furthermore, in courses besides those pertaining to the Middle East, this animus frequently permeates those classrooms as well. This book will provide much needed help for students (and concerned parents) going off to the university, along with other concerned readers as well. It is designed to be user friendly, as you will see below.

It is not unusual, for example, for students to take courses related to the Middle East and never be informed that the original Mandate for Palestine, as Great Britain received it on April 25, 1920, in the aftermath of World War I's breakup of the Ottoman Turkish Empire, included the modern Arab nation of Jordan as well as Israel, along with non-apportioned territories such as Judea and Samaria (which only since the last century has also been known as the West Bank). Since this does not sit well with the typical subtle or not so subtle academic Arabist lesson plan describing how Jews "stole all or most of Palestine," it is most often simply ignored. And forget about hearing how the Arabs themselves really stole much, if not most, of the entire region from its other native, non-Arab peoples.

Data, memoranda, and documentation from the League of Nations Permanent Mandates Commission, Colonial Secretary Winston Churchill, President Franklin Delano Roosevelt, and elsewhere that show that many, if not most, so-called "native Palestinians" were, in fact, Arabs who had poured into the Mandate from elsewhere in the region to take advantage of the economic development going on due to the Jews—Arab settlers setting up Arab settlements in Palestine—will also appear to be non-existent as students learn the fine details about a "colonial" and/or "racist" Israel instead. And again, those daring to disagree with the instructor's own polemic will then often have the tables turned on them as they wind up being branded the polemicist instead, an undesirable outcome for those pursuing academic careers at the mercy of such tenured "professionals."

Students will likely not study the Jews' age-old connections to the land of Israel, nor their tragic struggle against the Soviet Union of its day, the Roman Empire, for their freedom and independence. Missing from most academic syllabi will also be a discussion of the other side of the refugee coin, the half of Israel's Jews whose families fled Arab/Muslim lands as a result of the Arab attempt to nip a reborn Israel in the bud, but without roughly two dozen other states to potentially call their own, as Arabs have.

While Israel's admittedly imperfect struggle to survive will be closely examined under the high-power lens of moral scrutiny, the forced Arabization, subjugation, and/or slaughter of millions of native, non-Arab Imazighen/ Berbers, black Africans, Kurds, Copts, Assyrians, Jews, Semitic but pre-Arab Lebanese, and others in the region will likely never be mentioned at all. Neither will continuing black slavery in an Arab world, which likes to lecture (along with its champions in academia) about "racist Zionism" instead.

Sadly, I have been forced to criticize America's new president, Barack Obama, as you will soon see for yourself. My friends who know me also understand that if he were the first blue American president instead of black, the criticism would have been the same.

While there are policies of his with which I agree—such as the need for greater fuel efficiency in American automobiles (I was one of the first to own a hybrid Toyota Prius when they first arrived in Florida around 2001), stricter environmental protection based on sound science, and the need to develop and adopt alternative energy forms—too many of the president's friends, foreign policy appointees, and apparent foreign policy goals come with lots of baggage tied to them.

If I went to a synagogue where the rabbi spouted anti-black venom repeatedly for more than two decades while I belonged to that congregation, one would have the right to question my own beliefs regarding such issues.

Barack Obama did this in Chicago sitting in Reverend Jeremiah Wright's church, where he was a member since 1988, then claimed he never heard the latter's anti-Semitic/anti-American tirades. He then fumbled with and switched his story, yet this is the same Jeremiah Wright who is best buddies with the Nation of Islam's Louis "Judaism is a gutter religion" Farakkhan and who ran a Hamas ("Israel has no right to exist") manifesto in his church bulletin.

As I completed this book, President Obama continued to get fully immersed in the office of the presidency. He has recently had his first meeting with Israel's own new leader, Prime Minister Benjamin Netanyahu, and the results of this and earlier preparations perhaps suggest that the president may now possess a keener sense of balance and may be more aware of crucial issues and facts than he was before, given that long list of blatantly anti-Semitic and/or anti-Zionist friends and associates he indeed has. Only time will tell.

To criticize Israel and its policies is not anti-Semitic in itself. But, dishing out such criticism, holding Israel to standards few if any other nations are held to, and denying the state of the Jews the same rights which others are not denied is. (I.e., Arabs stake claim to almost two dozen states of their own, conquered and forcibly Arabized from mostly native, non-Arab peoples.) In this latter scenario, the age-old animus—both in the Muslim East as well as in the Christian West—for the Jew as an individual has simply been substituted for hatred and/or unfair treatment of the Jew of the Nations.

The chapters of the book are concise and to the point, focusing on key issues. Each is designed to stand on its own as much as possible, so some repetition of crucial facts is deliberately built in to allow for this and will resurface from time to time. The reader may thus open any chapter and quite possibly find crucial points to the conflict again carefully woven in and related to the main thrust of that particular chapter.

I will, at times, refer to the "good cop/bad cop" game that Arabs, the American State Department, and others play with Israel. This refers to the tactic known to be used by some police departments in which a supposedly more rational, level-headed officer, the "good cop"—in order to get information out of someone, or to sway him to do something—threatens turning him over to a more volatile "bad cop" partner if the person does not cooperate. Think Fatah's Abbas and Hamas, in that order. In reality, both "cops'" goals regarding Israel are the same.

Likewise, you will read about Foggy Bottom and/or the Foggy Folks. Foggy Bottom is one of the oldest of the nineteenth-century neighborhoods in Washington, DC. It is believed the area received the name because low elevation made it susceptible to substantial concentrations of fog. The name is often also used as a nickname for the United States Department of State, headquartered in that neighborhood, just to the northwest of Capitol Mall area.

Also, *Judenrein* is the term Nazis used to describe their goal to make the world Jew-free.

Since I mentioned the influence of my parents, I cannot end this Introduction without also paying tribute to my patient, wonderful wife, Elisabeth (Betsy), for putting up—for almost three decades now—with all the assorted problems and inconveniences the countless hours of my labors of love (and lost fishing trips) caused in our home. She has supported me in every way, often assuming responsibilities that perhaps should have been mine so that I would have time to work on editorials and articles. My brother, Dr. Joseph, repeatedly challenged me to delve deeper into the issues, sometimes in hot and heavy debate.

My children, Abigail Zipporah, Jessica Beth, Jonathan Ze'ev, and Elana Judith, lost too much precious time with me. I can only hope that they truly understand what their father was/is trying to achieve. I have tried very hard to prepare them for what they likely will encounter at the university. In this ever-shrinking world of intellectual exchange, Israel often is unfairly vilified, criticized out of context, and so forth, while the much greater sins of those who surround it are too often ignored.

My goal for my children—as for this book—has been to present them with the very human—and hence, imperfect—nature of their people's struggle to end their perpetual victim status with the resurrection of the nation their ancestors have called home for thousands of years, even during forced exile.

Sure enough, soon after the three oldest went off to the university, they soon found themselves enmeshed in conversation with others espousing the blatant anti-Zionism of the well-known Jewish professor, Noam Chomsky. Hence the importance—if one cares at all (which too many young Jews do not)—of knowing your stuff, somewhat, at least, before heading off to campus.

Rabbi Hillel, a contemporary of Jesus, summed it up when he said, "If I am not for myself, who will be? But, if I am only for myself, then what am I?"

I have always stressed the necessity of the pursuit of relative justice and have never claimed the absence of a case to be made for the other side, the broader perspective, fair compromise, and such. Again, this is what this book attempts to be all about. I believe that if Arab parents did likewise, this conflict could have been resolved many decades ago.

Quite a while back, I wrote a widely published article, "The Chicken or the Egg?" To my pleasant surprise, while doing a routine search of the progress of the article on the web, I found that it also appeared as the lead editorial in the late Dr. Tashbih Sayyed's print newspaper, *Pakistan Today*. Not long afterward, Tashbih called me on the phone from his new home in California, and a wonderful friendship with this courageous and amazing man began. Tashbih died an untimely death a few years ago, but his wife and daughter, Kiran and Supna Zaidi, picked up the cause for justice for all peoples in the region.

Tashbih and family have showcased scores of my editorials over the years in both *Pakistan Today* and *Muslim World Today*, a moderate Muslim response to the jihadis that reaches countless thousands of people who too often do not get to hear or see such messages. I am forever grateful. And there are other moderate Muslim voices out there as well these that need to be cultivated and supported.

I also must mention an amazing young man and friend of our family, Charlie Waserstein, whose intense prodding helped make me decide to act at this time.

I am indebted to Reverend John Jeyaseelan, Allen Springer, Nonie Darwish, Dr. Sherkoh Abbas, Brigitte Gabriel, Dr. Daniel Pipes, Dr. Allen Quain, Arie Ast, Esther Levens, Reverend Howard Chadwick, Robert Caggiano, Dr. Alexander Grobman, Dr. Rebwar Fatah, Ze'ev Shemer, Anne Sinai, Eric Rozenman, Bernard J. Shapiro, Delta Vines, Atalie Anderson, Virginia Maxwell, Amanda Lowell, Jihan Ruano, Michael Travis, Dr. Paul L. Williams, Jeff Bigman, Dr. Arthur Goldschmidt, Jr., H. Bendor, Diane Wolff, Jim Sesi, Nissan Ratzlav-Katz, Diane Dyer, Lior Ben-Ami, Faridon Abbas, Rabbi Gary Perras, Yugurten, Dr. Andrew Bostom, L.B. Neal, Michael Clark, David Cukierman, Frank Salvato, Rabbi Pinchas Ezagui, Simone Simmons, David Kramer, Jerome B. Gordon, Sarie Korf, Ted Belman, Charlie Cabiac, Bob Sharff, Mike Farb, Dr.

Fred Costello, and other friends who have encouraged me, challenged me, have spread their own message, and who have helped me to reach audiences all over the world who don't often get the chance to see the likes of it in their own societies.

Lastly, I dare not forget to mention again those more subtle but equally duplicitous, slanted, and hypocritical academics—such as those to whom I fell prey in the early eighties—whose classes convinced me that my own personal account of this multi-faceted story had to be written. While being deprived of a PhD dissertation advisor (and thus, a university career—no one person should ever have such power) by such folks, I remain, nonetheless, indebted to them as well for finally—decades later—forcing this book out of me.

Chapter 1

NAKBA: The Tragedy That Didn't Have to Be

*H*ONIGMAN, HOW CAN *you be so insensitive?* Perhaps the following can help explain. There has certainly been much suffering in this world, and I do not mean to downplay any of it. But, in regard to what Arabs and their supporters accuse Israel of—while the rest of the world betrays either a convenient lapse of memory or perhaps a willful ignorance, or worse—it is essential to expose these issues to a more revealing light, one too often deliberately shut off.

Shortly after Israel celebrates its Independence Day each spring (the exact date differs from year to year due to the Hebrew lunar calendar), the world faces another "celebration" of sorts: the Arabs' "*Nakba*" Day, May 15 of each year. That is what the Arabs call their catastrophe—Israel's rebirth—placing guilt for their own post-'48 predicament on Jews. They demonstrate all over, including in America and Israel itself, and assorted media give them as much, if not more, coverage than they do for Israel's Independence Day.

While I do not deny Arabs their audience, would the same protests of scores of millions of black Africans, Copts, Imazighen (Berbers), Kurds, Assyrians, Jewish refugees from Arab/Muslim lands (or the few Jews still remaining there), and other non-Arab victims of Arab imperial conquest, forced Arabization, murder, expulsion, genocide, and so forth over years (continuing to this day) get the same media publicity and attention?

In a word, no.

To start with, allow me just one case in point out of a zillion that could be cited. Who has heard anywhere—in the college classroom, in the media, from the State Department, or elsewhere—that the majority population of North Africa, the non-Arab Imazighen, are increasingly being ordered not to name their children with traditional names but must use Islamic/Arab ones instead?

Yet, if Israel sneezes too loud, it is on the front page.

Get the picture? Indeed, none of the Arabs' multitudes of victims dare to even demonstrate without placing their own lives on the line. And when they rarely do, few, if any, people elsewhere in the world get to see or hear about such things anyway. It literally takes Arab mass murder, such as in the Anfal campaign in Iraq or in the Sudan, before anyone even notices. So forget about what Arabs are doing to Kurds in Arab Syria right now without anyone saying a word; the murdered are not numerous enough yet, I guess. Forget, too, about their ongoing tragic subjugation.

All right, but still, didn't Arabs also suffer because of the Jews' insistence on casting off their perpetual, millennial victim and statelessness condition? And their children?

Yes, some did, but here is the main point. The Arab *Nakba* was a catastrophe that did not have to be. Arabs were and are mainly victims of self-inflicted wounds that occurred due to their own subjugating, racist attitudes toward all others daring to stake a claim, no matter how small, after the breakup of the four century-old Ottoman Turkish Empire in what Arabs proclaimed to be— as a result of their own earlier imperial conquests—"purely Arab patrimony."

While no one is squeaky clean once hostilities erupt, the post-'48 Arab predicament was sired overwhelmingly by themselves. The suffering Arab children witness is mostly due to their parents' and leaders' inability to conceive of possibilities by which others' children could have a better life as well, throughout the region, not just involving those of whom Arabs refer to as "their" *kilab yahud*—Jew dogs. More-than-fair compromises that would not have allowed for all of that suffering to occur were repeatedly rejected by the Arabs themselves. And the so-called Arab peace plan that President Obama currently says Israel would be nuts to reject is a plan for Israel's suicide, not peace. We will deal with those specifics later, in other chapters.

Squeaky clean? When you are attacked and enemies call for another genocide against you, bullets and bombs start to fly, and comrades start to fall, too often the chaos begins. But there is no military in the world that fights with greater ethical standards than that of Israel's—and any objective analysis would have no trouble confirming this. Is the record perfect? Of course not. Whose is?

Certainly not the Arabs'. Listening to news coming out of the Middle East, it is nearly impossible to hear reports about terrorist atrocities against Israeli civilians (and Jews elsewhere) without also hearing some academic or journalist justifying them in the name of alleged Arab grievances and the sham art of proportionate and disproportionate military response. Folks such as Richard Cohen, Nicholas Kristof, and others have written that the Arabs have been given no alternatives.

So, when Israel carefully targets, as best as possible, the deliberate murderers of women, children, and other innocents—as exemplified in the aftermath of what typically happens after the bombing of a bus or restaurant or mortar and rocket launches against Jewish civilian population centers—this somehow becomes equated with the next Arab "revenge" attack launched against additional Israeli civilians. Furthermore, few and far between are those who even call such Arab acts of barbarity "terrorism," not even when mothers and children are butchered at point-blank range or when Jewish body parts are toyed with by Arabs before television cameras.

When Israel puts its sons in danger by dropping leaflets telegraphing its punch, by going house-to-house to hunt terrorists in their strongholds to purposely avoid civilian casualties (when it has the capability of flattening those areas from a distance), and so forth, it gets accused of massacres anyway, while the real atrocities—terrorists' use of "human shields" when deliberately attacking Jews—are virtually ignored.

When faced with their own "problems," Arabs have gassed, bombed, and shelled their enemies from afar—à la Assad's Hama solution in Syria, Saddam's gassing of Kurds in Iraq, King Hussein's "Black September" in Jordan, and too many other examples to list, and all with no calls for investigations by the United Nations or trials in Geneva, as Israel has been subjected to. The latter are apparently reserved just for Israel's defensive responses aiming to prevent its innocents from being slaughtered. That Arabs consider the rebirth of Israel a catastrophe is, in reality, merely par for the course.

Having conquered and forcibly Arabized millions of non-Arab peoples and their lands in creating most of the almost two dozen states, which now possess millions of square miles of territory, at no time did Arabs ever consider that anyone else but themselves had any political rights in the region. This was so when what was promised to become an independent Kurdistan after World War I was turned into Arab Iraq instead, due mostly to the collusion of British petroleum politics and Arab nationalism. Thirty-five million Kurds thus remain stateless to date, often at someone else's mercy. Is the State Department insisting on a *road map* for them?

Millions of Imazighen in North Africa resisted the Arab onslaught for centuries. Their language and culture are still largely suppressed or outlawed today. Other millions in black Africa have died resisting this forced Arabization as well. The fight goes on as this book is being written, with millions of blacks having been killed, maimed, enslaved, turned into refugees, and the like over the decades.

You see, in most Arabs' eyes, theirs is the only justice. There are, thankfully, some very notable exceptions.

Read the Kurdish nationalist Ismet Cherif Vanly's book, *The Syrian 'Mein Kampf' Against The Kurds*, for further insight into this. The only safe Copt or Nubian in Egypt is one who knows his place. Ditto for the native Semite, but frequently non-Arab, Christian Lebanese.

The concept goes like this: once a land has been conquered on behalf of the Arab nation and the Dar ul-Islam, it can never revert back to its former status, the Dar al-Harb ("realm of war").

Perfect justice is an extreme rarity in the human realm. It was not present when scores of millions became refugees as a consequence of the last century's wars, nor when the Indian subcontinent was divided into Muslim Pakistan and Hindu India (and later, Bangladesh). It did not exist when millions of Greeks, Bulgars, and Turks exchanged populations, nor when half of Israel's six million Jews' families fled Arab/Muslim lands around the same time Arabs were fleeing in the opposite direction during Israel's war of independence as a result of the combined Arab attack in May 1948. They are the other side of the Middle East refugee problem that no one ever talks about. All of these examples, and many more not mentioned, represented imperfect attempts to arrive at compromise solutions so that the rights of both parties to any given conflict could be addressed.

Ze'ev Vladimir Jabotinsky, the pre- and mandatory era, no-nonsense realist and patron saint of the modern Likud Party in Israel (to whom academics, such as at least one who controlled my academic future, referred to as a fascist or at least attributed a fascist leaning), perhaps said it best when he spoke of appetite versus desperation, starvation, and need. If this does not sound familiar, check out the dustjacket of this book again. He was *that* important—as much as the difference between Prime Minister Netanyahu and his predecessor, Ehud Olmert, today.

Love him or hate him, Jabotinsky was honest. And, unlike many of his starry-eyed Zionist colleagues almost a century ago (and their head-in-the-sand contemporaries today), he saw the true nature of the conflict between Arab and Jew in the Middle East.[1]

Earlier, in the nineteenth century, Leo Pinsker spoke of the need for the "autoemancipation" of the Jews, the perpetual, unwanted guest—never host—ghost people, even before the harsh realities of a supposedly enlightened France opened Theodore Herzl's eyes.[2] The Dreyfus Affair would soon lead Herzl, the father of modern political Zionism, to write *Der Judenstat—The Jewish State*.[3]

Jabotinsky, likewise, understood all of this as well when he spoke of the Jewish condition both during the pre-and mandatory period for Palestine. Contrary to what some accuse him of, he knew that Arabs also had rights in the region. Where is the Arab leader who says this of the Jews?

It was understandable that Arabs, who remembered their own proud, conquering, and Caliphal imperial past (imperialism is evidently only nasty when non-Arabs so indulge), should want to return to those earlier days of dominance after the collapse of their own rival successors—the over-four-centu-ries-old Ottoman Turkish Empire, the Seljuk Turks, and other non-Arab rulers even earlier. Indeed, after the fall of Iudaea (Judea) to Rome, only varieties of imperial successors ruled the land. No one but the Jews ever established the likes of a "nation state" there since their fight for freedom and independence against the Soviet Union of its day.

That Arabs would want to make Palestine their sixth, seventh, or eighth state (today number twenty-two) made perfect sense to Jabotinsky.[4]

But Jews did not have this luxury. For them, the familiar pattern of millennial existence—most violently manifested in the pogroms of Eastern Europe and Russia and hints of what was yet to come in Germany—added desperation and necessity to the quest for the rebirth of their own sole state. And while the frightened mellahs of dhimmi Jewish existence in the Arab/Muslim world experienced no "Holocaust" per se, their experience over the ages was also not without memories of massacres, forced conversions, subjugation, humiliation, and existence as *kilab yahud* "Jew dogs" of their Arab neighbors.[5]

While it is true that the Arab suicide/homicide bomber, who today deliberately kills innocents, also does this out of "passion" and perhaps "desperation," Jabotinsky, long ago, saw the difference, something that too many others today still don't—or won't—see: there was no need for this situation to have arisen among Arabs. Honorable partitions and solutions had repeatedly been offered—and turned down—by the Arabs themselves. The reality has been that any solution that did not translate into another *final solution* regarding Israel and its Jews was unacceptable to them. In the predominant Arab mindset, theirs remains the only justice.

There are those today who like to make the argument (especially academics—whom I've personally heard say this), "If Jews can have a state, why not Palestinians?" For some, this is simply honest ignorance, pathetic though it is. But for far too many others, it represents something far worse, for they know better.

While I will not get into argument over whether a distinct Palestinian Arab nationalism exists today, it certainly did not exist before the rise of modern political Zionism. In fact, the former arose specifically to negate the latter. There are volumes of evidence to support this. Virtually all the writings of politically conscious Arabs on the eve of the collapse of the Ottoman Turkish Empire spoke of a greater Syrian Arab or Pan Arab identity.[6] The "Palestinians" were the Jews.

When the Middle East and North Africa were being divided after the collapse of the Ottoman Turkish Empire after World War I, the hopes and dreams of many diverse subject peoples were reawakened. Britain's Sir Mark Sykes, America's President Woodrow Wilson, and others fueled the fires with talk of self-determination for those populations.

Arabs made out very well in the long-term aftermath. Unfortunately, they refused to grant anyone else even the right to think in such terms in what they declared to be "purely Arab patrimony," be they Kurd, Jew, Imazighen, black African, and so forth. We are dealing with the tragic consequences of this today. Thus, ironically, it was their own subjugating attitudes and greed that sired what the Arabs today call their *Nakba*.

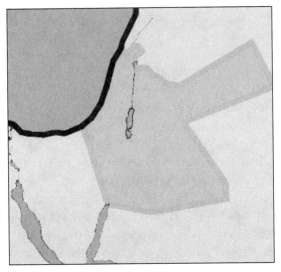

Pre-1922 Partition

In 1922 Colonial Secretary Churchill, to reward Arab allies in World War I, chopped off nearly 80 percent of the original Palestinian Mandate issued to Great Britain on April 25, 1920—all the land east, across ("trans-") the Jordan River—and created the purely Arab Emirate of Transjordan, today's Jordan. Emir Abdullah, who received this gift on behalf of the Hashemites of Arabia, attributed the separation of this land from the area promised to the Jews to an "act of Allah" in his memoirs. Sir Alec Kirkbride, Britain's East Bank representative, had much to say about this as well.[7]

The Jordan-Palestine connection is just one of many well-documented facts (not "Zionist propaganda") completely ignored or distorted by Arab and pro-Arab spokesmen and, unfortunately, little known by the rest of the world. Prominent Arab spokesmen, such as the PLO's Marwan Barghouti, for example, typically claim that Jews got 78 percent of all of the land, the standard Arab line. Leading newspapers typically prepare segments on the Middle East ignoring this crucial Jordan-Palestine connection as well.

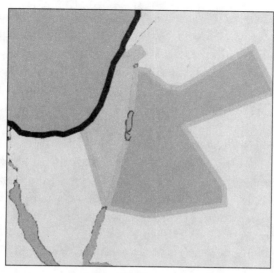

Post-1922 Partition

In reality, not only do Arabs today have almost two dozen states, but they have had one in most of "Palestine" for well more than half a century. What is now being debated is the creation of a twenty-second state, the second Arab one in "Palestine." And for this to occur, they expect Israel to consent to nothing less than national suicide. Any guarantees that others make to Israel—including President Obama's recent ones—won't be worth recalling down the line if history is a precedent.

After the Sinai campaign in 1956, Israel received American "guarantees" regarding its right to passage through the Suez Canal and the Straits of Tiran and the Gulf of Aqaba. In 1967, when Egypt again blocked Israel at the latter two points (a casus belli), America declared itself "neutral." So much for guarantees.

As it has been rehashed many times, in 2000 Prime Minister Ehud Barak offered Arafat some 97 percent of the territories, half of Jerusalem, and other far-reaching concessions for the sake of peace. U.S. chief negotiator Dennis Ross, who was present at Camp David and subsequent negotiations at Taba, revealed that a $33 billion fund was also to be made available to the Palestinian Arabs as well in a contiguous state, not "disconnected cantons" as Arab spin doctors and their Western stooges now claim.[8]

This, of course, all begs the question: what compromises did Arabs ever make with any of their own non-Arab competitors mentioned above? Did Kurds get a state in at least part of Iraq? Are black Africans in the south of the Sudan to be free from slaughter, enslavement, and forced Arabization? Am I the Passover Bunny?

The Arab response to Barak and Clinton was to tell Israel to agree to take in millions of Arab refugees, real or alleged, so that the Jews would be overwhelmed. Decades later, this is now part of the Saudi "peace" plan that President Obama claims Israel would be nuts to refuse. Despite recent allegations to the contrary, the Arabs have not given up on this. After the earlier Geneva Initiative, when the Jews refused suicide, the Arabs next launched the intifada as their follow-up counteroffer.

Keep in mind that if Arabs had agreed to the 1947 partition, which divided the roughly 20 percent of Palestine left after Arabs had already received the lion's share of the land in 1922 (Transjordan) into another Arab and one, miniscule Jewish state, there would not be one Arab refugee today. Instead, surrounding Arab states immediately attacked a reborn Israel and told their people to clear the way for a quick victory.

While no one fights a totally guilt-free war (and once bullets start to fly and comrades start to die, sometimes not all goes as originally planned), overwhelming evidence exists that it was the Arabs themselves, with their rejection of Israel and their invasion of the nascent Jewish state, who mostly created their own refugee problem.[9] And after they created it, unlike hundreds of millions of other refugees around the world, the Arab refugee problem was deliberately not allowed to be solved by the Arabs themselves.

An Israel about the size of New Jersey wound up absorbing more Jews, who fled Arab/Muslim lands and left far more property and wealth behind, than Arabs who fled Israel as a result of the hostilities. Yet, the Arabs' only "solution" was to create squalid camps for their own refugees and, with few exceptions, refuse to integrate them. They were to be used, instead, as perpetual, tragic pawns—political ammunition in the Arabs' greater war against the Jews.

It must also be noted that many, if not most, so-called "native Palestinians" were themselves recent immigrants into Palestine. The records of the League of Nations Permanent Mandates Commission and other sources give ample testimony to this. Sheikh Izzedine al-Qassam, for whom Hamas's militant wing is named, was from Latakia, Syria. A good amount of evidence exists that points to Egypt as the birthplace of Arafat. We know for sure that thousands of Egyptians settled in the land in the wake of Muhammad Ali and his son Ibrahim Pasha's invasions in the nineteenth century when Jews were starting to pour millions of dollars into it for development.[10]

While Arabs consider it to be their natural right to settle anywhere in the "realm of Islam," when hundreds of thousands of native Middle Eastern Jews did likewise—coming from Egypt, Syria, Iraq, Yemen, Libya, Morocco, Tunisia, and other lands as well—Arabs considered this to be an "injustice."

How dare anyone else but Arabs, especially "their" *kilab yahud*—"Jew dogs"— want a degree of national dignity in the region!

To understand the meaning of reborn Israel to the Jew, one needs to know what Jewish history was like for two thousand years after the Jews dared to take on the conqueror of much of the world for their independence. Most people are totally ignorant of this. A reading of the contemporary Roman-sponsored historians—Tacitus, Dio Cassius, Josephus, and so forth—gives a mostly "non-Zionist" account of the fervor with which Jews fought for the freedom of their land.

Here's Tacitus:

> Vespasian succeeded to the command, it inflamed his resentment that the Jews were the only nation that had not yet submitted.

This was during the first revolt in 66–73 C.E. The Arch of Titus stands in Rome to this very day to commemorate this victory over the Jews.[11]

The emperor, Hadrian, became so enraged at the Jews' persistence that in 135 C.E., after the second major (and even more costly) revolt, he renamed Judaea *Syria Palaestina*—Palestine—after the Jews' historic, non-Semitic enemies, the transplanted Aegean "sea people" Philistines, in an attempt to end the Jews' hopes once and for all.

Forced conversions, being branded the "deicide people," inquisitions, demonization, dehumanization, ghettos, blood libels, massacres, expulsions, the Holocaust, and existence as perpetual stranger in someone else's land became the plight of the "wandering Jew," his own *Nakba*. But, unlike that of the Arabs, it was not of his own making.

So, is a victim any less a victim because his victimization has been the longest enduring?

Would that he had possessed two dozen other states like Arabs have. Perhaps then there would have been no need for the rebirth of Israel. But the Jew did not possess even one, let alone almost two dozen.

Since "perfect justice" never existed in the community of nations but is now only demanded of the Jews, does relative justice demand no state for Jews (as tiny as that state is) and some two dozen for Arabs? That's still even the "moderate" Arabs' long-term plan, regardless of the claims of those now tightening the screws on Israel from abroad. If the answer is yes, then such bias against Israel as is frequently experienced in academia or in the media (CNN, BBC, National Public Radio, NBC, written publications, and so forth) might be understandable. But if one disagrees with this one-sided vision of justice, then how can one justify much of the media's (and others') apparent acceptance of what the Arabs

call their *Nakba*—Israel's rebirth—since whatever catastrophe occurred was
primarily of their own making, due to an Arab self-centered unwillingness to
grant anyone else—Kurd, Imazighen, Jew, black African, or whomever—even a
tiny sliver of the rights they so fervently demand for themselves?

The borders of any additional state that may emerge for Arabs in "Palestine"
must not come at the expense of the security of the sole state of the Jews. Keep
this in mind regarding ongoing debates over the path of Israel's security fence,
the attempts to shove the current Saudi Peace (of the grave) Plan down Israel's
throat, and other like issues.

In the wake of the '67 War, UN Security Council Resolution 242 did not
demand that Israel return to the suicidal armistice lines of 1949. Among other
things, those lines made Israel a mere nine to fifteen miles wide at its strategic waist, where most of its vulnerable population, industry, and so forth are
located. It called, instead, for the creation of "secure and recognized" borders
to replace those lines. Israel was not expected to withdraw from all of the territories in question, though Arabs and their supporters tried—and failed—to
have wording to accomplish this attached to the final draft of the resolution.[12]

Furthermore, those lands where much of the compromising would have
to be done after Israel already withdrew from the Sinai—Judea and Samaria,
the "West Bank"—were not "purely Arab" lands but non-apportioned territories of the Mandate, open to settlement by Jews, Arabs, and others as well.
Leading international legal scholars such as Eugene Rostow, Arthur Goldberg,
and others have written extensively about this.[13] The demand that those lands,
where Jews have thousands of years of connecting history, become *Judenrein*,
the Nazi term for "Jew-free," is unwarranted and troubling. And, besides the
Arabs, that is just what the European Union, the current American administration, and others are presently calling for.

The reality is that this conflict continues for one reason only: Arabs are
fighting the 1948 war for Israel's rebirth all over again. Even the Palestinian
model "moderate," the late Faisal al-Husseini, openly admitted that an Arab
Palestine from the river to the sea was the real goal.[14]

At meetings for the so-called roadmap and later at President Bush's Annapolis initiative, the European, Russian, and American state departments planned
to create a second Palestinian Arab state. Arabs refused to even talk about Israel
being a "Jewish" state, while demanding yet another of their own. Palestinian
Arab Authority Prime Minister Mahmoud Abbas, Ahmed Qurei', and others
continue to refuse to recognize Israel's Jewish identity to this very day—and
they are the alleged "good cops." We will take a closer look at this important
issue in one of the next chapters, "À la Alaa."

Hence the problem with talk about the creation of a Palestinian Arab state, the roadmap, the Saudi Plan, and the like. Arabs have repeatedly said since their "one fell swoop" strategy failed as of the '67 war, they would adopt a destruction-in-stages (or phases) strategy instead. They will accept any land "diplomacy" (pressure on the Jews) will yield and that will make their real, final goal—the destruction of Israel—easier to achieve. That is what the earlier so-called peace initiatives and the Arabs' current one were/are all about. In the Arabs' own words, it is a "Trojan horse."[15]

Again, while peace is worthy goal, the aim is not the peace of the grave.

So, one more time then: when is a catastrophe not really so? When it is—or was—totally avoidable and brought about primarily by oppressive attitudes and actions of the alleged victims themselves. Unlike what Jews have faced over the millennia, the Arab *Nakba* was basically a tragedy that did not have to be. It was very much a self-inflicted wound.

While tragedy occurred, it was born of a subjugating mind-set that declared virtually none besides Arabs worthy of dignity and political rights in the region. And again, for Arabs, colonialism and imperialism are deemed nasty only when someone else besides themselves are the perpetrators.

Unlike Arabs, who were offered repeated compromises, no such accommodations were ever offered by Arabs to their own national competitors. Think hundreds of thousands of massacred and gassed Kurds, even greater genocide in the Sudan, burned down Egyptian Coptic churches, and murdered Copts. In other words, precisely what the real struggle is also largely about in pre-Arab Lebanon. King Solomon built the temple of the Jews in Jerusalem from his Phoenician ally, King Hiram's famed cedars. There was the murder, subjugation, and denial of the very identity of North Africa's majority Imazighen/Berber population, and so forth.

Again, had Arabs not repeatedly attacked Jews and invaded a reborn Israel in 1948, the Arab *Nakba* and the flight of Arab refugees would not have come to pass.

Massive, non-Zionist contemporary evidence (including from Arabs) testifies to this. And some Arabs (mostly new-comers themselves into the Palestine Mandate) would have come to live (as many now do) in one Jewish state—which made Arabic a second official language and where Arabs who side with Hamas sit in Israel's Parliament—as millions of non-Arabs (including many Jews) have lived in almost two dozen "Arab" states. Jabotinsky pointed this out eloquently.[16] Contrast the Israeli Arab example with many non-Arabs who had and still have their own languages and cultures outlawed in "Arab" lands.

In one of numerous examples of the above Arab testimony to their own largely self-inflicted wound, according to the West's current darling and alleged "good cop," Mahmoud Abbas's, own words:

> The Arab armies entered Palestine to protect the Palestinians, but instead they abandoned them, forced them to leave, and threw them into prisons (refugee camps) similar to the ghettoes in which Jews were earlier forced to live.[17]

Had Arabs been willing to grant Jews a miniscule slice of the same human dignity that they so forcefully demand for themselves, the problem could have been resolved decades ago.

So, the day that Arabs confess their own, much greater original sin for all of the above is the day that they will gain the right to protest others' imperfect struggles to obtain a modicum of justice for themselves.

In striving to create a world in which the relative rights of hopefully all the diverse peoples in the Middle East and North Africa will be addressed, the sole Jewish state in existence should not be expected to sacrifice itself on the petroleum-greased altar of international hypocrisy so that the Arabs' twenty-second state—and second in "Palestine"—can be born, regardless what the rest of the world demands.

Chapter 2

À LA ALAA

(Note: The following three chapters address a key element
in the Arabs' perpetual campaign to deny Israel's right to
exist—that Jews are not a distinct people and thus not entitled
to a distinct political existence in their own land.)

A TRANSLATION BY THE highly respected Middle East Media Research Institute (MEMRI) on July 3, 2003, dealt with an interview with Ahmed Qurei', aka Abu Alaa, who a bit later became one of Arafat's chiefs. He is now an official in Mahmoud Abbas's Palestinian Authority. Among other things, he was asked about the Arabs' problem with having the word *Jewish* placed in front of the words *State of Israel* at the summits leading up to the roadmap. Here was (and remains) his response, "What is the meaning of a Jewish state? Do we say, Sunni state? Shi'ite state? Christian state? These are definitions that will bring turmoil."

More recently, the current chief Arafatian in a suit, Mahmoud Abbas, repeated virtually the same lines in Ramallah on April 27, 2009 upon his own restatement rejecting Israel as a Jewish state, "A Jewish state, what is that supposed to mean? You can call yourselves what you want, but I don't accept it and I say so publicly."[18]

Keep in mind that while most Arabs demand that a twenty-second Arab state be born, they eternally deny Jews their one. We will develop this idea much more as we proceed.

It is not unusual to hear critics of Israel, including academics, proclaim, "If Jews can have a state, then why not Catholics, or Protestants, or Hindus, and so forth?" À la, Alaa. Indeed, this was one of a prominent Ohio State University law professor's favorite lines in his frequent presentations against Israel. I had the pleasure, on several occasions in the seventies, of following him around while in Columbus and nailing him in public on this and other issues.

Dr. Daniel Pipes' Campus Watch reported on December 13, 2003, that several additional professors—Joseph Massad, Erica Dodd, and others—had also come out very publicly on this matter as well. It is a favorite piece of anti-Israel ammunition.

Now think about this for a minute. Someone from England is English; from Poland is Polish; from Sweden is Swedish; from Ireland is Irish. While there are other ways of describing one's nationality or ethnicity (we're not Americanish), the addition of the suffix *-ish* denotes this as well. Indeed, that is how *Webster's Collegiate Dictionary* primarily defines it.

So what is the "moderate" Abu Alaa's, Mahmoud Abbas's, and their buddies' problem here?

It is really very simple. If they admit that the Jews are a nation or a people, it makes Arab rejection of their national movement—Zionism—more difficult to defend. In other words, how could Arabs demand some two dozen states for themselves while denying Jews their one? Well, they could, as they do with Imazighen, Kurds, and everyone else living on what Arabs claim to be "purely Arab land." But it makes the selling of the argument to reasonable minds that much more difficult.

So let's take a closer look at this issue.

Jew comes from the name *Judah*, originally the Hebrew tribe named after one of Jacob's twelve sons and later Judah/Iudaea/Judaea as the land was known in the times of the Greeks and Romans. After the death of King Solomon some three thousand years ago, the kingdom of the Jews split in two. The ten tribes in the north formed Israel, and those of Judah and Benjamin formed the southern kingdom. *Judaean* equals "Jew."

When Rome suppressed the first major revolt of the Jews for their freedom and independence after 73 C.E., it issued thousands of Iudaea Capta coins that can be seen in museums all over the world today. As the Roman historians themselves wrote, Iudaea/Judaea (not Palaestina) was the land, and Judaeans (not Palestinians)—Jews—were the people of that land.[20]

Iudaea Capta coin

Now here's the somewhat confusing part. That particular people—the Jews—also had a peculiar set of religious beliefs: they worshiped a totally spiritual G_d, who no man could see and who demanded that man live by a strong moral code. The Roman historians Tacitus or Dio Cassius, living at that time were amused and spoke of this peculiarity in their writings and had lots more to say about the Jews as a people.[21] We will return to Tacitus a bit later on.

While Abraham and the Hebrew patriarchs lived centuries earlier, Jews emerged as a people/nation after the experience at Sinai, some thirteen hundred years or so before Jesus. They came to inhabit a distinct land, had their own culture, language, history—and, again, their own distinct set of religious beliefs.

The *Amarna Letters*, an amazing archaeological treasure from ancient Egypt, show repeated correspondence between Pharaoh and surrounding Hittite, Hurrian, Babylonian, Canaanite, Assyrian, and other kingdoms. Guess what comes out, among other things, in the correspondence. Complaints about invasions by the "Habiru" and "'Apiru," quite possibly the Hebrews. And while there is some scholarly debate about the derivation of those names (along with the identities of those peoples and their relationship to each other), the exact timing of the Exodus, and some other details as well, the letters date back to the general time period that the biblical conquests of Joshua and the Hebrew people are thought to have occurred. More recent excavations in Jericho tighten the connection even more.[22]

Jumping ahead a thousand years or so, again to Roman times, listen to just this one brief quote from the many pages the contemporary Roman historian, Tacitus, devoted to the Jews, "It inflamed Vespasian's resentment that the Jews were the only nation who had not yet submitted."[23]

Do you think Tacitus was talking about the Jews' "religious affiliation"—to quote Abu Alaa or his mouthpieces in academia—or their identity as a people? Actually, we don't have to even ask. Tacitus tells us. Are you listening, Abu Alaa and Co.? Look carefully at the above quote once again for your answer, from the historian who wrote the account right around the same time period in which the events were unfolding.

While it is true that one may join one's destiny to the peoplehood/nationhood of Israel via religious conversion to the faith of that people, faith itself—while a part of the picture—is still just that. It is one part of the picture. So, Ruth the Moabitess became a convert when she told Naomi in the Hebrew Bible, "Whither thou goist I shall go, your people shall be my people, your G_d, my G_d."

Note, please, that even here, in the sacred writings of the Jews, peoplehood is mentioned before religion. Perhaps a coincidence? Probably not.

When Jews were repeatedly humiliated, massacred, demonized, and so forth throughout subsequent centuries, as soon as Napoleon released them from the mandatory ghettos and granted them citizen rights, many tried to redefine themselves so that their peoplehood identity would not cause them additional future problems.

But that frequently did not work, either.

"Kanes" or their counterparts were tossed into the same ovens as Cohens, and the modern political Zionist movement gained its momentum because Alfred Dreyfus, "the Frenchman of Jewish faith," was still seen by his fellow Christian Frenchmen—including enlightened ones—as simply another dirty, G_d-killing Jew.

The late nineteenth century Dreyfus Affair opened another assimilated Jew's eyes, those of Theodore Herzl, who subsequently wrote *Der Judenstat*—"The Jewish State"—in response.

It is indeed ironic when Arabs such as Abu Alaa and their supporters bring this identity issue up. As usual, they rely on the innocent ignorance of most of their audience on such matters.

Consider, for example, how you identify an Arab. Because of their widespread conquests and forced Arabization (still going in places like North Africa, where the once majority Imazighens' language and culture have been frequently suppressed or outlawed; in the Sudan, where millions of black Africans have been killed, enslaved, driven out, and so forth resisting this; the gassings, massacres, and such in Syrian and Iraqi Kurdistan), the definition regarding *Arab* has come down to language spoken, paternal (so to claim the children of those conquered as their own) ancestry, and/or one's own actual or willingly adopted identity as such.[24] It is not exactly precise.

As just one example of this, take a close look at the pictures the next time you see "Arabs" on television, in magazine articles, or wherever. Frequently you will see some very obvious Arabs of black African ancestry—many born of slave mothers, grandmothers, and so forth. Black slaves are still arriving into Arab lands via the Sudan and perhaps elsewhere. Now recall that these are the same folks who speak of alleged "Zionist racism" and who have been able to sell this to much of the world.

The point is that there is no purity of blood, genes, and/or nation demanded for the Arabs' own collective self-definition (even though there are ethnically pure Arabs). Yet they and their supporters demand this of the Jews.

Last but not least, Islam is the forcibly imposed official religion of state in virtually all of the almost two dozen Arab states that exist so far. Check out their constitutions and other official documents. And they let it be known in the latter that the states are "Arab" as well—despite the blurriness of what that term really means and the presence of often millions of native non-Arabs in those lands. Nevertheless, this does not stop those like Mr. Qurei' or that Ohio State law professor from raising such issues of identity with the sole, microscopic state of the Jews.

The reality, of course, is that this is all just another ploy in the Arabs' perpetual campaign to deny Jews their one, sole state and to delegitimize Israel.

Chapter 3

What Would Ibn Khaldun Say?

(Note: While Arabs deny both the peoplehood and nationhood of Israel, let's see what perhaps the leading Muslim scholar of all time had to say about such matters.)

ZIONISM HAS MEANT different things to different people over the millennia. The connecting thread woven throughout all variations, however, has always involved Jews being in their land and at least somewhat in control of their own destinies. Whether they were biblical tears shed by the rivers of Babylon some two thousand years before Ibn Khaldun lived or writings such as those of the medieval poet Yehuda HaLevi, proclaiming a desire to be a pauper in Zion rather than a prince in Muslim Spain (where Jews had it relatively good), these ancient ties have bound Jews to Israel for most of man's recorded history. The animosity that often greeted them in the Diaspora helped to assure that those ties would not be forgotten.

For religious Zionists of all degrees and persuasions, the hand of G_d was—and is—at work in all of these events throughout the ages leading up to and after the rebirth of Israel in 1948. It took, after all, the rejection by the non-Jewish world of even the most assimilated of Jews—men like Captain Alfred Dreyfus—before the rebirth of political Zionism could become a reality in the late nineteenth century. But not all were religious Zionists.

Many Jews had indeed tried just about everything to gain acceptance in the non-Jewish world, but the Dreyfus Affair, pogroms, and numerous other problems culminating in the Holocaust kept on occurring in the "enlightened " and "modern" age, anyway. It was as if G_d were sending a message: "You will have no alternative. Israel must be reborn, whether you Jews like it or not!"

So Zionism came to have another meaning. It represented for many a chance for Jews to simply bring a semblance of normalcy into their lives. Since the fall of Judaea to Rome, too often bloodbaths, forced conversions, expulsions, inquisitions, blood libels, demonization, ghettoization, and every other imaginable humiliation were the plight of the Jew in the Diaspora.

There are churches to this very day that have stained glass windows or murals depicting Jews stabbing the Host of the Christian Communion in order to supposedly kill Jesus yet again. And the Arab world provides widespread anti-Semitica to its people as well. They were G_d killers in the Christian West and "sons of apes and pigs," killers of prophets in the Muslim (especially Arab) East. Thus, not all who dreamt of a return to Zion did so out of an urge to become "a nation of priests" or a "light unto the nations."

While the high ideals of religious Zionism still remained in many a Jewish heart and soul (even among agnostics), the chance to change their age-old tenuous existence in both the Christian and Muslim halves of the Diaspora was also a major motivating factor. Besides wanting to escape the mandatory ghetto (and, subconsciously, the evolved ghetto mentality) of the former and the mellah of the latter—and the negative effects and consequences such existence both produced on and brought out from themselves over the centuries—Jews just wanted to have a nation like all others. More than three thousand years earlier, when most other folks were still worshiping stone idols and practicing fertility rites, the Jews' ancestors were pleading with the prophet Samuel to intercede with G_d to allow them to have a worldly king, and for at least some of the same reasons.

Jews wanted to be farmers (in the Christian West, especially, they had largely not been allowed to own land), barbers, street cleaners, policemen, doctors, scholars, soldiers, statesmen—whatever—but above all else, masters of their own fate, and not the perpetual stranger in someone else's land, nor a pawn being played in someone else's games (usually with deadly consequences to themselves). Jews had often been allowed to settle in a land only after agreeing to take on unpopular tasks and jobs.

Some, like Karl Marx, would seek solutions to these problems in a broader context, via political and socio-economic reform. Ironically, while Marx despised his Jewish roots, he sounded like a Hebrew prophet in his demand for justice for the poor and the oppressed. Isaiah, Micah, and others would have understood his passion well. Indeed, they were his teachers.

Zionism meshed together all of these diverse fears, hopes, and dreams. And the key to its future had everything to do with transforming the powerless state of the Jews as a people.

Enter 'Abd-ar-Rahman Abu Zayd ibn Muhammad ibn Muhammad ibn Khaldun, born in the early fourteenth century C.E. He was one of the most important philosophers, jurists, and scholars Islamic—or any—civilization would ever produce. His name surfaces in the contemporary West every once in a while. On March 19, 2003, for example, an Associated Press (AP) story mentioned the release of an Egyptian-American human rights activist, Saad Eddin Ibrahim, from a seven-year sentence in prison. He had founded the independent think tank called the Ibn Khaldun Center and proved to be too independent for the Egyptian government's wishes. Ibn Khaldun had spent much of his later life in Cairo.

Graduate students in Middle Eastern studies usually come to know Ibn Khaldun through his work, *The Muqaddimah*. It is actually the introduction to and book one of his *Kitab al-'Ibar, The History of the World*. Besides simply giving an account of events, he offers a rational explanation of the "hows" and "whys" they occurred. He uses frequent historical illustrations to make his points. It is here that this great Muslim scholar, who died almost six hundred years ago, has some very important things to say about Jews and Israel.

Among other things, Ibn Khaldun detailed the prolonged, bloody conquest and forced Arabization process of Amazigh/Berber North Africa, the consequences of which we are dealing with to this very day. Here's one tiny example: "the Arabs outnumbered and overpowered the Berbers, stripped them of most of their lands."[25]

While he offers good critique and discussion about biblical and other accounts regarding Jews in general (he speaks of the Roman conquest of Jewish Jerusalem—something even the "moderate" latter-day Arafatians, such as Mahmoud Abbas, deny ever existed), it is his perspective on issues we have already covered above that is now of special relevance.[26]

Before *The Muqaddimah* was introduced above, I had reviewed the powerlessness of the Jewish experience and the negative consequences that derived from this. Ibn Khaldun spoke clearly to this matter as well:

> Students, slaves, and servants brought up with injustice and tyrannical force are overcome by it. It makes them feel oppressed, induces them to lie and be insincere. Their outward behavior differs from what they are thinking. Thus they are taught deceit and trickery. They become dependent on others. Their souls become too indulent to acquire good character qualities. Thus they fall short of their potentialities and do not reach the limit of their humanity. That is what happened to every nation that fell under the yoke of tyranny and learned the meaning of injustice. One may check this out by observing any person who is not in control of his own affairs and has no authority on his side to guarantee safety. One may look at the Jews (as an example). The reason is what we have said.[27]

However one chooses to respond to his assessment, Zionism's non-religious raison d'etre would have been obvious to Ibn Khaldun, one of the world's most important thinkers six centuries ago. He devoted much time and effort to the evolution and development of the Jewish nation, its early struggles with its adversaries, and its later fight for freedom with the mighty Roman Empire, and its consequences. He then followed this with an analysis of the Jews' tragic condition of powerlessness throughout subsequent generations.

Ibn Khaldun would have well understood the rebirth of Israel and the 'asabiyah—group consciousness (emphasized throughout his writings)—which made it possible, even if it was a consciousness born not only out of a "noble house" but also from the desperation of the Jews' perpetual victim, scapegoat, and whipping-post status. While he commented that the Jews, who had one of the most "noble houses" in the world, had subsequently lost their 'asabiyah and for centuries suffered constant humiliations as a result, he would have surely applauded and understood their desire to end this unfortunate turn of events.[28]

The Muqaddimah emphasizes that the Jews were forced to wander in the desert for forty years due to their "meekness." Ibn Khaldun stressed that this was necessary so that a new generation would arise with a new, more powerful 'asabiyah.[29]

At a time when Arabs are demanding their twenty-second state (most having been created by the conquest of non-Arab peoples and their lands), chances are more than good that this great Muslim scholar would have approved and viewed the resurrection of Israel as an answer to the unique plight of stateless Jews, and the end of an even more tragic and extensive wandering and period of meekness and powerlessness in the desert.

Israel's leaders would do well to heed his advice.

Chapter 4

ARAFAT'S JESUS

"Now Jesus, having been born in Bethlehem of Judea in the days of King Herod," is how the account of Jesus' birth begins in the second chapter of the Gospel of Matthew. Note, please, the location is Bethlehem of Judea, not the "West Bank," not "Palestine," but Judea.

As the year 2003 began, Greek Orthodox Metropolitan Irineos sought appointment as patriarch of Jerusalem. Letters with his signature on them to Yasser Arafat contained, among other things, the following:

> You are aware of the disgust all the Holy Sepulchre fathers feel for the descendants of the crucifiers of our Lord Jesus. Crucifiers of your people. Jewish conquerors of the Holy Land of Palestine.

Irineos claimed that his above letter, dated June 17, 2001, and published in the Israeli newspaper, *Maariv*, was a forgery. Unfortunately, there were evidently many other documents of the same flavor making the rounds as well.

Irineos's attitude, unfortunately, is not uncommon among Christians in the Middle East and elsewhere. Indeed, the quote above is virtually the same as words often spoken by the Greek Catholic archbishop of Jerusalem, Hilarion Capucci, a few decades earlier. All of these quotes and positions can readily be found on the Internet. So it is safe to assume that many people still share these beliefs. Some have simply inherited and modified them from traditional Christian teaching. Others, feeling exposed and vulnerable themselves living among real or potentially hostile dominant Muslim populations, sought/seek common ground with their own off again/on again persecutors by turning the focus on a common demon, the Jew.

Christians played an important role in the nascent Arab nationalist movement in the late nineteenth and twentieth centuries, and the above explanation was certainly one of the main motivating factors. This was not unlike some Jews seeking to be absorbed under the potentially protective, inclusive umbrella of various socialist movements in Christian Europe around the same time, and thus, for some, the attraction to communism as well.

A number of years ago, during the pope's visit to Israel, the media reported one of many of Arafat's own frequent comments on this subject. Speaking of the apostle Peter, Arafat explained the "Palestinian"—non-Jewish—identity of

Peter and company. The Arabs have constantly tried to portray themselves as the "originals" in the land.

Now for a reality check. There was no country nor nation known as "Palestine" during the time of Jesus. The land was known as Judaea, and its inhabitants were Judaeans. Jews.

Tacitus and Dio Cassius were famous Roman historians who wrote extensively about Judaea's attempt to remain free from the Soviet Union of its day, the conquering Roman Empire. They lived and wrote during or not long after the two major revolts of the Jews in 66–73 C.E. and 133–135 C.E. They make no mention of this land being called "Palestine," nor its people "Palestinians." And they knew the differences between Jews and Arabs as well. Check out this quote from Vol. II, Book V, *The Works of Tacitus*:

> Titus was appointed by his father to complete the subjugation of Judaea. He commanded three legions in Judaea itself. To these he added the twelfth from Syria and the third and twenty-second from Alexandria. Amongst his allies were a band of Arabs, formidable in themselves and harboring toward the Jews the bitter animosity usually subsisting between neighboring nations.[30]

After the first revolt (see also the contemporary accounts of the Roman-sponsored Jewish historian, Josephus, in his extensive *Antiquities of the Jews* and *Wars of the Jews*), Rome issued thousands of Judaea Capta coins that can be seen today in museums all over the world. Again, notice, please, their name is Judaea Capta, not "Palaestina Capta." Additionally, to celebrate this victory, the Arch of Titus was erected and stands tall in Rome to this very day.

Inside Arch of Titus, menorah

When, some sixty years later, Emperor Hadrian decided to further desecrate the site of the destroyed temple of the Jews by erecting a pagan structure there, it was the grandchildren's turn to take on their mighty conquerors.

The result of the struggle of this tiny nation for its freedom and independence was, perhaps, as predictable as that which would have occurred had Lithuania taken on the Soviet Union during its heyday of power. Check out this next quote from Dio Cassius:

> 580,000 men were slain, nearly the whole of Judaea made desolate. Many Romans, moreover, perished in this war [the Bar Kochba Revolt]. There-fore Hadrian in writing to the senate did not employ the opening phrase commonly affected by the emperors, "I and the legions are in health."[31]

The Emperor was so enraged at the Jews' struggle for freedom in their own land that, in the words of the esteemed modern historian Bernard Lewis, "Hadrian made a determined attempt to stamp out the embers not only of the revolt, but also of Jewish nationhood and statehood, obliterating its Jewish identity."[32] Wishing to end, once and for all, Jewish hopes, Hadrian renamed the land itself from Judaea to "Syria Palaestina"—Palestine—after the Jews' historic enemies, the Philistines, a non-Semitic sea people from the Greek isles of the Aegean Sea. So, sorry, Arafatians and Hamasniks. Trying to hijack the Philistines' identity, as you have tried to do with that of the Jews, will not work either.

All of this did not occur until after 135 C.E., with the defeat of Judaea's char-ismatic leader, Shimon Bar Kochba. And, as with the breathtaking discovery of the Dead Sea Scrolls practically at the moment of Israel's rebirth over six decades ago by an Arab shepherd boy, Bar Kochba's letters to his troops, his minted coins "For the Freedom of Israel," and other archaeological treasures were also soon unearthed.

"Palestine" became largely "Arab" the same way that most of the roughly two dozen other states that call themselves Arab today did—by the earlier conquest, occupation, settlement, and forced Arabization of other native, non-Arab peoples and their lands. Muhammad and his successors' imperial Caliphal armies burst out of the Arabian Peninsula in the seventh century C.E. and spread in all directions. Massive numbers of native peoples were slaugh-tered in this process.

The Ottoman Turks were the latest in a long series of imperial conquerors to rule the land of Israel since the Jews fought for their freedom against Rome. They did so for some four centuries up until World War I. From the tenth century onwards the Arabs lost control of the land themselves. And when the Arabs' own Caliphal empires ruled, it was from Damascus or Baghdad. There was not and never has been an independent entity of Arab Palestine.

During the mandatory period following the break-up of empires after World War I, the League of Nations Permanent Mandates commission recorded scores of thousands of Arabs pouring into a largely depopulated Palestine from surrounding countries to take advantage of the economic development going on because of the Jews. Many more entered under cover of darkness and were never listed. All of these folks were preceded in the nineteenth century by many thousands of Egyptians who came with Muhammad Ali and Ibrahim Pasha's invading armies and never left. More Arab settlers were moving into Palestine. Arafat himself was one of them, coming from Cairo. So was Hamas's "patron saint," Izzeddine al-Qassam, arriving from Latakia, Syria.[33]

And so much for Arafat's Jesus.

Arch of Titus

Chapter 5

ATTACK OF THE AMNESIACS

IN LIGHT OF repeated acts of megabarbarism deliberately directed against Israeli innocents, it is far past the time to take a closer look at some of the underlying issues that have frequently been ignored. Consider the following, for starters.

Pick your paper—as diverse as the *Washington Post*, or the *Daytona Beach News-Journal* (Florida). Chances are pretty good that editors and columnists are ready to give advice or offer condemnation regarding Israel on the matter. And this just reflects the American press. It is often far worse elsewhere. Take the BBC, for instance.

The *Post's* Richard Cohen, *The New York Times'* Nicholas Kristof, and many of their colleagues elsewhere did not like Israel's now-comatose Prime Minister Ariel Sharon very much, especially those settlements he had frequently insisted upon.

The *News-Journal's* editorialist Pierre Tristam—one of the point men for the paper's own slant—writes such objective essays as "Barbarism Beneath Israel's Boot." Keep in mind that when Jews were earlier being blown up on buses, in restaurants, in teen night clubs, and such, I never once noticed Tristam using that *b*-word, and I monitored his writing very closely. But those horrible Israeli checkpoints Jews set up to stop the real barbarism—now *that* was just intolerable.[34]

After being bombarded by me and some others on the local media watch committee formed at my house soon after that particular Tristam article appeared, both the *News-Journal* and Pierre started to watch themselves a bit more. All of a sudden, Pierre was soon writing about Islamic extremists too, not that there's any real comparison between them and deliberate Arab disembowelers of Jewish children and the Jews.

Kristof compared Sharon to Arafat. In a piece that appeared in the *News-Journal* on May 27, 2004, he blamed Sharon for "knocking the legs out from under the Palestinian moderates."

The fact that the Arabs had responded to Camp David and Taba 2000, in which they were offered everything but the kitchen sink and responded by starting the bloody intifada instead, "of course" had nothing to do with hurting the so-called peace camps on both sides of the conflict for those of Kristof's persuasion. More about him later.

More often than not, attempts by the public at a meaningful response to such "truths" are suppressed. And those few snippets that are permitted usually appear in the paper long after the original extensive editorial and op-ed attacks, skewed news reporting, pictures, and the like have had a chance to be digested and absorbed as "fact" by readers.

While living in the safety and comfort of their own homes and having to travel farther to work than the width of Israel by its pre-'67, 1949 UN-imposed armistice lines, such folks as these in the media, academia, and in our own State Department seem to prefer a breed of Jew that bares the necks of his kids much easier. But, then again, most of them complained about former Prime Minister Ehud Barak as well, even though, had Arabs agreed to have a state alongside Israel instead of in place of it under his instead of Sharon's watch, virtually all of those settlements would have been history by now. Not to mention the fact that when Sharon himself earlier believed that Israel had a true partner for peace, he dismantled settlements in Sinai for Menachem Begin in order to achieve "peace" with Egypt. Yet to no one's surprise, it was totally ignored by the Richard Cohens, Nicholas Kristofs, and Molly Moores of the media world.

It is also worth noting that it is from "peaceful" Egypt, recipient of more than sixty billion dollars in American top-of-the-line armaments and aid, that those tunnels into Gaza originate from which supply Hamas, Islamic Jihad, & Co., with explosives and armaments to carry out a continuous terror campaign against Jews. So much for what kind of trust Israel can place in any other alleged "peace" agreements Israel is being pressured to make with other Arab regimes. A noticeable exception involves the agreement made with the late King Hussein's Jordan—but that was largely because the same folks who want Israel for dinner tried to roast Hussein's Hashemites as well.

As of April 2004, Sharon had gotten into political trouble in Israel for declaring, in the absence of another Arab partner for peace, that he would dismantle settlements in the strategically important Gaza Strip and West Bank anyway. Many saw this as simply a unilateral reward for terrorism, thereby only encouraging more of it.

True to form, there was no gratitude shown by Arabs for these concessions, just more one-sided demands. Their post-'67 destruction-in-phases scenario was playing out nicely. Nevertheless, the media largely kept up its attacks upon Sharon anyway.

So, all of this begs yet another question: why is there seldom any attempt, in the name of fair journalism, to determine why those Jews are so adamant on the issues of territory and settlements?

As a concession to the roadmap, it had earlier been reported that Arafat and his former (and now current) Holocaust-denying prime minister, Mahmoud Abbas, were seeking to limit Arab terror and incineration of Jews to "just" the West Bank and Gaza. They would thus supposedly be able to show the world that they were only against "occupation and settlers," not Israel itself. A mere look, however, at the material in their own Web sites, textbooks, newspapers, sermons in mosques, and the like quickly reveals and explains what occupied territory really means— Tel Aviv, as well as Hebron. This is even more so for the Hamas crew.

Now, think about the following: after its war to oust Saddam from Iraq, America, many thousands of miles away, banned the Baath Party in Iraq. Regardless of one's thoughts about this, both Hamas and Abbas, located right on miniscule Israel's doorstep, openly declare that no Jewish Israel, regardless of size, has a right to exist. So what should a much more vulnerable Israel insist upon?

For those without a grasp of history, both recent and a bit farther back, this ploy focusing on occupation and settlements will work. And it will do so for those who simply like to believe that Israel is the devil incarnate as well. Unfortunately, it also seems to work with a media afflicted too often with a severe case of amnesia when it comes to such issues. The reality is that this proposed gesture by Arafat was just another staged fiction for, at best, a naïve West.

Just who is a settler in the Middle East, and how is that word defined? Of course, Arabs, Cohen, Tristam, the Foggy Folks, anti-Israel academics, and so forth point to Jews.

Unless the West Bank is ethnically cleansed of the Jewish presence, as the fiction goes, there will be no chance for peace. Much, if not most, of the press constantly supports this position. Countless editorials and columns have appeared spouting such wisdom, and it provides the meat for common lectures as well in academia. The fantasy is also an essential element in the current alleged Saudi peace plan—the one now fully endorsed by President Obama.

Look at just one example of how the media had presented this situation. Consider the November 16, 2002, AP report by Nasser Shiyoukhi. Check out his description of the situation in Hebron, the site at which the Hebrew patriarch, Abraham, purchased a burial site for his family: "The Muslims here are among the most devout and the Jewish settlers among the most radical."

Notice the adjectives as well as the nouns. Unlike the Arabs, the Jews— who know that they are risking their lives living among hostile Arabs but do so anyway for deep religious conviction and faith—were not described as "devout," a positive concept, but were labeled, instead, as being "radical," with negative connotations. Yet Hebron's Tomb of the Patriarchs was sacred to Jews for more than two thousand years before the Prophet of Islam ever lived and before the vast majority of Arabs ever knew that Abraham (whom they now claim to have been Muslim) even existed. The same folks who claim that there was no Temple of Solomon in Jerusalem (Arabs call it Buraq's Mount in honor of Muhammad's winged horse, who supposedly took him on a flight to the holy site and then to heaven) deny any Jewish connections to Hebron as well.

Now for another dose of reality. Arafat was born in Cairo, Egypt. Thousands of other Arabs came from Egypt earlier in the nineteenth century with Muhammad Ali's armies, and many, like Arafat a bit later, settled in Palestine.[35]

During the mandatory period after World War I, the League of Nations Permanent Mandates Commission recorded additional scores of thousands Arabs entering into Palestine and settling there. It is estimated that for each one of these people who were recorded, many others crossed the border under cover of darkness to enter into one of the few areas in the region where any economic development was going on because of the influx of Jewish capital.[36] These folks later became known as "native Palestinians." As just one of many quotes that could be cited regarding this important but most often ignored issue (how many academics bring it up in class? none of mine—even at the doctoral level), consider President Roosevelt's memorandum to his secretary of state on May 17, 1939: "Arab immigration since 1921 has vastly exceeded the total Jewish immigration during this whole period."[37]

While this is not to say that there were not native Arabs also living in Palestine, it is to say that many, if not most, of these folks were also newcomers—settlers—themselves. Many of the villages set up in the West Bank and elsewhere were settlements established by Arab settlers. And there were Jews whose families never left Israel/Judaea/Palestine as well over the centuries—despite the tragedies of the Roman Wars, forced conversions by the Byzantines, the Diaspora, Crusades, and so forth.

So, why is it acceptable to Cohen, Kristof, Tristam, and—at best—their fellow amnesiacs for Arabs from the surrounding lands to settle in Palestine, but not for Israel's Jews, half of whom were refugees themselves from Arab/Muslim lands?

Jews owned land and lived in Judea/Samaria until they were massacred by Arabs in the 1920s. Those lands were not known as the West Bank until British imperialism made its presence there in the twentieth century and purely Arab Transjordan—itself created in 1922 from almost 80 percent of the original Mandate for Palestine Britain received on April 25, 1920—annexed the west bank of the Jordan River after the 1948 fighting.

Saying Jews have no rights in places like Hebron or on the Temple Mount is like claiming that if China conquers the Vatican, then Catholics will no longer have rights there.

Again, the world would not know of the significance of places like Hebron if not for the holy Scriptures of the Jews. If more than one million Arabs can live as citizens without fear in Israel, then why is it that Arabs and President Obama insist that lands where both peoples have historical ties must be made *Judenrein*? If Judea's Jews must leave, then why should Israel's Israeli Arabs (many of whom who are hostile to the state) stay?

UN Resolution #242 emerged in the aftermath of the Six Day War. It did not call for Israel to return to those suicidal, pre-'67 armistice lines.[38] Among other things, those lines had made Israel a mere nine miles wide, a constant temptation to its enemies.

Notice, please, that the vast majority of the settlements are built on strategic high ground areas designed to provide precisely what Israel is entitled to under Resolution 242, a slightly increased buffer from those who would destroy it. Furthermore, any eventual Israeli withdrawal was to be linked to the establishment of "secure and recognized borders" to replace those fragile lines. Many of those nations now demanding Israel to forsake this have conquered nations and acquired territories hundreds or thousands of miles away from home in the name of their own national security interests.

Legal experts such as William V. O'Brien, Eugene Rostow, and others have repeatedly stated that the non-apportioned areas (the West Bank in particular) of the Palestinian Mandate were open to settlement by all residents of the Mandate, not just Arabs.[39] That Arabs disagree is not a shock. They do not believe Jews have rights in any part of Israel. I will provide a constant reminder that most of the almost two dozen so-called Arab states were themselves conquered and forcibly Arabized from non-Arab peoples like the Imazighen/Berbers, Copts, Kurds, Jews, black Africans, and others as well.

Lastly, at Camp David 2000 and Taba, Barak's Israel offered to end the occupation. Recall that 97 percent of the disputed (not "occupied") territories, half of Jerusalem, a $33 billion fund, and other concessions were offered to Arafat in a contiguous state, not disconnected cantons, as Arab spin doctors now claim. Ambassador Dennis Ross was there as U.S. chief negotiator and confirmed all of this.[40] I will take his word over Arafat's—so much for "occupation" being the cause of the problem.

Unfortunately, the predominant Arab "vision of peace" still has no room for a permanent Israel. Some have made a tactical decision to play the game to win as many concessions diplomatically (and to acquire billions of dollars in foreign aid) from Israel as possible, making their end goal that much easier to achieve.

Arafat and others speak of the "Peace of the Quraysh." The Quraysh were a pagan tribe with whom the Muslim prophet Muhammad made a temporary peace until he gained enough strength to deal the final blow. Even the PLO's late showcase model moderate, Faisal al-Husseini, called for a purely Arab Palestine "from the River to the Sea."[41]

If one is really interested in seeing what Arab thinking is in these regards, all that is required is an online visit to the "moderate" Palestinian Authority Web sites or a look at their textbooks, maps, insignias, and such. There is no Israel present. And these are the "good cops." Go to the Hamas site and then understand why the sole, miniscule state of the Jews cannot be expected to commit national suicide so that Arabs can obtain their twenty-second state—and second in Palestine.

Chapter 6

In Defense of Bantustan

(Note: The following three chapters are especially useful to help place events and situations into a more balanced and wider perspective.)

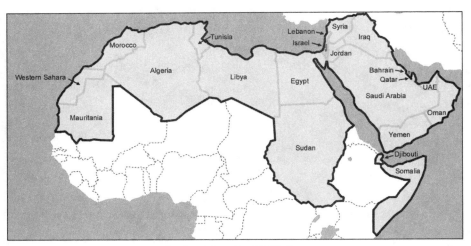

Israel and the wider Middle East

A WHILE BACK, PRESIDENT Bush and Secretary of State Powell made the point at "roadmap" summits that the prospective twenty-second Arab state was to be no Bantustan. They and others have repeated this many times in voicing concerns that Israel's security fence, being built to keep Arabs from deliberately blowing up Jewish innocents aboard buses, in restaurants, teen night clubs, pizzerias, shopping malls, and the like does not follow the "green line" which demarcated Israel's pre-'67, nine-mile-wide armistice line (not border) existence. The original Bantustan was a disconnected entity created for blacks under the apartheid regime in South Africa and no substitute for a real state.

Before we proceed, let's first look at the above regional map. Try to find Israel without the aid of a magnifying glass. On a map of the world, you might need a microscope.

While all people should be able to live in dignity, this applies to Jews, also. This, unfortunately, proved often to be impossible both in the Christian West, where Jews were considered to be the deicide people (and were treated accordingly), as well as in the Muslim East, where they were considered to be persecutors of prophets and *kilab yahud*—"Jew dogs." Hence the necessity of the rebirth of Israel on less than one-half of one percent of the territory of the Middle East and North Africa.

As will be constantly stated, in creating those "Arab" states on more than six million square miles of territory, millions of non-Arabs—Imazighen, Copts, Kurds, black Africans, Jews, and so forth—were slaughtered and/or conquered and forcibly Arabized, often having their own native cultures and languages outlawed, violently suppressed, and so forth. It continues to happen, even as this book is being completed, not just in the past.[42]

Please be sure to check out this past footnote. All of it. And then ask yourself the following question: how could any professor, claiming objectivity, ignore all of this—as is routinely done in the typical Middle East Studies class taught by the typical Middle East Studies Association (MESA) professor—while pontificating about such things as checkpoints and the security barrier Israel has been forced to set up to prevent its kids from being blown apart, racist and/or imperialist Zionism, and so forth?

Once you deliberately change lenses (these folks are not stupid and have even more access to such information as you see in footnote 42 than I do) when comparing the alleged sins of Israel to those of the "Arab"/Muslim world that surrounds it (which, if the lens switch were not done, would then place Israel in line for canonization), you lose—or should lose—all academic credibility. Yet, again, this happens routinely. Such academic duplicity and hypocrisy is the rule, not the exception, on the typical university campus—and those who dare to disagree or protest do so at the risk of their own academic careers.

Been there, done that.

While Arabs and their supporters use 1947 as the starting point for discussion about the partition of Palestine, this is blatantly dishonest—for reasons already cited. As we have seen, the land called Palestine by then represented only about 20 percent of the original, as it existed in 1920 before the separation of Transjordan—all the land east of the Jordan River, given as a reward to Britain's World War I Hashemite Arab allies in 1922. An Arab state has thus existed on some 80 percent of Palestine since 1922—today's Jordan—regardless of the distaste of this fact by the Israel bashers. Transjordan's ruler, Emir Abdullah, attributed this to an act of Allah in his memoirs.

Are there local differences between Arabs? Sure, just as there are differences between South Carolinians and Georgians, or Californians and New Yorkers. Jews did not ask for dozens of different states because their people came from dozens of different countries (including Jews whose families never left the land of Israel since the Roman wars). Arabs are not entitled to dozens of states at the expense of one for Jews, Kurds, Imazighen, and so forth. Yet that is precisely what Arabs expect. In fact, they call not achieving this their *Nakba*—catastrophe.

Despite all of this, Arabs rejected the 1947 partition as well, even though Jews would have wound up with about 10 percent of the original area of the 1920 Palestinian Mandate with various Arab nationalists receiving some 90 percent of it.

Then, as now, for the vast majority of Arabs, it is not how big Israel is that is the crux of the issue. It is that Israel, in fact, *is* that poses their problem.

So Mr. Bush's, Mr. Powell's, and all the more recent statements coming out of the European Union and the White House regarding the "two-state" solution (which Arabs do not accept, despite the whitewashing) have been largely misdirected.

It has not been Jews who have rejected fair and honorable solutions over the decades. And similar compromise partitions and such between competing national movements elsewhere have not been uncommon, involving population exchanges and the like. All of them left personal heartaches in their wakes for the sake of arriving at justice for the bigger picture. The compromise that created Hindu India and Muslim Pakistan at the same time Arabs rejected the 1947 partition plan for Palestine especially comes to mind.

At the close of hostilities after the invasion by Arab states of a nascent Israel in 1948, the UN-imposed armistice lines made Israel a mere nine miles to fifteen miles wide at its waist, a constant temptation to its enemies. Most of Israel's population and industry lies in that narrow waistband. I travel three times that distance—one way—just to go to work.

In the aftermath of the 1967 Six Day War, Israel was forced to fight after it was blockaded at the Straits of Tiran and other numerous hostile acts. UN Resolution 242 did not demand that Israel return to the status quo ante. It called, instead, for the creation of "secure and recognized borders" to replace those fragile '49 armistice lines. And any Israeli withdrawal was to be made in the context of real peace treaties, not *hudna*-shmudna jokes the Arabs offer— temporary ceasefires designed only to strengthen the Arab position while endangering Israel even further.

Any such true peace agreement must take all of the above into account. Keep this in mind as well regarding the path of Israel's security fence. Israel's main airport, Parliament, and so forth must not be exposed to what southern Israel has been receiving since Israel unilaterally withdrew from Gaza years ago, non-stop terror deliberately aimed at Israeli civilians via thousands of rockets and mortars. Ask the ghost of General Patton about what he would do with such an enemy. Or, for that matter, any general in charge of any nation's defense.

Israelis have no desire to rule over several million Arabs in the disputed territories. But they also do not want one or two good cop/bad cop, Mahmoud Abbas-disguised, Fatah/Hamas state or states set up in their backyard and side porch that only temporarily allow for a relative quiet to further its still retained destruction-in-stages goals.

More than lip service is required to grant an extremely vulnerable Israel the security any other nation would demand.

This means—or should mean—that Arabs are not going to be able to get all that they want on the West Bank and elsewhere as well. That is what is meant by "compromise." And this also means that the additional Arab state will not be very large and will have some restrictions placed upon it. Truth be told, there is obviously not really room for a third state to be created within the original borders of 1920 Palestine—a second Arab one to be created there.

The contiguity, viability, and such of that proposed twenty-second Arab state must not come at the expense of the security and viability of the sole, minuscule state of the Jews—one half of whom, in Israel, were refugees themselves from so-called "Arab" lands. And that is the missing half of all the statements about a "two-state solution," "bantustan," and such that those of us who care about the quest for relative justice and the long-term health of Israel and other victims of Arab conquest and subjugation in the region worry about.

Chapter 7

RESOLUTION TO KILL THE RESOLUTION

A T A DAILY briefing on January 9, 1992, State Department spokesperson Margaret Tutwiler was asked about accepting the word *Palestinian* when referring to the territories of the West Bank, Gaza, and Jerusalem. Her answer was that the U.S. had accepted this usage since 1979, but that it was for "descriptive" purposes only. Typical Foggy Folk gobbledygook.

When later asked, "If it is a long-standing policy, why wasn't the word *Palestinian* used in UN Security Council (UNSC) Resolution 338 or in 242, which underpins the current peace process?" Tutwiler replied, "I do not know why, and I'll be happy to ask somebody for you."[43] Some five years later, in a May 21, 1997 briefing, the State Department's spokesman, Nicholas Burns, focused on the "settlements" issue.[44]

Interesting, don't you think, that in numerous similar briefings by the State Department over the decades—and in all the discussions and elaborations that ensued—the ties seem to never be made between those settlements the new Obama administration also lectures Israel about and the spirit and intent of UNSC Resolution 242. Perhaps it is a coincidence, but I think not.

It seems to have taken Secretary of Defense Donald Rumsfeld to remind his State Department counterparts in an August 6, 2002, speech, "If you have a country that is a sliver and you can see three sides of it from a high hotel building, you've got to be careful what you give away and to whom you give it...."[45]

Much has been written about 242. Some claim it is ambiguous. Not so. Adopted in the wake of the June 1967 War—started when Arabs blockaded Israel at the Straits of Tiran and the Gulf of Aqaba (a *casus belli*); threw the UN Peacekeeping Force out; and amassed one hundred thousand troops, armor, planes, and so forth right up to Israel's border while calling for a war of extermination; and so forth—242 is as famous for what it did not say as for what it did.

As anyone who has studied this subject knows, among other things (and besides the references above), there was no mention of a total withdrawal by Israel to the 1949, UN-imposed armistice lines, which were never meant to be final political borders. This was reinforced by a call for the creation of "secure and recognized borders" to replace those lines—lines that turned Israel into that nine-mile wide rump state, forever at its neighbors' mercy.

As we've already discovered, a reading of Lord Caradon, Eugene Rostow,

Arthur Goldberg, and other architects of 242 clearly shows that Israel was not expected to return to the deadly and absurd status quo ante.

As Ambassador Dore Gold and others have pointed out, President Lyndon Johnson summarized the situation this way on June 19, 1967: "A return to the situation on June 4 [the day before outbreak of war] was not a prescription for peace but for renewed hostilities." He then called for "new recognized boundaries that would provide security against terror, destruction, and war."[46] Johnson was backed up by General Earle Wheeler of the Joint Chiefs of Staff and many others as well. Here's a brief excerpt from Wheeler's Pentagon document prepared for Secretary of Defense Robert McNamara on June 29, 1967: "Israel would require retention of some captured Arab territory to provide militarily defensible borders."[47]

Keep in mind that on the West Bank, Israel took these lands in a defensive war from an illegal occupant—Transjordan—which subsequently renamed itself Jordan as a result of its 1949 illegal acquisition of non-apportioned lands of the original 1920 Mandate west of the Jordan River, which Jews as well as Arabs were legally entitled to live on. Indeed, Jews have thousands of years of history connecting them to these lands and owned property and lived there up until their massacres by Arabs in the 1920s and 1930s. Additionally, many, if not most, of the Arabs themselves were also relative newcomers, pouring in from Syria, Egypt, and elsewhere in the region.

General Wheeler's document also envisioned Israel acquiring an adequate buffer zone atop the West Bank mountain ridge, in command of the high ground, giving it at least some semblance of in-depth defense.

During President Richard Nixon's term in office, official U.S. policy seemed to erode vis-à-vis Johnson's position. Whether this was due to Nixon himself or the State Department's Arabists (who opposed Israel's rebirth in the first place) reasserting themselves, on December 9, 1969, Secretary of State William Rogers allowed for only "insubstantial alterations" regarding the 1949 armistice lines. After having to answer to Senator Henry "Scoop" Jackson and others as well, soon afterwards—until recently—the U.S. refrained from such deviation from both the wording and intent of 242.

Moving ahead, and once again utilizing Ambassador Gold's useful summary, here is what President Ronald Reagan had to say about all of this on September 1, 1982: "In the pre-1967 borders, Israel was barely ten miles wide. The bulk of Israel's population was within artillery range of hostile armies. I am not about to ask Israel to live that way again."[48]

In 1988, Secretary of State George Shultz declared, "Israel will never negotiate from or return to the 1967 borders."[49]

In the 1990s, during the Clinton years (and despite the later pressure brought to bear on Prime Minister Ehud Barak to sweeten the pot by offering Arafat far more than 242 called for at Camp David and Taba in 2000), official policy, as expressed by Secretary of State Warren Christopher in 1997, was that, "Israel is entitled to secure and defensible borders"—à la 242.

So, what happened between the days of Reagan and his latter day successors? From Reagan's 1982 statement that Israel would never be expected to return to its former ultra-vulnerable existence, we progressed to President George W. Bush's May 26, 2005, White House statement that the 1949 armistice lines must be the basis of peace between Israel and the twenty-second Arab state—the second Arab one in "Palestine"—which both Bush and, even more so, his successor, President Barack Obama, are determined to create, no matter what.

President Obama's first phone call in early 2009 to a foreign leader was to the alleged good cop, Mahmoud Abbas—a Holocaust denier who still refuses to ever recognize a Jewish Israel and expects the latter to consent to being swamped by millions of "returning" Arab refugees, after Israel also forsakes 242 and withdraws back to the '49 armistice lines.[50]

A year before his turnaround, Bush had echoed Reagan himself, stating virtually the opposite of his May 26, 2005, statement in a much-publicized letter he gave to Prime Minister Sharon as the latter was preparing for the unilateral Israeli withdrawal from Gaza.

So, as Rogers and Hammerstein's King of Siam said in *The King And I,* "'Tis a puzzlement!"

Indeed.

Yet, prior to the Obama Administration (with its own anti-Israel folks appointed to key positions; failed attempts to place others like Chas Freeman there; Rashid Khalidi-types present in the wings; and so forth—besides the presence of Jews the president can point to, but who really do not matter for such things), there was one constant ingredient that seems to have worked for the erosion of support for both the vision and the spirit of 242 over the previous years—James A. Baker III.

During President George W. Bush's dad's days in office, good buddy Secretary of State James Baker III promised the butcher of Damascus, Hafez al-Assad, a total Israeli withdrawal from the strategically important (and once part of the original Palestine Mandate) Golan Heights. This was his idea about what to do with 242. Unfortunately, that also now seems to be President Obama's as well, if he could just get a bit more cooperation from Damascus on Iraq and Lebanon.

Baker has been in the background for decades, especially since his close friends, the Bushes, gained ascendancy in American politics. His law firm represents Saudi and other Arab interests in this country and typifies how people move through the revolving doors of businesses tied to Arab interests back and forth into government positions—especially those in Foggy Bottom. Baker's law partner, Robert Jordan, was appointed ambassador to Saudi Arabia by President Bush in 2001. George Shultz, Casper Weinberger, and many others have been through these lucrative doors as well. Most often, their influence has spelled trouble for an Israel trying to get a fair hearing and has been involved in eroding such positive developments as Resolution 242 and so forth.

In a *Time* magazine article on February 13, 1989, Baker spoke of Israel as being a turkey to be hunted and carefully stalked. He has referred to Jews working for him and doing his bidding (including the recent American ambassador to Israel and Obama friend) as his "Jew boys." But Baker is perhaps best known on this topic for his following piece of wisdom, "[deleted] the Jews, they don't vote for us anyway!"[51]

You know it is true because—as a zillionaire, high-power lawyer who likes also to talk about those Jews and their money (nah, he's not interested in such stuff; just ask his Arab petrodollar moneybag friends)—he would have sued long ago over this revelation if he could. And if you believe that Baker is alone among the power brokers with these attitudes, I have two bridges to sell you.

This, indeed, says it all regarding what Israel can expect from such circles. If you wonder why the vision of justice in 242 has been replaced by a constant bickering over settlements instead—never tying the two together—look no further. Please take another look at that map in chapter #6. Is this fight really about territory?

George W.'s winning a second term in office and his appointment of Baker as his special Middle East envoy combined with the recharged influence of the State Department's old and new generation Arabists and the Bush family's massive oil connections to negate any alleged influence of Evangelical Christians seeking justice for Israel. Furthermore, realizing that he would not have to run again and need the latter's support, he probably calculated that he basically had nothing to lose and much to gain financially down the road. Just ask Presidents Carter and Clinton about such Arab "appreciation," if further explanation is needed. Shafting Jews pays nicely.

Only time will tell how this will all play out.

But, at this point, Israel will have to depend on the integrity, courage, and fortitude of its own leaders (missing lately—until very recently), expecting them to act as the leaders of any other nation faced with the same circumstances would act. Only they can insist that Israel gets the justice Resolution

242 promised it. And, while it would be nice to have support from elsewhere, that is the way it should be anyway.

I believe that newly-elected Prime Minister Benjamin Netanyahu and Foreign Minister Avigdor Lieberman have what it takes to resist the enormous pressure that will be placed upon Israel (including and especially by its friends) to forsake basic national security interests—not thousands of miles away, but a stone's throw from its kids—that none of those making these demands on the Jewish state would ever consider doing themselves.

Chapter 8

MISSING: ONE ARAB *ALTALENA*

BACK IN FALL 2003, news reports were circulating about "behind-the-scenes" peace plans that supposedly had been worked out by left-wing Israelis and some Palestinian Arab politicians and academics, notably Yasser Abed Rabbo and Sari Nusseibeh.

As a result of the Arab invasion of a newborn Israel in 1948, two refugee situations were created: Arabs who fled Israel and a like number of Jews who fled "Arab"/Muslim lands. Unlike the former, however, the latter did not have some two dozen other states to potentially choose from, including one carved out of some 80 percent of the original Palestinian Mandate issued to Britain on April 25, 1920, and today known as Jordan.

Nusseibeh is perhaps best noted for his advice to Arab refugees—some real and many fudged—to give up their claim to return to Israel proper in order for peace to occur.[52] Arabs still believe that they will be allowed to do just that and overwhelm the Jews with their numbers. And why shouldn't they believe this? After all, it is part of the current alleged Saudi "peace" plan that President Obama claims Israel would be nuts to reject.

Earlier, President Bush sent the same message as Nusseibeh in his April 2004 televised public announcement to the world while responding to Prime Minister Sharon's disengagement plan for Gaza and parts of Judea and Samaria, aka the West Bank. Nusseibeh has also called for an end to suicide bombings. The American State Department—grasping at straws to blow some life into its all but dead "roadmap"—had also given its own blessings to these initiatives.

The problem, of course, is that, unlike Israel, where there is strong grassroots sentiment for an honorable compromise to be found, poll after poll among Arabs still reveal that even if Israel agreed to withdraw to its pre-'67, nine-mile-wide, armistice line existence, most Arabs would still not accept its right to exist anyway and would continue to support attacks upon its people.

The sad reality is that folks like Nusseibeh continue to live only because Hamas, Islamic Jihad, al-Aqsa, and Mahmoud Abbas's latter-day Arafatians themselves do not take them seriously. And Nusseibeh has also been caught playing tricks with his words. Maybe he had to—if you get my drift.

Isam Sartawi and other previous rare voices of reason were eliminated as soon as they appeared to be a real threat to the overwhelming Arab rejectionist mentality. Mahmoud Abbas's allegedly moderate Palestinian Authority has done nothing to change this climate. The latter's schools, media, mosques, and so forth continue to assure that the possibility of an Arab "grassroots" campaign for an honorable peace with a viable Jewish neighbor will be an impossibility for at least a long time to come. Instead, the "moderates" play a game and speak only of a temporary "Trojan horse" truce—a *hudna*—designed to gain concrete tangibles from Israel on the ground while retaining their destruction-in-stages goals toward the Jewish state.

Nusseibeh is like the Eugene McCarthy of American politics back in 1968, but not as influential. He is tolerated only as long as he is useful to be show-cased as a voice of alleged Arab moderation and reason to a naïve West. As we've already discussed, the late Faisal al-Husseini served in a somewhat similar capacity, although his "vision" was still a purely Arab Palestine from the river to the sea. Rabbo can be seen as just another Arafatian marionette. Don't look for anything really "new" from this direction either.

As long as the Nusseibeh types can be used to win additional concessions from Israel, they are safe—since they serve an important purpose in helping to create the façade of Fatah moderation. But they better have some solid tricks up their sleeves if they actually expect either the Abbas or Hamas crews to have to live up to such pipe dreams.

Will Yossi Beilin, Yasser Abed Rabbo, Sari Nusseibeh, Secretary of State Clinton, or President Obama feel safe boarding a bus in Jerusalem or eating in a restaurant in Haifa once Israel is forced back to its suicidal '49 armistice lines, removes checkpoints, and the like? That's the real test of any such peace plan or "deal" that is proposed.

Thus, little of the above should be taken seriously until something crucial occurs to change the current reality. Let's step back again to the days of the Mandate to truly understand what is needed at this time.

It was early May 1948, coincidently almost at the very moment of my own birth. Surrounding Arab countries invaded a reborn Israel to nip it in the bud. The Jews had no choice but to immediately emerge out of the shock of the Holocaust in order to deal with yet another harsh reality.

David Ben-Gurion, leader of the new state, made countless historic decisions, but one particularly painful one involved the ship *Altalena*—a pen name for his Labor Zionist Party's rival, the late Ze'ev Vladimir Jabotinsky.

Jabotinsky's heirs were determined to repay the Arab slaughter of Jews in kind and to hasten the end of British rule and anti-Israel policies by any means necessary. Among other things, they purchased an American ship and landed it near Marseilles, France. It was expected that the vessel would be making repeated trips between France and Israel carrying arms and new recruits gathered from the survivors of Europe's nightmare and the frightened mellahs of *kilab yahud*—"Jew dog"—Jewish existence in "Arab" North Africa and the Middle East.

Israel desperately needed the arms and manpower aboard the *Altalena*. But Ben-Gurion insisted that there would be but one unified command. On June 20, Ben-Gurion made a decision to resist the Irgun's challenge concerning the ship's precious human and material cargo. In the ensuing tragic battle, scores of Jews were killed by fellow Jews for the sake of shaping the infant state's future and character. There is a big debate still going on today over this incident.

Holocaust-denying author, first Arafat-appointed, now currently-elected Palestinian Authority Prime Minister Mahmoud Abbas had given lip service to the need to end attacks on Jewish innocents—for whatever his reasons. He and his earlier Arafatian successor, Ahmed Qurei' (Abu Alaa—remember him?) specifically did not like the bad press that comes along with suicide bombings. Arafat, the master puppeteer, had long been exposed as saying one thing to Western ears and quite another to his own people in these regards. He trained his comrades well.

Both the supposedly "moderate" Abbas and his then-security chief, Mohammad Dahlan, had past ties themselves to terrorist activities. Yet the hope was, that was yesterday's news and that there could be a chance for a better tomorrow. But Hamas is Hamas, and latter-day Arafatians have the former's same intentions for the long term. Meanwhile, they will enrich themselves and, by playing the game, currently have America itself constructing, training, and supplying a Palestinian Arab Army—among other things. Billions of dollars more in aid are at stake as well, coming from the European Union and so forth. As Mel Brooks said in his movie *History of the World*, "It's good to be the king,"—er, moderate.

The truth is that neither the good cops nor the bad cops above have any intention of arriving at an agreement in which a viable Jewish state exists on the morrow. That has been proven over and over again. And there will be no better tomorrow with any of these folks still calling the shots. Literally.

That better tomorrow will not arrive unless new leaders arise in that would-be twenty-second Arab state with the willpower to make the decisions a stateless and millennially persecuted people and its leaders—literally, at the end of their collective rope—made more than sixty years ago.

What will the real and alleged peaceniks and assorted world hypocrites do the day after the next Egged bus blows up loaded with innocent Jews aboard? Or another father is murdered having dinner with his children? Or mother assassinated at point-blank range, along with her kids in a car? Or when

Tel Aviv, Ben Gurion Airport, Haifa, the Knesset, or Jerusalem is hit by the same—or better, U.S.-supplied—rockets, mortars, suicide bombers, and so forth after Israel has been forced to withdraw to its microscopic, '49 armistice line existence yet again?

The Oslo days of the Trojan horse "peace" (President Clinton's legacy) that Arabs played with Jews are over. The more Israel gave, the more it continuously bled.[53]

Despite Arab visions of the much-touted and now highly endangered "roadmap" or the current push for the Saudi "peace (of the grave) plan" to the contrary, there can be no Oslo II.

How many nations would tolerate the virtually continuous terror and such that Israelis are simply expected to put up with? Israel constantly prevents attacks you do not get to read about in the news practically daily. The decrease in incidents is largely the result of that security fence and those checkpoints the world wants it to dismantle or render virtually useless. As soon as Israel caves in to show flexibility, Jews are typically soon massacred afterwards.

Until Arabs make clear their intention to live peacefully alongside a secure Jewish state with concrete measures that are actually taken to stop the murder of Jews, the constant promotion of hatred and violence among the Arab masses (from kindergarten up), and so forth, then Israel should not be expected to become a party to its own demise by caving in to Arab demands and those who support them.

No other country would expect less under the circumstances Israel has been constantly faced with.

What's missing, you see, is the Arabs' own *Altalena*.

Chapter 9

THINKING JERUSALEM

IF YOU THOUGHT the security barrier Israel is building to try to keep Arabs from deliberately murdering its kids was an international hot potato, just wait. While it keeps getting shoved onto the back burner for fear of the intense heat that it will generate, there is no doubt that Jerusalem will be one of the most difficult issues to resolve in any so-called "peace process."

A while back, Yossi Beilin and some other fellow delusional Israelis brought the subject up in their Geneva fiasco with some of Arafat's conscious and unconscious marionettes. As with the rest of that initiative, Jews would give up concrete tangibles—in this case sacred ones—in return for vague Arab promises à la the earlier Oslo disaster. Given this, it is time to take a look at some candid facts regarding Jerusalem, despite the risk of ruffling even some friendly feathers.

While Christians, Muslims, and Jews all have ties to Jerusalem, these ties are in no way "equal." In religious Jewish sources, for instance, Jerusalem is mentioned more than six hundred times, but it is never mentioned even once in the Quran. It is alluded to in the latter in passages about the Hebrew kings David and Solomon and the destruction of the temples of the Jews. Arafat and his latter-day Arafatians (Abbas & Co.), as well as the Hamasniks, deny a Jewish temple ever existed there. They call the Temple Mount "Buraq's Mount," after Muhammad's legendary winged horse. But a mention of Jerusalem itself is nowhere to be found in the Muslim holy book; interesting, since it was recorded in many other places besides the writings of the Jews themselves for more than 1,500 years before the rise of Islam.

Religious claims of both Christians and Muslims to Jerusalem exist primarily because of both of their links to the Jews. Political claims, based upon facts on the ground, are, admittedly, more complicated. Even so, throughout over three millennia since King David conquered it from the Jebusites, renamed it, and gave it its Jewish character, no other people except the Jews has ever made Jerusalem their capital, despite its conquest by many imperial powers, including that of the Arab Caliphal successors to Muhammad as they burst out of the Arabian Peninsula in the seventh century C.E. and spread in all directions. Damascus and Baghdad were the seats of Arab Caliphal imperial power, and Mecca and Medina the holy cities. This is not to say that Jerusalem was ignored by its Muslim conquerors, such as the Umayyads, who built the Dome of the Rock/Mosque of 'Umar on the Temple Mount, making it Islam's allegedly third holiest city. But it is to say that Jerusalem was, and is, in no way the focus for Muslims and Islam that it is for Jews and Judaism.

Since David made Jerusalem his capital and it became the site of his son Solomon's temple, Zion became the heart and soul of Jewish national and religious existence. Jews from all over the early Diaspora made their pilgrimages and sent offerings to its temple.

"By the Rivers of Babylon we wept," and "If I forget thee, O Jerusalem, may my right hand forget its cunning," were just a few of the many biblical expressions of the Jews for Zion. Such yearning persisted throughout subsequent millennia in the Diaspora as well. "Next year in Jerusalem," sustained the Jew throughout countless degradations and humiliations culminating in the Holocaust, in the Muslim East, as well as the Christian West.

There is no Muslim parallel to these claims, despite efforts today to portray Palestinian Arabs (many of whom were new arrivals—settlers—in the land themselves) as the "new Jews."

Jews coming from a hundred different lands (including those native to Israel itself) did not have almost two dozen other states, as Arabs have, to potentially choose from and suffered dearly for this statelessness. Most Arabs claim sole rights over Jerusalem the same way they want sole rights over Tel Aviv. In their eyes, only they have legitimate political rights anywhere in what they regard as the Dar ul-Islam.

Regardless of whatever theology one clings to, Jesus' historical experiences in Roman-occupied Judaea and Jerusalem were those of a Jew living under extremely precarious conditions. Thousands of his countrymen had already been killed, crucified, and so forth in the subjugation/pacification process. The contemporary Roman and Roman-sponsored historians themselves—Tacitus, Josephus, and Dio Cassius—had much to say about all of this. Recall, again, this one telling quote from Tacitus, "Vespasian succeeded to the throne, it infuriated his resentment that the Jews were the only nation who had not yet submitted." And during this tumultuous period, regardless of the nature of the leadership role one assumed or was perceived as assuming—worldly, heavenly, or otherwise—if such a leader appeared as any kind of threat to Roman rule whatsoever, that leader was soon history.

These oppressive conditions led to open revolts and guerilla warfare to rid the land of its mighty pagan conqueror—wars which would eventually lead the Roman emperor, Hadrian, to rename the land itself from Judaea to Syria Palaestina in 135 C.E. in an attempt to stamp out any remaining hopes for Jewish independence and national existence. Judaea was thus renamed after the

Jews' historic enemies, the Philistines, a non-Semitic sea people from Aegean region, to drive home the point.

For a modern analogy, imagine Lithuania as it was engulfed by the Soviet Union in the latter's heyday of power. Or a Hungarian freedom fighter or Greek partisan taking on the Soviets or the Nazis. Think of the sympathy and admiration normally given to such situations.

Now also think about the treatment Jews have received over the ages for longing for this same freedom and dignity. Whatever Jesus did or did not mean in his statement, "Render unto Caesar," this passage and others in the New Testament have been used to belittle this same desire for freedom and independence among the Jews.

Judaea Capta (not "Palaestina" Capta) coins were issued, and the towering Arch of Titus was erected after the first major revolt in 66–73 C.E., showing, among other things, the Romans carrying away the giant menorah and other objects from the Jewish temple that at least many, if not most, Arabs and other Muslims claim never existed. It stands in Rome to this very day to commemorate Rome's victory over the Jews and Jewish Jerusalem.

When Muhammad, the prophet of Islam, fled Mecca to Medina in 622 C.E. (the Hijrah), the inhabitants welcomed him. Medina had been developed centuries earlier as a thriving date palm oasis by Jews fleeing the Roman assault in Judaea (the banu-Qurayzah and banu-al-Nadir tribes, etc.), and its mixed population of Jews and pagan Arabs had thus become conditioned for a native prophet conveying a similar message.

Muhammad learned much from the Jews. While the actual timing of his decision on the direction of prayer may never be known, during his long sojourn with the Jews of Medina, his followers were instructed to pray toward Jerusalem. Early prominent Islamic historians, such as Jalaluddin, came right out and stated that this was done primarily as an attempt to win support among the influential Jewish tribes (the "People of the Book") for Muhammad's religio-politcal claims.[54]

It is from the Temple Mount in Jerusalem that Muslims believe Muhammad ascended to heaven on his winged horse. A mosque, the Dome of the Rock, would later be erected on this Jewish holy site after the Arab imperial conquest of the land in the seventh century C.E.

There is no doubt among objective scholars that Jews had an enormous impact on both Muhammad and the religion that he founded. The holy sites for Muslims in Jerusalem (the mosques erected on the Temple Mount of the Jews) are now deemed holy precisely because of the critical years Muhammad spent after the Hijrah with the Jews. The Temple Mount had no prior meaning to pagan Arabs. While there was some early Christian influence as well, intense scholarship has shown that the holy Law (*Halakha*) and holy Scriptures of the Jews had a tremendous influence on the Quran, Islamic Holy Law (Shari'a), and the like.

Muhammad's "Jerusalem connection" was most likely not established until after his extended stay with his Jewish hosts. This was no mere coincidence, Muslim religious beliefs regarding Muhammad's conversations with the Angel Gabriel and such notwithstanding.

When the Jews refused to recognize Muhammad as the "Seal of the Prophets," he turned on them with a vengeance. Before long, with the exception of Yemen, there were virtually no Jews left on the Arabian Peninsula. And the direction of prayer was soon changed away from Jerusalem and toward the Kaaba in Mecca instead.

While it may be more politically correct these days to do so, to state that Jerusalem has the same meaning for Muslims as it has for Jews is to simply tell a lie.

In modern times, Jews constituted the majority of Jerusalem's population from 1840 onward. When Jordanian Arabs—whose nation itself was formed from almost 80 percent of the original Mandate for Palestine issued to Britain on April 25, 1920—seized east Jerusalem after their invasion of reborn Israel in 1948, they destroyed dozens of synagogues and thousands of Jewish graves, using tombstones to pave roads, build latrines, and so forth.[55]

When Jews were denied access to their holy sites for almost two decades, the whole world remained silent. After Israel was forced to fight a defensive war in 1967 due to its being blockaded by Egypt's Nasser at the Straits of Tiran (a *casus belli*) and other hostile acts, Jerusalem became reunited. Access to all peoples and faiths subsequently became unhindered. It was at this moment that much of the world next chose to rediscover Jerusalem, demanding its redivision, internationalization, and such. Now there's justice for you! It is sickening, but, unfortunately, not really shocking or unexpected in the Jewish experience.

For centuries, Jews were forcibly converted and/or expelled, massacred, humiliated, demonized, inquisitioned, ghettoized, declared the "deicide people," and so forth—to one extent or another—in both the Muslim East and the Christian West. They are determined that their rights in the sole capital of the sole, microscopic, reborn state that they possess will not be sacrificed on behalf of any twenty-second state created for Arabs, especially since the latter show, in poll after poll, that regardless of how much more Jews will bare their necks for peace, Arabs will not accept the legitimacy of a viable Jewish Israel anyway.

Chapter 10

CHUTZPAH—ARAB STYLE

D R. AARON KLIEMAN'S book, *Foundations of British Policy in the Arab World: The Cairo Conference of 1921* should be "must reading" for those who truly want to make sense out of the conflict between Arab and Jew in the Middle East today. It is one of those references that other prominent scholars used to cite in their own works.[56] Nowadays, however, with much of this field being hijacked by a blatantly anti-American and anti-Israel fraternity, things have changed.

The chief tenured honcho who taught this subject while I was doing my own doctoral studies, for instance, managed to teach an entire graduate course on the Palestine Mandate without ever bothering to mention either Klieman's important work or the crucial facts within it, which you soon will be reading. That was almost three decades ago, and—as I feel a need to reiterate time and again so folks truly understand how such courses are often run in such classes—woe unto thee if you dared bring such things up.

Things have perhaps gotten even worse today, as Dr. Daniel Pipes' Campus Watch can testify to. But back when I was trying to complete my doctoral studies, I was left hanging in the wind with no Campus Watch or any other organization like it—and all at a university where wealthy Jewish benefactors forked over millions of dollars in contributions to the university.

The Associated Press report headlined in the *Daytona Beach News-Journal* on February 25, 2004, read as follows: "Jordan Joins Chorus Against Israeli Wall." It was Jordan's turn to lay it on the Jews.

Prince Zeid al Hussein complained that the security fence/defensive barrier Israel was erecting to help prevent its innocents from being blown to bits on buses, in restaurants, and the like might send Palestinian Arabs fleeing into his own kingdom. He also justified the suicide bombings by blaming them on the four decades' old Israeli occupation.

Now for a reality check. Indeed, the Hashemites would do themselves a service by not addressing this issue to anyone with any knowledge of the actual facts and history involved. Since many, if not most, folks do not possess this, Arabs and their supporters feel free to rant.

To appreciate what comes next, first find a map of the Middle East and North Africa (such as that provided in chapter 6). One of the world will do, but everything will be much smaller. Find Jordan and then find Israel to its west.

As I've repeatedly emphasized throughout this book (yes—it is that important), in 1922, Colonial Secretary Winston Churchill, to reward Arab allies in World War I (remember the movie *Lawrence of Arabia*?), chopped off almost 80 percent of the original Mandate of Palestine issued to Great Britain on April 25, 1920—all the land east of the Jordan River—and created the Arab "Emirate of Transjordan," today's Jordan. This was engineered by Churchill a year earlier at the Cairo Conference. See the maps again in chapter 1.

Emir Abdullah, who received the land on behalf of the Hashemites of Arabia, attributed this gift to an "act of Allah" in his memoirs.[57] Sir Alec Kirkbride, Britain's East Bank representative, had much to say about this separation of the lion's share of the Palestinian Mandate as well: "In due course the remarkable discovery was made that the clauses of the mandate relating to the establishment of a National Home for the Jews had never been intended to apply to the mandated territory east of the river."[58]

So, as will be reiterated time and again (since anti-Israel spokesmen repeatedly state that the Jews wound up with most of the land), right from the get-go, Arab nationalism was awarded the bulk of the Palestinian Mandate. While it officially remained tied to the whole unit, Jordan, nonetheless, became a virtually separate entity. So, from 1922 onward—after already having been handed most of the territory—Arabs would point to what was left of "Palestine" (the name Rome gave to Judaea after the Jews' second revolt for freedom in 135 c.e., to try to bury their hopes once and for all) to make yet further claims on the land.

Arabs answer by citing geographical and other differences between some Arabs and others, since adjacent Arabs from the Arabian Peninsula—the Hashemites—came to rule over the Transjordanian portion of the Palestinian Mandate instead of locals.

Using such logic, since there are Jews in Israel from over a hundred different countries (including one-half who were refugees from "Arab" lands and some whose families never left Israel since the days of the Roman conquest), then Jews are therefore entitled to multiple states as well, including in the so-called "Arab" world.

Think of it. Less than one-half million Arabs were entitled to an independent state of Kuwait, and ditto for even less in Oman, Qatar, Dubai, and some other places. Some two and one-half million Jews can therefore also stake a claim to parts of Morocco, Iraq, Tunisia, Algeria, and so forth—where they pre-dated the seventh-century Arab conquests of those lands.

Instead of calling themselves Jews, perhaps these Jewish refugees from "Arab" lands (the refugees you do not hear about) need to play the Arab game. As Arabs, for political purposes and to negate historical claims of the Jews, only recently renamed themselves "Palestinians" (indeed, many, if not most, came from elsewhere in the region), Jews should also consider renaming themselves as well to stake their own additional claims on territory.

Arab and pro-Arab professors typically ignore all of the above when teaching this topic. The main starting date for them is not 1920, but 1947, the proposed partition of "Palestine." Of course, they conveniently omit telling students that this was the second partition of the land (which the Arabs rejected) and pretend that Jordan was always a separate state. And their student sponges mostly soak it all up.

The Jordan-Palestine connection is just one of many well-documented facts (not "Zionist propaganda") completely ignored or distorted by Arab spokesmen and, unfortunately, little known by the rest of the world. Arabs typically claim Jews got 78 percent of all of the land, and leading newspapers typically prepare segments on the Middle East ignoring this crucial Jordan-Palestine connection as well.

While discussion now revolves around a two-state or even a one-state solution to the conflict between Jews and Arabs, the reality is that Jordan is historically and demographically Palestinian. So there is a third solution, though it is kept hushed up these days.

Jordan has been a reasonable neighbor of late—relatively speaking at least—so Israel hasn't made an issue of this. Indeed, it was Israel that saved the Hashemites' collective derrieres in 1970 when the Palestinian Liberation Organization (PLO) of both Arafat and his close pal Mahmoud Abbas decided to cash in on this third alternative.

Palestinian Arabs "fleeing into Jordan," à la Prince Zeid's remarks, would therefore be, in reality, simply moving from one part of Palestine to another.

And did anyone ask why Israel is obliged to provide work or anything else for the butchers of its kids? That supposedly would be one of the main reasons for the Arab flight into Jordan, to find work.

Arab workers have killed their Jewish employers, hijacked bulldozers to kill other innocents, destroyed property, and so forth. Yet Israel has taken pains to create passageways for these people through the security fence, usually at the American State Department's insistence.

When, in collusion with Syria, Egypt's Nasser decided in 1967 that it was once again time to try to destroy Israel, his boasts of victories and massive Israeli casualties led Jordan's King Hussein (some of his calls were intercepted and taped) to join in the prospective massacre. Israel, through the United Nations, begged Hussein to distance himself from Nasser's plans. The king did not listen and instead launched an attack on the Jewish half of Jerusalem instead.[60] The rest, as they say, is history. And that's how Jordan lost the West Bank—which it seized in the 1948 fighting—in the first place. Transjordan, led by British officers, joined other Arab countries in attacking a reborn Israel, trying to nip it in the bud.

So the prince would be better off not bringing this subject up, at least not to those with any sense of fair play. When you launch a war and lose, there's a price to pay, especially if the land you launched your attack from was not yours in the first place.

Whatever will or will not become of the land in question, it must be noted that this is indeed disputed territory, not "occupied purely Arab" land as Arabs and their supporters claim. Jews lived and owned property in these areas until their slaughter in the 1920s and 1930s. Judea and Samaria, only recently in history known as the West Bank (largely as a result of British imperialism and Transjordan's later annexation), were non-apportioned parts of the Mandate open to settlement by Jews, Arabs, and other residents of the Mandate alike. Indeed, numerous Arabs poured into the area from all over the Middle East and North Africa.

Recall that the Records of the League of Nations Permanent Mandates Commission documented scores of thousands of Arabs entering Palestine from just Syria alone. Hamas's "patron saint," Sheikh Izzedine al-Qassam, was one of those new arrivals. Many more Arabs entered the Mandate to take advantage of the economic development going on because of the Jews. Under cover of darkness and never recorded, more Arab settlers set up more Arab settlements in Palestine. Why are these "legal" and appropriate but those of the Jews not?

The good cop/bad cop team of Arafat's and, now, Mahmoud Abbas's Fatah and Hamas/Islamic Jihad created the Israeli security barrier that the hypocrites of the world placed on trial in Geneva several years ago. And there is no doubt that it has saved many innocent Israeli lives.

Until those above leopards change their spots, Israel must do what any other nation would do to protect its citizens from massacre. Indeed, many other nations have constructed such fences for far less compelling reasons. As just a few of many examples, Saudi Arabia has one; so does India, and the United States as well.

As for the route of the fence, in the wake of the June '67 War, UN Resolution 242 expressly did not call for Israel to return to the status quo ante and the suicidal armistice lines imposed upon it at the close of hostilities in 1949. As has been pointed out many times, among other things, those lines made it a mere nine to sixteen miles wide at its waist.

What 242 did call for was the creation of "secure and recognized borders" to replace those vulnerable lines. Adding a few more miles of buffer in strategically important areas of the West Bank, on the Golan, and elsewhere is precisely what that resolution had in mind. The architects of the final draft of the resolution (Lord Caradon, Rostow, Goldberg, etc.) have stated this themselves.[61]

Israel does not seek to control millions of Arabs' lives. What it does want is a reasonable territorial compromise over these disputed lands—not the unilateral, Munich-style "solution" too much of the rest of the world now has in mind.

Chapter 11

BEWARE OF GREEKS—ER, ARABS—BEARING GIFTS

I HAD TO SEE this movie. As a decades-long student of classical history, as well as contemporary Middle Eastern affairs, the chance to see the tragic clash between Achilles and Hector on the big screen was too much to resist

With all the fuss over Brad Pitt as Achilles in *Troy*, I did not realize that one of my favorite actors, Peter O'Toole, also starred in the movie as Priam, the Trojan king.

I had recently been able to locate a set of video tapes of a made-for-television movie starring a much younger O'Toole as the Roman general who besieged the Jews in their last stronghold at Masada in 73 C.E., during the first of two major revolts they launched for their independence from the Empire. Judaea had fought this other tragic war, but for far more important reasons than raging hormones.

The contemporary Roman or Roman-sponsored historians—Tacitus, Josephus, Dio Cassius, and others—lived right around the time of those latter revolts. A reading of their extensive works shows that the amazing story of the quest of the Jews for their freedom against the conqueror of much of the known world played second to none.

The fortress of Masada overlooks the Dead Sea to this very day and appears just as those ancient historians described it. The Arch of Titus stands tall in Rome as well, depicting the Roman victory over the Jews and the conquest of Jerusalem. Judaea Capta coins can be found in museums all over the world, minted by Rome to also commemorate its subjugation of the Jewish nation. So, if anything, there's far more historical corroboration for this story than that told by the Greek's Homer. All that awaits is for some producer doing it justice and putting it on the big screen.

But briefly, for now at least, back to the Greeks.

Virgil, the most famous poet in Ancient Rome, wrote one of the greatest epics of all time, *The Aeneid*. In Book II, the priest Laocoon warns the Trojans not to accept the giant wooden horse placed outside the impenetrable walls and gates of Troy. His legendary speech has been paraphrased in the now-common saying, "Beware of Greeks bearing gifts."

We all know how ignoring Laocoon's advice turned out for Troy. Now let's turn the clock ahead some three thousand years for a look at another Trojan horse.

On June 24, 2001, the much-showcased model "moderate" of the Palestinian Arab team, the late Faisal al-Husseini, gave an interview in the Egyptian newspaper *Al Arabi*. He was commenting about the so-called Oslo Agreements in which Israel was largely expected to yield concrete tangibles, essential to its security, in return for vague Arab promises. As it turned out, the more Israel gave and ceded for the sake of peace, the more it bled.

Arabs interpreted Israeli conciliatory moves as signs of weakness.

Many more Jews were soon deliberately butchered by Arab terrorism—blown up at Passover seders, at bar mitzvahs, on buses, in restaurants, shopping malls, night clubs, and so forth—during the time of the Oslo "peace" than at any other. Arabs envision all such future peace "deals" as being one version or another of Oslo II, including the new "Saudi peace plan" endorsed by the new American president himself.

Listen to how al-Husseini, who labeled dealings with the Jews a Trojan horse, further described the earlier unfolding events: "When we are asking all the Palestinian forces and factions to look at the Oslo agreement and other agreements as 'temporary procedures,' or 'phased goals,' this means that we are ambushing the Israelis and cheating them. Our ultimate goal is the liberation of all of historical Palestine from the [Jordan] River to the [Mediterranean] Sea, even if the conflict will last for another thousand years."[62]

Now I'd like to ask all of those many international critics and hypocritical masters of the double standard who still insist that Israel cave in to virtually all that Arabs demand for the creation of their twenty-second state if they really believe that those currently running the latter-day Arafatian Fatah/Hamas, good cop/bad cop team have changed their approach toward peacemaking with the Jews for the better since Faisal al-Husseini gave his by now infamous quotes.

Any fair, sane person knows what the answer is to this.

If amnesia has set in and one needs an additional reminder, just look at the well-publicized Arab rage at President Bush's fleeting April 2004 remarks—since largely and pathetically retracted—which suggested that, just maybe, the sole state of the Jews shouldn't have to return to its 1949, UN-imposed, nine-mile-wide armistice line existence again, or be overwhelmed by absorbing millions of real or fudged Arab refugees after all. Half of Israel's Jews were refugees from Arab/Muslim lands, but without some two dozen other states to potentially choose from.

While it is long past due for a fair and just peace to finally be worked out between Arab and Jew in the Middle East, justice does not demand that the sole, resurrected state of the Jews deliver itself on a silver platter, à la Czechoslovakia

1938, so that Arabs can have their twenty-second state, and the second—not first—one in "Palestine." In case you don't know, just ask the Hashemites in "Jordan" what this last comment is all about.

And in case you can't get an audience with the young King Abdullah II or find other "Jordanians" to be deaf, dumb, and blind regarding your question, just find yourself a map of the original Mandate for Palestine as Britain received it on April 25, 1920, before Colonial Secretary Churchill decided to give his Hashemite World War I allies from the Arabian Peninsula (who were in the process of getting their own derrieres booted out of the peninsula by the rival clan of Ibn Saud—as in Saudi Arabia today) a "reward" in 1922.

As for now, unfortunately, there is a good piece of advice Israel simply cannot afford to ignore. And shame on those calling themselves Israel's friends, or even just objective observers, if this is what they demand the Jews to do. Beware of Arabs bearing gifts.

Chapter 12

Too Predictable

(Note: This chapter is definitely not for the politically correct. It was written in anger, is blunt, and, unfortunately, is all too true.)

ANOTHER RANDOM BUS bombing. This one a day before Israel was to be "brought to court" in Geneva about five years ago to defend itself for building a fence designed to keep Arabs from blowing its kids apart.

More incinerated and maimed innocents, whose only crime was their existence in a land where their ancestors have lived for more than three thousand years. Another hollow condemnation by the alleged good half of the Arafatian/Hamas–Islamic Jihad, good cop/bad cop team. Not that they really object, but it is bad publicity for their cause.

I believe it was Martin Niemoller, a German theologian, who wrote something like the following: "First they came for the communists, and I did nothing. Then they came for the Jews, and I remained silent. And by the time they came for me, there was no one left to protest."

Coincidentally, a bit earlier, on August 19, 2003, another Arab bought his ticket to "paradise" and its seventy or so virgins supposedly awaiting him (what do the girls get?) by blowing Jews apart on a bus, while yet another was doing likewise to United Nations workers in Iraq. Now, what was the lesson from Reverend Niemoller's remarks again?

This is the same UN that, at best, has seen a "moral equivalence" between Jewish babes and grandmothers being deliberately and wantonly slaughtered and Israeli steps taken to try to stop that slaughter. That latest Arab suicide bomber above had claimed he did this to avenge Israel's killing of armed Hamas fighters in Gaza; you know, the folks who play soccer with Jews' heads and assassinate, at point blank range, pregnant Jewish mothers and their children. Real heroes.

While what I am writing is admittedly being written in anger, there is no doubt regarding the truth of the words.

Israel has become too darned predictable.

Earlier, the now-comatose Prime Minister Sharon, the old valiant warrior, caved in to pressure, in Gaza and elsewhere, from so-called "friends"—the same ones who would have leveled the source of these atrocities, had it been done to their own nations and peoples.

Arabs, who refuse to dismantle their terrorist infrastructures and who still

65

do not accept the permanency of a Jewish state (that goes for the "moderate" good buddy of Presidents Bush and Obama, Mahmoud Abbas as well), also demand that Israel stand by and do nothing while Jews get murdered. They cannot seem to figure out why Israel must have such things as a security fence or real borders instead of armistice lines, which made it, among other things, a mere nine-miles wide—a constant temptation to those aiming to destroy it. As if the answer were not obvious.

How many other nations would continuously tolerate such horror without exacting just and devastating retribution? Think about the daisy cutter and bunker-buster bombs and so forth America has used against its own enemies in Afghanistan and Iraq, as just a few recent examples.

Despite all that the Arabs accuse Israel of, they know that the Jews will try their best to just target the rats in their dens. They will go house to house, endangering their own sons, and try to pluck out the exact murderers and wannabes as best as possible. That is what typically happens in Gaza and elsewhere; yet those operations become the Arabs' next excuses for future bus bombings, blown up restaurants, rocketed civilian centers, and so forth.

The Geneva Conventions make perfectly clear that militants are not permitted to use their own non-combatants as human shields, that those non-combatants do not prevent an army from pursuing terrorists, and that any harm occurring to the civilian population as a consequence falls on the heads of the cowards using their own people this way. But you would never know this by listening to the accounts in the press or even by America's own State Department from time to time.[63]

Given all of the above, there is, again, only one conclusion: Israel has indeed become too darn predictable.

Arabs know that their own wives and children will not be deliberately targeted on buses, in restaurants, shopping centers, or markets. So what I will state next, I regret, but will say anyway—it is time, given the Arab track record of barbarity, for them to reap what they have sown.

The next Arab outrage must be accompanied by massive Israeli retaliation—employing America's own Powell Doctrine on war, for example. It is time for Israel to do what is necessary to protect its citizens, regardless of how much aid the U.S. decides to suspend. Hopefully, many a U.S. citizen will convey the proper message to politicians if Foggy Bottom is allowed to have its Arabist-dominated way with Israel over this. Ditto regarding the new American president, Barack Obama, who unfortunately seems intent on pressuring Israel to accept a so-called Arab peace agreement (the Saudi plan) that is anything but.

As this book gets ready to go to print, there is a hint of perhaps some positive changes that President Obama may have in mind, such as not expecting Israel to consent to being inundated with allegedly "returning" Arab refugees—a part of that Saudi plan that the president has said Israel would be nuts to reject. President George W. Bush stated the same thing regarding refugees a while back as well. But, so far, it is still just a hint—for which Israel will be expected to cave in concretely on every major issue. Furthermore, all the Arab players—with the possible exception of Jordan—have stated that they will accept no changes to the current Saudi peace (of the grave) plan.

Poll after poll taken among Arabs have constantly shown that even if Israel withdrew to the nine-mile wide armistice lines imposed upon it after the 1948 fighting (having been invaded by surrounding Arab countries immediately upon its rebirth)—something UN Resolution 242 expressly does not require it to do—Arabs would still reject its right to exist and support ongoing terror against it anyway. So who's kidding whom here regarding the security barrier/fence? And Israel's "friends" know this as well.

It is time for Israel to tell the hypocrites around the world (much of which also has had plenty of Jewish blood on its hands) that it does not care what they think, and then act to protect its own people as best as it can, as any other nation would.

And while it sounds harsh, perhaps it is time for Israel not to worry about being too precise in its targeting, for it is time that Arabs fully understand that if they harbor and support barbarous terrorists (who gleefully play with the body parts of their victims on camera) as heroes, then they will share in their fate. President George W. Bush said almost those exact words regarding America's own fight in Iraq a while back.[64]

When dealing with their own "problems"—à la Assad's "Hama Solution" in Syria (in which ten times more people were killed in a month than Israel killed in two years of intifada); King Hussein's Black September in Jordan; Saddam's murder of Kurds in Iraq (five thousand in Halabja alone, hundreds of thousands of others); the slaughter of millions of black Africans in the Sudan (still going on as this book is being written); and so forth—Arabs have massacred literally millions by poison gas, bombs, and artillery from afar. And all without a peep from the United Nations. And no trial before an international court of justice either, as Israel was subjected to for its defense barrier.

It is time for Israel to make clear that it will use its own air force, tanks, and such—the way America has—to target the rats' dens instead of risking the lives of its own nineteen-year-old infantrymen by futilely trying to do the job as "morally correct" as possible. This has gained it nothing among the world's hypocrites and cost it the lives of more of its own soldiers instead. Witness the aftermath of Israel's latest incursion into Gaza because of the thousands of rockets and mortars launched from Gaza into Israeli civilian centers.

Israel is fighting a war it did not want. It repeatedly has offered more than fair compromises to its enemies, far more than Arabs have ever offered to any of their own national competitors. But nothing short of Israel's suicide will, unfortunately, satisfy most Arabs, including the alleged "moderates."

Arabs do not worry about "ethical choices" when disemboweling Jews. Again, poll after poll show that the vast majority of Arab non-combatants support such acts of terrorism against Jews. On the contrary, the more innocent the Jewish victim, the more preferred he—and more often, she—is for shock value as a target.

So, it is time for Arabs to get massive doses of at least a modified version of their own medicine. While I do not advocate blowing up Arab buses, restaurants, or schools, any building, town, and such harboring murderers and their collaborators must be recognized for what the Geneva Conventions say it is: a fair military target.

Article #51/7

The presence of the civilian population shall not be used to render certain points or areas immune from military operations, in particular in attempts to shield military objectives from attack.

Article #58b

The parties to the conflict shall...avoid locating military objectives within or near densely populated areas." [The rats' dens are typically set up in, or adjacent to, civilian apartment buildings, hospitals, mosques, schools, etc., as America has learned for itself in Iraq.]

Article #51/2

The civilian population...shall not be the object of attack. Acts of violence the primary purpose of which is to spread terror among the civilian population are prohibited...Indiscriminate attacks are prohibited.[65] [Arabs typically target Israeli and other Jewish civilians.]

And those famous funeral processions showing hundreds of the dead butcher's colleagues firing weapons into the air?

It is time for Israel to see them for what they really are—one big, legitimate military target. It is time for Israel to stop letting Arabs dictate how the game will be played. If mothers and infants are fair game for Arabs, then what are the murderers' collaborators for Israel? It should be a no brainer.

It is time for Israel to send the press packing, tell the UN to go fly a kite (or worse), finish the security barrier as quickly and as strongly as possible with an adequate buffer (permitted by UN 242)—so it does not have its absurd, suicidal nine-mile-wide existence again—and ask its friends in the United States to stop having one set of standards for themselves and another one for Jews in their sole, microscopic state. When America thought it knew where Saddam Hussein was dining, it bombed the restaurant to smithereens, innocent diners present and all. And what's that thingamajig America has constructed along its own southern border to keep Mexicans out who are just seeking work and a better life, not coming across to blow American children up? (By the way, I am all for that American security fence.)

In other words, the more unpredictable the Israeli response to Arab barbarity, the better. I truly wish it had not come to this. But, when volumes of Arabs start dying relatively randomly (Arabs outnumber Jews sixty to one in the region; they know that Israel loses a war of attrition, so do the math) as Jews have been doing, perhaps they will be less likely to treat their own cowardly butchers who hide behind the skirts of women and carriages of babes as heroes and less likely to open up a new intifada. If the latter or any semblance of it once again erupts, the gloves must come off in a quick, devastating response.

While this harder approach to Arab terror may also not be the solution, Israel has tried just about everything except consenting to its own demise—and nothing else worked, either. Arabs simply replaced a pre-'67 War, one-fell-swoop strategy for a "destruction in stages" plan for Israel instead, using "negotiations" to win from the Jews what couldn't be won on the battlefield.

So, summing this up, it is time for Israel to lose its predictability and for Arabs to get a mega-taste of what they have been dishing out. And, last but not least, it is time for Israel to draw its own lines in the sand and let all know them—especially its alleged friends.

If that second Arab state in Palestine emerges on the West Bank and Gaza—as President Obama is pushing for (and as did his predecessor)—Israel must let it be known clearly from the get-go that it will treat any acts of violence originating from that new sovereign state not effectively dealt with by that new state's authorities as an act of war and handle it the way America's own General Colin Powell has stated wars should be fought—conclusively.[66]

Chapter 13

A Lesson from Kosovars and Palestinians for Atlasians

With a new president and his long list of anti-Israel friends and advisers, a few key issues needed to be placed into their proper perspectives. Now tell me, what would you do in the age of nationalism—which came relatively late to the Middle East—if your national group already had almost two dozen states on over six million square miles of territory (conquered mostly from other national groups) and wanted to create at least one more, but another people's sole, tiny, resurrected nation state stood in the way?

Well, please take a look—like many of us have over the decades—at the answer through the oft-quoted words of a spokesman for that above national group itself, PLO executive committee member Zuheir Mohsen, on March 31, 1977, in the Dutch newspaper *Trouw*. For anyone with functioning neurons, it is one of those clubs designed to waken you into reality.

> The "Palestinian people" do not exist. The creation of a Palestinian state is only a means for continuing our struggle against the state of Israel for our Arab unity. In reality today there is no difference between Jordanians, Palestinians, Syrians, and Lebanese. Only for political and tactical reasons do we speak today about the existence of a Palestinian people, since Arab national interests demand that we posit the existence of a distinct "Palestinian people" to oppose Zionism.[67]

Before having to deal with the politics and sensitivities of at least some in the West, Arabs simply gave no thought to Mohsen's tactics.

As you have surely noticed, and as I deliberately like to reemphasize time and again (for those who like to place Israel under the high-power lens of moral scrutiny while playing deaf, dumb, and blind to what surrounds it), millions of native peoples were simply conquered and forcibly Arabized in the name of the Arab Nation and the spread of its Dar ul-Islam—raw imperialism and colonialism, pure and simple—and are still suffering the consequences of this murderous subjugation.

In a post-Holocaust age, however, in the struggle to win over hearts and minds from abroad, how could Arabs demand twenty-two states while denying Jews their one? The answer: as Mohsen so correctly stated above, reinvent yourselves. From now on, you're "Palestinians"—and then depend on the ignorance (real or voluntary) of most of the rest of the world to back your claim that "if Jews can have a state, why not Palestinians?" And, furthermore, don't you know that "Palestinians" are the new, formerly stateless Jews?

Forget the facts—especially if you are depending upon most Middle East academics to provide them.

For example, most Arabs never saw the land of the Jews—Judaea—until their own murderous imperial conquests brought them out of the Arabian Peninsula in the seventh century c.e. when they spread out in all directions. They acquired the land of the Jews the same way they conquered parts of black Africa, all of Berber North Africa, Syrian and Mesopotamian Kurdistan, Iran, Coptic Egypt, India, pre-Arab Lebanon, and so forth.

Or that the very name *Palestine* was dubbed upon Judaea by the Roman Emperor Hadrian after the Jews' costly second revolt for freedom. To pour salt onto their wound, he renamed the Jews' land after their historic enemies, the Philistines—a non-Semitic sea people (not Arab) from the area around Crete. Tacitus, Dio Cassius, and other contemporary Roman historians wrote all about Judaea and Judaeans—not "Palestine" or "Palestinians." Recall one of my favorite telling quotes about the Jews' first revolt in Vol. II, Book V, *The Works of Tacitus*: "Vespasian succeeded to the command. It inflamed his resentment that the Jews were the only nation that had not yet submitted. Titus was appointed by his father to complete the subjugation of Judaea. He commanded three legions in Judaea itself. To these he added the twelfth from Syria and the third and twenty-second from Alexandria. Amongst his allies were a band of Arabs, formidable in themselves and harboring toward the Jews the bitter animosity usually subsisting between neighboring nations."[68]

Not having endured the forced exile and Diaspora of many (but not all—many still remained in the hill country and elsewhere clear up to the Arab conquest)[69] of the Jews, still many Arabs were newcomers themselves to the Mandate of Palestine after World War I. When the United Nations Relief Works Agency UNRWA was set up to assist Arab refugees after a half-dozen Arab states invaded a nascent Israel in 1948 to nip it in the bud and their attempt backfired, the very word *refugee* had to be redefined from its prior meaning of persons normally and traditionally resident to those who lived in the Mandate for a minimum of only two years prior to 1948 to assist these people.[70] Recall that Hamas's own patron saint, for whom its terror brigade and rockets are named, Sheikh Izzedine al-Qassam, was born near Latakia in Syria. Arafat was from Egypt. And both "native Palestinians" had plenty of company, pouring into the Mandate because of the economic development going on due to the Jews.[71]

Now, using this same tactic, Serbs have been similarly shafted. Albania is an independent nation southwest of the former Yugoslavia. The Serbs fought their first major battle for Kosovo against the spread of the Dar ul-Islam (this time led by Turkish imperialism) in 1389—more than six centuries ago. Albania had become at least nominally converted to Islam via the Ottoman conquest. Over the centuries, ethnic Albanians encroached upon traditionally Serbian lands.

Enter the late twentieth century. Everyone knew that with the death of Tito, Iraq's twin, artificially glued-together state of Yugoslavia would fall apart.

Now, if you're an Albanian in Serbia and you already have an ethnic Albanian state in existence (so you can't claim "statelessness"), how do you stake your claim for additional territory—at another people's (Serbs') expense?

Hitler played a somewhat similar game with the large population of ethnic Germans in Czechoslovakia's Sudetenland. World War II soon followed, as his sights were set far beyond the Czechs' and Slovaks' domain.

According to this line of reasoning, America also better watch its own southwest very carefully—especially since it really was once part of Mexico anyway, President Bush's ranch and so forth. And what's Russia up to these days, since we're on this subject? Think Moscow's recent invasion of Georgia and other non-Russian peoples' lands. With Russian ethnic minorities, this could be how this game would be played out in the Kremlin.

The answer, however, regarding Albanians in Serbia is, you follow Zuheir Mohsen's advice. But instead of renaming yourselves "Palestinians," you, of course, call yourselves Kosovars instead. And then get assorted jihadis from the rest of the Arab/Muslim World to assist you—along with America and NATO.

There is no doubt that too much of the conflict regarding the breakup of Yugoslavia was deliberately biased against the Serbs for a number of reasons. Atrocities occurred (as they had for centuries)—but on both sides, with Serbs often the victims, victims the State Department ignored as it sought Muslims it could point to as championing while America was fighting others in Iraq, Afghanistan, and elsewhere. American bombers led the final dismemberment of the Yugoslavian nation.

There's a lesson here—and Jews, Kurds, Imazighen/Berbers, and others need to pay close attention.

So, following the Arab game plan, instead of demanding just the rebirth of their one state, Jews need to demand others as well.

Jews have a long history in Morocco, as just one example—long before Arabs conquered both Jews and Imazighen alike there.

More than six hundred thousand Moroccan Jews now live in Israel—part of the other side of the Middle East refugee problem few ever talk about—more

Moroccan Jews than Arabs who got their own nation states in Kuwait or Abu Dhabi when they were first created. Additionally, many more Moroccan Jews live in America, France, and elsewhere today, including Morocco.

Why multiple states for Arabs and not for Jews?

As early as Roman times, Jews fleeing the Roman wars in Judaea began to travel inland in North Africa and forged both economic and cultural ties with the Imazighen—especially in the Atlas Mountains. Some of the latter folks even adopted the faith of their Jewish neighbors.

When Arab Muslims invaded, Jews and Imazighen fought them together. Across the Atlas Mountains, Queen Dahlia al Kahina (whom the famed Muslim scholar, Ibn Khaldun, called "the Jewess") led both Jews and Imazighen in battle against invading Arabs, who would later massacre and subjugate both peoples.

Why not states for Atlasians—at least one for Jews and one for Imazighen—in North Africa?

Today, the Imazigen—the majority population—are being told that they cannot even name their kids with their own traditional names and have to use Islamic—Arab—ones instead.[72] Imagine if Israel were doing this to its Arab citizens. Would there be the same non-response and silence in academia or the mainstream press? Does this question really even need to be asked?

Why "Palestinians" and "Kosovars," but not "Atlasians?" And while we are at it, some thirty-five million stateless Kurds need to jump aboard as well.

Kurds predate Arabs in "Arab" Syria as well as in "Arab" Iraq and "Turkish" Turkey. But we all know what happened/happens when Kurds try to assert their rights there. Their best hope right now is in the place where they were indeed promised independence after World War I—in northern Mesopotamia, part of today's renamed Iraq. The most sympathy they typically get from academics such as those with which I studied is being called extremists, rebels, or separatists. Those same voices of moral authority who also cry aloud over a sole, miniscule Jewish state's rebirth and/or the absence, so far, of the Arabs' twenty-second state—and second, not first, one in Palestine.[73]

While I do not really expect much of what I have described above to happen, it is worth asking those academics, folks at the State Department, and other hypocritical practitioners of the double standard, *why not*? If thirty-five million used and abused stateless Kurds played the Arab game regarding trading "Arab" for "Palestinian," how many Kurdish states might they be entitled to? At least four?

The reality, of course, is that Kurds, Imazhigen, black Africans, Copts, Assyrians, Jews, and all of these peoples are still struggling to maintain or obtain basic political and human rights in what Arabs call "purely Arab patrimony."[74]

That others buy into their subjugating mind-set is the real travesty.

Chapter 14

QASSAM, KASSAM—SO, WHAT'S IN A NAME?

EVER SINCE A now-comatose Prime Minister Sharon announced plans for a unilateral disengagement from Gaza about five years ago this past April, adjacent towns in Israel proper have come under increasing attack. Qassam rockets and mortars have been frequently fired into communities such as Sderot and Ashkelon, deliberately aimed at terrorizing civilians. Whereas Israel tries its best to carefully target those responsible for the murder of its people, the Arab targets of choice are the most innocent. Not only is greater shock value derived from this, the reality is that in Arab eyes there are no Jewish innocents. Jewish preschoolers were killed in such a volley, helping to set into motion Israel's earlier assault on Gaza's terror apparatus, and thousands more of these attacks led to Israel's broader 2008 incursion.

Now, when choosing this weapon of terror, Hamas (which, like most other Arabs, denies a Jewish state of Israel's right to exist with or without the disputed territories) gave careful thought to the name that it should go by. Since the "militant wing" of the organization (the folks that actually launch the rockets and blow up the buses, teen night clubs, pizzerias, and such) was named after Sheikh Izzedine al-Qassam, it made sense to name this weapon in honor of him as well.

Surely such a man must have had some great credentials in the "Palestinian" Arab movement, don't you think?

Of course. Ol' Izzy made his name via butchering and disemboweling "Zionist invaders" during the early mandatory period after World War I. So, what else do we know about this legendary leader of the "Palestinians"? Well, for starters, how good is your memory, class? Hamas's hero—like many if not most other "native Palestinians"—was born elsewhere. In his case, somewhere around Latakia, Syria.

Recall as well that in just one three-month period alone, the League of Nations Permanent Mandates Commissions documented scores of thousands of other Syrian Arabs pouring into the British Mandate of Palestine.[75]

Like numerous other Arabs moving in from elsewhere, they came to take advantage of the economic boom going on because of the influx of Jewish capital. And for every Arab newcomer—settler—that was documented, many more slipped in under cover of darkness and were never recorded. Add to this the fact that, for a number of reasons, the Brits were more concerned about entering Jews than entering Arabs. Despite this, lots of evidence exists that shows that—like the murderous sheikh—most "Palestinian" Arabs were no more native than most of the returning, forcibly exiled, Diaspora Jews.

Now, let's again reiterate. So many Arabs were recent arrivals into the Mandate that when the UNRWA was created to deal with the Arab refugee situation, created as a result of the invasion by a half-dozen Arab states of a reborn Israel in 1948, it adjusted the definition of *refugee* from the prior meaning of persons normally and traditionally resident to those who lived in the Mandate for a minimum of only two years prior to 1948. Also keep in mind that for every Arab who was forced to flee the fighting that the Arabs started in their attempt to nip a nascent Israel in the bud, a Jewish refugee was forced to flee Arab lands, but with no UNRWA set up to help them.

Indeed, scores of thousands of Jews fled the same Syria that the sheikh immigrated to Palestine from. Greater New York City alone now has tens of thousands of these folks. Many others moved to Israel and elsewhere. The superstar celebrity Paula Abdul is from a Syrian-Jewish refugee family.

But, while Arabs see it as their natural right to settle anywhere in the Dar ul-Islam and what they claim as purely Arab patrimony (despite the fact that scores of millions of non-Arabs also live in the area and have been conquered and forcibly Arabized by them), when Jews moved into their sole, reborn state (as opposed to some two dozen for Arabs), Arabs declared this to be *al Nakba*—the catastrophe.

Hundreds of millions of Hindus and Muslims could arrive at a less-than-perfect modus vivendi in the 1947 partition of the Indian subcontinent—at virtually the same moment in history that Arabs were rejecting a similar offer over what was left of the Palestine Mandate after Arabs had already been awarded the lion's share in 1922 with the separation of Transjordan—yet the mere thought of anyone else gaining even a sliver of the very same political rights that Arabs demand for themselves was out of the question. The conflict we have in the Middle East today is mostly all about this subjugating Arab mind-set that refuses to understand no other justice but its own.

So, the next time you hear about those "Qassam" rockets, consider the irony here. And, oh yes, I almost forgot. Remember also that Arafat himself was born in Cairo. And tens of thousands of other Egyptian Arabs had preceded his own migration and settlement in Palestine somewhat earlier in the wake of Muhammad Ali and his son Ibrahim Pasha's military excursions in the latter nineteenth century.

Chapter 15

EVOLUTION OF THE SUICIDE/HOMICIDE BOMBER

WHILE THE YEAR 2004 brought other issues back to the front burner that also demanded immediate attention (the future of the Gaza Strip and the rest of the disputed territories, as just a few examples), it is worth rethinking another all-too-real fact of life that had driven events over recent past years, especially since the onset of the era of the so-called Oslo peace in late 1993. I am speaking, of course, about the Arab suicide/homicide bomber.

Unfortunately, we have heard too much about suicide/homicide bombers in the Middle East, and when Israel pursues the deliberate murderers of its innocents, this then becomes the next excuse for Arabs to kill yet more innocents. Of course, the way many—if not most—Arabs see all of this, there are really no Israeli "innocents." They're all simply Jews who have allegedly stolen purely Arab land. That is the way it is taught in their textbooks, preached in their mosques, and inbred into the next generation from kindergarten on up.

After the September 11, 2001, tragedy, when nineteen Arabs (mostly Saudis) hijacked commercial aircrafts and flew them as guided missiles into the World Trade Center and the Pentagon, killing some three thousand Americans and others as well, the situation has become even more of a concern. Officials believe that it is just a matter of time before the United States once again becomes victimized this way. The Arab suicide/homicide bomber has also since made his (or her) debut in other places as well—notably in the fight for the future of Iraq and Afghanistan. Young children have been used as living bombs, having earlier been encouraged to become martyrs.

There is no doubt that the Arab–Israeli conflict represents horrendous human tragedy. But while Arabs and their supporters place the blame for this on Israel, the truth is actually far more depressing.

As in many other places, there are conflicting historical and political claims over the land contested between Arabs and Jews. There are hundreds, if not thousands, of scholarly books written about the connection of the Jews to the land of Israel. The very name *Jew*, itself, comes from the later name of the land, Judaea, which in turn was named for the Hebrew tribe of Judah, one of Jacob's sons. Judaean equals Jew. Early Muslim Arab historians recorded this in their works, as does the Quran itself, the holy book of Islam.[76]

Similarly, there are many books that deal with the imperial Arab conquest, settlement, and incorporation of the land of Israel/Judaea/Palestine—and much of the rest of entire region as well—into the two earlier Arab caliphates based in Damascus and Baghdad.

Suffice it to state, therefore, that a quest for relative justice demanded some sort of compromise over the land in question. Unfortunately, that was too much to ask.

Arabs saw themselves as the only legitimate heirs to a defeated Ottoman Turkish Empire that had replaced the Arabs (and others) as imperial rulers and had controlled most of the region for some four centuries prior to the end of World War I. After the Allied defeat of the Turks, Arabs subsequently treated the region, despite the presence of scores of millions of non-Arab peoples, as "purely Arab patrimony" and acted accordingly.

Recall just a few of many other examples discussed already of what next transpired: both Amazigh (Berber) and Kurdish languages and cultures have been periodically "outlawed;" churches of the Copts have been burned down; black Africans in the Sudan and Kurds in Syria and Iraq have been subjected to genocide and massacred; and more Jews would wind up fleeing so-called "Arab" lands than Arabs who fled Israel, the other side of that famous refugee problem that few ever talk about. Those who resisted this forced Arabization process were simply killed, turned into refugees, and the like. There have been millions over the decades, and it continues to this very day.

Returning to the chapter's main topic, the Arab rejectionist response to the question of a compromise with the Jews over the question of Israel/Palestine falls into the same pattern as those above. Arabs rejected any solution that would grant Jews any rights at all. Indeed, some Arabs equated Kurdish national rights with the potential birth of "another Israel."[77] They attacked a miniscule, reborn Israel in 1948, giving birth to the continuing problem regarding Arab refugees. But it didn't have to be this way.

Hundreds of millions of people became refugees in the course of the last violent century (not to mention the millions before then). Many were displaced between the two world wars. Scores of millions were uprooted in the 1947 partition of the Indian subcontinent into Hindu India and Muslim Pakistan.

Many more examples exist, like that involving Turks and Greeks. But, as I've already hinted at above, one truly stands out in light of the current turmoil in the Middle East—the one involving one-half of Israel's six million Jews, whose families fled Arab/Muslim lands around the same time Arabs fled in the opposite direction due to the invasion of Israel by five Arab states upon its rebirth in 1948. This does not include another million of these Sephardim who fled to other lands in the Diaspora, notably France and the Americas. They were known as *kilab yahud*—"Jew dogs"—in those "Arab" lands. So much for what Arabs like to claim was their alleged tolerance of "their Jews" before the rise of modern political Zionism. How dare anyone else but Arabs demand a sliver of national dignity in their region!

At virtually the same time that the partition of the Indian subcontinent was taking place, the Arabs rejected a similar plan that would have created a second state for themselves in historic Palestine. Take another look at those earlier maps in the book. What would later rename itself Jordan had already emerged on almost 80 percent of the original territory of the Mandate issued to Great Britain in the wake of the Paris Peace Conference on April 25, 1920. Colonial Secretary Churchill had separated all of Palestine east of the Jordan River and handed it over to Britain's Hashemite Arab allies in the creation of Transjordan in 1922.

Read what Sabri Jiryis, a prominent Palestinian Arab researcher at the Institute for Palestinian Studies in Beirut, had to say about all of this in the Lebanese newspaper, *Al-Nahar*, on May 15, 1975: "While it is estimated that seven hundred thousand Arabs fled the 1948 war, against this Arabs caused the expulsion of just as many Jews from Arab states whose properties were taken over, a population and property exchange occurred and each side must bear the consequences."

Much more evidence for this exists in books written by Arab kings, officials, and others as well. So, why is it that over a half century later, Arabs—who have been receiving billions of dollars in aid from the United Nations, the European Union, America, oil revenues, other international funds, and elsewhere—still have not relieved the plight of their own refugees, a problem which, by their own rejectionist attitudes, they overwhelmingly created themselves?

Arabs like to cite an alleged massacre by Israelis at Deir Yasin, a village that controlled the road to Jerusalem from which Arabs were attacking Jews. Truth be told, Jewish forces were attacked from within the village itself, and then chaos broke out. Arab "militants" are famous for setting up shop amid their non-combatants. Witness how they conducted themselves in the recent war in Gaza, earlier in Lebanon, and so forth. Video tape is available showing Hamas launching rockets from school grounds while a headquarters was set up in hospitals and the like.[78] The same deal occurred a while back regarding Jenin.

That Arabs habitually use their own civilians as human shields is beyond dispute. More recently, the actions of Hamas, Hizbullah in Lebanon, the various Fatah factions, America's own experiences in Iraq, and so forth amply testify to this. Again, schools, apartment buildings, mosques, hospitals, and so forth are frequently used by Arab combatants—against the Perfidy and other clauses of Geneva Conventions, by the way—and then the Arabs invite the press in to see the casualties that they themselves caused. And the latter useful idiots buy into it.

Was Israel squeaky clean once it was invaded and fighting for its very life? What nation could make such a claim? But Israel tried as hard as humanly possible to avoid the conflict in the first place. What other nation that you know of calls its enemies on the phone and tells them to evacuate first or drops leaflets telegraphing its punch in advance? Those "devil" Jews do, and the Arabs know it, too.

Unfortunately, the only thing Israel could have done to avoid this conflict would have been to consent to its own abortion. Arab refusal to recognize justice in any hue but their own created the Arab refugee problem.

Keep in mind that volumes of solid documentation exist that show that Jews pleaded with their Arab neighbors, both in and out of the Mandate, for something much better. Some Arab leaders themselves—including Mahmoud Abbas—have admitted to their own responsibility for this mess.[79]

Again, Arabs have almost two dozen states on some six million square miles of territory—lands that belonged mostly, as we have already noted, to other non-Arab peoples before they were conquered in the name of the Arab nation. Jews absorbed their own refugees (half of whom came from the "Arab"/Muslim world) into a sole, tiny state roughly the size of New Jersey, virtually invisible on a map of the world.

The answer to the above question regarding why there are still Arab refugees can perhaps best be illustrated by Arab actions.

Some years back, with the status of the disputed territories Israel found itself in control of in the aftermath of the 1967 War still unresolved, Israel offered to knock down the dilapidated refugee camps and replace them with new housing and better living conditions.

It is worth remembering that Egypt and Jordan occupied these territories from 1948 to 1967 and not only did nothing about this problem for almost two decades but never discussed the creation of that additional Palestinian Arab state there, either.

So, how did the Arabs respond to that Israeli offer? They demanded that Israel do nothing to remedy life in the camps. Luckily, Israel ignored them and did indeed do much to improve life there.[80]

But, again, why would Arabs do this? It is really not hard to understand. Quite simply, and as it has been known for decades, Arabs have used their own refugees as pawns in their perpetual war to delegitimize Israel.

Arabs do not want the refugee problem solved, not as long as it means that a viable Jewish state of Israel will still exist on the morrow. That is why they tacked on the "right of return" of millions of real or alleged Arab refugees to the so-called Saudi peace plan a few years back and Arafat walked away from an offer to get some 97 percent of the disputed territories, half of Jerusalem, a 33 billion dollar sweetener, and other major concessions as well at Camp David 2000 and Taba in 2000.[81] And that is why even President Obama's "moderate" Arab buddy, Mahmoud Abbas, today still refuses to recognize a Jewish Israel—even if Israel caved in to all of his demands, all the while demanding the birth of the Arabs' twenty-second state.

The result of both Arafat's and the "moderate" Saudis' so-called peace plans still envisions Israel's Jews being overwhelmed so that a second Arab state will replace Israel, not live side by side with it. This should come as no surprise since all Palestinian (and many other) Arab maps, schoolbooks, Web sites, and the like omit Israel as well. This is also why talk about creating a "provisional Palestinian Arab State" under these circumstances is scary. Recall that Faisal al-Husseini, the late showcase moderate of Abbas's folks, said that while he would accept any land diplomacy would yield, a purely Arab Palestine from the river to the sea was the real goal, the same old "destruction of Israel in stages" strategy dominant since after the "one fell swoop" alternative collapsed as a result of its failure in the 1967 Six Day War.[83]

Thus, tragically, this conflict still really has no end in sight. And the horrendous human costs specifically associated with suicide/homicide bombings for both sides have been created and sustained by the Arabs themselves.

Reasonable compromises have been repeatedly offered—and rejected—to end the Arab–Israeli conflict, certainly light years more than anything Arabs have ever offered to the numerous native, non-Arab peoples they have conquered and forcibly Arabized in carving out most of the almost two dozen states they now call their own.

Chapter 16

Hunting Quail and Sitting Ducks

An American president—the first since Harry Truman in 1948—finally took a political stance in April 2004 that might still, in the long run, actually further the peace process between Arab and Jew if given half a chance. Regardless of some backtracking, President George W. Bush's public announcement that Israel should not be expected to slit its own throat by absorbing millions of real or fudged descendants of Arab refugees, nor have to return to the UN-imposed Auschwitz/armistice lines of the post-1948 fighting was a positive development. Unfortunately, newly-elected President Obama's endorsement of the so-called Saudi peace plan—which demands these very things of Israel—is a step backward. While he hints at possibly some modifications, I would not hold my breath waiting for Arabs to accept any that affect those crucial issues above. I hope I'm wrong.

While the precise wording of UN Security Council Resolution 242 has been known for quite some time (and both the resolution itself as well as commentaries by its architects—Eugene Rostow, Arthur Goldberg, Lord Caradon, and others—are readily accessible), the State Department spent decades trying to distort the interpretation of it to require Israel to return to its absurd nine to fifteen-mile-wide, mostly armistice line (not border) existence. The final draft of the hotly-debated 242 that was adopted in the wake of the June 1967 Six Day War—a war started by Arabs with their blockade of Israel, a *casus belli*, and other hostile acts—expressly did not call for this, although Arabs and their supporters (the French, Russians, and so forth) attempted to have it do so—and failed.[83]

What 242 did call for was the eventual withdrawal (in the context of moves toward real peace, not *hudna* ceasefires) of Israel from "territories"—but not *all* or *the* territories—to "secure and recognized boundaries" to replace those vulnerable armistice lines.

The main problem that immediately followed in the wake of the president's televised April 2004 announcement was all the pandering to the predictable Arab "rage" that subsequently took place by the media, anti-Israel academia, and others.

The Arabist Foggy Folks also quickly began to muddy the waters. No surprise here. They opposed Truman's recognition of Israel in the first place, and not a few multinational oil and other big-business folks with lucrative ties to the Arab oil sheikhs have made it into the highest ranks of the State Department and other areas of government as well. A lucrative revolving door, indeed. Just ask James Baker III.

If President Bush's comments had been left intact (which, unfortunately, they were not), the following might have eventually occurred. Faced, at long last, with the solid reality that America's policy toward Israel would not reincarnate that of Allied Europe, when Czechoslovakia was sacrificed by its "friends" at Munich in 1938 over a heavily German-populated Czech Sudetenland, the Arabs—when the dust finally settled—would likely have to either fish or cut bait if they expected to ever gain anything beyond the pleasure of simply butchering more Jews from all of this mess.

Despite some unfortunate backtracking by Bush himself (the Iraqi prison scandal broke right around the same time as did stories about Arab "rage" over his remarks—so it was once again time to soothe Arabs at the Jews' expense, and it seems to have remained so ever since), the above scenario was, and may still be, the very real possibility arising from the president's comments. Once more, however, this largely depends on whether or not the Foggy Folks will be allowed to emasculate the potential here and whether Bush's successor, President Obama, will follow through on this as well. As of April 2009, I wouldn't bet on the latter. But, again, I'd like to be mistaken here.

To understand at least some of what's at stake better, let's review some related events and issues.

As the new year, 2004, began, President George W. Bush spent the holiday hunting quail with President George H. W. Bush and James Baker III—a close family friend, his father's secretary of state, and his own special Middle East envoy. Chances are pretty good that they traveled farther in their hunt than the State of Israel is in width. Indeed, it is been said that there are some Texas driveways larger than the latter.

Now, I have nothing against hunting per se, as long as it is done in a sustainable way to put food on the table. My dad, G_d rest his beloved soul, brought home quail, pheasant, and so forth from time to time. Only vegetarians have a right to protest, and I'm not quite there yet. My brother, Dr. Joseph, is. Furthermore, while I voted for the other guy the last time around, I'm no Bush-basher either, although I have problems with the family's oil ties and related worrisome environmental record.

So, what was bothering me wasn't the quail that were being hunted nor the hunters during that New Year's holiday. My problem was/is with the influence James Baker continued to have on the Bush family. I have an even more bothersome worry that the family (for sure at least some of the older members) shared many of these same ideas with or without his influence.[84]

I have a feeling that Daddy and James are, at least somewhat, peas of the same pod, but I was hoping, despite the odds, for something better from the son. George W. quotes, after all, from Joshua in the Hebrew Bible, but then (up until his 2004 announcement) apparently flipped and espoused Judea becoming mostly *Judenrein* in the next breath.

To anyone concerned about Israel not being shortchanged in terms of justice, it was indeed worrisome to see the reemergence of James Baker III on the political scene. Having said this, however, too many of President Obama's buddies are as bad or worse. Before even taking office, for example, he sent his good pal and newly-appointed envoy, Robert Malley, to Syria to do some horse trading—with pressured Israeli concessions on the Golan Heights as the likely American carrot. Malley was a close friend of Arafat and is rabidly anti-Israel.[85] Too many of the new president's friends and appointees thus share that same Baker trait.

Baker had been appointed as Mr. Bush's special envoy to the Middle East, and if the latter got reelected in November 2004, then anything was possible. Bush would have nothing to lose in terms of angering a large segment of his Evangelical Christian supporters if he followed Baker's above earlier foul advice and Foggy Bottom's lead since this would be his last term in office. Unfortunately, on this same issue in that election, the Democrats were even worse. Former President Jimmy "Apartheid Israel" Carter was likely their future main man in the Middle East, and he has yet to meet an Arab disemboweler of Jewish babes and grandmas he hasn't blamed the Jews themselves for.

Headaches. And they continue now as well—as bad or worse—with what's apparently on President Obama's agenda.

Baker had been in the background for decades, especially since his close friends, the Bushes, gained ascendancy in American politics. His law firm represents Saudi Arab interests in this country and, again, typifies how people move through the revolving doors of businesses tied to Arab petrodollars back and forth into government positions—especially those in Foggy Bottom.

Baker's law partner, Robert Jordan, was appointed ambassador to Saudi Arabia by President Bush in 2001. Casper Weinberger and many others have been through these lucrative doors as well. Most often, their influence has spelled big trouble for an Israel trying to get just a fair hearing.

While President George H. W. Bush was at the helm, widespread reports circulated that Secretary of State Baker promised Hafez al-Assad, the butcher of Damascus and master of Lebanon, the same deal on the Golan Heights as Egypt's Sadat received in the Sinai Peninsula—a complete withdrawal of Israeli forces.

Once again, please remember what 242 did not call for. And this was prior to negotiations between the parties themselves, a promise Baker evidently made to Saddam Hussein's above virtual twin, author of the "Hama Solution," and such.

Hama was the town that dared oppose Papa Assad and suffered tens of thousands of casualties within a month or so as a result, far more than Arabs have suffered after years of intifada, Gaza wars, and terror launched against Israel. And then there were also Syria's past and renewed subjugation and atrocities against its own non-Arab Kurds (also à la Saddam in Iraq) to consider, with no United Nations inquiries or trials in Geneva either.

In a *Time* magazine article on February 13, 1989, Baker spoke of Israel as being a turkey to be hunted and carefully stalked. He has referred to Jews working for him and doing his anti-Israel bidding (including the recent American ambassador to Israel and good friend of President Obama, Daniel Kurtzer) as his "Jew boys." I think you get the picture. But I'm getting sidetracked, so back to Baker's comments about the Golan.

What most folks do not understand is that the Golan was a hotly contested region ruled by many different peoples—including Jews—over the millennia. Furthermore, it was part of the original Mandate of Palestine Britain received after World War I until imperial politics prompted a tradeoff with France in 1924.

The Bush presidents, Baker, and now President Obama know full well how Syria used its acquisition and position on the Golan prior to '67 to rain death on Israeli kibbutzim and fishermen in the Sea of Galilee below. And they also know the losses Israel took to end that state of affairs when war was forced upon it— largely via Syria's instigations and game-playing with Nasser's Egypt—in 1967.

A bit later, had it not been for Israeli forward positions on the Golan, it was an easy downhill assault into Israel proper when Syria attacked in the Yom Kippur War in 1973. And if you believe that Israel was attacked to simply retrieve "occupied lands," I have not one but two bridges to sell you.

The passes Israel now controls greatly prevent a renewed Syrian assault. Additionally, much of Israel's water supply originates in this area, a vulnerability Syria is well aware of and has tried to cash in on in the past. Indeed, when Israel later offered almost an entire retreat from the Heights, negotiations broke down because of Syria's insistence that it be allowed to hold Israel virtually captive this way.

What's even more worrisome is that if Syria had not blundered into supporting Saddam against America in Iraq, the Bush administration—with Baker's and Foggy Bottom's active prodding—would have been all set to turn the screws on Israel vis-à-vis the Golan. Indeed, there were reports to this effect periodically coming out of the State Department prior to Syria's support of the Iraqi opposition forces against America. And now the new President seems poised to attempt to deliver Israel as well in return for a quid pro quo regarding more Syrian cooperation in Iraq and/or Lebanon.

So what gives here?

For a while, it looked like George W. was able to distance himself from the troublesome record of the past. His dad's venomous attack against Israel, when the latter launched its surgical strike against Saddam's Osirik nuclear reactor in Iraq in 1981, still haunts the memory. It angered too many of his Arab oil buddies and their allies at the State Department. Just think what a nuclear-equipped Saddam would have meant to not only his region but to the world at large. Yet that didn't stop the Foggy fulminations, nor those from George H. W. Bush against Israel either. And now we have a nuclear Iran to worry about.

But as the months progressed after the 2003 toppling of Saddam in Iraq, the president's line in the Middle East sounded more and more like the same one constantly pushed by his father, Baker, and Foggy Bottom: "Justice for Arabs and [blank] everyone else."

Again, has anyone heard of a roadmap, for instance, for some thirty-five million stateless Kurds, America's best friends (despite our manhandling of them) in Iraq, and the folks the Arabs are likely to slaughter yet again when America finally withdraws? Or one for the Imazhigen, the majority, subjugated, non-Arab native people in forcibly Arabized North Africa?

Is there a course at the typical university where Israel is routinely dissected under the microscope set up to study the plight and quest for justice of any of these non-Arab folks? And how many pre-Ottoman, Ottoman, and modern Turkish specialists even utter the word *Kurd* in their classes? Coincidence? Guess again.

Arabs must have their twenty-second state, but the ongoing subjugation of those scores of millions of native, non-Arab peoples is merely swept out of the window of your typical ivory tower.

What's wrong with this picture?

Shameful—but "justice," State Department and too often Middle East Studies Association (MESA) style. Thus the need for a strong, more balanced executive at home in the White House.

While Mr. Bush's above 2004 remarks in relation to Sharon's Gaza plan were promising, as we have already seen, there was major backsliding regarding them. Nothing he said, after all, was even legally binding. In a virtual state of panic, the Foggy Folks were quick to point out themselves that Israel had received promises before from American Presidents in return for important concessions it was largely coerced into making, only to see them evaporate when they were needed in the crunch. Whoops.

America—the most powerful nation on Earth, three thousand miles wide from coast to coast, largely separated from its likely enemies by expansive oceans, and so forth—can acquire, conquer, or *whatever* land and manipulate, topple, or *whatever* governments in the name of its own national security interests, manifest destiny, and such. But, how dare an Israel that one needs a magnifying glass to find on a world map build a fence to keep Arab bombers from blowing up its kids or insist that a compromise is in order to assure that Assad Jr. doesn't follow in papa's footsteps. As of 2009 he has an incentive not to do so. Israeli long-range artillery on the Golan are in a position to potentially do unto Damascus what Damascus actually did unto Jews for two decades prior to '67. Think of all the shameful flak Israel has caught over these issues.

Every military expert who has visited the Golan from abroad has given the same advice: Israel would have to be suicidal to return to the status quo ante here. Israel simply does not have the wiggle room on the Golan or in Judea and Samaria/West Bank that it had, at least somewhat, in the Sinai. Egypt got all of the latter back—plus the oil fields Israel developed, etc.—in return for a very cold peace. Most of the smuggling of arms, explosives, and the like come through tunnels into Gaza from Egypt to attack Jews in Israel who totally withdrew from Gaza years ago. Nice peace, partner. Yet reports were soon circulating that Washington was concerned that Israel was solidifying its position on the Golan and would eventually put the squeeze on here, as it has done vis-à-vis the West Bank and elsewhere.

Of course, one could have hoped that if President Bush eventually stood by and solidified his April 2004 comments regarding Israel being entitled to territorial compromise on the West Bank à la what UNSC Resolution 242 actually called for, he'd also take the same position regarding the Golan. Unfortunately, the results were very mixed on all of this as President Bush left office. And it appears that the mix has gotten even more worrisome now.

Gaza, after all, since the days of the Egyptian pharaohs, has been used as an invasion route into Israel proper and is presently a rejectionist terrorist stronghold, one that launched thousands of rockets and mortar shells into Israel proper after the Israeli withdrawal.

Mubarak, the current Pharaoh, rules a blatantly anti-Semitic as well as anti-Zionist nation of over sixty million people, armed to the teeth with top-of-the-line American warplanes, other weaponry, and such, and is no friend of Israel either.

While a case could have been made for both retention of or withdrawal from Gaza, in the long run, it is not only Hamas, the latter-day Arafatians in suits, and Islamic Jihad that Israel has to fear here. Not by a long shot.

Gaza is a spear leading into Israel proper, and very often throughout history that spear has been wielded by a powerful Egyptian army. And it still remains to be seen just how much of the strategically important West Bank, even under the best of potentially evolving scenarios, Israel would actually be allowed to retain as well. President Obama loves the Saudi plan—which calls for a return of Israel to the '49 Auschwitz/armistice lines.

Turning the clock back again, as the summer of 2004 approached, all of this had the potential of another Baker/Foggy Folks "done deal" scheme in the making, with G_d knows what kind of behind the scenes pressure had been exerted on Prime Minister Ariel Sharon. Something certainly seemed to have shaken the old warrior into making some major policy shifts, especially since they would likely be seen by Arabs as unilateral concessions to their rejectionist policies, thereby only encouraging more of the same.

Summing up, as of mid-2004, one had to think long and hard about what might very likely be going on if the Syrians weren't continuing to behave as Lebanon's virtual master and acting so foolishly regarding American policies in Iraq. Or what might also be occurring if things continued to go sour for America in its attempt to rebuild that post-Saddam nation. Israel likely would have, and still could, become the desired sacrificial offering by America to improve its Arab relations.

So, my problem really never had anything to do with hunting quail. It was about demanding that Israelis remain forever as sitting ducks—for that's what a return to the pre-'67 armistice lines would amount to, whether in Judea, Samaria, or on the Golan. It was—and is—a matter about justice for somebody else besides Arabs in the region for a change.

Chapter 17

APPETITE VERSUS STARVATION

ARABS HAVE SPENT decades trying to convince the world that they are both the old and the new Jews. Arafat and others have claimed that Jesus, Peter, and their comrades were actually Arabs—"Palestinians" to be exact—and not Jews. It seems that planes were not the only things that Arafat's crew decided to hijack.

Too bad that besides the Jews themselves, the Romans, who ruled the land in Jesus' day, also left a clear record of the land belonging to the Jews—whom they were in the process of conquering—and also made a clear distinction between Jews and Arabs as well.

Recall that Tacitus and Dio Cassius were famous Roman historians who wrote extensively about Judaea's attempt to remain free from the Soviet Union of its day, the conquering Roman Empire. They lived and wrote during or not long after the two major revolts of the Jews for independence in 66–73 C.E. and 133–135 C.E. They make no mention of this land being Arab, of it being called "Palestine," or its people "Palestinians." On the contrary, they detailed the difference between the native Jews Rome was fighting and the Arabs from surrounding lands who decided to join the massive Roman assault on their Jewish neighbors.

Here is this important quote again from Vol. II, Book V, *The Works of Tacitus*: "Titus was appointed by his father to complete the subjugation of Judaea. He commanded three legions in Judaea itself. To these he added the twelfth from Syria and the third and twenty-second from Alexandria. Amongst his allies were a band of Arabs, formidable in themselves and harboring toward the Jews the bitter animosity usually subsisting between neighboring nations."[86]

After the first revolt, Rome issued thousands of Judaea Capta coins that can be seen in museums all over the world today. Notice, please, "Judaea Capta," not "Palaestina Capta." Additionally, to celebrate this victory, the Arch of Titus was erected illustrating legionnaires carrying away the spoils of the Jewish temple in Jerusalem. It stands tall in Rome to this very day. The Arafatians and Hamasniks, of course, deny that such a temple ever existed.

When, some sixty years later, Emperor Hadrian decided to further desecrate the site of the destroyed temple by erecting a pagan structure there, it was the grandchildren's turn to take on their mighty conquerors.

Recall this next quote from Dio Cassius: "580,000 men were slain, nearly the whole of Judaea made desolate. Many Romans, moreover, perished in this war [the Bar Kochba Revolt]. Therefore Hadrian, in writing to the senate, did not employ the opening phrase commonly affected by the emperors, 'I and the legions are in health.'" [87]

The emperor was so enraged at the Jews' struggle for freedom in their own land that, in the words of the esteemed modern historian Bernard Lewis, "Hadrian made a determined attempt to stamp out the embers not only of the revolt but also of Jewish nationhood and statehood, obliterating its Jewish identity." [88]

Wishing to end, once and for all, Jewish hopes, Hadrian renamed Jerusalem Aelia Capitolina, and the land itself from Judaea to "Syria Palaestina"— Palestine—after the Jews' historic enemies, the Philistines, a non-Semitic sea people from the Aegean area around Crete. [89]

The reality, of course, is that the vast majority of Arabs did not even begin to enter into the picture regarding the land of Israel/Judaea/Palestine until almost seven centuries after the fall of Jewish Jerusalem—during the beginning of the Arabs' own extensive imperial conquest, forced Arabization, and colonialist settlement of much of the region. As I like to point out, imperialism is only nasty when non-Arabs so indulge in it.

Ditto for settlement and such.

As we have already seen, most so-called "native Palestinians" today came into the land only relatively recently themselves. [90]

While the story of the Arabs' attempt at establishing themselves as the "aboriginals" of the land could be developed further, I'll let it rest for now. So we'll end the discussion about their attempt at becoming the old Jews.

Let's next turn to the Arab attempt to become the new Jews. After Judaea's fight for freedom against the mighty Roman Empire and the conversion of the latter to Christianity, forced conversions, being branded the deicide people (and treated accordingly), inquisitions, autos da fe, demonization, dehumanization, ghettos, blood libels, massacres, expulsions, and existence as perpetual stranger in someone else's land became the all-too-frequent plight of the stateless "wandering Jew."

Estimates have placed the number of Jews murdered as a result of these experiences prior to the Holocaust in both the Christian West—where they were considered to be "G_d killers"—or in the Muslim East, where there was no Holocaust per se but where Jews were still frequently regarded as "killers of prophets" and *kilab yahud*, "Jew dogs," in the millions. And this was without the benefit of twentieth-century methods of mass extermination aiding the process.

Arabs have tried to convince the world that their experiences and the plight of Palestinian Arab refugees is somehow the equivalent of that of the Jews. It has worked to a great extent with a world largely—and too often willingly—deaf, dumb, and blind to the obvious differences.

Let's turn the clock back some seventy years to hear how one great Jewish leader explained these differences in his *Evidence Submitted to the Palestine Royal Commission in London* in 1937. Still recovering from the murderous pogroms and massive Jewish refugee problem that accompanied them just a bit earlier, it had by now become evident that even worse was yet to come. Let's take a look at how this visionary dealt with all of this:

> Three generations of Jewish thinkers have come to the conclusion that the cause of our suffering is the very fact of the Diaspora, the bedrock fact that we are everywhere a minority. The phenomenon called Zionism may include all kinds of dreams, but all of this longing for wonderful toys of velvet and silver is nothing compared with that tangible momentum of irresistible distress and need by which we are propelled and borne.
>
> Whenever I hear a Zionist accused of asking too much, I really cannot understand it. Yes we do want a State; every nation on earth, they all have States of their own, the normal condition of a people. Yet, when we, the most abnormal of peoples, and therefore the most unfortunate, ask for only the same, then it is called too much. We have got to save millions, many millions. I do not know whether it is a question of one third, half, or a quarter [indeed, one third of world Jewry would be eliminated within just a few years of his remarks].
>
> I have the profoundest feeling for the Arab case, in so far as that case is not exaggerated. I have also shown to you that there is no question of ousting the Arabs. On the contrary, the idea is that Palestine on both sides of the Jordan should hold the Arabs and Jews. What I do not deny is that in that process the Arabs of Palestine will become a minority. What I do deny is that that is a hardship.
>
> It is not a hardship on any race, any nation possessing so many National States now and so many more National States in the future. One fraction, one branch, and not a big one, will have to live in someone else's State: Well, that is the case with all the mightiest nations of the world. That is only normal and there is no "hardship" attached to that. So when we hear the Arab claim confronted with the Jewish claim, I fully understand that any minority would prefer to be a majority.
>
> It is quite understandable that the Arabs would also prefer Palestine to be the Arab State No. 4, No. 5. or No. 6, but when the Arab claim is confronted with our Jewish demand to be saved, it is like the claims of appetite versus starvation.[91]

The presenter of this evidence was Ze'ev Vladimir Jabotinsky, the patron saint of Israel's modern Likud Party, Prime Minister Netanyahu's folks. And, as can be seen above, unlike too many other starry-eyed Labor Zionist thinkers, he was a realist regarding what could and what could not be expected in the Jews' relationships with Arabs.

As Jabotinsky correctly forecasted, Arabs made out quite well after the breakup of the Turks' four-century-old empire at the end of World War I. To date, as is constantly stressed throughout this book, they have almost two dozen states belonging to their Arab League. Most of these were conquered and forcibly Arabized from scores of millions of non-Arab peoples.

Furthermore, guess how those non-Arab Muslim states, like Iran, Indonesia, Afghanistan, and Pakistan became Muslim in the first place?

Remember that these are the same folks who proclaim that the Jews are "imperialist colonizers" and get their assorted stooges in academia and elsewhere to promote this hypocritical travesty.

Appetite, indeed, Mr. Jabotinsky, and at everyone else's expense.

As we've already explored, with a few powerful fellow Muslim exceptions, Arabs declared the region to be solely theirs and launched jihad and killed anyone who stood in their way, millions to date.

In failing repeated attempts to destroy militarily the sole, miniscule state the Jews managed to get as a refuge, the Arabs next turned to another ploy. In the quest to defeat Israel on the battlefield of ideas, the Arabs virtually transformed themselves into the new stateless Jews.

In a like manner, Israel's attempts to survive and suppress repeated acts of Arab terrorism and assaults on its life were also twisted to be equated with the Nazis' treatment of the Jews. Arabs allegedly became the new David to an Israeli Goliath, despite the fact that there are some 170 million of the former on more than 6 million square miles of territory opposed to 6 million Israeli Jews in a state that one just about needs a magnifying glass to locate on a map of the world.

Along these lines, there are those who make the argument, "If Jews can have a state, why not Palestinians?" For some, this is simply ignorance. But for too many others—academics included—it represents something far worse, for they know better.

While I won't get into argument over whether a distinct Palestinian Arab nationalism exists today, it certainly did not exist before the rise of modern political Zionism a little over a century ago. In fact, the former arose specifically to negate the latter. There are volumes of evidence to support this. Virtually all the writings of politically conscious Arabs on the eve of the collapse of the

Ottoman Turkish Empire spoke of a greater Syrian Arab or Pan Arab identity. And there never was an Arab country, state, or nation of "Palestine." Indeed, the "Palestinians" were the Jews.[92]

As in Jabotinsky's day, currently, and before, this conflict has never been about Jews wanting to deny Arabs their own fair share of relative justice. On the contrary, it is always been about Arabs not allowing anyone else even a tiny sliver of those very same rights they so fervently demand for themselves. But, could you really blame them, given most of their own mind-sets and the realities at play?

Who among the world's leaders, for example, is demanding a "roadmap" for a single state for those thirty-five million truly stateless Kurds, whose one best chance at independence was nixed by a collusion of British petroleum politics and Arab nationalism?[93] Where are those holier-than-thou academics demanding Kurdish rights on campus like those—either subtly or more explicitly—doing so for the creation of a twenty-second Arab state on the ashes of Israel?

Yet earlier, in light of the above, Arabs also came to understand that they needed to change perceptions a bit.

In the war of ideas, the Arabs realized that the very identity of the conflict would have to undergo some major modifications.

In their attempt to create their additional state—in place of Israel, not alongside of it (nothing has really changed to this very day)—Arabs understood that it would make better press and public relations to speak in terms of creating a state for "stateless Palestinians" rather than calling for the creation of a twenty-second Arab state at the expense of the one of the Jews'.

Hocus pocus.

Arabs, with some two dozen states, would next be transformed into the likes of previously subjugated, perennially victimized, stateless Jews.

Again, recall Zuheir Mohsen, a PLO official, in his interview with the Dutch newspaper *Trouw* on March 31, 1977, and review how he explained this Arab-to-Palestinian transformation strategy: "There are no differences between Jordanians, Palestinians, Syrians, etc. It is only for political reasons that we now carefully underline Palestinian identity. This serves only a tactical purpose, a new tool in the continuing battle against Israel."[94]

Despite the passage of time, these basic truths do not change.

The Arab-Jewish (or Arab-Kurdish, Arab-Imazhigen, Arab-black African, and so forth) conflict is still all about Jabotinsky's appetite versus starvation, a conquering, subjugating appetite on the part of the Arabs to deny anyone else their own share of justice in the region.

By rejecting repeated compromises over the approximately 20 percent of the

Mandate of Palestine left after they had already received the lion's share of it in 1922 with the creation of purely Arab Transjordan (almost 80 percent of the whole), the Arabs created the impasse we are still living with today. They invaded a reborn Israel in 1948 in an attempt to nip it in the bud, thereby creating two refugee crises in the process: Arabs who fled Israel, often from just one part of "Palestine" to another, and a like number of Jews who fled "Arab"/Muslim lands. But, unlike the Arabs, the Jews didn't have other multiple states on millions of square miles of territory of their own to potentially choose from.

What's even more depressing is that in many crucial ways nothing has really changed for well over a half-century, as a look at Arab Web sites, textbooks, maps, television programs, and such illustrates. Israel simply does not (or shouldn't) exist. And the most that will be offered to it will be a temporary respite, a *hudna*, like that the prophet of Islam, Muhammad, allowed his enemies until he could muster the strength to deal them the final blow, Arafat's so-called "Peace of the Quraysh." As we've seen, even the Arabs' own moderates admitted to this, calling any and all such moves for "peace" a Trojan horse.

Again, the basic truths of this struggle do not change. They are eternal. And the Arab-Jewish conflict is still all about appetite versus starvation.

Chapter 18

MIND-BOGGLING—THE HYPOCRISY AND DOUBLE STANDARDS

The timing was just too much. I had just read of Western journalists crying uncontrollably at the news of Arafat's death in November 2004, watched as the murderous ghoul's carefully-nurtured masses cried out slogans for Israel's destruction at his burial in Ramallah, and read repeated editorials virtually canonizing the Egyptian master butcher of Jews. Next, I heard someone interviewed about the situation in Iraq referring to the Pesh Merga—the fighting force of the Iraqi Kurds—as being the most effective army of its kind in Iraq. Then, to top it off, I came across an article about the Kurds in the November 14 *Boston Globe* by Thanassis Cambanis. While the article was informative and fairly balanced, please note its title: "Kurds' Separatist Ambitions Pose Challenge to Iraq."

It just all came together.

Once again, the stench of hypocrisy and double standards was unbelievable. Nothing had changed since I was exposed to the same sickening duplicity in the allegedly hallowed halls of the ivory tower decades earlier. There, Israel was routinely taken to ask, while the so-called Arab world around it most often got a free pass. Ditto today.

For decades, the very same journalists, academics, politicians, Hollywood-types, and other would-be sources of ethical enlightenment who have been in the forefront of the fight for the creation of the Arabs' twenty-second state (second, not first, one within the original 1920 borders of the Palestinian Mandate) have either totally ignored or denigrated the aspirations of some thirty-five million truly stateless and much oppressed people, the Middle East's Kurds.

While slanting courses on the Middle East to the tipping point in favor of the Arabs and "Palestinians" in particular (and woe unto thee if you disagreed), the only time I ever heard the tenured chief honcho and specialist on Turkey ever even mention Kurds during my resurrected doctoral studies in the early eighties was when he mocked their plight, telling of his travels in so-called Turkish "Kurdistan."

Unlike Arabs—who could have had that additional state decades ago if they just didn't keep on insisting upon denying Israel's Jews (half of whom who were refugees themselves from "Arab"/Muslim lands) their sole, microscopic one—Kurds were never offered such a deal or partition over lands in which they have lived for thousands of years, long before a Turk or Arab ever arrived, conquered, and settled there.

Kassites, Hurrians, Guti, Medes, and other Kurdish ancestors predated the Arabs by millennia in Mesopotamia. Yet, when the Middle East was partitioned after World War I, while Arabs wound up with the lion's share of Palestine after Colonial Secretary Winston Churchill convened the Cairo Conference in 1921 and orchestrated the award of Transjordan—almost 80 percent of the total—to his Arabian Peninsula Hashemite Arab allies the following year, there would be no such division in the much larger Mandate of Mesopotamia—despite earlier promises made to the Kurds. The Arabs received the whole shebang, the oil-rich Kurdish areas included.

While spread out over a half-dozen modern states and having their own internal differences and divisions the same way that Arabs and others do, the Kurds sought only one Kurdistan for their scattered people, similar in many ways to the Jews. With the emergence of both a powerful Turkey under Musa-tafa Kemal ("Ataturk") in the West and a similar situation in the East with the rise of Reza Shah Pahlavi, Mesopotamia became the only realistic hope for Kurds in the age of nationalism and the collapse of former empires.

Arabs, on the other hand, insisted that all lands that they formerly conquered in their own age of Caliphal imperialism and conquest were destined solely to be part of the "purely Arab patrimony" of the region—despite the presence of scores of millions of native, non-Arab peoples.

For a Kurd, Copt, Amazigh, Jew, black African, and so forth to gain some semblance of acceptance in such a polity, they had/have to play along with the rules of the Arabizing game. As we have seen, the ongoing genocide against blacks in the southern and western parts of the Sudan, and the plight of North African Imazighen, Syrian, and Iraqi Kurds, *kilab yahud* (native "Jew dogs"), Egyptian Copts, and others as well are the result of this subjugating mind-set.

So, why is it that while the "moralists" of the world shed tears to the cause of either that next Arafatian or Hamas Arab state, they remain largely deaf, dumb, and blind to all the above?

Where are the Michael "Israel is one of the top three world evils" Moores and their pathetic Jew stooge choirs on such matters?[95]

Where is the New Left regarding these things? How about President Jimmy "Apartheid Israel" Carter, Jesse "Hymietown" Jackson, & Co.? They all certainly have plenty to say about "oppressive Israelis" who dare to inconvenience Arabs by setting up checkpoints and a security barrier to prevent Jewish kids from being blown apart.

How can the allegedly liberal press and media, United Nations, European Union, and others as well (including the Sate Department) insist that Israel cave in to all that Arabs demand (known today as the Saudi peace plan, which Arabs insist Israel must accept as a whole), while ignoring the plight of Kurds who have been repeatedly slaughtered en masse by the very same Arabs (and others as well) whom the world still insists that Kurds not separate from? Indeed, most scholars—who, of all people, should know better—simply call them "separatists" if they bother to mention them at all, those same sources of ethical enlightenment who don't hesitate to take Israel to task.

Did those same above folks insist that Serbs, Croats, Albanians, and other mutually hostile groups stay together for the sake of the unity of Yugoslavia after the death of Marshall Tito? If the latter nation was said to be an artificial state (pieced together after the collapse of the Austro-Hungarian Empire in World War I), then so too—most certainly—is so-called Arab "Iraq."

The latter was largely created to further the goals of British petroleum politics in cahoots with Arab nationalism, especially after British Mesopotamia was awarded the oil-rich areas around predominantly Kurdish Mosul in 1925 in the wake of the collapse of the Ottoman Turkish Empire and the rise of modern Turkey under Mustafa Kemal Ataturk.[96]

With the Arab portions of Iraq once again likely to erupt after America's departure, is it reasonable for the world to insist that the Kurds stay united with Arabs who have repeatedly massacred and gassed them, periodically outlawed their culture and language and such in years past, and who have already promised yet more revenge against them for being America's staunchest allies in Iraq?[97]

While "Palestinian"—regardless of how you define the term (most were Arabs who migrated into the Mandate from elsewhere)—Arabs form the overwhelming majority of Jordan's population, and Jordan itself comprises the bulk of the original 1920 Mandate of Palestine, the world insists that yet another state for Arabs be created in "Palestine."

Those above Arabs, by whatever name, share the same culture, language, religion, and history (but also with local loyalties and stories to tell). Yet, the world accepts their "need" for some two dozen separate states. Think about that *Boston Globe* article's title again that we started this chapter with.

And at the same time that most of the world still debates whether or not Arabs, who have deliberately targeted Israeli cities, blow up civilian buses, and such are militants or terrorists, folks like David Ignatius of *The Washington Post* have no problem using the "T-word" for Kurds. While these same voices insist that there be that twenty-second state for Arabs, somehow tens of millions of Kurds remain, forever, undeserving of one. Furthermore, their quest is more often than not negatively labeled as that of mere extremists, rebels, or separatists, as we have seen.

Ignatius, while writing on September 16, 2003, of the danger in playing America's Turkish card in Iraq, when referring to Kurds, labeled them only as terrorists or rebels.

Too many other examples of this hypocritical, double standard treatment abound.

More often than not, the Kurds, Copts, Imazighen, and other victims of Arabs are simply ignored by the very same academics and others who readily demonize and seek to divest from Israel. And besides Ignatius's comments, we have seen more recent ones similar to them in the *Boston Globe* and elsewhere.

Even more pathetic was an op-ed in the March 26, 2003, *New York Times* in which Thomas Friedman advised that Kurds should be told point blank, "What part of 'no' don't you understand? You Kurds are not breaking away." This is the same guy who—up until some recent rude awakenings—has written volumes demanding that Israel cave in to virtually all Arab territorial demands despite the fact that in the wake of the '67 War UN Resolution 242 itself recognized the need and allowed for a compromise here.

The last time America abruptly pulled out of Iraq after the first Gulf War in 1991, the Kurds were massacred while American forces were still a stone's throw away. This happened after President George H. W. Bush told them to revolt against Saddam and then left them holding the bag. A few years earlier, Saddam and his Sunni Arabs gassed and slaughtered Kurds en masse in their 1986–1989 genocidal Anfal Campaign.

America had used and abused them again even earlier after we encouraged the Kurdish revolt under Mullah Mustafa Barzani in the seventies. That time they were manipulated to help our friend the Shah of Iran in his dispute with Iraq.[98] Overall, hundreds of thousands of Kurds have been killed and maimed by Arabs during these episodes, used and abused by the same State Department that specializes in shafting Jews as well.

Unlike the chances that Arabs repeatedly have at least had, up until recently, Kurds have never been able to progress beyond what Richard Cottam of *Nationalism in Iran* calls "negative nationalism," primarily because they have never been granted even one lasting territorial base in the modern age of nationalism in which they could have an opportunity—such as Arabs blew away after the total Israeli withdrawal from Gaza years ago—to work out and achieve a more positive variety.[99]

The autonomy Iraqi Kurds have recently achieved in millennia-old Kurdish lands in the north of the country in the aftermath of America's overthrow of Saddam under George W. Bush holds great promise to improve this situation. If America's earlier federal plan for Iraq collapses or is abandoned by the dominant Shi'a Arabs upon our withdrawal (which allowed for that autonomy), America must not abandon Washington's best friends over there—the Kurds—yet again.

During these days when we wonder what will happen next in an Arab-dominated Iraq after America's exit, is it not time for the Kurdish question to at long last get the full and fair support and attention that it deserves, the same treatment that the Arab quest for a twenty-second state has already received for decades now?

Chapter 19

April Magic

I DON'T KNOW. MAYBE it was just an exercise in rallying support among millions of key Evangelical Christian voters and winning over some Jews in what promised to be a very close election back in November 2004. President Bush, after all, had won the last time around in a highly controversial election by, literally, just a few handfuls of votes here in Florida. But maybe—just maybe—while it undoubtedly involved this, perhaps there was something else astir as well.

Israel's prime minister, Ariel Sharon, made a very hard decision in April 2004. After decades of supporting the construction of Israeli settlements in disputed territories Israel wound up with as a result of having to fight a defensive war for its life in June 1967, the Old Warrior decided that the costs outweighed the gains of keeping Jews in Gaza.

While it is true that, while their numbers drastically fluctuated, Jews had lived in Gaza for millennia; that, since the days of the Pharaohs, Gaza had been used as an invasion route into Israel proper by those aiming to destroy or subjugate it; that Gaza had become a hotbed for terrorists aiming to destroy Israel; that Jewish communities set up in Gaza were not on Arab-owned land; and so forth; it is also true that many—if not most—Israelis were looking for a way out of Gaza if the proper conditions presented themselves.

Israel had long been under pressure to take some steps to revive the all but dead, so-called roadmap for peace with Palestinian Arabs. While the latter was seen, at least in a few circles, to exist in such a moribund state due to the unwillingness and/or inability of the Arabs to control their own murderers of Jews, this key factor did not matter nearly as much as it should have. So the squeeze—as usual—was put on the Jews. While such hypocrisy was by now expected from Europe and much of the rest of the world, the folks at Foggy Bottom also habitually indulge in this sort of behavior, coming up with absurd alleged "moral equivalencies" and the like.

Lacking any Anwar Sadat or King Hussein-type to deal with among Palestinian Arabs (i.e., Arab leaders willing to allow for a viable Israel still existing on the morrow after a peace treaty is signed), Sharon decided to make a bold, unilateral move to break the stalemate while also supposedly enhancing Israel's overall security position. The latter assertion was/is hotly debated given certain "facts of life," such as the thousands of rockets and mortars, which were subsequently launched from Gaza into Israel proper after Israel's total withdrawal.

In April 2004, Sharon thus came up with his Gaza withdrawal plan. In addition to the removal of Gaza's eight thousand Jews, some settlements in Samaria, the northern West Bank, were also placed on the eviction notice. The world had been clamoring for such Israeli moves for decades.

Those who had conquered territories sometimes hundreds or thousands of miles away from home in the name of their own nations' security somehow couldn't figure out the life-threatening problems Israel was constantly faced with due to the armistice lines imposed upon it in 1949 by the United Nations, lines that simply marked where the invading Arab armies were stopped (by Israel—not the UN) during Israel's rebirth in 1948. As is well known by now, those lines made Israel only about nine to fifteen miles wide at its strategic waist, where most of the nation's population and industry are located.

One needn't be Napoleon nor General Patton to figure out what this all meant to a nation grossly out-manned and out-gunned, surrounded by enemies sworn to its demise. And, as would become the norm, the United Nations had only stepped in after the Jews turned the tide of the Arab invasion in 1948 to snuff out both their own lives and the life of their sole, miniscule, resurrected nation.

Israel was never meant to be a nine-mile-wide rump state—but that's how it was left when the lines were drawn in '49, marking the point where the Jews finally turned back the invasion of a half-dozen Arab armies supplied to the teeth with weaponry left over by the Allies from World War II and led, in Transjordan, by British officers. The UN stepped in to limit Arab losses, not to prevent their blatant aggression. This behavior would be repeated in subsequent decades as well.

Arab settlers from elsewhere then, once again, poured into these disputed territories. As we've seen, leading international legal scholars like Eugene Rostow have pointed out, the latter had largely been non-apportioned state lands belonging to the original Mandate, open to settlement by Arabs, Jews, and others as well. After 1949, however, only Arabs were able to move here with Transjordan's internationally unrecognized land grab.

Recall that purely Arab Transjordan, comprising all the land on the east bank of the river, had already been created by the British in 1922 from almost 80 percent of the original 1920 borders of the Mandate of Palestine, and Jewish communities in Judea and Samaria—the West Bank—had been massacred by Arabs in the 1920s and 1930s. During this same time period, massive waves of Arabs poured into the Mandate from Syria, Egypt, North Africa, and elsewhere. Many more Arabs entered under cover of darkness and were simply never recorded—more "native Palestinians." Thanks to the Jews, the Mandate was economically booming, drawing Arabs in from the entire region.

While what follows has been repeated ad nauseam, it must be stated yet again.

The architects of famed UN Security Council Resolution 242 (Lord Caradon, Rostow, Arthur Goldberg, etc.) carefully worded the final, accepted draft so that Israel would not be expected to have to return to its pre-'67, suicidal armistice lines. Indeed, the resolution called for the creation of "secure and recognized borders" to replace those lines and deliberately left out the words *all* and *the* in a discussion of eventual withdrawal in the event of peace.

The bulk of Israel's settlements have been placed with such an eventual strategic territorial compromise in mind. While some may have to go as a tradeoff for a real peace agreement, others will have to stay, but not if President Obama apparently has his way. The current Saudi peace (of the grave) plan—which the new president says Israel would be nuts to reject—calls for a full Israeli return to the '49 Auschwitz/armistice lines in return for basically a promise of good Arab behavior.

Let's be honest. The area under discussion is extremely tiny to begin with. There have already been two states created in the area of the original 1920 Mandate of Palestine, one for Arabs, Jordan (some 80 percent of the whole), and a much smaller one for Jews, Israel.

When Egypt held Gaza and Jordan (the name changed after it came to hold both banks of the River) held the West Bank for almost two decades after grabbing those territories in the 1948 fighting, no one called for the creation of an additional Arab state, the Arabs' second, not first, in "Palestine." But, after 1967, the world suddenly demanded the latter of the Jews—expecting them to bare their necks to bring this about. Furthermore, the American Foggy Folks constantly make the point that that second Arab state in Palestine must be no Bantustan.

Guess what?

Justice does not demand that the boundaries and such of any twenty-second Arab state—that there really is no room for—must come at the expense of the security of the sole, miniscule state of the Jews. And any Israeli leader with his spine and some other parts still intact must be crystal clear in conveying this message—regardless of whom it must be addressed to.

Despite all of this, back in 2004, Sharon sought to break the logjam with his April withdrawal proposals. So, the assorted world hypocrites really should have applauded Arik's (Ariel Sharon's nickname) decision, correct?

Guess again. And the Arabs, themselves, of course, viewed Sharon's unilateral withdrawal from Gaza decision simply as another victory to be credited to their destruction-in-phases scenario.

Terrorism works, Lebanon encore, and so forth.

That's the message, unfortunately, they got from Arik's gesture of goodwill. And rather than feeling compelled to come up with some real conciliatory moves of their own (such as some real steps toward nation-building and other elements of "positive" nationalism), the Arabs simply made more demands for additional, unilateral Israeli concessions that would make the Jews even more vulnerable.

As a teacher, I can say that post-Gaza, the Arabs flunked yet another test of trustworthiness as a neighbor with flying colors, which, in turn, taught Jews (at least those with heads not stuck in the sand, ostrich-style) the same old lesson they had learned already: no Israel, regardless of size, would ever be acceptable to those who claim the whole area as simply being purely Arab patrimony and/or part of the Dar ul-Islam.

Since the failure of their one-fell-swoop plan for Israel's destruction in June 1967, Arabs adopted a strategy to politically force (via pressure from Israel's "friends" during "negotiations") a return to the indefensible armistice lines of 1949. Given new technologies, massive buildups of Arab armed forces, the continuing booming Arab birth rate, and the like, the return of Israel to its pre-'67 lines, coupled with a demand for a "return" of millions of Arabs to the Jews' rump state, would be the beginning of the end for the Jewish state.

Unfortunately, President Obama apparently thinks the above is all just grand since all of this is what's expected of Israel in the so-called Saudi peace plan—which the president is preparing to try to shove down Israel's throat as this book is being proofed. As of late May 2009, the latest news I can report is that I think I heard the president mention something about some possible "modifications" to that plan, something all the Arab players have repeatedly said is unacceptable. But still, a glimmer of hope?

Arabs have openly acknowledged all of the above. Recall that even their showcase "moderates" have called Oslo and other so-called plans for peace merely part of their Trojan horse, designed to bring about Arafat's so-called "Peace of the Quraysh," the temporary *hudna* designed to buy time while weakening the Jews for the same final blow Muhammad dealt to his pagan enemies almost fourteen centuries earlier.[100]

That Arabs have responded this way was no shock. But they have been supported in this behavior by most of the world as well.

And then there was the magic of April 2004. There had been talk before Sharon came up with his withdrawal plan that he would get some backing from Washington on some other key matters.

Now, pay close attention: there is a simple yet indisputable set of facts regarding the Arab–Israeli conflict. If there will ever be peace between Arab and Jew, Arabs will have to give up their eternal plans for Israel's destruction. Had they done this, Arabs could have had their second state in the original Mandate of Palestine decades ago.

Fair and just plans were presented to and rejected over the decades by the Arabs themselves—far more than Arabs had ever offered to any of their own perceived competitors. The reality is that they still want their additional state to exist in place of, not along side of, the Jewish one. And that's the Arab–Israeli conflict summed up in twenty-two words—one for each member of the Arab League, including that of the observer PLO's state-in-waiting, the proposed new, second, Arab state in Palestine.

Enter George W. Bush.

Standing near Sharon, in a news conference being watched and listened to all over the world, an American president—the first since Truman in 1948— finally took a political stance that may someday still lead to peace.

George W. stated before millions watching him the two key ingredients for such a recipe:

1. Israel should not be expected to return to the indefensible armistice lines of 1949, and the President called them just that, not "borders."

2. Real and fudged Arab refugees would have to go to the proposed new Arab state, not overwhelm the Jews in Israel. Too bad President Obama evidently doesn't understand this, for, again, the latter is part of that current Saudi non-peace plan, which he said he fully endorses. Recall that half of Israel's Jews were refugees from Arab/Muslim lands who left far more wealth and property behind than Arabs fleeing a war which they and their surrounding brethren had themselves started.

Einstein was not needed to figure all of this out. But Arabs had long been given reason via the world's (including and especially America's of late) actions to hope that Israel would yet become an updated Czechoslovakia with the West Bank as its Sudetenland. All that was missing was a proper Chamberlain-like leader and conditions allowing for another Munich sellout to achieve "peace." I fear that perhaps America has recently elected such a leader—no matter how many Passover seders he attends, Jew frontmen he gets to play along, or Holocaust speeches he delivers. James Baker III had his "Jew boys" too—as did the grand inquisitor, Torquemada. Perhaps things will unfold better than the evidence so far suggests. I hope so. But, as the expression goes, talk is cheap. What really counts are the actions one takes.

Yet, the problem resurfaced even before President Obama was elected in late 2008.

President Bush's two key ingredients spoken four years earlier, as simple as they were, will always remain the necessary magic if there is ever to be peace between Arab and Jew in the Middle East.

Unfortunately, they proved to be fleeting, practically from the get-go. No sooner than they were spoken, the Foggy Folks began to water them down. Again, no surprise here. The State Department fought President Truman over the very rebirth of Israel over a half century earlier and has frequently acted to undermine it ever since.

But, to make matters worse, something even more disturbing next transpired. America's Iraq prison scandal erupted. This, added to an already increased overall level of Arab animosity surfacing regarding Iraq, the Arab–Israeli conflict, and so forth, led the State Department to quickly search for additional ways to appease the Arabs.

Poof. Gone. Apparently only for an instant was the magic of April 2004.

Both the State Department and the President himself soon made statements that basically retracted much of what President Bush had said earlier.

What did/does this say to Israel—then, as well as what President Obama seems to be up to now—after Israel cedes all of the concrete, essential tangibles of security and survival in return for Arab and American promises that subsequently vanish into thin air?

The troubling fact is that at the first sign of problems America is too often willing to retract its support for Israel to have what all other nations naturally expect—the right to protect itself from any alleged peace that is really designed to bring about its very destruction.

If Arabs ever expect to get anything meaningful in terms of that additional state they demand, they will have to come to terms with that earlier April magic President Bush spoke of and understand that others, besides themselves, also have a right to a slice of justice in the region.

When they do this, they will find an Israel forthcoming in its willingness to meet them far more than halfway.

Chapter 20

AL CHAIT SHECHATANU, WE HAVE SINNED AGAINST YOU

JEWS BEGIN THE Ten Days of Awe, which fall between Rosh Hashanah and Yom Kippur, each new year, with a confession of sins committed in the eyes of G_d. Additionally, it is required that transgressions committed against fellow human beings be addressed as well. Without a true turning of the heart (*Tshuvah*) in attempts to rectify both, the confessions and fasts associated with the High Holy Days remain just meaningless words.

In terms of Arab–Israeli politics, Jews have been accused of countless sins by much of the world today, the same world that largely ignores the relatively moral dung heap that surrounds the Jewish state. This is especially true in the world of academia. Sound like "sour grapes," or too strong of a statement?

No, the grapes are fine, and the statement isn't strong enough. Ask scores of millions of the region's Arabs and non-Arab victims whom they would rather be victimized by—Arabs or Jews. Hands down. No contest.

As just one of too many examples, Arafat's boys (many with blood on their hands from killing Jews) fled into Israel to escape King Hussein's forces when the PLO's (and Mahmoud Abbas's) Fatah and others attempted to overthrow the Jordanian ruler in Black September 1970. Not that Israel got any thanks from the Arafatians for this.

As far as I'm concerned, this represented just another on a long list of mistakes too many starry-eyed Lefty Jews have made in a conflict with their totally rejectionist enemy. Israel had Arafat's murderous crew in a crossfire and should have taken advantage of it. Many survived, found refuge with the Jews—only to target and murder them and their children later. Dumb.

By the way, Jordan killed more "Palestinian"—however that term is defined—Arabs in Black September (like Hafez al-Assad slaughtered Arab enemies in his "Hama Solution" in Syria) in a few weeks than Israel has done fighting Fatah and Hamas in years.

So, as is noted in terms of yet another Jewish holiday, Passover, while it is regrettable that any hardship had to be suffered even by enemies who would destroy us, as Jews symbolically remove drops of wine from our cups at the Seder dinner to diminish our joy of deliverance, I offer no apologies for wanting to put an end to the Jews' two-thousand-year-old nightmare of massacres, forced conversions, expulsions, ghettoization, pogroms, dehumanization, inquisitions, dhimmitude, demonization, Holocaust, and being labeled either killers of G_d by the Christian West or "Jew dog" killers of prophets in the Muslim East by doing what was necessary for our own survival, working, with G_d's timely help, for the rebirth of Israel. The Prophet Ezekiel's vision of the resurrected Israeli phoenix of his valley of the dry bones arrived just in the nick of time.

At a time when most Arabs and their hypocrite supporters elsewhere offer no confessions and ask no forgiveness from neither G_d nor man for blowing up buses, restaurants, and schools, deliberately targeting innocents, subjugating, enslaving, and massacring millions of non-Arab peoples just in the last half-century alone, in the Middle East and North Africa on behalf of the Arab nation and what they claim as "purely Arab patrimony," Jews can honestly say that they have truly attempted—repeatedly—to reach an honorable and just solution to their problems with Arabs. To any truly objective observer, this is not debatable. I would gladly share a platform with anyone—which I have earlier already done (occasionally on television) with some leading Arab and other anti-Israel scholars and spokesmen—to debate this issue.

While wanting to put an end to their own perpetual *Nakba* (Arabs refer to the rebirth of Israel as the "catastrophe"), Jews nevertheless agreed to one compromise after another over the past century so that Arabs could gain their twenty-second state. Those of us who are knowledgeable are tired of reminding the world (and each other) that this included Arabs being granted the lion's share of the original 1920 Palestinian Mandate itself with the creation of purely Arab Transjordan—today's Jordan—from some 80 percent of "Palestine" (the name the Roman Emperor Hadrian renamed Judaea after the Jews' second major revolt for freedom in 133 to 135 C.E.) in 1922.

By early 2001, Arabs had rejected an offer that would have created that additional Arab state, eliminated most of the Israeli settlements on disputed—not "purely Arab"—lands, handed them over thirty billion dollars, and would have turned over some 97 percent of those lands to Arab control.[101]

Unfortunately or fortunately, at least some of us were not shocked at this.

As we have seen, that Arabs have always wanted their new, additional state to exist in place of Israel (regardless of the latter's size), not along side of it, has always been the problem. So "occupation" and "settlements" are not the core issues of the debate. Since Arabs see all of Israel proper in those latter terms, however, we have an even more serious dilemma in these regards. Only Arabs are entitled to settle, colonize, and occupy, remember?

This defining problem has always involved Arabs refusing to grant anyone else but themselves political rights in the region, with the possible exception of some of those whom they successfully Islamized centuries earlier.

While this holds true for Turks, Afghanis, Pakistanis, some two hundred million Indians, Iranians, and others for example, this is largely not the case with Kurds, black African (Muslim and non-Muslim) Sudanese, and Imazighen/Berbers. For the latter, the issue becomes more of a clash of ethnic nationalisms than of religion—with the Arabs' still-ongoing forced Arabization process still under way centuries after they burst out of the Arabian Peninsula in their imperial conquests of the region.

Kurds, blacks in the Darfur region of the Sudan, and the majority Imazhigen (Berbers) of "Arab" North Africa are largely Muslim—but not Arab. And while Arabs demand that others confess their "imperial" sins, Arabs see their own conquest, forced Arabization, colonization, and settlement of other peoples' lands simply in terms of their own just due.

So, as the current Hebrew New Year 5769 began, Jews had lots—both individually and collectively as a people and community—to work on to make better, both before the eyes of G_d and man. The latter also included continuing to search for a fair and honorable solution to problems involving Arabs.

To do this, however, Jews must have true partners for peace, ones who recognize Israeli rights as well as their own, again, understanding that others besides Arabs are entitled to a bit of justice in the region. Unfortunately, as we have seen and will continue to explore, this is not how the vast majority of Arabs have ever perceived this. And everything that most officially say, write, teach, and preach to their own people (with a few wonderful exceptions) works against this change in mind-set from ever happening. Under such circumstances, no amount of Israeli concessions will ever be enough, regardless of what the new American president's friends and advisors tell him.[102]

Until the day of that above required Arab epiphany arrives, however, Israel must do what it must do to thrive, not just survive, amid a sea of those aiming to destroy it.

The frequent demand, for example, that a miniscule Israel fight with one hand constantly tied behind its back must be rejected by Israel's leaders, even when such demands come from its "friends."

A while back, when Israel carefully targeted a Hamas training camp right after the latter blew up two more buses filled with children and other Jewish innocents, none other than the other so-called Palestinian Arab moderate, Abbas's predecessor and then-prime minister/Arafatian chief marionette Ahmed Qurei', endorsed further barbarism against Jews as being justified because of the Israeli counter-assault.

Using Qurei' and other Arabs' logic, murderers should thus never be pursued nor dealt with. So, even in "moderate" Arab eyes, Jews are supposed to just allow themselves to continuously be slaughtered with no response.

What Israel really needed to do then—and afterwards, in response to similar barbarism—was to follow the above assault on the murderers of its kids quickly, with ever more devastating blows. The day of the Hamas funerals comes to mind, with hundreds more Hamas members and their supporters crying out during the procession for additional murder and firing weapons into the air. Many with Jewish blood already on their hands and wannabes were likely in that procession. If Jewish kids at home, on buses, in schools, restaurants, and other civilian centers are fair game for Arab "heroes," then why is such a gathering of armed would-be assassins not a legitimate target?

Will such actions make Arabs hate Jews any more than they do already?

Well, nobody likes to have their own nose bloodied, but these folks are already dedicated to the Jews' destruction—both individually and collectively. The only thing that prevents more atrocities is Israel's nonstop vigilance. So, Israel must fight—somewhat at least—to win and must ignore the hypocrites elsewhere who will always condemn it, no matter what. The latter would have leveled Gaza years ago if their own countries were subjected to the same treatment Jews have been told to constantly endure. Imagine your own town or city having over ten thousand rockets and mortars fired at it, as Israel recently experienced from Gaza. What would you expect America or any other country to do to those launching those unprovoked attacks—the Arab idea of positive nation-building?

If Fallujah was a fair target for American air force fighter bombers day after day in Iraq (ditto for Afghanistan) because we believed our enemies were located there, then what are hundreds of Hamas folks, dedicated to Israel's destruction crying out for revenge and announcing their planned intentions to butcher more Jews at such funeral processions?

Unlike a huge, three thousand mile-wide America, thousands of miles away from its Iraqi Arab enemies, tiny Israel faces these problems right in its very own backyard and side and front porches. While 9/11 changed this reality a bit, it is still far better to be in America's position than that of Israel's. Furthermore, any alleged innocent Arabs killed as a result of their support of those who are openly dedicated to the murder of Jews and the destruction of their sole state are not exactly innocent. President Bush acknowledged this truism himself in former statements.[103]

On the other hand, women, children, and others aboard Israeli buses, in pizza parlors, in shopping malls, at home, and such are not dedicated to the murder of Arabs or denial of Arab rights. Yet they are the preferred targets of choice of Arabs.[104]

The problem has always been that Arabs have seen their rights as being exclusive, negating those of others, a classic case of negative nationalism if ever there was one.

There is no room for a true compromise with this mind-set, only for a temporary *hudna*—ceasefire—until the time for total conquest better presents itself for the Arab cause. Under these unfortunate but very real circumstances, Israel's six million Jews (again, that disturbing number) cannot afford to simply fight a war of attrition with an Arab world that is numbered in the hundreds of millions, with one of the highest birthrates anywhere. Arafat talked of the Arab mother as being his best weapon. Sick.

While I hate to stoop to such thinking, taking out fifteen murderers after a like number of Jewish innocents have been massacred and scores more maimed is a losing tactic.

On the other hand, sending hundreds of them at the same time, however, to their own idea of paradise sends quite a different message. And when Hamas follows through with the next inevitable attack, the Israeli response must increase exponentially.

This is not to say that all hope must be given up regarding a peaceful solution to the Arab–Israel conflict. But it is to say that deceiving ourselves by yet again placing our heads in the sand (as too many delusional Jews are still prone to do) and believing that the new cattle cars will yet lead elsewhere besides the "showers" will only lead to the demise of the Jewish state. Take another look at the response, above, of the alleged "moderate" Ahmed Qurei'. His current successor, Mahmoud Abbas, the present alleged good cop, is definitely on his same page, regardless of all the attempted whitewashing from abroad.

Of all real sins that Jews must seek forgiveness for during the Ten Days of Awe, the High Holy Days, they must remind themselves that the rebirth of the Jewish state and their struggle to survive are not to be counted amongst them. And the latter requires decisive action, not just words.

A security fence, for example, that does not allow for the protection of Israel's main airport, Parliament, and the rest of its narrow, strategic waist, where most of its population and industry are located, comes to mind (which the American Foggy Folks insist upon), as does a barrier that does not grant Israel at least a minimally adequate protective buffer zone between itself and millions of Arabs still sworn to its destruction—a buffer, by the way, envisioned by the final draft of UN Security Council Resolution 242 itself.

What other nation would be asked to forsake such things?

For those who think otherwise, well, read my mind. They already know what my response will be. Recall the difference mentioned in the book's Introduction between anti-Semitism and anti-Zionism?

Issues related to the survival of the Jews in their sole, reborn nation should not be debatable to fair-minded observers, especially given the repeated attempts by Jews to reach a fair solution to their problems with the Arabs and also considering that it was a murderous and dehumanizing millennial anti-Semitism practiced by much of the rest of the world that, ironically, led to the very rebirth of the Jewish state in the first place.

Chapter 21

UNCLE BOUTROS AND UNCLE TOM: A LESSON IN ARAB TOLERANCE

A FEW YEARS BACK, a friend sent me a note alerting me to Diane West's great article in the *The Washington Times* referring to the essential historian Bat Ye'or's writings on *dhimmitude*. Having written somewhat myself on the subject of the forced Arabization and Islamization of much of the region's lands and peoples, events sired by the publication of some Danish cartoons, at which Muslims took offense, also had me thinking anew on this subject.

How deadly absurd that Arabs and their lackeys—who habitually demonize both Jews and their religion in the media, religious sermons, cartoons, and elsewhere—explode in world-wide rage because some Danes suggested that since many, if not most, of the conflicts going on in the world today involve Muslims, their religion might just have something to do with this. And as if the age-old concept of the conquest of the Dar ul-Islam over the Dar al-Harb was just a Zionist concoction or such.

A listening to or a reading of even the so-called "moderate" Arab media in Jordan, Egypt, Saudi Arabia, and so forth routinely appears as if it has been lifted right out of Hitler's *Der Sturmer*. The same goes for the land of the Shi'a Iranian Islamists, not that there's really any love lost between most Arabs and Aryans.

While *dhimmitude* primarily refers to the plight of conquered, native Christian and Jewish populations, the People of the Book, keep in mind that Arab subjugating (if not outright racist) attitudes also extended to those non-Arabs who—to join the victors, escape taxation, share in the booty, and so forth—became Muslims, the Mawali.

As with the contemporary historian, Bat Ye'or, Professor Julius Wellausen's much earlier classic work, *The Arab Kingdom and Its Fall*, is also priceless background—especially for the early period of this still-lingering problem. And those who were not Ahl al-Kitab either usually converted or were massacred.[105]

If anything, the modern age of nationalism only made matters worse in these regards. Saladin, the medieval terror of Christendom and the Crusaders in the Middle East, was a Kurd who jumped on the Arabization/Islamization bandwagon. As we have already discussed, had he lived in his native Iraq or later Syria (where a large statue of him mounted on his horse stands in

Damascus) today, he would have likely witnessed his own native language and culture outlawed, his people gassed and otherwise massacred, and so forth—all done by his fellow Muslims.

The Abbasid Revolution in the eighth century C.E. largely occurred because of early disgust of the converted Mawali populations with the blatant Arabism of the Umayyad successors to Muhammad. And, once again, in modern times, hundreds of thousands of Muslims—but non-Arabs—would continue to be slaughtered, oppressed, and so forth in the name of the Arab nation.

Keep in mind that these are the same folks who like to continuously lecture about alleged Zionist racism; you know, those same Jews who made Arabic the second official language of their state, have Arab representatives in the Knesset who routinely side with Hamas (which denies Israel's very right to exist).

All of the previous discussions on Arab subjugation of non-Arab conquered peoples made me think about some famous quotes I came across during my earlier own doctoral program days.

In Amos Elon's *Flight into Egypt*, he reviewed his encounters with the late President Sadat's foreign minister, Dr. Boutros Boutros-Ghali. The latter would later become secretary general of the United Nations.

A Copt—a descendant of Egypt's now-subjugated, ancient, pre-Arab Christian people—it was largely believed that Boutros-Ghali was chosen for this post precisely because of his unquestioned, assured loyalty. Centuries of *dhimmitude* could be expected to have done its thing. And it did.

Listen carefully to some excerpts regarding this Copt's advice to Elon, a prominent Israeli journalist: "In his office, there is a map of the Middle East on which Israel is still blacked out. Israel must integrate by accepting the nature of the area that nature that is Arab. In a tape of a long discourse delivered in 1975 to Professor Brecher he proclaimed that in the vast area between the Persian Gulf and the Atlantic Ocean everyone had to be Arab or risk continuing strife. Still, Boutros-Ghali felt that there might be a solution. How? Well, Israel could become an Arab country. Most Israelis were (Jewish) immigrants from Arab countries anyway."[106]

While this might be a great answer to Iran's Mahmoud Ahmadinejad—who, besides openly calling for Israel's destruction also likes to claim a European origin for all of Israel's Jews—please pardon my nausea anyway. Again, think about what's going on all around the Middle East and North Africa, the subjugation and at times outlawing of fellow Muslim—but non-Arab—Kurdish, Imazhigen (Berber), and other languages and cultures, and continuing slaughter of both Muslim and non-Muslim black Africans in the Sudan and elsewhere.

Meanwhile, the Arabs' oil-addicted sycophants and/or fellow anti-Semites look on and act as if they're all brain-dead. If Israel were involved, there would be trials in Geneva, United Nations hearings and resolutions, demonstrations on university campuses, and whatever—with the State Department likely joining the chorus.

The United Nations General Assembly passed Resolution 3379 equating Zionism (the national liberation movement of the Jewish people) with racism on November 10, 1975. I'll never forget the eloquent response of America's United Nation's representative, the late Daniel Patrick Moynihan. Many of us wore "Proud to Be a Zionist" buttons from then for quite some time.

While walking down the streets of Manhattan on a lunch hour break, guess who I bumped right into doing likewise? There he was, in the flesh, Ambassador Moynihan. I couldn't control myself. I ran up to him, smiled, and thanked him with a tear in my eye. He smiled back and grabbed my hand. I cannot remember what words were subsequently spoken. But what a moment it was.

The UN has continuously indulged in such "fairness" regarding Israel right up to this very day (as we'll explore more deeply later on). So, in light of what you've read above, I have a few questions:

- When's the UN's Arabism Equals Racism meeting being scheduled for?
- When are academia's Middle East scholars going to highlight such things in their classes the way they regularly focus upon and demonize Israel?

(You gotta be kidding.)

- And where's that worldwide broader, fairer perspective this book is largely all about?

Answer: Who says I don't have a sense of humor?

To learn more about the plight of non-Arab peoples in the region, other scholars, besides the Egyptian Jewess Bat Ye'or, have also made important contributions. One, in particular, Professor Albert Memmi, a Tunisian-born Jew, wrote a short but powerful work also exposing firsthand, like Bat Ye'or, *dhimmitude*—and what needs to be done about it. Memmi supported Tunisia's struggle for independence from France, and the mere four lines on page V at the beginning of his book *Jews and Arabs* say it all:

> To my Jewish bothers
> To my Arab brothers
> so that we can all
> be free men at last[107]

Compare this to Boutros-Ghali's pathetic advice. In fairness, in contrast to Copts who daily fear for their very lives in Egypt, a reading of what they have to say about these things when they flee abroad is telling as well. Ditto for Christian, pre-Arab Lebanese, Assyrians, Armenians, and others.

In 1852, Harriet Beecher Stowe authored a famous antislavery novel, *Uncle Tom's Cabin*, in which she wrote of the blacks' expected servile behavior toward their white masters. Indeed, this is the Arabs' predominant idea of tolerance—creating a whole non-Arab region of Uncle Boutroses.

So, those explosive episodes regarding the cartoons in Denmark should really not have been unexpected, nor their outrage at the pope's later remarks about the violent nature of Islam, either.

Arabs and too many of their non-Arab but fellow Muslim wannabes typically believe that others may not indulge in what they routinely do to others—often light-years worse. The frequent litmus test for the Muslim non-Arab too often becomes out-Arabing the Arab in hatred of the Jew (seen often on campus, in Iran and Pakistan today, and so forth), subjugation of the dhimmi, and/or defense of the faith—a faith which, by the way, was shoved down their own throats, either directly or indirectly, centuries earlier by the imperial conquests of the Arabs.

Hopefully, the eyes of even the most naïve will at last open to the consequences of continuing to allow Arabs free reign with their hypocrisy and double standards.

And that thorn-in-the-side state of the scorned *kilab yahud* "Jew dogs"—as Arabs like to call it—is on the front lines for all the rest of the Dar al-Harb, the realm of war, in Islam's eyes.

While there are Muslims who disagree with the jihadists, the sad fact is that the militants are very much in the ascendancy, forcing all but a relatively few brave souls into silence or to cower behind them.

Wise up, world, before it is too late.

Chapter 22

LONG LIVE ARABISTAN

IRAN'S PRESIDENT, MAHMOUD Ahmadinejad, sent a letter to President George W. Bush on May 8, 2006, in which, among other things, he restated Israel's alleged original sin and the need to create another state for Arabs in its stead in the region. He often mouths such wisdom.

Well, since he insists, there's a way to meet at least some of his demands—sort of.

Recall, once again, that the lion's share of the original 1920 Mandate of Palestine was handed over by Colonial Secretary Churchill to Arab nationalism in 1922 with the creation of what would later be renamed Jordan—a more than just partition of the land favoring the Arabs. Indeed, Arabs wound up with almost 80 percent of the total area.

So, the real place where justice for Arabs has not yet been addressed and still remains to be achieved is in—hold on to your seats—Ahmadinejad's Iran itself.

As we have already discussed, during the seventh century C.E., Arab Caliphal imperialist armies burst out of the Arabian Peninsula and colonized, settled, forcibly Arabized, and spread Islam by a conquering sword in all directions.

Judaea, renamed Palestine (for the Jews' historic enemies, the Philistines) by conquering Romans after the second revolt of the Jews for their freedom, became occupied by Arabs at this time. They took it from Rome's successor, the Byzantine Empire. Arab imperialism targeted Iran likewise, and from there moved eastward into the Indian subcontinent.

Using southern Iraq as a springboard, southwestern Iran—Khuzestan province in particular—traded back and forth between invading Arab and Iranian rulers for centuries.

While it became subsequently linked to Iran despite repeated Arab invasions over the centuries, Khuzestan became so extensively Arabized that, in Safavid times (sixteenth–eighteenth centuries C.E.), the province was commonly known as Arabistan. In modern times, not until Iran's Reza Shah defeated him in 1924, the Arab Sheikh of Muhammarah ruled much of the area.[108]

Arabs have remembered all of this very well. Indeed, once again Iraqi-based Arabs—this time under Saddam's banner—launched the long and bloody Iran-Iraq war of the 1980s that was largely fought over this oil-rich and strategically important area—Khuzestan for Iranians, Arabistan for Arabs. To deal with this problem, Iran has ruthlessly suppressed any manifestations of Arab nationalism by any and all means necessary. By the early twentieth century, a proposal had been put forward to even outlaw the Arabic language.[109]

More recently, here's an excerpt as to how the British Ahwazi Friendship Society reported the situation on July 29, 2005, and in more detail in 2007: "The Unrepresented Nations and Peoples Organisation (UNPO) released a statement condemning the recent violent repression of ethnic minorities in Iran following the election of right-wing hardliner Mahmoud Ahmadinejad. Pointing to clashes between security forces and Ahwazi Arabs and Kurds, Nicola Dell'Arciprete, UNPO Assistant General Secretary, said: 'The UNPO condemns the Government's repressive policies against all the Iranian citizens. Iran is a multi-ethnic country in which half of the population belongs to ethnic minorities such as Azeri, Gilaki and Mazandarani, Kurds, Arabs, Lurs, Balochis, Turkmen.'"[110]

Now recall how Ahmadinejad likes to sit on his moral high horse, constantly lecturing Israel and others about such things. He did so in his letter to President Bush as well as recently before the United Nations in April 2009—and a thousand other times in between.

The original 1920 Mandate of Palestine had already undergone partition (first in 1922, with the virtual separation of Transjordan), so—as on the Indian subcontinent, with the creation of Hindu India and Muslim Pakistan—and later, Bangladesh as well) and elsewhere—the political rights of competing nationalisms could at least be addressed.

Recall that had Arabs accepted the additional 1947 partition plan, they would have wound up with about 90 percent of the borders of the original 1920 Palestine Mandate. They rejected the 1947 division of the remaining 20 percent of the land left because, once again, in Arab eyes, there is no justice other than their own.

Jews—like Kurds or Imazighen or Assyrians or Copts or black African Sudanese, and so forth—were entitled to no political rights in lands which Arabs claimed a monopoly on for themselves. Recall, as well, that many—if not most—Arabs were newcomers into the Mandate themselves, as the Records of the Permanent Mandates Commission of the League of Nations and other solid documentation testify to, though all will swear that they were there—as the title of Joan Peters's book says—from time immemorial. Arabs happen to specialize in *taqiyya*—permitted lying to "infidels" for the cause—which they have repeatedly been exposed as doing.[111]

Ahmadinejad refuses to acknowledge any of the above, claims all Israeli Jews were from Europe (tell that to Israel's Iranian-born former army chief of staff, General Shaul Mofaz, and its former president, Abraham Katsav), and the like, yet answers the political aspirations of millions of other non-Iranians living on his own soil only with massacre and repression.

Hypocrisy at its worst.

Turning to the Arabs of Khuzestan/Arabistan in particular, at any hint of unrest, Iran has been quick and deadly to act in its own national interest. Arabs have also been ethnically cleansed from the area and replaced by others.

As just one of many examples, when Arabs of the *Nahda* (renaissance) movement bombed Iranian targets in Ahwaz and elsewhere, Iran arrested thousands of them and set out to "fix" the problem by any means necessary.

Iranians continuously do likewise to Kurds, Baluchis, and any others who dare to assert their own political rights. Thousands have been killed as a result over the years in the name of Iranian nationalism.

So, this all begs the question of both the man and the nation he represents. Why does justice supposedly demand that the sole, microscopic state of the Jews—half of whom were refugees from the "Arab"/Muslim world (many from Iran itself; more than one hundred thousand live in America today, about another hundred thousand in Israel)—consent to national suicide so Arab settlers and colonizers can have their twenty-second state and second one in Palestine, but Arabistan should not gain independence from Iran as well?

If a Palestine much smaller than Iran could undergo partition in the name of justice for diverse peoples, then why not Iran? Again, Arabs were already handed over most of "Palestine."

So Ahmadinejad is indeed correct. It is time for that twenty-second state for Arabs to be born—long live Arabistan!

Chapter 23

PANTSIL, DARFUR, AND THE ARAB MAN'S BURDEN

SOMETHING AMAZING HAPPENED during the 2006 king of all sports events, the World Cup. A young black African football, aka soccer, star, John Pantsil, celebrated his Ghanaian team's victory over the Czech Republic by taking out a concealed Israeli flag and, with the help of his teammates, ran it around the field with untold millions watching all around the world.

There's a name for that sort of thing, and it is called courage.

At a time when much of the world—and Pantsil's Third World in particular—demonizes the Jew of the Nations, Pantsil stood up to tell it like it is.

Arabs, in particular, are especially incensed. They, who have massacred, raped, maimed, turned into refugees, and enslaved millions of blacks for centuries (still going on as this article is being written), like to lecture others about alleged Zionist racists.

John Pantsil knows better, as do many others too intimidated to speak up.

Israel has indeed aided black Africa tremendously for over half a century. Like many other football players (including Arabs), Pantsil also plays for another team besides that of his native country. His other team is in Israel.

Related to this story, an article appeared just a few days earlier dealing with how Arabs have dealt with some of Pantsil's fellow black Africans in the Sudan.

Tucked into an article on page nine of my local Florida paper (*Daytona Beach News-Journal*) on June 15, 2006, was a classic line, but I doubt if it was noticed by most. It was, after all, nowhere near the front page or an op-ed, editorial, or such. And it wasn't the sports section or the comics.

I mean, if Arab civilians in Gaza get killed (due to a war waged by leaders they themselves elected whose goal is to exterminate their Jewish neighbors and who use those civilians deliberately as human shields), then there's a real story—big pictures, detailed accounts (using only Arab sources, of course), editorials, the whole shebang. That's the typical deal if Israel is the alleged bad guy.

But, those in that above June 15 story were not Arabs allegedly killed by Jews; these were, instead, blacks murdered by fellow Arab and/or willingly Arabized Sudanese. So, a buried blurb on page nine would do nicely.

While the media is running more articles about the old but continuing tragedy in the Sudan of late, the message still doesn't seem to sink in to those who are at least now covering the story.

The June 15 article by Nick Wadhams of the Associated Press dealt with the findings of the UN-backed court probing war crimes in Darfur. In the middle of the article, Luis Moreno-Ocampo, chief prosecutor for the International Criminal Court, was quoted in his report as stating that eyewitnesses told of the perpetrators of the atrocities telling victims such things as, "We will kill all the black[s]. We will drive you out of this land."[112]

But, try as you may, one would be at a loss to determine who those above racist perpetrators were. No need for a magnifying glass or guesswork, however, when the articles are about Israel or Jews. The perpetrators, of course, were/are Arabs and Arabized blacks who have waged war in Africa in the name of the Arab nation for over four decades (actually, for centuries).

For whatever reasons, too often that detail is left out when Arabs are involved, and for the same reasons why the average reader doesn't get to read about Kurdish schoolchildren being forced to sing songs praising their alleged "Arab" identity in Syria, the plight of non-Arab Imazighen, Assyrians, Copts, native *kilab yahud* "Jew dogs," and so forth throughout the "Arab" world.

Rare was the student who heard anything about the war in the Sudan in the 1960s when its modern version erupted big time. Periodically the public would be tossed reports of Anya-Nya "rebels" who began a revolt against the imposition of Arab rule in the south in 1963—like those now coming from some columnists today.[113]

Similarly, the typical Middle East Studies, history, or political science class never learned much about the plight of non-Arabs in the region either.

Recall, for example, the only time that I heard about Kurds (some thirty-five million of them and, unlike Arabs, truly stateless) from the tenured chief honcho while resurrecting my own earlier doctoral studies in the early eighties was when he mocked their own national aspirations, speaking of his travels through Turkey. But "Palestine" and the "plight of the Palestinians" were more often than not up front and center; indeed, he taught a whole course largely about them.

Another relatively more balanced professor spoke to me privately about Kurdish issues. As his doctoral T.A.(teaching assistant), he asked me to prepare a one-day lesson on the Kurds for his classes. I did—explaining who they were, their own political aspirations, and so forth—and then the proverbial manure hit the fan.

I was rebuked for upsetting the many Arab students in those classes. And notice please, the good professor did not dare teach anything to his classes about the Kurds (or other non-Arab victims of forced Arabization and the like) himself. He had his T.A. do it. But he was, indeed, the relative good guy; the other simply ignored Kurds unless he could mock them.

Since I brought both of these folks up, let me further elaborate my personal connection here. A little while earlier I had been invited to be one four presenters on a major program on the Middle East in a major city in the near-midwest. One of the local main university's professors was also on the panel of presenters. He completely ignored what the program was supposed to be focused on and turned his presentation into a "Jews stole Arab land" song and dance instead.

Following him in the speaking order, I had no choice but to throw my original presentation up into the air ("The Turkish Straits and NATO") and wound up exposing his *taqiyya* fairy tales instead.

Afterward, another professor came up to me and introduced himself. He inquired about my own academic credentials, where I did my previous M.A. and doctoral studies, and so forth. He then asked why I didn't resume my doctoral work at his university (a big one!).

I laughed and responded, "Did you not just hear what came out of the mouth of your colleague?" I told him that I also knew of the well-known, one-sided slant of another colleague of his before even moving to town in 1976. I had done my previous graduate work at the Kevorkian Center for Near Eastern Studies, a consortium, in those days, of Princeton, Columbia, and New York Universities based at NYU's Washington Square campus across from the law school. Illness and financial problems interrupted my earlier doctoral program in late 1975, and I accepted a more lucrative consulting position, which would allow me to use my Middle East studies background elsewhere just a bit later.

Based out of the midwest, I became a consultant specializing in Middle Eastern affairs for an organization covering my region's three states. I was flown or drove in to dozens of colleges and universities to balance some resident professor such as the ones described above; appeared on television and radio; gave numerous public presentations; had dozens of major op-eds published in leading newspapers throughout my region; debated numerous one-sided, anti-Israel professors and other spokesmen. The presentation mentioned above, at which I was later engaged in conversation with an inquiring professor, was part of what I did in my professional position.

Returning to that conversation about the possibility of my resurrecting doctoral studies at this new university and my concern over the obvious bias of some of the professors, my inquirer responded, "They're just a few of a number of people in this field that you could hook up with. When PhD dissertation time comes along, they'll be others with whom you can work."

As the song goes, like a fool, I believed. The man who told me this was the good professor for whom I would later be a T.A. When dissertation time did come along a few years later, guess who I was told could be the only one whom I could turn to for this help? Three guesses and the first two don't count—the chief tenured honcho. So guess who never got a doctoral dissertation advisor?

I was a subtle—but still very present—thorn in his side, even though I tried not to be.

I believed that within the walls of academia there should be room for open and free exchange of ideas and debate on all issues. Too bad said professor and his ilk do not see things that way.

I tried to heed my late father's (of blessed memory) advice about keeping the sword sheathed until the proper moment. But this "expert's" seminars were so obviously slanted, I had no choice but to interject key information he repeatedly and deliberately left out. There were students much younger than myself present in those seminars without my own deep background in research in the subjects of study. If I had remained silent, they would have never heard the various other sides, nor received the broader perspective. That was enough to place me on his blacklist, and I was thus slated to be nipped in the bud in terms of a future academic career at the university level.

So much for academic freedom between the walls or in the halls of academia. And those were the days before Dr. Daniel Pipes' Campus Watch, and so forth, so, I was just left hanging in the wind. We moved to Florida not long afterwards and wasted years, money, effort, and so forth. No one person should be allowed to have such power over another.

So, as we've seen with my own personal story, too often it is Israel, alone, that is targeted to be constantly placed under the high-power lens of moral scrutiny, despite the fact that—unlike how Arabs have treated their own perceived nationalist competitors—the Jews indeed made repeated, honorable attempts at compromise with them. And watch out if you dare to suggest otherwise, *you, you, polemicist you* (direct quote from that professor; that's what happens when your "polemic" disagrees with that of your subtle or not so subtle resident MESA polemicist).

Think about numerous blacks in Africa alone—not only in the Sudan—who suffered quite a different fate at the hands of Arabs whose idea of compromise involves total subjugation to their own cause. Millions of these people have been massacred, enslaved, turned into refugees, and so forth over the centuries. Now ask yourself how many times Arabs have been taken to task by the international community—always quick to accuse Israel for any and all alleged sins—for such things. Or by those above intellectuals in the ivory tower.

In contrast to those above Arab versions of compromise, think about what the Jews have done (or were handed a fait accompli about) over the past century to reach an honorable accommodation with Arab nationalism.

Did Arabs ever offer any such thing to their own nationalist rivals?

But there's no mystery here.

As we have seen, in Arab eyes, no one but themselves could be rulers or perceived as equals in their neck of the woods—not "their" Jew dogs, gassed Kurds, massacred black Africans, intimidated Copts, nor whomever.

A few years ago, David Ignatius of *The Washington Post* wrote on September 16, 2003, of the danger in playing America's Turkish card in Iraq. When referring to Kurds, he managed to label them only as terrorists or rebels.

At a time when most media folks still debate whether or not Arabs—who deliberately blow up Jewish innocents—are "militants" or "terrorists," folks like Ignatius have no problem using the "T-word" for Kurds. Imagine if these were Jews committing those atrocities in the Sudan? We don't have to imagine.

Think of the Muhammad al-Dura affair, the alleged earlier Deir Yasin and later Jenin massacres, and so forth, front page news, editorials, and op-eds for months. It turns out that solid evidence now shows that the Arabs lied through their teeth about all of these (*taqiyya*), and an all-too-gullible West simply accepts the Arab version of any given story over and over again. Think BBC, NPR, CNN, NBC, *The New York Times*, and so forth. And recall that, related to this issue, it is long been a given that Arab "militants" typically hide behind the skirts of their women and the baby carriages of their children, then cry crocodile tears before a hundred television cameras from all over the world when Israel is forced to strike back. Better yet, you've heard of Hollywood and Bollywood. Now look up Pallywood on any Internet search engine to see *taqiyya* on stage. Check out the footnote here for some ideas—you won't be sorry.[114]

Why is the world so willingly gullible?

Is it that after massacring and victimizing Jews (often allegedly in G_d's name) for millennia, Gentiles need to convince themselves that Jews are indeed as bad as themselves?

As an example of this mess and the West's collaboration in demonizing the Jew of the Nations several years ago, while Arabs hastened to cart off most of the evidence from a Gaza beach tragedy, it turned out that they lied again. Surviving evidence pointed to Arabs mining the beach to prevent Israeli commandos from launching another attack, which took out Arab rocket crews earlier. Thousands of mortars and rockets had been deliberately launched against Israeli civilians over the previous months during the Arabs' earlier alleged "cease fire." It appears that those Arab picnickers blown up on the Gaza beach had likely encountered one of their brothers' own mines.

So, again, what's up? I think I know but will be accused of being a paranoid Jew if I say it.

Let's return to the Sudan.

Back in early March 2006, I came across Nicholas Kristof's *New York Times* op-ed dealing with the Darfur genocide. And, unlike the above June 15 article, he did manage to mention the word *Arab* (once) as well. Compared to most others, Kristof has shown more responsibility in at least portraying the broader perspective regarding the struggle for political rights in the region. His vision, however, is still obstructed when it comes to Arab–Israeli issues.

Despite this, Kristof still doesn't get it, and if he doesn't, most of the others of his ilk certainly don't.

Is it a genetic defect of this species that dictates seeing the entire region only through Arab lenses? Perhaps a current or future payoff of sorts from Arabs (others, for example, habitually move through the revolving door of politics and big business tied to Arab petrobucks, Bechtel, as just one example)?

Is it that perpetual Jew thing again?

Given the policy of most of the alleged "liberal" (I was, until my recent listing as an Independent, a registered Democrat who drives a hybrid Toyota Prius and has a solar collector on his roof) media to treat others in the region, besides Arabs, as mere interlopers, rebels, or separatists, their audiences remain ignorant of the atrocities committed against any and all who don't accept subjugation and forced Arabization as their fate.

And even most, like Kristof, who finally write exposés about particular Arab actions, still can't make the next essential leap—that others are also entitled to what Arabs demand exclusively for themselves.

While I share the concern about earlier effects of imperialism Western style, the media, the ivory tower, and so forth have too often ignored the scores of millions of non-Arab peoples and/or lands that have been conquered, massacred, enslaved, turned into refugees, colonized, and such by the Arabs' own centuries-old imperialist policies—creating new victims daily.

In case there are any doubts as to what the game plan is for the African part of what Arabs like to call "purely Arab patrimony," pay close attention below.

The Third World likes to chastise the West for its condescending attitudes. Again, I agree with much of that criticism, Rudyard Kipling's poem "The White Man's Burden," and so forth.

But while the media and academics are quick to agree, why are writers even like the more tuned-in Kristof mum about such things as President Nimeiry's statements during the slaughter of more than a half-million blacks in the Sudan in the 1960s and 1970s (much more since) that the Sudan is the basis of the Arab thrust into black Africa, the Arab civilizing mission.[115]

Is it that the Arab man's burden is acceptable, but the white man's isn't?

Or why, over the decades, has there been no response to this all-too-typical subjugating Arab approach, as expressed in Article 7 of the Syrian Arab Constitution of the ruling Ba'ath party?

> The Arab fatherland belongs to the Arabs. They alone have the right to direct its destinies. The Arab fatherland is that part of the globe inhabited by the Arab nation which stretches from the Taurus Mountains, the Pacht-i-Kouh Mountains, the Gulf of Basra, the Arab Ocean, the Ethiopian Mountains, the Sahara, the Atlantic Ocean, and the Mediterranean Sea.[116]

Help me out. I still can't tell for sure—are there any Eskimos included in that above Arab imperial vision? Probably not, but think about Mindanao in the Philippines, or much of Europe if it doesn't watch out. France had its own little intifada not long ago.

Again, keep in mind that these are the same folks who condemn alleged expansionist, racist Zionists who dare to assert that Jews deserve a state more than nine miles wide. These are the same Jews who made Arabic the second official language of their sole state and who have Arab representatives in the Knesset who regularly side with Hamas (which rejects the existence of a state for Jews for the same reason Arabs reject one for Kurds or black African Sudanese, and so forth) against the country in the region that has the freest Arabs, Israel.

The June 15 AP article ended by stating that Sudan's national courts have shown little desire to investigate crimes against humanity in Darfur. Appalling. But consider also the travesty committed for decades by those alleged moral watchdogs in academia, the media, the UN, and so forth who too often ignore such happenings unless it involves Israel.

Recall that the latter was brought to the International Court of Justice in Geneva for building a fence designed to keep Arabs from deliberately blowing apart its children. Oh, yes, the inconvenience the fence causes Arabs was/is just too much. Rather, Jews should tear down the defensive security barrier (guess what the U.S. has on its border with Mexico?) and watch their innocents being butchered and terrorized so Arabs won't have to be inconvenienced.

I see. How could I be so insensitive?

Think about how much attention has been given by the media, academia, and so forth for decades to the cause of the Arabs' twenty-second state; that additional one in "Palestine," which Arabs demand take the place of the Jewish one, not live in peace beside it.

Now ask yourselves when the last time was that you heard of something similar being demanded for any of the Arabs' numerous victims mentioned above.

Just Jewish "paranoia" again? I think not.

Racist Zionists? Don't think so.

Just ask John Pantsil.

Chapter 24

PARTNERS: THE ULTIMATE TROJAN HORSE

CAROLINE GLICK'S MASTERPIECE, "Grounded in Fantasy," appeared in the June 18, 2007, edition of the *Jerusalem Post*. It is still must reading for all interested in what's happening in Gaza and beyond these days.

While many of us have been writing about these things, the gal definitely has a way with words. I was almost convinced not to write my own editorial analysis at the time, since between what I and others penned earlier and Glick's later column, all bases—for heads not buried ostrich-style in the sand—should have been already covered.

Leave it to the Associated Press and Israel's then Prime Minister Ehud Olmert, however, to convince me otherwise. On the same day Glick's editorial appeared, Olmert was quoted in an AP article stating that Israel would be a "genuine partner" of a new Palestinian government and promised to consider releasing millions of dollars in frozen tax funds to it.

As has repeatedly been pointed out, there's no real difference between what our State Department would have us believe to be Mahmoud Abbas's latter-day Arafatian good cops and Hamas's bad cops. President Obama has since joined others in scolding Israel for not buying into this sale.

There is no doubt that both seek the destruction of the state of the Jews. And both have been honest about this (Hamas more than the Arafatians' Fatah). Abbas's Palestinian Authority boys simply play the game better for Western consumption to gain all kinds of support—and, again, have said so. Right now, besides all the money and other assistance pouring in to the alleged good cops, America is building up their army for them—so they can later kill more Jews, no doubt.

Why won't the Foggy Folks listen? Or all subsequent American presidents after Ronald Reagan?

As has been repeated often—but not sinking in to those creating the fiction of Fatah "moderates"—Abbas's folks have called any and all dealings with the Jews merely a Trojan horse, each unilateral concession gained from Israel since the Oslo fiasco bringing them one step closer in their openly admitted destruction-in-stages plans. Pressured by its American friends, up until the 2009 election, Israel's weak leaders had played along with this dangerous game. It still remains to be seen if Netanyahu and Lieberman won't wind up doing the same. I don't think so.

With Hamas in control in Gaza—and in possession of huge quantities of American military equipment it received courtesy of our friend Abbas (from whom they stole it when they bounced his forces out of Gaza), besides what's being smuggled freely via Egypt from other (especially Iranian) sources—Washington is now insisting that Jews allow Judea and Samaria (the "West Bank") to be turned into another Gaza.

But, it will be said by some that Fatah and Abbas really are different from Islamic Jihad and Hamas.

Who's kidding whom here? Take a quick look at any of their Web sites, maps, or books, hear their sermons, and so forth—just for starters.[117]

Fatah's goals for creating "Palestine" from the river to the sea have never changed and won't. The main disagreement between Hamas and Abbas is over who gets control of the moolah (not to be confused with mullah).

Forcing Israel back to its 1949, nine-mile-wide armistice line existence will simply bring most of its population and industry within easy range of Fatah's (or probably later Hamas's) American weapons. And that, along with the moderate Abbas's pledge that he'll never stop demanding that Israel agree to be swamped by millions of alleged returning jihadi refugees, makes any such "peace deal" a deadly joke. Fatah and its affiliates have as much or more Jewish blood on their hands as Hamas.

And what, pray tell, does Israel get for this proposed "partnership"?

A *hudna* ceasefire.

Again, as the Arafatians—not Hamas—like to point out, it's the same thing their prophet, Muhammad, granted to his enemies until he was strong enough to conquer them. And this is not to say that an actual treaty with Fatah would be worth the paper it would be written on, considering the agreements Abbas's "moderates" have already reneged upon before the ascendancy of Hamas in Gaza.

Unfortunately, the same questions need to be repeatedly asked over and over again.

Where is the evidence the Foggy Folks and now a new American president offer for Fatah's alleged moderation and acceptance of a permanent Jewish state as its neighbor?

There is none—all evidence points to the contrary. Abbas has recently repeated this himself.[118]

Are Fatah's Web sites, schools, mosques, television and radio stations, press, and so forth spreading this message of "acceptance" around to their own people—whom, poll after poll show, would mostly seek Israel's destruction anyway if Israel withdrew from all of the disputed lands?

No, they definitely are not.

Webster's New World College Dictionary defines *partner* as a person who takes part in some activity in common with another sharing its profits and risks. Unfortunately, as we saw once again in that AP article, the wrong party jumped at the opportunity at "partnership" here.

Ex-Prime Minister Olmert lived the leftist fantasy of Arabs giving up their claim of virtually the entire region as being part of the Dar ul-Islam and/or purely Arab patrimony.

Please, pretty please, Arabs, tell us what we can do to have you accept us.

Sickening. Pathetic. The Gentiles' vision of the groveling Jew personified.

Because of Israel's military actions against Hamas, Fatah was at least temporarily pulled out of the Hamas fire. Recall that Abbas & Co. got the boot from Gaza by the former.

Someone not tuned in might actually think that it should be Abbas and Fatah, themselves, who should be seeking a sort of partnership with Israel.

After all, the massive destruction Israel waged against Hamas in retaliation for thousands of rockets and mortars launched against its civilians certainly helped Fatah and Abbas—increasingly less popular than Hamas—in its contest for control (and the billions of dollars in foreign aid).

"No! No! He can't do that," some will say. "It will make Abbas a traitor!"

Precisely. And that's the point.

Israel would be suicidal granting such huge concessions in land, aid, and so forth to folks who still can't reconcile with the right of Jews to have in one, tiny, reborn state what Arabs insist upon having almost two dozen of for themselves. It is bad enough that many others (i.e., America) are now insisting upon this; the Jews, themselves, don't have to be a partner in their own demise.

Who will stop, for example, that independent Fatahland or successor Hamasistan from importing all kinds of sophisticated arms (missiles and such) and placing them right in Israel's backyard, where every plane from Ben-Gurion Airport, for example—just a few miles away—will have to worry about being shot down?

Don't count on the Foggy Folks, President Obama, or anyone else.

There must be no more pressure on Israel to merely accept some Arab sweet talk in exchange for very real, concrete concessions that bare the necks of Jewish kids to those who repeatedly and deliberately target them. Yet this is what an American president himself is now doing. As we have seen, that the State Department continues along this path also is simply par for their usual course. Recall that they opposed Israel's rebirth from the very start and have too often tried to undermine it—both covertly and overtly—ever since.

Unfortunately, Abbas's idea of partnership means getting the gift of the ultimate Trojan horse handed to him: Jews building up the very folks who will bring about their own destruction.

For Abbas and his latter-day Arafatians in suits and ties, both Jews and Arabs "partner" just for the Arabs' advantage and against the Jews' own interests. Another look at *Webster's* definition above may be in order.

Perhaps that's why it was ex-Prime Minister Olmert bowing to Washington by pleading for partnership and not Abbas.

Chapter 25

SETTLERS, NOW THINK ABOUT
THIS LONG AND HARD

SETTLERS. LET'S SEE, now what's a good synonym for this? Hmmmmm. *Jews!* Now there's a good one, correct? I mean, almost every time you hear the word mentioned these days, it's got Jews associated with it. Not so? Think long and hard, however, about what follows.

Not that the information hasn't been known before. Indeed, some get tired and upset at having to rehash it over and over again. Me, too.

It is just that only a relative few have cared enough to find out, and the mainline press, most of the rest of the media, academia, and much of the rest of the world are either indeed ignorant of these facts or deliberately sweep them under the rug for one reason or another.

As just one of countless examples over the past three quarters of a century regarding the Arab–Israeli conflict, the headline of the February 21, 2005, *Orlando Sentinel* was a case in point and read as follows: "Israel Approves Ousting Settlers."

Jews were/are the settlers and Arabs are the allegedly abused aboriginals. You've heard it many times before.

Now for a reality check.

Just who is and who is not a settler in these regards?

Please recall that when the United Nations Relief Works Agency— UNRWA—was set up to assist Arab refugees (after a half-dozen Arab states invaded a nascent Israel in 1948 to nip it in the bud and their attempt back-fired), the very word *refugee* had to be redefined to assist those people.

So many Arabs were recent arrivals themselves into the Palestinian Mandate that UNRWA had to adjust the very definition of *refugee* from its prior meaning of persons normally and traditionally resident to those who lived in the Mandate for a minimum of only two years prior to 1948. Do you truly understand what this is saying? Furthermore, Arab refugees have been handled very differently than scores of millions of others worldwide—to their much better benefit.[119]

Now also keep in mind that for every Arab who was forced to flee the fighting that Arabs started (after all, how dare Jews want in one tiny, resur-rected state what Arabs demand for themselves in some two dozen others), a

130

Jewish refugee was forced to flee Arab/Muslim lands into Israel and elsewhere, but with no UNRWA set up to assist them.

As just one of many examples, greater New York City alone now has tens of thousands of Syrian Jewish refugees and their descendants. And while many, if not most, of France's pre-World War II European Jews perished in the Holocaust (rounded up too often by the French themselves), much of France's now newly-endangered, post-war Jewish population also consists of refugees from the "Arab" world.

As for those "native Palestinians," as we've discussed earlier, recall that Arafat himself was born in Cairo, Egypt. Scores of thousands of other Arabs came from Egypt earlier in the nineteenth century with Muhammad Ali and his son Ibrahim Pasha's armies and, like Arafat a bit later, many settled in Palestine.

During the mandatory period after World War I, as we also noted earlier, the Minutes of the Permanent Mandates Commission of the League of Nations recorded additional scores of thousands of Egyptian, Syrian, and other Arabs entering into Palestine and settling there. Indeed, this influx of Arabs into the land is well documented, but few—except scholars—usually delve into these sources.[120] Furthermore, too many academics these days have an anti-Israel bias and agenda—so such facts are usually simply ignored. To pour additional salt onto this wound, and as you've also already read, too often a grad student brings such things up at his own future professional risk.

Ready for more "native Palestinians"?

Hamas' patron saint, Sheikh Izzedine al-Qassam, for whom its militant wing (the folks who blow up the teen clubs, pizzerias, buses, and so forth) was named, was from Syria. (The exact location—Latakia, Jableh, etc.—is debatable.) He, too, settled in Palestine.[121] This is the same Hamas that butchers Jewish "settler" babes and grandmas. And the same Hamas that says no Israel—regardless of size—has a right to exist. In this, however, as we have seen, it has company in the alleged "moderate" Mahmoud Abbas and his Palestinian Authority as well. Abbas ran on a platform calling for Israel's destruction, but by "other," more acceptable means.

Blown buses bring bad press.

Recall that President Obama's friend (the alleged good cop)—to whom he made the first foreign phone call of his new presidency—still insists that a Jewish Israel is unacceptable and expects Israel to allow itself to be swamped by real and fudged Arab refugees to "peacefully" undo its Jewish identity, all while demanding that a twenty-second Arab state, the second Arab one in Palestine, be born.[122]

It is estimated that for each one of those incoming Arabs above who were recorded, many others crossed the border under cover of darkness to enter into one of the few areas in the region where any economic development was going on because of the influx of Jewish capital. These folks later became known as "native Palestinians." Meanwhile, hundreds of thousands of Jewish refugees from some of those same "Arab" countries—Syria, Egypt, Iraq, Morocco, Yemen, and so forth—became settlers.

While this is not to say that there were not native Arabs also living in Palestine, it is to say that many, if not most, of the Arabs were also relative newcomers—settlers—themselves.

Many of the villages set up in the West Bank and elsewhere were settlements established by Arab settlers. And there were Jews whose families never left Israel/Judaea/Palestine either over the centuries, despite the tragedies of two, well-documented major wars for their freedom and independence with Rome, forced conversions of the Byzantines, the Diaspora, Crusades, and other nightmares as well.

So, why is it acceptable for Arabs from surrounding lands to settle in Palestine (where Arabs, by the way, never had an independent state), but not for Israel's Jews, half of whom were refugees themselves from Arab/Muslim lands?

Jews owned land and lived in Judea and Samaria until their massacre by Arabs in the 1920s and 1930s.

And for those who make short shrift of the Jews calling those lands by the above names (I heard one commentator on National Public Radio doing so on the very same day of the cited *Orlando Sentinel* article), Judea and Samaria didn't become known as the "West Bank" until British imperialism made its presence there in the twentieth century and purely Arab Transjordan—created itself in 1922 on the east bank from 80 percent of the original 1920 Mandate for Palestine—annexed the west bank of the Jordan River after the 1948 fighting. The United Nations had imposed mostly armistice lines—not borders—which made Israel a mere nine miles wide at its waist in some parts. Jews were then barred from living on lands where they had thousands of years of history and as much right as Arabs to live.

Whatever will or won't become of the disputed lands in question, it must be noted that this is disputed territory, not "Arab" land, as the media, the United Nations, the State Department, and others like to insinuate. Again, Jews lived and owned property there until their slaughter by Arabs.

Recall that Judea and Samaria were non-apportioned parts of the Mandate, and leading authorities such as Eugene Rostow, William V. O'Brien, and others have stressed that these areas were open to settlement by Jew, Arab, and other residents of the mandate alike.[123] Indeed, as we've already discussed, hundreds of thousands of Arabs poured into the area from all over the Middle East and North Africa. Having one of the highest birth rates in the world, those "native Palestinians" soon greatly increased their numbers even further. Again we see more Arab settlers setting up more Arab settlements. So why are these legal and acceptable but those of the Jews not?

UN Security Council Resolution 242, in the aftermath of the 1967 War that Arabs started with their blockade of Israel—a *casus belli*—and other hostile acts, called for the creation of secure and recognized borders to replace Israel's vulnerable armistice line existence. All the architects of that resolution, from Lord Caradon to Eugene Rostow and others, concur here. Israel was not to be forced to withdraw to the suicidal status quo ante.[124]

Any renewed discussions about the so-called roadmap, Saudi peace plan, or whatever must take all of this into account. The Israeli settlements issue everyone—Mr. Obama, included—is making such a stink about is all about Israel getting those buffer lands 242 allows for so Israel does not become a sub-rump state once again.

And those truly in search of justice would do well to reconsider the very words they choose to discuss this conflict.

Chapter 26

CHANUKAH CORROBORATIONS

THE YEAR WAS 1887. An Egyptian woman discovered a treasure-trove of over three hundred clay cuneiform tablets that would shake the world of religion and the study of ancient history. Named for a local Bedouin tribe, the Tel el-Amarna tablets (which can now be found mostly in the Berlin and British Museums) were mostly the official correspondence between Pharaoh Amenhotep IV—Akhenaten—and his governors and vassals from places such as Canaan, Syria, Babylonia, and so forth. They date mostly from around 1380 B.C.E. and were written in Akkadian, the language of diplomacy of the era.

So, what does all of this have to do with Chanukah?

Patience.

Now, guess what repeatedly comes out in this official correspondence between Pharaoh and his vassals in Canaan and the surrounding areas?

Complaints about invasions of Habiru, including, very likely, those who would later come to be known as Hebrews.

While some scholars debate the details, most agree that the time—with even newer confirmations via excavations in Jericho—fits into the period of Joshua's conquests of Canaan.

Like many other accounts in the Hebrew Bible, we indeed have good supporting evidence from elsewhere to support the Jews' own version of these events. And what makes it even better is that this often comes from those viewing the events from the "other side" of the picture.

This is no small point.

Corroboration is very important to any serious scholar. Not many religio-historical texts can match the corroboration found in those of the Jews.

Jumping ahead about eight centuries, Babylon became a powerhouse, and the Jews' remaining southern kingdom, Judah, fell captive to Nebuchadnezzar. The northern kingdom, Israel (the ten "lost tribes"), fell to the Assyrians a few centuries earlier.

The Jews would next find a hero in—hold on to your seats—an Iranian ruler, Cyrus the Great, who allowed their return to Judah in 539 B.C.E.

Not exactly current Iranian President Ahmadinejad's type, if you know what I mean.

Again, while the Hebrew Bible gives the Jews' own account of this episode, we also have it from the "other side" as well.

Take a look at this ancient quote from an Iranian source, *The Kurash Prism*, courtesy of the Iran Chamber Society and other historical sites:

> I am Kurash ["Cyrus"], King of the World, Great King, Legitimate King, King of Babilani, King of Kiengir and Akkade, King of the four rims of the earth, Son of Kanbujiya. I returned to these sacred cities on the other side of the Tigris the sanctuaries of which have been ruins for a long time, the images which used to live therein and established for them permanent sanctuaries. I also gathered all their former inhabitants and returned them to their habitations.
>
> Furthermore, I resettled upon the command of Marduk, the great lord, all the gods of Kiengir and Akkade whom Nabonidus had brought into Babilani to the anger of the lord of the gods, unharmed, in their former temples, the places which make them happy.[125]

Now, check out the Jews' own version of this in Ezra 1:1–8 in the Hebrew Bible:

> In the first year of Cyrus, king of Persia, in order to fulfill the word of the Lord spoken by Jeremiah, the Lord inspired King Cyrus of Persia to issue this proclamation throughout his kingdom, both by word of mouth and in writing: "Thus says Cyrus, king of Persia: "All the kingdoms of the earth the Lord, the God of heaven, has given to me, and he has also charged me to build him a house in Jerusalem, which is in Judah. Whoever, therefore, among you belongs to any part of his people, let him go up, and may his God be with him! Let everyone who has survived, in whatever place he may have dwelt, be assisted by the people of that place with silver, gold, and goods, together with free will offerings for the house of God in Jerusalem."[126]

Corroboration.

The names of Israel, Judah/Judaea, and Hebrew kings are also found in the records of the Jews' ancient neighbors and adversaries.

There are indeed many examples of this, but the last few I'd like to review for now before tying all of this together are some of my favorites. You've seen them repeatedly. They're especially relevant because these "non-Zionist" sources—indeed, anti-Zionist sources—contradict the Arab claim that Arabs were the original "Palestinians." And while these quotes are deliberately referred to elsewhere in this book (for reasons explained in the Introduction), they truly deserve repeated consideration.

There was no separate country nor nation known as "Palestine" during the time of Jesus. The land was known as Judaea and its inhabitants were called Judaeans. Jews.

Recall that Tacitus and Dio Cassius were famous Roman historians who wrote extensively about Judaea's attempt to remain free from the Soviet Union of its day, Imperial Rome. Both lived and wrote around the time of the two major revolts of the Jews in 66–73 C.E. and 133–135 C.E., and they make no mention of this land being called "Palestine" nor its people "Palestinians." Furthermore, they showed that they knew quite well the differences between Jews and Arabs in their accounts.

Recall this earlier footnoted quote from Vol. II, Book V, *The Works of Tacitus*, "Titus was appointed by his father to complete the subjugation of Judaea. He commanded three legions in Judaea itself. To these he added the twelfth from Syria and the third and twenty-second from Alexandria. Amongst his allies were a band of Arabs, formidable in themselves and harboring toward the Jews the bitter animosity usually subsisting between neighboring nations." And, some sixty years later, after Hadrian decided to further desecrate the site of the destroyed Temple of the Jews by erecting a pagan structure there, the Jews took on their mighty conquerors again.

From Dio's *Roman History*.

> More than 580,000 men were slain, nearly the whole of Judaea made desolate. Many Romans, moreover, perished in this war [the Bar Kochba Revolt]. Therefore Hadrian in writing to the senate did not employ the opening phrase commonly affected by the emperors, "I and the legions are in health."[127]

Corroboration.

Enraged at the Jews' persistence in their quest for freedom and wishing to finally end their hopes once and for all, after 135 C.E., Hadrian renamed the land itself from Judaea to "Syria Palaestina"—Palestine—after the Jews' historic enemies, the Philistines, a non-Semitic sea people from the Aegean area.

And now (drum roll please), let's see what all of this has to do with Chanukah.

In the seventies, while a doctoral student at the Kevorkian Center for Near Eastern Studies, I had the privilege of having Dr. F. E. Peters as one of my professors.

A leading expert of the ancient Near East (along with other related subjects as well), one of his specialties was ancient Greece.

Fluent in the language and immersed in the primary sources, Peters's *The Harvest of Hellenism* largely supports the Jews' own accounts of their struggle for independence against their latest conqueror prior to the appearance of Rome, the Syrian Seleucid successors to Alexander the Great. After the latter's death, his generals had fought for the pieces of the pie. Ptolemy wound up with one of the other main prizes, Egypt.

Listen to these scattered quotes from Peters, who devoted a good portion of this over eight-hundred-page book to the same subject found in the Jews' own writings in the *First and Second Books of Maccabees.*

> The Seleucids, like all other Hellenistic monarchs, with the exception of the Macedonian Antigonids, were worshiped as gods. Jew and Hellene clashed on the issue of conduct. Hellenism could allow almost any eccentricity in private behavior; however, the polis found it difficult to accept a large-scale and public refusal to share in its life and rites.[128]

Whatever else may or may not have happened in Judaea during the time of Antiochus IV Epiphanies ("the god made manifest"), and while the good professor takes issue with some aspects of the Jews' own accounts, both he and Jewish tradition agree that the clash he himself wrote about above inevitably led to the first war ever fought—at least partially—over religious freedom.

Proclaiming yourself a god among pagans was one thing. They could just add Antiochus to a long list.

But to do this with Jews, whose religion teaches that no man—regardless of how great—could be divine, was explosive. Add to this his attempt at squashing their determination to retain their own way of life and religious practices, and the revolt of the Maccabees became inevitable.

Here's the Roman historian, Tacitus, a few centuries later on the same subject, writing after the Jews next took on the Romans: "The Jews acknowledge one God only, and conceive of him by the mind alone, condemning, as impious, all who, with perishable materials, wrought into the human shape, form representations of the Deity. That Being, they say, is above all, and everlasting, neither susceptible of likeness nor subject to decay. In consequence, they allow no resemblance of Him in their city, much less in their temples. In this way they do not flatter their kings, nor show their respect for their Caesars."[129]

That above passage, by the way, explains the main schism between Judaism and Christianity today as well. So, read it again carefully.

Corroboration.

At a time when Israel—which was making history and causing a revolution in religion, ethics, and morality millennia before most peoples had even made their historical debuts—still has to fight for its right to take its place among most newcomers on the world scene, the story of Chanukah and its message of rededication is as important today as it was when Judah the Hammer took on his mighty pagan rulers over two thousand years ago.

So, *Chag sameach*! Happy Chanukah, regardless of whatever month it is.

Chapter 27

Focus on the Here and Now

A GOOD FRIEND AND I had a discussion some time ago about Christian support for Israel. Neither of us is naïve, and both of us are seasoned observers of the Jewish scene. The focus was not so much the mainline churches—which have shown growing hostility over the past years (divestment from Israel, buying into an Arab "David" vs. an Israeli "Goliath," and so forth)—but the Evangelicals, more than fifty million of them.

I remember growing up and having Christians knocking on my door telling me that my family was going to hell, in Philadelphia no less, with some four hundred thousand Jews in its environs. Imagine what it is like out yonder ways.

As a graduate student, I remember studying Christian theology as part of my interest in first-century Judaism and the struggle of the Jews for their freedom and independence against Rome. So I know the theological reasons for at least some Christian support for Israel, as well as the fate of Jews after the Second Coming in that theology.

While doing those graduate studies, I also worked for years for an organization that monitored Christian proselytizing groups (among other things). So, when it comes to skeptics on this issue, I'm definitely no greenhorn.

Having said this, I'm convinced that groups like Pastor John Hagee's Christians United for Israel (CUFI) and Christian Action for Israel (CAFI) are among the best friends both Israel and Jews have right now—at a time when any friends at all are a rarity.

CAFI has helped spread such articles as "Thinking Jerusalem" of mine around for years now. And check out CUFI's Nights to Honor Israel on a Web search. I dare you to tell me that you see something other than good there, unless, of course, you are opposed to Israel's existence.

Few things are ever clear-cut or risk-free, and many Christians still embrace replacement theology. Jews are cursed, wandering G_d killers for them as well. But here in the United States, tens of millions of Evangelicals have more clout than a relative handful of Jews—more than half of whom do not really care about Israel anyway.

Indeed, some very influential alleged members of the tribe, the George Soros and Noam Chomsky types, are downright hostile. I deal with the latter, too. They funded (and 78 percent of Jews voted for) President Barack Obama's campaign, knowing full well the long list of anti-Semitic and/or anti-Israel close friends and associates he has, crying about those "poor Palestinians" Israel allegedly abuses, asking Israel to make suicidal, one-sided concessions to enemies who deny its very right to exist, spewing vile anti-Semitism from various pulpits, and so forth. The Nation of Islam's rabid anti-Semite, Louis Farrakhan, has called Obama the Messiah.[130]

Now that President Obama is in office, it has become obvious that at least some of our main fears regarding Israel were well founded. He's pressuring Israel to accept a Saudi peace (of the grave) plan, which is a virtual clone of another such "peace plan" pushed by alleged "friends" who sold out the Czechs to Hitler at Munich in 1938. Substitute the Sudetenland for Judea and Samaria (the West Bank), and the analogy is indeed chilling.

While there has been a slight hint of late that President Obama may have something else in mind (an American peace plan?), there is still too much to be deeply concerned about here. Arabs have made it quite clear that they are not open to such key revisions to their virtual ultimatum for "peace" with Israel.[131]

So, I worry about head-in-the-sand Hebrews more than I do Evangelicals right now—especially since there are plenty of the former in Israel, too.

I have worked with local pastors here in Florida, such as Reverends John Jeyaseelan, Howard Chadwick, and others involved in annual in Peace for Israel festivals, interfaith pilgrimages to Israel, and other programs for years now. I've seen tears in their eyes as they and their flocks embraced Jews and asked them for forgiveness for past Christian sins toward the Jewish people. Thousands of folks—mostly Christians—attended these local events. Not a Jewish dime was involved, it was all Christian sponsored, raising huge amounts of dollars for Israel at the same time. And this is happening in many other places all around the country as well.

But again, as I stated, I'm not naïve.

I understand Christian theology quite well. I wish I could say the same about most Christians regarding Judaism. They believe what they believe; we believe what we believe. But as long as they're not forcing it upon us (as was done too often in the past) and they're focusing on what they're focusing on instead, I don't know what else one can ask for, given the huge amount of crucial support they give us.

These particular folks are not actively proselytizing Jews. Indeed, I have openly discussed this with them. Some have rejected replacement theology and frequently speak of this rejection. Do some other Christians engage in proselytizing, including some associated with CUFI? No doubt, I'm sure. But that's more our problem than theirs. Would they like us all to be good Christians? Probably. And I'd like them all to see where they perhaps strayed as well from Hebraic monotheism.

So what?

On this issue, the real question is, What are we doing wrong if the beauty and messages of our Hebraic prophets, psalms, and Torah are being ignored or simply bypassed by our own people?

Sorry, Jews, but if you want someone to blame, then start with our own religious leaders.

If our Hebrew Bible (aka "Old Testament") teaches such lessons as "love thy neighbor as thyself;" "what does the Lord require of thee but to do justice, love mercy and walk humbly with thy G_d;" "offer me not vain sacrifices if ye do not justice for the widow and the orphan;" and much, much more and our kids still think they have to go elsewhere to find a G_d of love, then whose fault is it?

Not Reverend Hagee and CUFI's, that's for sure. If one has never seen thousands of Christians at their frequent rallies for Israel, lobbying the White House and Congress, traveling to Israel when even Jews from other countries were staying away, and so forth, then please try to imagine it. I have seen all of this.

Such support is absolutely critical here in the States, and thus for Israel, too.

We have too many Jews in the government and elsewhere—especially in crucial areas like the media, academia, and so forth—who, to advance their own careers, accept the oil-tainted State Department's view that to be pro-America one has to be hostile to Israel, or simply don't care either way.

I would bet that at President Obama's Passover Seder—conducted as he was apparently preparing plans to push a very dangerous Arab "peace" plan down Israel's throat—he had a number of those above types of Jews at the table.

Again, I hope I'll be proven wrong about all of this. I would love to look back later and conclude that, despite all the evidence at hand, the president surprised his doubters, including me.

For now, however, I'll still take my chances with Reverends John Hagee, John Jeyaseelan, and Howard Chadwick any day over such fellow tribal members as described above. CUFI and other similar organizations are fighting for a better here and now for the Jew of the Nations—something too many *landsmen* themselves don't think twice about undermining and treating unfairly, especially those in academia.

Are such organizations as John Hagee's concerned about the hereafter, the

Second Coming, and such too? Sure. But the deal is that, in their theology, they don't get the latter without the former.

So, along with my valued Christian friends (and not all Christians are our friends), I'll worry about the world to come after this one is made safer for Israel, Jews, and hopefully the rest of the world as well—Arabs included—in the here and now.

Chapter 28

SAMIR KUNTAR AND OTHER
LESSONS FOR THE DIASPORA

LIKE A BROKEN record, the same story replayed over and over again, ad nauseam. Israel captures live Arab disembowelers and wannabes of Jews, then other Jews pay to keep them alive in jail.

Until the inevitable happens. Arabs capture more live Jews, then offer a swap for hundreds of their jailed comrades.

If the Jews are lucky, they get back a live prisoner or so.

In just one example, in 1985 they exchanged almost twelve hundred Arabs for three of their own. In January 2004, they handed over more than four hundred Arabs for one Israeli businessman and the bodies of three soldiers abducted along the Lebanese border in 2000.

Usually, the deal involves remains of a few dead Jews for hundreds of Arab killers and collaborators—who are soon back in the Jew-killing business.

And I bet you thought Jews were smart.

In 2006, the swap was for a few more Israeli soldiers (their remains) kidnapped by Hizbullah in another cross-border raid from Lebanon. Recall the war this triggered during that summer.

Among others Israel has supplied free room and board to over the years was Samir Kuntar, a Lebanese who the Jews had held for almost three decades. Good way to either directly or indirectly spend Jewish Diaspora funds, right?

Kuntar's relevant bio is educational—and only emphasizes how beyond dumb Jews can really be.

On April 22, 1979, Kuntar led a terror team that entered Israel from Lebanon by boat. Around midnight they reached coastal Nahariya, killed a policeman, and entered a high building. They next split into two groups, one breaking into the apartment of the Haran family. Danny Haran was taken hostage, along with his four-year-old daughter, Einat. His wife, Smadar, hid in a crawl space with their two-year-old daughter, Yael, and a neighbor.

Kuntar's group next dragged Danny and Einat to the beach. Kuntar shot Danny at close range in front of Einat and drowned him to ensure that he was dead. Next, he smashed the four-year-old girl's head on beach rocks, crushing her skull with the butt of his rifle. Meanwhile, back in the crawl space, two-year-old Yael Haran had been accidentally suffocated to death by her mother's

142

attempts to quiet her whimpering so as not to reveal their hideout.[132]

While Kuntar's exploits rank "up there" with Arabs as far as heroics against Jews go, he's no exception to the rule. As just one of too many other examples, in May 2004 Arabs gunned down a pregnant Jewish mother and her four terrified little daughters. After spraying their car with gunfire, they next ran up and blasted each of their victims' heads to make sure they had finished the job.

One of the Arab heroes next deliberately shot the swollen belly of the eight-months-pregnant mother, Tali Hatuel, at point-blank range.[133]

Note, please, that all of these Jewish victims were/are deliberately targeted—they're not accidentally caught in the middle because their own folks routinely use them as human shields—a favorite tactic used by Arab "militants" that victimizes their own non-combatants.

Now, combine this above lunacy (knowing what predictable blackmail awaits, the Samir Kuntars should never be taken alive, and if they are, after a quick trial, should be executed soon afterwards) with the additional death wish of still too many Israelis and other Jews who believe that if they just keep on making one-sided concessions after concessions on crucial security issues, Arabs will finally let the microscopic Jewish sub-rump state that's left live in "peace."

Peace of the grave. And it is that obvious.

That others pressure Israel to act against its own basic needs is no surprise—the State Department, Dhimmi Europe, some American presidents, and so forth. The Jewish state should be used to this.

That Israel allows itself to be bullied this way—regardless of the American aid issue and such—is beyond pathetic. It truly borders on suicidal, and such behavior should not be repeatedly rewarded by the Diaspora.

Why, by early 2009, was Ehud Olmert still in office as Israel's prime minister, for example? Why couldn't the selfish portions of his fragile coalition see the forest of their miniscule state's survival for their own individual trees?

While Gaza 2008 was in full bloom and boom, Olmert also apparently sought to appease Bashar al-Assad—the late butcher's son—with the gift of all the territory Syria has repeatedly used in order to attack Israel from, the Golan Heights. President Obama now expects Israel to cave in on this as well. He sent his virulently anti-Israel pal, Robert Malley, to make nice to Assad in Damascus before he was even in the White House. Now, let's see. What might President Obama offer the Syrians in exchange for their better behavior in Iraq and Lebanon and some steps away from Iran?[134]

Think about how borders have constantly changed all over the world due to such aggressive, murderous behavior as Syria's—not to mention that the Golan Heights were to be part of the original 1920 Mandate of Palestine after World

War I until the Brits and French did some imperial trading. Or that numerous peoples besides Arabs ruled the Golan Heights over the centuries, including Jews.

And what of Syria's continuous, oppressive shenanigans in Lebanon, burying hopes of those who wanted an independent, more peaceful path for their country? Or their continued murderous suppression of millions of Syrian Kurds?

Should Israel ignore all of this too in its quest to become a state like all others, with no friends, just interests? That's where its recent anti-Jewish, post-Zionist path has been leading it. Let's hope the new Netanyahu government will be true to its campaign promise and end that disgraceful behavior.

So, how to get the message across that such consistent, self-destructive behavior cannot be supported?

Think about it. Perpetually victimized Jews waited millennia to finally live to see the Hebraic prophetic resurrection of Israel, only to see spineless leaders with delusional supporters undo the dream.

If the Benjamin Netanyahu–Avigdor Lieberman team also drops the ball (and they're probably the best leaders Israel could have given this moment in time), then perhaps it will be time to send a real wakeup call to Israel from abroad, and it will indeed be a hard one for the Diaspora to deliver.

Yet such things as the refusal to enact the death penalty for deliberate butchers of innocents (and please don't sing to me about allegedly stooping to their level) and the recent refusals to demand the reasonable territorial compromises allowed by UNSC Resolution 242 require drastic action at this time.

Diaspora Jews have poured many billions of dollars into Israel for well over a century now. While this doesn't give them the right to dictate Israeli policy, on the other hand, the Diaspora does not have to continue to support policies that are obviously a dead end—both figuratively and literally.

Israel doesn't have to continuously try to prove how much "better" it is than the mostly giant moral dung heap surrounding it.

Yet it continues to act this way—not that it makes any difference to the world's hypocrites. For the latter, murderers and those who seek to bring them to justice are morally equivalent. Just ask the State Department, the European Union, *The New York Times*, the United Nations, the BBC, many academics, and so forth.

Furthermore, don't you know, they're not murderers. They're just Arab freedom fighters resisting those Nazi Jews.

Compare civil and political rights and freedoms in an admittedly imperfect Israel with any Arab or other country surrounding it. I dare the doubters. If this were done, Israel should be canonized instead.

If Samir Kuntar was a Jew, Kurd, Amazigh (Berber), Copt, black Sudanese, or such and committed these acts against any of those "Arab" states in which these non-Arab peoples have lived, he would not have lived to see the light of day.

Misguided Jews kept him alive for decades and then set him free to kill again. The man shot and drowned an innocent father, crushed the skull of his young daughter, and was responsible for the death of his infant. One quick shot to the head—on the spot.

The Diaspora does not have to continue to pump money into a post-Zionist, anti-Jewish state that insists it is going to out-Christian the Christians, turning cheek after cheek to enemies who will never accept a permanent Jewish neighbor, regardless of size. That's the way it was for far too long up until the 2009 elections, which brought Netanyahu and Lieberman into office.

Furthermore, the actions of recent Israeli leaders who have played along with the Arabs' well-known destruction-in-phases plans borders on treason—regardless of the non-stop, outside (American) pressure they were subjected to, the same pressure the Obama team is now applying as well.

Something is needed to open up the eyes of too many who have forgotten what life was like for Jews all over the world before the miraculous phoenix arose from the ashes of Auschwitz-Birkenau and the frightened *kilab yahud* "Jew dog" mellahs of the Arab world.

Perhaps a severe shock is what's really needed to bring the forest back into vision, and one long enough to drive home the message.

I realize it is controversial. It is hard to say no to the many worthy charities and such pulling at Diaspora heartstrings.

But if business stays as usual regarding recent pathetic Israeli behavior after the return of Benjamin Netanyahu and the emergence of Avigdor Lieberman, Iran's Ahmadinejad will be correct regarding his death forecast for the Jewish state.

And the Jews will largely have done it to themselves.

If Israel can no longer count on Diaspora money to fill the many social gaps in society that depend upon it and it then has to use state funds targeted for defense and elsewhere to cover those internal costs, perhaps the message will finally get through. Hopefully, with this new team running the show in Jerusalem, it won't have to come to this.

The heir of Jabotinsky, Begin, and a younger Ariel Sharon has come to the fore to take his rightful place.

These are extremely dangerous times for Israel—even worse than usual. If Netanyahu does what he knows in his heart as well as his mind he must do for the very survival of the Jewish state, he will find an Israeli public, finally awoken from its slumber, that will know how to respond.

And I believe that that response will resonate abroad as well, with many positive consequences here on the critical American scene.

Chapter 29

ISRAEL OWES GAZA NOTHING EXCEPT AN ULTIMATUM

IN MAY 1948, Egypt was one of about a half-dozen Arab states that tried to nip a nascent, resurrected Israel in the bud. And for the same reasons, Arabs and those willingly (most weren't) Arabized have slaughtered, subjugated, and committed genocide against Kurds, black Africans, Imazhigen/Berbers, Assyrians, Copts, and others besides "their" Jew dogs who dared to insinuate that they too—besides Arabs—have rights in a region proclaimed by the latter to be solely their own. Recall that one-half of Israel's Jews consists of Jews who pre-dated Arabs in that region but who fled to Israel, the refugees few ever talk about. Over another million of these Jewish refugees from "Arab" lands fled abroad to the Americas, France, and elsewhere.

Armed to the teeth with weapons left over by the Brits from World War II, Egypt seized Gaza while a British-officer–led Arab Legion in Transjordan (created itself in 1922 from almost 80 percent of the original 1920 Mandate of Palestine) seized Judea and Samaria on the west bank of the Jordan River. Transjordan, now controlling both banks, soon renamed itself Jordan. Its occupation of those non-apportioned (not purely Arab) parts of the Mandate was recognized by only two other nations, Great Britain and Pakistan.

The same above Arab pair—along with Syria and a few others as well—took another shot at their 1948 goal in June 1967. Big mistake.

In collusion with Syria, Egypt blockaded Israel at the Straits of Tiran (a *casus belli*), amassed one hundred thousand troops, tanks, and aircraft on Israel's border, and convinced Jordan to jump on board. It then ordered the United Nations peacekeeping force out of the area so it would be able to invade the Jewish state unimpeded. Like a fireman who flees the moment a fire starts, the UN simply complied. It would repeat its uselessness this way many times later—stepping in only after Israel turned the tide of repeated Arab aggression, not preventing it or punishing the aggressor. Indeed, the UN did just this in 1948. That's how Israel wound up with mostly Auschwitz/armistice lines—making it virtually invisible on a world map—not real borders.

And that's how Israel wound up in Gaza and in the West Bank—turning the tide on Arab plans of genocide—in all of six days. I have all of the original newspaper articles from that time period stored in a box.

As has been written many times, during the almost two decades that Egypt and Jordan occupied those areas, no one clamored for the creation of a second state for Arabs within the borders of the original 1920 Palestinian Mandate. In 1947, Arabs were offered about half of the 20 percent of the territory left after the creation of Transjordan and rejected this partition. Some 90 percent of the total area wasn't enough. They had to have it all. Jew dogs were entitled to nothing.

That was over sixty years ago—and, as we have seen up to the present moment with an alleged Saudi "peace" plan that is basically a recipe for the Jewish state's suicide—nothing has really changed regarding that same Arab mind-set, which refuses to grant scores of millions of non-Arabs living in the region even a tiny sliver of the same political rights Arabs demand for themselves. That, in a nutshell, is the Arab–Israeli conflict.

Let's review.

A few years back, a now-comatose Prime Minister Sharon—under intense pressure from Washington—agreed to unilaterally withdraw from Gaza, a coastal area that had been repeatedly used since the days of the pharaohs to invade the land of the Jews. It was also the land of Goliath's non-Semitic, Aegean "sea people," the Philistines (as in "Palestine"), who gave both Egyptians and Jews earlier shared headaches.

Sharon's withdrawal plan was highly controversial, but there were enough potentially positive aspects to it that it seemed to at least some folks worth a try. The problem is that all of the worst-case scenario results soon emerged instead.

Gaza was a test—a chance to see if Arabs wanted to build their twenty-second state more than they wanted to destroy the sole, tiny nation of the Jews. And (no shock here) they flunked it horrendously.

Given this as background, now consider President Obama's current pressure on Israel to repeat this scenario of withdrawal in practically all of Judea and Samaria, known only for less than a century as the West Bank.

Regardless of the threats from its friends, Israel must stand its ground and insist on the territorial compromise it must have in that vulnerable area—which UNSC Resolution 242 allows for. Bordering the West Bank is Israel's narrow-as-a-zipper strategic waist. A tank thrust coming from the east could dissect it here at the virtual blink of an eye. And Israel faced just such assaults like this in the past.

Being the target of repeated Arab attempted destruction, Israel was under no obligation to return any territories used for those purposes before treaties of real peace—not *hudna*-type ceasefires—were signed.

Borders and territorial possessions all over the world have historically been changed for far less than what Israel has faced—including America's. And does anyone remember the Falkland War the Brits fought with Argentina? Now imagine the Brits (along with numerous other hypocrites) lecturing Israel—as they constantly do—about what the Jews allegedly need to do in their own very backyard (not thousands of miles away from home) regarding Arabs who deliberately terrorize and slit the throats of their kids and other innocents.[135]

With the withdrawal of Jewish organic farmers and so forth, leaving advanced greenhouses and such behind (Gaza thus becoming *Judenrein*), did the Arabs offer Israel any semblance of peace?

The only thing Arabs did was congratulate themselves about how nicely their well-known destruction-in-stages scenario for Israel was playing out, courtesy, especially, of American pressure on the Jewish state. They're counting on a replay of this on the West Bank and on the Golan with help from the new Obama administration as well.

Recall that prior to the setback in '67, they called for a one-fell-swoop plan for the Jews' demise. Afterward, this was replaced with a strategy to force Israel—via diplomacy (i.e., arm-twisting by its "friends")—back to its 1949, UN-imposed, microscopic armistice line, not border, existence. The final version (as opposed to the French and Russian one) of UNSC Resolution 242 was drafted in a rare display of true justice to rectify that wrong after the Six Day War.

Thus, any withdrawal of Israel from territories was to be in the context of real peace treaties and to secure and somewhat defensible and recognized real borders—not armistice lines. It was expected that the travesty of the '49 lines would be reversed as Israel withdrew from territories—not *all* territories and not *the* territories. Indeed, as we already discussed, the UN fought very hard over the precise wording of 242 for just this reason. A reading of its architects, such as Lord Caradon, Eugene Rostow, and others, makes this very clear. Here's Lord Caradon:

> It would have been wrong to demand that Israel return to its positions of June 4, 1967, because those positions were undesirable and artificial. After all, they were just the places where the soldiers of each side happened to be on the day the fighting stopped in 1948. They were just armistice lines. That's why we didn't demand that the Israelis return to them.[136]

Nevertheless, for a very cold peace, Israel handed Egypt back the best tank trap it had, buffering itself from latter-day pharaohs, as well as oil fields it developed, major airbases, and some decent semblance, at last, of strategic depth. With Sinai thus returned, Gaza was the next piece to fall in the post-'67 Arab destruction-in-stages game plan.

Indeed, Gaza was a failed test.

Arabs had an opportunity to prove doubters such as myself wrong, and we really wanted that to happen, though we knew better. We would have loved to have seen Arab steps toward real, positive nation-building, improvements for the masses on the ground, and so forth. Had Israel observed this, there is no doubt it would have been a good neighbor. It has wanted this from the get-go.

The actual "peace offering" Arabs gave Israel in return for its total withdrawal, however, was to elect Arabs to power in Gaza who didn't even feel it necessary to play Mahmoud Abbas and his Fatah and Palestinian Authority's phony game of acceptance. Actually, Abbas and his crew don't do this either and still refuse—to this very day—to accept a Jewish Israel. Arabs can claim almost two dozen Arab states (created mostly from non-Arab peoples' lands), but how dare Jews speak of one miniscule, reborn state of their own, a state where over three thousand years ago King David made Jerusalem his capital.

Yet, to prop up the West's sweet-talking, latter-day Arafatian darlings in suits, Mahmoud Abbas (Holocaust denier and one of Arafat's chief lieutenants and terror planners) and Fatah had to be made the good cops by a State Department long hostile to even the very idea of Israel to the Hamas bad ones to help make the sale and twist the arms of the Jews. In reality, both have the same long-term plans for Israel.

While attacks against Israel from Gaza were launched before Hamas gained control there, they increased afterward. Thousands of rockets and mortars were launched against Israel proper after the complete, unilateral Israeli withdrawal.

Instead of a hand being offered to an Israel that could indeed be very generous in peace, Arabs elected those who openly (to their credit—no game playing here) call for Israel's total destruction, the same folks who were blowing up school kids and others on buses, in restaurants, nightclubs, and such a while back. They even set up a museum commemorating their heroism, complete with fake Jewish body parts hanging from ceilings for all to sing praises to.[137] These are the folks to whom President Obama expects Israel bare the necks of its children. And that museum, by the way, was set up on the Abbas's Fatah-dominated West Bank—not in Gaza.

Think about what Israel really needs to do with such an enemy. Does America's own Powell (as in Colin) Doctrine ring a bell? Here are some excerpts to check out.

Powell expanded upon the doctrine, asserting that when a nation is engaging in war, every resource and tool should be used to achieve decisive force against the enemy, minimizing US casualties and ending the conflict quickly by forcing the weaker force to capitulate. This is well in line with Western military strategy dating at least from Carl von Clausewitz's *On War*.[138]

As of late 2008, there was supposedly a ceasefire in effect. Hamas got tired of losing too many of its folks to Israel's pinpoint strikes. Yet, during this "ceasefire," Israel ceased, but the Arabs still fired.

Because of this, the Jews stopped the flow of goods and services to the people who elected those who want both Jews and the Jewish state dead and who cause death, maiming, and destruction in nearby Israeli towns and cities.

How unreasonable of those Jews!

Just ask the UN's Ban Ki-moon, the European Union's Benita Ferrero-Waldner, NGO Oxfam's Jeremy Hobbs, and so forth. Again, as we've seen before, they simply expect Jews to keep on out-Christianing Christians by turning cheek after cheek after cheek, not that any "Christian" country would ever put up with such murderous manure that Israel is simply expected to keep on accepting from Arabs.

Tit-for-tat responses have never worked well with Arabs. They know there are hundreds of millions of them and about six million Israeli Jews. Now, again—why am I nervous about that number? Recall that Arafat praised the Arab mother as his best weapon, and Mahmoud Abbas was the late Egyptian ghoul's close confidant and chief lieutenant.

To be taken seriously, Israel must treat Gaza's Hamas and those who eagerly elected it according to America's own Powell Doctrine. Again, if firing thousands of rockets, mortars, and such at one's cities are not considered acts of war, then what is? If calling for the death of a nation and its people and acting on those threats are not acts of war, then what is?

If ever a nation had reason to level an enemy from above and afar, then who if not Israel?

Think about what America and Great Britain did to Germany's Dresden in World War II—not to mention a nuked Japan.

Israel certainly has the means, and not doing so, trying to be humane to the inhumane, only brings hypocritical charges leveled against Jews anyway. Who else do you know telephones its enemies and drops leaflets from the sky to save their lives? Jews do. And there are few innocents in Gaza. There are terrorists—excuse me, "militants"—and mostly others who willingly elect and hide them. See the Jamie Foxx movie *The Kingdom* for a good idea of how this works.

Arab non-combatants hide murderers who in turn use the former as human shields (willingly or not) after they deliberately attack Jewish civilians—all contrary to the Geneva Conventions, by the way. Think Perfidy Clause and such.

Yet, none of this ever matters to the UN, the European Union, Oxfam, the State Department, the BBC, NPR, academic hypocrites, and so forth.

Arabs and those willingly Arabized are still committing atrocities, waging genocide, subjugating non-Arab native populations, and so forth throughout that entire region, and all those above can do is insist that Jews allow the resupply of rejectionist enemies who would butcher them if they had the chance. No doubt.

Egypt, which Israel has an alleged peace treaty with due to the courage of the late (assassinated) Egyptian president, Anwar el-Sadat, has allowed hundreds of tunnels to be dug from its territory to supply Gaza with the means to kill Jews.

Imagine if this were reversed. Again, Pharaoh now supposedly has a peace treaty with Israel.

Here's an idea, let them smuggle food and so forth instead. Furthermore, why smuggle? Let Pharaoh supply his own Arab brothers with those supplies. By the way, Israel has been permitting essentials to cross into Gaza anyway, despite the Arab mortar and rocket attacks.

And why are Jews obligated to supply their executioners and executioner wannabes with anything?

Would any other people be expected to do this? Would America? Should be a no brainer, right? But, it is that Jew thing again.

David Ben-Gurion, Golda Meir, Ze'ev Vladimir Jabotinsky, and Menachem Begin must be rolling in their graves.

Before the return of Benjamin Netanyahu, propped up with Avigdor Lieberman as foreign minister, Israel's recent leadership acted too much like those who traditionally guarded Arab sheikhs' harems—if you get my drift.

Prior to the November 2008 American elections, Prime Minister Olmert had some additional last minute arm-twisting done by another soon-leaving official, Secretary of State Condoleezza Rice. President Bush himself had also lately joined the "gang-up on the Jews" party as well.

Hey, President Clinton received millions of dollars for his library and such from the Arab oil spigot as a gift for forcing Jews into the deadly Oslo "peace" debacle and agreeing to forsake 242's promise of secure borders, not to mention the funds Jimmy "Apartheid Israel" Carter milked the same Arab petro-teat for, so why not the scion of the Bush oil family as well? George W. was certainly acting that way those past few years—and I (with reservations) voted for him.

Like many other State Department types, Secretary of State Condoleezza Rice's career of squeezing Jews into making self-destructive decisions is sure to pay off later also. Just ask James Baker III (Dubya's virtual uncle). As I like to remind folks, Rice has already had one oil tanker in the Chevron fleet named after her. Shafting Hebrews and Arab potentate derriere-kissing have been lucrative business decisions for over half a century.[139]

Israel must have new leaders who will act boldly—regardless of the consequences. If America threatens to cut off aid, then so be it. So Netanyahu and

Lieberman must live up to their potential, no matter what.

With a man who has numerous anti-Semitic and/or anti-Israel friends, advisors, and supporters now in the White House, Israel must draw its lines in the sand, beyond which it will no further retreat. It can hope for the best, but—given the apparent hand held in the current American corner—it must definitely prepare for the worst.

Think of it.

A three-thousand-mile-wide America buffered by two huge oceans—which toppled President Manuel Noriega so that its security interests, almost two thousand miles away, would be better served in the Panama Canal zone—is now pressuring Israel to once again become a nine-mile wide, sub-rump state, exposing most of its population to close and predictable Arab terror and fire.

Jerusalem, Tel Aviv, Ben Gurion Airport, Haifa, the Knesset, and such (adjacent to the West Bank) must not be subjected to what Sderot and Ashkelon in Israel's south have, until recently, frequently received—daily bombardment. And that realistically is what is to be expected if Israel does in Judea (land of the Jews) and Samaria (aka, the other part of the West Bank) what it did in Gaza—unilaterally withdraw. And that's what the Obama-supported Saudi peace plan calls for. Recall that the President said Israel would be nuts not to embrace it.[140]

Israel must insist on reasonable but effective territorial compromises regarding the remaining territories in dispute, be they the Golan Heights or the West Bank. Presidents Johnson and Reagan, along with Secretary of State Shultz (an amazing exception to the Foggy Bottom rule), military commanders, and others understood this quite well. It appeared that President Bush II did too—at least for a while.[141]

Arabs (even those few Israel has "peace treaties" with) still refuse to accept the permanent reality of a '49 armistice line, nine-mile-wide Jewish state—let alone anything beyond the virtually microscopic. Think, once more, about that racist, imperial Arab claim to practically the entire region, the Dar ul-Islam vs. the Dar al-Harb, and so forth. And, again, think gassed Kurds, cultural subjugation (and worse) in North Africa, genocide in Darfur and southern Sudan, and so forth while you're at it in case you think that Arab claim isn't taken seriously by them.

Given all the above, as for Gaza Israel must send an ultimatum, not supply it.

And that will be even more true for whatever happens in the future vis-à-vis Abbas and his alleged latter day "good cop" Fatahniks (who still swear they'll never recognize a sole Jewish state next to their twenty-second Arab one) on the West Bank in terms of Arab sovereignty there.

Tens of thousands of Abbas' American-trained and supplied forces will be right next to Israel's narrow strategic waist, where some 80 percent of its population and industry are located.

There's no room for half measures in Israel's response to Arab aggression there. All of Israel's main population centers fall within reach of Arab artillery, rocket, and other fire from there, and all upgraded courtesy of Uncle Sam—Israel's best friend.

Once that new Arab entity gains full sovereignty, then any attacks emanating from that area must be dealt with as an act of war and treated the same way America would handle rocket attacks on Texas launched from Mexico. And yes, there is a difference between the two.

Almost three dozen Israels would fit into just Texas alone. Israel is far more vulnerable than America, and it faces enemies who, for the most part, appear to see no justice other than their own. Israel's fight is still, literally, over its very existence.

In late 2008, Israel finally held Gaza accountable for those ten thousand rockets and mortars launched against Israel proper after Israel's total withdrawal years earlier. Israel cut short its extensive operations as a gesture to the newly-elected American president. If the terror continues, Israel must exponentially up the ante.

And the UN, Oxfam, the European Union, and other assorted hypocrites and practitioners of the double standard who'll criticize Israel no matter what—unless it rolls over and plays dead?

Let them go to where they're really needed but to where they never will to relive the real—not mostly self-inflicted—plight of scores of millions of non-Arab peoples still being slaughtered, enslaved, subjugated, and so forth throughout the region on behalf of Arab nationalism and its "purely Arab patrimony."

Chapter 30

No, Mr. Jihadi—Gaza Isn't Warsaw

'Twas the second week in January 2009—I forget the exact date—and I was treated to a disturbing sight. It happened just before Israel abruptly stopped its offensive in Gaza to appease the new incoming American president.

Fox News interviewed an Arab spokesman about the Gaza thing to get that side of the then-current fighting. Israel had finally overdosed on about ten thousand rockets and mortars being fired at its civilian populations in Israel proper since its total unilateral withdrawal from Gaza years earlier. I can't remember Mr. Jihadi's name. It doesn't matter.

His response was typical, one that anyone who has followed the Arab–Israeli conflict over the last century could recite: the "Palestinians" (Arabs) are the new Jews, and the Jews are the new Nazis.

But Arabs already have almost two dozen states on over six million square miles of territory, you reply—including one sitting on some 80 percent of the original 1920 Mandate of Palestine renamed Jordan. And Jews were stateless until the resurrection of their sole, tiny nation.

Shhh.

Don't ruin a good Arab fairy tale. Besides, don'tcha know, these ain't Arabs, they're "Palestinians." Back to Fox News.

Mr. Jihadi's version of Arab Jews and Jew Nazis is the now popular "Gaza is the Warsaw Ghetto" claim.[142]

Given this ignorance, prejudice, and idiocy, a bit of background is in order.

In 1940, the Nazis began to concentrate most of Poland's three million Jews into several ghettos. The word *ghetto* itself comes from a much earlier church legacy vis-à-vis the Jews. One of the debates among the church fathers had to do with what should be done with the "deicide people." Guess who they allegedly were/are? Buchanan certainly knows—as does his fellow pea in the same pod, Mel Gibson.

The "gentle" St. Augustine won out—at least at some times and in some places.

So, instead of Jews being burned alive in their synagogues and such (which others suggested and which happened anyway), they were to purposely be kept alive—but in such a lowly state, that when people looked upon them, all would be reminded of their crime and recognize the deicide people.

The ghetta (today's ghetto) was where the iron foundries were located in Italy—the smelliest, most unhealthy areas of the city. Perfect for god-killers (I won't insult G_d by capitalizing the previous word), gated and locked as well. These soon spread throughout Christendom, while the "Arab" world constructed its own versions, mellahs, for its *kilab yahud*—Jew dogs. The origin of the notorious Jew badge the Nazis forced Jews to wear was actually in the Arab world.

Does anyone still seriously wonder why Israel had to be reborn?

The ghetto in Warsaw was the largest. It held about four hundred thousand Jews who were told that they would be "resettled" to the East or, at worst, would be going to forced labor camps to work for the Germans.

By 1942, however, word of the Nazis' true plans had made it into the ghetto. The cattle cars were heading for extermination camps, part of the Final Solution. While some still kept their heads in the sand (not unlike too many Jews to this day), many faced reality and joined the resistance. This was harder for Jews since they often faced the anti-Semitism of the other folks as well—not only the Germans. The road to Auschwitz was indeed paved by many ingrained "religious" teachings in Islam as well as in Christianity. By the way, President Obama's good friend and Israel's alleged "peace (of the grave) partner," Mahmoud Abbas, is also a well-known Holocaust-denier.[144]

The full-fledged uprising of David vs. Goliath began in 1943 in the ghetto. Armed with some pistols, revolvers, homemade weapons, and explosives, and some Polish rifles and such, paid for dearly, the Jews took on their tormentors and embarrassed them profusely until the Nazis blasted every place they could possibly hide.

During the Holocaust, the Nazis singled out the women and children first. The attractive of the former might be used for pleasure before being murdered. The kids were killed right away, as they were of no use, unless they wound up in the labs of Nazi doctors to be turned into human guinea pigs for all kinds of grotesque experiments. All of this is well documented. One and one-half million of the six million slaughtered—for no other reason than they were Jews—were babies and children.

OK, so now let's take a look at Mr. Jihadi's alleged Gaza "Warsaw Ghetto." Unlike the Jews, who were not trying to kill any Germans, the Arabs of Gaza eagerly elected an organization—Hamas—dedicated to blowing both Jews and the Jew of the Nations apart.

The Arabs killed in the fighting had been mostly fighters—despite Arab claims. The non-combatants who were killed were deliberately and repeatedly used as human shields by their own "heroes." Where were the UN, International Court of Justice, academic, and other voices crying out about this blatant Arab war crime?[145] They are continuously as useless here as they are in stopping Arab genocide in black Africa.

Unlike the Nazis, who sought out every last Jew for extermination, Israel deliberately telegraphs its punch (dropping leaflets warning civilians to evacuate the combat area, cell-phoning residents, and so forth), knowing full well that it will expose its plans to its enemies as a result; sends its own soldiers to their deaths on the ground, fighting door-to-door knowing in advance of booby traps waiting for them but trying to avoid the deaths of non-combatant Arabs as best as possible; and so forth. When the Allies fought the Nazis and Japan, they firebombed German cities and nuked the latter.

Israel's fight is with Arabs who want it dead and who continuously act upon their wish. No Jewish state, regardless of size, is acceptable. Arab kids are brainwashed from the diaper to the day camps to the schools to the mosques to murder Jews. Nothing Israel does humanely—treating Arabs in Israeli hospitals, supplying its Arab enemies (who else does that?), attempted compromises, and so forth—matters. Sad, but true.

So, why waste young Jewish lives? The world's hypocrites will condemn Israel's self-defense anyway. Gaza should be taken care of from above or blasted by artillery from a distance.

Actually, perhaps Israel should follow the Arabs' own Hama Solution. When Syria's Hafez al-Assad had "problems," he wiped out some forty thousand of his enemies (Arabs!) in about a month by leveling the town of Hama with artillery and so forth. Who screamed about that? I never heard any of my professors mentioning it.

Unlike Nazis, who targeted Jews for just being Jews (as Arabs do as well), Israel has tried its best—given the Arab women and children human-shield game—to target just jihadi combatants rather than just plain jihadis. (Sorry, but Arabs who openly embrace and elect other Arabs who are dedicated to the murder of non-Muslim, non-Arabs in the name of a combination of Arabism and militant Islam fall into this category.)

If killing Arabs was Israel's goal, does anyone seriously doubt that the Jews could have made Gaza "Arabrein" by now as the Nazis earlier made much of Europe *Judenrein*?

Finally, as already noted, as I was still working on this book, Israel agreed to a ceasefire on behalf of the incoming new American president. Unfortunately, all this will accomplish will be to give Hamas time to rearm and regroup. This was not a good idea, especially since many of those tunnels delivering weapons from Egypt's Sinai were/are still functional. Imagine if this were reversed and

Israel allowed its territory to be used against Egypt—with which it supposedly has a peace treaty—this way?

Israel should not have accepted any ceasefire unless it made it very clear to all of the parties—especially an America under President Obama—that the next missiles fired against Israeli towns (as some ten thousand had already been since Israel's full withdrawal from Gaza several years back) would see Gaza turned into a remake of Dresden 1945, after the American and British firebombing. Germany finally got the message and the war soon ended.

Sometimes there's no other way—especially if your enemy has genocidal intentions toward you. It has been said that the two atomic bombs dropped on Japan actually saved many more lives than it cost in the long run. I don't know about that, but I do know that, unlike the "civilian" Arabs' murderous attitudes toward Jews and Israel, which polls continuously confirm, Dresden's German and Hiroshima's Japanese civilians probably didn't seek the destruction of America or want to kill individual Americans.

Arabs have had years and billions of dollars in aid to begin building that twenty-second state they say they must have. They have used the time and the money to prepare for and conduct hostilities against their Jewish neighbor instead. Again, a test of peaceful intent Arabs flunked with flying colors. They are indeed the masters of negative nationalism.

All of this must be kept in mind for the inevitable next round. When it comes, regardless of what the hypocrites around the world will scream and of the threats from its friends, which also will arrive, Israel must deliver the closest thing to a knockout punch that it can. And that will mean paying Hamas's leadership hiding in Syria a visit as well.

Chapter 31

BETWEEN ANKARA AND JERUSALEM

THE TURKS ARE, once again, upset with Israel. Among other things, while hosting a banquet in honor of the visiting United Nations Secretary General, Prime Minister Recep Tayyip Erdogan urged the world "not to turn a blind eye toward Israel's savagery." He was commenting on Israel's long-overdue retaliatory strike on Gaza in late 2008.

In reality, the Arabs killed in the fighting had been mostly fighters, despite Arab claims—the non-combatants killed were deliberately used as human shields by their own fighters. Where had the United Nations, International Court of Justice, academic, European Union, and other voices been about that above blatant Arab war crime? The same place most of academia has been, I guess.

Unless it is Israel they can all jump upon, they're about as useless here as they have been in stopping Arab genocide in black Africa and Arab subjugation and atrocities in Kurdistan, North Africa, and elsewhere as well.

Let's review a bit.

After putting up with thousands of mortars and rockets being deliberately fired at their civilian population years after a full Israeli withdrawal from Gaza and the UN doing nothing to stop this, the Jews had no other choice but to move in to try to stop the murder, destruction, and terror themselves. How long would Ankara itself have put up with these deliberate acts of war before reacting?

The Arabs who elected Hamas—an organization which exists primarily to destroy Israel—have been used by Hamas to commit a double war crime: Israeli civilians have been deliberately targeted from Arab civilian centers, while the latter have been used as human shields. The Perfidy and other clauses of the Geneva Conventions speak clearly about such cowardice and barbarism.

While I do not advocate adopting the Arabs' own tactics used against Jews (such as blowing up Arab buses, restaurants, shopping malls, schools, and such), any building, town, home, and so forth harboring murderers and their collaborators must be recognized for what the Geneva Conventions say it is—a fair military target.[146]

Before I proceed with a reality check, let me state clearly that I am in favor of good relations between Turkey and Israel, but relations based on equality and the highest moral standards of behavior humanly possible by *both* parties toward others in the region.

Now, let's begin.

Unfortunately, the same folks who have declared over one-fifth of their own non-Turkish, Kurdish population (some fourteen million people) to be "non-existent" in the past—they're really just "Mountain Turks, don'tcha know?—and have taken steps to outlaw Kurdish language and culture (Arabic is one of Israel's two official languages), are, once again, enraged at Israel for going after both Arab terrorists and their infrastructure in Gaza. These are the same folks who have killed tens of thousands of Kurds (and many others as well) over the years in the name of their own security, have invaded neighboring Iraq for similar reasons, and so forth.

I favor American, NATO, and Israeli alliances with Ankara, but the particular relationship with the latter must not be an unbalanced affair, something for Turks to use when relations are on the downswing with Syrian Arabs, for example. As of April 2009, they were definitely on the upswing. Turkey held joint military exercises with Syria.

Ankara complains about Israel being forced to take steps to prevent Gaza from becoming one giant base to launch death, destruction, and terror from (while Israel has agreed, short of consenting to suicide, to an Arab state being set up there), but totally nixes the idea of an independent Kurdish state being set up in adjacent northern Iraq for the Turks' own security reasons. Think about that for a minute. We will return to this point later.

For several years now, Arabs had a chance to begin to create that twenty-second state they demand to have in Gaza and the West Bank (actually, their plans include all of Israel as well). All they did with the time and billions of dollars in aid that poured in was to use both to terrorize their Jewish neighbor. As I find necessary to repeat—Gaza was a test that Arabs flunked with flying colors.

So, it is time to use that American expression and really "talk turkey" (speak candidly) to Turkey, if you know what I mean.

Israel has neglected a brave people who have helped many Jews in the past. Just ask the hundreds of thousands in Israel who originated in Iraq. Israeli leaders have done this largely to not anger the Turks over this painful issue. So Ankara's policies toward the Kurds (especially those in Turkey itself) were treated in a hands-off manner, the same way most academics handle the subject—those same sources of enlightenment who do not hesitate to tear Israel apart in their classes. Indeed, Israel has helped Ankara fight Kurds who have resorted to violence in order to achieve their own political rights in Turkey (the PKK, for example), a highly controversial policy.

Since the Turks, however, insist on joining much of the rest of the world in applying hypocritical double standards toward the Jewish state, the time has come for certain truths to, at long last, come out in the open. Some thirty-five million Kurds remain stateless today, often at someone else's mercy. At a time when much of the world insists that justice demands that there be yet another Arab state, there is a nauseating silence—in most of the media, in academia, at the United Nations, and so forth—over the plight of this people.

Spread out over a region that encompasses parts of southeastern Turkey, Syria, Iraq, Iran, and other adjoining areas as well, these modern-day descendants of ancient Medes, Guti, and Hurrians continue to find themselves in very deadly and precarious circumstances.

Kurdish culture and language have periodically been "outlawed" in attempts to Arabize or Turkify them, and in an age when other dormant nations/national groups were able to seize the independence moment with the collapse of empires and such, Kurds were repeatedly denied self-determination by an assortment of alleged "friends" and foes alike. The world—including America—still clamors for a twenty-second Arab state but turns a blind eye to thirty-five million used and abused Kurds.

As we have already noted, having been promised independence after World War I, the Kurds saw their hopes dashed after the British received a favorable decision from the League of Nations on the Mosul Question in 1925.[147] Mosul and Kirkuk were where most of the northern oil was located, and the main arm of British imperial power—the navy—had recently switched from coal to oil.[148]

The Brits decided that their long-term interests involved not angering Arabs, who—by their own writings—declared that the rise of an independent Kurdistan would be seen as the equivalent of the birth of another Israel.[149]

Regardless of scores of millions of non-Arabs living in the region (including one-half of Israel's Jews who were refugees from "Arab"/Muslim lands), Arabs declared a political monopoly over what they regarded as purely Arab land.[150] We are living with the consequences of this mind-set today, along with the related confrontation of the Dar ul-Islam vs. the Dar al-Harb. Hamas and the Gaza mess are but the latest manifestations of this.

For a number of reasons—such as not angering Arabs and Turks alike—the State Department insists, after hundreds of thousands of Kurds have been maimed, gassed, and slaughtered in other ways by Arabs just in Iraq alone over the last half-century (not long ago, Syrian Arabs and Iranians renewed their own previous slaughter of Kurds as well), that Kurds will never gain independence. Recall that the heartland of ancient Kurdistan had been in the oil-rich region around Kirkuk, an area hotly disputed today between Kurds and Arabs in post-Saddam Iraq. Both Ankara and the State Department insist that Kurds remain part of a united Iraq, regardless of the bloody consequences this will likely have for them in the future yet again once America leaves the scene.

America's autonomous federal dream, while looking good on paper, probably will not last far beyond America's withdrawal. The majority Shi'a, like the Kurds, massacred and long suppressed by Saddam's Sunni Arabs, have other plans. Furthermore, as the Brits earlier armed Arabs in their confrontations with the Kurds, America has now done likewise in rebuilding Iraq's Shi'a Arab-led army.[151]

The same State Department—which also fought President Truman over America's recognition of a reborn Israel in 1948—insists that there be no partition of Mesopotamia/Iraq.

Britain had earlier received the Mandate for Mesopotamia at the same time it received the Mandate for Palestine in the post-World War I era upon the breakup of the Ottoman Turkish Empire. But, unlike Palestine (the name Rome gave to Judaea after the Jews' second revolt for freedom), which would have proposed or actual partitions in attempts to arrive at a compromise solution between Arab and Jew, a much larger Mesopotamia was/is somehow declared to be incapable of doing this same bit of justice for its Kurds.

The main reason put forth for why Mesopotamia/Iraq is incapable of this sort of partition is the potential for instability it will cause in the region. Not only will oil-rich Arabs be miffed at someone else gaining national rights in "their" region, but the Turks, in particular, will supposedly have a fit due to their own large Kurdish minority. Not to mention that Iranian mullahs have been collaborating with Ankara to suppress Kurds as well. Iran also has a substantial—and oppressed—Kurdish population.

While strong Turco-American and Turco-Israeli relations—if not alliances—are worthy of support, the Turks are wrong on this matter, and too many others, so willing to accuse Israel, have granted them a moral free pass on this for too long—my university professors, for example. Somehow those same folks teaching students about those nasty Israelis seem to develop a complete case of amnesia when it comes to the Kurdish question in Turkey and elsewhere. And don't think that funding, research opportunities, and so forth don't impact what is and is not included on the academic syllabus of study.[152]

While it is understandable that Ankara is nervous about the potential problems, this does not give it the right to have a veto power over the plight of some thirty-five million long-oppressed, stateless, and politically abused Kurds. Recall that besides Turkey, there are a half-dozen or so other Turkic nations, and zilch for Kurds.

Again, think of the irony here regarding Ankara's outrage at Israel over its fight with unabashedly rejectionist Arabs, who could have had their additional state decades ago had they just not continued to work toward the destruction of the sole, tiny nation of the Jews.

An independent Kurdistan set up in northern Iraq—under the right conditions—might actually be a blessing for the Turks.

Those Kurds—like those Diaspora Jews, Greeks, and Armenians—wishing to live in an independent state of their own could migrate to it. An arrangement could be made whereby the oil wealth of the area could be shared with the Turks as well, since they feel they got robbed via the earlier decision by the League of Nations on the Mosul Question.

Putting things into an even more important and broader perspective, consider the following facts.

The CIA shows Israel to have a population of about seven million people, of whom some 20 percent are Israeli Arabs. Among the latter (the freest Arabs, by the way, anywhere in the region) are some extremely hostile elements. Israel's territory is about 20,770 square kilometers.

Turkey has a population of about sixty-nine million people, of whom about 20 percent are Kurds. Turkey's territory is about 780,580 square kilometers. About thirty-eight Israels can fit into Turkey.

Yet, despite its miniscule size, Ankara, Washington, the Europeans, and others have no problem demanding that Israel allow the creation of another Arab terrorist state, dedicated to Israel's destruction, right on its doorstep. Ignored are the repeated proclamations by even so-called Arab "moderates" that Oslo and all other such peace initiatives are but Trojan horses, steps along the way in the Arabs' post-'67 destruction-in-phases strategy for Israel.

Now, how will the fifth of Israel's population that is Arab react to this adjacent potential development? And how will the majority of Hashemite Jordan, which is also mostly Palestinian Arab (however you define that, since many, if not most, "Palestinians" were simply Arabs who entered Palestine from elsewhere in the region during the Mandatory Period), react to this?

Arafat's successors (Mahmoud Abbas's alleged current Fatah "moderates") had already tried a takeover of Jordan in 1970. They were crushed in King Hussein's Black September. And Israel's mobilization in the north sent a message to Fatah's Syrian allies at the time as well. Yet no one seems to be worried about any destabilizing effects here.

The same hypocrites who declare that Israel must grossly endanger itself so that yet another Arab state might be born insist that Kurds must remain forever stateless because of some problems their freedom might cause to a Turkey nearly forty times Israel's size in territory and over eleven times its size in population and with the exact same 80 percent to 20 percent mix of potential headaches.

Case in point. In Carter Findley's book, *The Turks In World History*, in his far-too-brief reference to this people at all (some thirteen to fifteen million of Turkey's seventy million total population), this well-known scholar of the Turks summed up the Kurds' status by simply referring to them as extremists and a separatist threat to their occupiers and conquerors.[153]

Recall that Kurds lived in the area for thousands of years before the Turks ever arrived from Central Asia or the Arabs burst out of the Arabian Peninsula. Such academics frequently also teach courses about Arab–Israeli politics, showcasing the plight of Arabs and setting Israel up for the micro-critique in the process. I know. I was there. And they do, indeed, indulge in such blatant hypocrisy.

Changing the lenses and the rubric of moral scrutiny on controversial issues to fit one's own personal biases—for whatever the reasons—should be a big no-no for anyone, let alone those with a captive audience paying lots of money to get a supposedly objective education. I guess they call that academic freedom. Too bad they often don't extend that freedom to their students, as well.

Where is the demand for justice and the micro-critique of Turkey regarding stateless, subjugated Kurds, who have even been denied being able to speak their mother tongue, coming from those academic practitioners of the double standard? Again, they routinely take Israel to task regarding the birth of Arab state number twenty-two (the second, not first, Arab one in "Palestine") and often do likewise regarding the very right of existence of the Jewish state at all—sometimes subtly, yet frequently not.

Perhaps all of this also represents a case of knowing who's helping to support your career and butter your bread. Like the Arabs, the Turks have been generous in a variety of ways to academics who know what to teach and also know what to play deaf, dumb, and blind to.

Some progress, so to speak, regarding this subject appears in a letter sent by Zachary Lockman, president of the Middle East Studies Association of North America (MESA) to Turkish Prime Minister Erdogan. It involves Turkey's handling of a Finnish scholar, Dr. Kristiina Koivunen, who dared to cross the line. She is a specialist on the Kurds—especially those of Turkey.[154]

While letters such as that of MESA's Lockman in support of a Finnish scholar on the Kurds are important, how many students taking a typical course taught by a typical MESA academic dealing with the Middle East in America get to share in her information?

Recall that the only other time in all of my undergraduate, master's, and doctoral studies at several different institutions I ever even heard the word *Kurd* mentioned—besides that one time when their plight was mocked by a MESA academic—was when the professor who I was a doctoral T.A. for allowed me one day to give a presentation to our classes. And afterward, the proverbial manure hit the fan. The Arabs in the class went ballistic. How dare others besides those Nazi Israelis be placed under the high-power lens of scrutiny!

There is no moral defense for this duplicity and hypocrisy, and the average student sitting in a class today in Middle Eastern Studies, history, or political science hears nothing of such things. I do understand, however, that life is simply a lot easier for academics—for all kinds of concrete reasons—if they know what subjects are "safe" and which ones are not. But that does not make this situation any less appalling.

Getting back to Ankara's own positions vis-à-vis Israel, the Turks definitely need to review the wisdom regarding those living in glass houses not throwing stones. That they have not learned this yet is but further testimony to the hypocrisy of others who have let the Turks get away with their own duplicitous attitudes and actions. And I say this as a supporter of the Turks and a strong Turco-American alliance.

Friendship, however, should not give a free pass to injustice.

Again, isn't it odd that in all the graduate-level courses I took involving the Ottoman Turkish Empire and modern Turkey, I heard not a peep of any of the above from all of those professors, either at the NYU-based Kevorkian Center for Near Eastern Studies or at Ohio State University, those same shining lights who were never shy about placing Israel under the high-power lens of moral scrutiny.

Odd isn't the word.

Asking Kurds to forsake the creation of their one, sole state for the pipe dream of an egalitarian Iraq is a travesty of justice if ever there was one. Historically, Arab nationalism has always triumphed over a more inclusive, more tolerant, Iraqi nationalism.[155]

Regardless of their religious coloration, the vast majority of Arabs are in no sharing mood when it comes to questions about what they see as "purely Arab patrimony." They are the rulers; the rest are the ruled. Period. End of conversation.

Unlike what a much smaller Israel faces, Kurds do not aim to destroy Turkey in order to see their own dreams of independence—or, at minimum, a highly entrenched, sustainable autonomy in Iraq—come true.

The reason Israel has fought war after war with Arabs is because the latter refuse to grant millions of other non-Arab peoples in the region even a tiny sliver of the very rights they demand for themselves. Many people besides Jews have been slaughtered and victimized by Arabs this way.

Ankara would be wise to reconsider its stance on all of these issues—especially since it insists on seating itself upon a moral high horse.

Chapter 32

HAMAS, GAZA, AND THE UNN
(UNITED NAUSEATING NATIONS)

As soon as Israel was reborn in the wake of the Holocaust, it was attacked by a half-dozen Arab nations—most of which had gained their own independence only recently as well. From that moment on, with a few (but important) rare exceptions, the UN would work to basically try to undo its "mistake" of permitting the resurrection of the Jew of the Nations.

Can't help it. Visions of the Hebrew prophets pour though my mind. Here are some excerpts from Ezekiel 37:

> The hand of the Lord was upon me. set me down in the midst of the valley full of bones... very many. and, lo, they were very dry.
> And He said unto me, "Son of man, can these bones live?" And I answered, "O Lord God, thou knowest."
> Thus saith the Lord God unto these bones; 'Behold, I will cause breath to enter into you, and ye shall live: And I will lay sinews upon you, bring flesh upon you, and cover you with skin, and put breath in you.'
> So I prophesied. there was a noise...shaking, and the bones came together, bone to bone...sinews and flesh came up upon them, and skin covered them above: but there was no breath in them.
> Then said He unto me, "Prophesy unto the wind, Son of man, and say to the wind, 'Thus saith the Lord God: 'Come from the four winds, O breath, and breathe upon these slain, that they may live.'"
> So I prophesied, and the breath came into them, they lived, and stood up upon their feet.
> Then He said unto me, "Son of man, these bones are the whole house of Israel: behold, they say, 'Our bones are dried, and our hope is lost... Therefore prophesy and say, 'Thus saith the Lord God; Behold, O My people, I will open your graves, and cause you to come up out of your graves, and bring you into the land of Israel.'"

Whoa! Heavy stuff. Written some twenty-six centuries or so ago, if this wasn't the resurrected phoenix of the Jews—Israel reborn—then what? And when Jews from the remote corners of the "Arab" world—where they also didn't know what the morrow would bring and were commonly known as *kilab yahud*, Jew dogs, killers of prophets—were gathered to be flown to Israel, with tears they recited the Hebrew prophecy predicting that they would return to Israel on the wings of eagles as they boarded the planes used in Operation Magic Carpet.

One of those above 1948 Arab attackers, Transjordan, only became independent itself two years earlier. Its army was led by British officers and, like Egypt's, was well equipped with Allied armaments left in the region after World War II.

Since the Emirate's own story is crucial for understanding attempts made to try to balance Arab and Jewish claims over that part of the Turks' empire that emerged as the Mandate of Palestine after World War I, I frequently reference this in my work. And since Arabs and their academic and other cheerleaders bring up their tale of how Jews allegedly stole all of the land over and over again, I'm forced to repeatedly remind various audiences of the truth as well.

Colonial Secretary Winston Churchill convened the Cairo Conference in 1921. As a result of this and other machinations of the latest empire (the Brits') to acquire the land of the Jews—Judaea—since the fall of the latter to Hadrian's Roman armies in 135 C.E., Britain's Hashemite Arab allies were awarded all of the original 1920 Mandate of Palestine east of the Jordan River—almost 80 percent of the total area—in 1922.

As we noted earlier, Transjordan's King Abdullah attributed this gift to an act of Allah in his memoirs. Along with other observers, Sir Alec Kirkbride, the Brits' east bank (of the Jordan River) rep, had much to say about this as well in *A Crackle of Thorns*.

Not long afterwards, Abdullah's brother, Emir Faisal, was gifted with all of the Mandate of Mesopotamia—renamed Iraq. Millions of Kurds thus saw their own best chance at independence shattered on behalf of Arab nationalism and British petroleum politics as well.[156]

The Ottoman Turkish Empire had ruled most of the region. And again, most of those above invading and other "Arab" states had, in turn, become Arab by the conquest, subjugation, and forced Arabization of millions of native peoples who survived earlier jihads in the wars of the Dar ul-Islam against the Dar al-Harb.

Similar stories could be told all over the region, millions of native, non-Arab peoples, within the power vacuum created by the collapse of empire, seeing their own hopes for freedom and independence in the new nationalist age swept away on behalf of the Arab nation. Some later fought alongside Arabs against the Mandatory Powers. It did them little good after the French and the British left the scene, however.

From Egypt, through North Africa into the Sudan, to Lebanon, Iraqi, Syrian

Kurdistan, and elsewhere, scores of millions have all been forced to consent to this forced Arabization process. Some took to it to gain from their association with their conquerors, many, if not most, did not.

Recall that Egypt's most famous native "Uncle Tom" Copt, the late President Sadat's foreign minister, Dr. Boutros Boutros Ghali, basically summed it up for Israel (as well as all others) in an interview with an Israeli author. Paraphrasing Amos Elon in *Flight into Egypt*, Ghali instructed, *If you want to be accepted in the neighborhood, you have to consent to Arabization.*[157]

From post-1922 up to the current day, therefore, the question has not been about Arabs achieving statehood in Palestine, but about Arabs getting a second state for themselves in what was left of the original 1920 Palestine Mandate after the creation of Transjordan in 1922 from the lion's share of the land, the Arabs' twenty-second in total spread out over six million square miles of territory.

Back to the United Nations.

In 1947, another partition plan was presented that would have divided the roughly 20 percent of the Mandate of Palestine left after the creation of Transjordan in half between Jews and Arabs.

Had Arabs accepted this, they would have wound up with some 90 percent of the total original area, quite a different story than you'll hear when Arabs and their assorted stooges explain how Jews stole most of the land.

They rejected this offer on the grounds that all the territory was part of the Dar ul-Islam and/or their "purely Arab patrimony." The rest is history.

Some things change; others never do. Israel's fight with Hamas, Fatah, and others today is the same as it was back then.

Back to May, 1948.

The UN watched its newest reborn babe brutally attacked upon birth. It did nothing to stop the onslaught and only finally stepped in after the Jews turned the tide of the battle.

Afraid that the Jews would push the Arabs back even further and take more of the non-apportioned territory of the Mandate, the UN finally acted. Keep in mind that these were not "purely Arab" territories.

The armistice lines drawn up by the UN in 1949 simply marked the point where hostilities were stopped.

As we have seen, they left Israel extremely vulnerable with a very narrow strategic waist where most of its population and industry are located. Many people travel farther than that just to go to work. It should not be a surprise, therefore, that these became known as the Auschwitz Lines—a constant invitation to Arabs to attack and a recipe for a second Holocaust. With few exceptions, the lines were never expected to be Israel's real political borders but transition steps along the way as peace evolved in the region.

Recall that as a result of its 1948 assault, Arab Transjordan grabbed the non-apportioned west bank of the Jordan River (where both Jews and Arabs had roots, owned land, and were allowed to live). Holding both banks, the Emirate changed its name to Jordan (since it now held territory from other parts of the Mandate besides those *across* the river)—and made all the land it now held *Judenrein*—including east Jerusalem. Numerous age-old synagogues were destroyed, ancient Jewish tombstones were used to pave roads, build latrines, and so forth.[158]

While Jordan thus emerged above, Pharaoh reincarnated—who had used Gaza to invade the land of the Jews for thousands of years before—once again grabbed that coastal strip.

Recall that during the time Jordan and Egypt held Gaza and the West Bank—almost two decades—no one demanded the birth of the Arabs' second state in Palestine in those areas. Not a peep from the United Nations, either.

As another result of the Arab attempt to nip a microscopic, resurrected Israel in the bud, two refugee situations were created, another point that needs to be reemphasized constantly. The Arabs have continued to this day to thrust the plight of their own refugees—created primarily as a result of their own actions—into everyone else's faces—people who were pawns (willingly or unwillingly) of the Arabs' own murderous schemes that backfired. They call this their *Nakba*—catastrophe.

Scores of millions of non-Arab peoples also became refugees as a result of wars over the last century or so. Yet the folkswho have received the most aid and who have deserved it the least—the Arabs—have become the biggest whiners.

When your "catastrophe" is the result of your own largely self-inflicted, self-centered, genocidal schemes to deny all others even a tiny slice of the same justice you demand for yourself, please pardon me if my tears remain reserved for the scores of millions of subjugated, intimidated, Arab victims—Jews, Kurds, black Africans, Assyrians, Copts, Imazhigen/Berbers, and so forth—instead.

Arab refugees, right from the start, were made virtual wards of the world—unlike all the others above. The United Nations Relief Works Agency (UNRWA), whose spokesmen readily vilify Israel, was created just to cater to these folks—many, if not most, of whom were newcomers themselves entering into the land because of its economic development by the Jews.

Recall that so many Arabs were recent arrivals themselves into the Palestinian Mandate that UNRWA had to adjust the very definition of "refugee" from its prior meaning of persons normally and traditionally resident to those who lived in the Mandate for a minimum of only two years prior to 1948.

Now, keep in mind that for every Arab who was forced to flee the fighting that Arabs started (after all, how dare Jews want in one tiny, resurrected state what Arabs demand for themselves in some two dozen others), a Jewish refugee was forced to flee "Arab"/Muslim lands into Israel and elsewhere but with no UNRWA set up to assist them.

Again, why not?

UNRWA has been openly hostile to Israel from the get-go. It has long allowed the promotion of anti-Western and anti-Semitic attitudes among the Arabs it serves and has done little to help solve the problem of their refugee status—unless giving shelter and employment to those who would terrorize and destroy their Jewish neighbor counts in his regard.[159]

Before Israel's later rounds of fighting in Gaza, back in 2004, UNRWA Commissioner-General Peter Hansen told the Canadian Broadcasting Company, "I am sure that there are Hamas members on the UNRWA payroll and I don't see that as a crime."[160]

Solid evidence and documentation obtained from Arabs on the spot have revealed that UNRWA has turned a blind eye to Arabs setting up mortar and rocket firing positions adjacent to UN schools, hospitals, private homes, and so forth. Additionally, in that late 2008 round, Israel had solid intelligence that Hamas leaders were hiding in the basement of such a hospital.

Similarly, when Israel was forced to go after Hizbullah in Lebanon in 2006, it turned out that the UN force there, UNIFIL, not only did not prevent attacks on Israel but allowed Hizbullah to set up its positions right next to UNIFIL units. After a UN position got hit as a result, pictures made the rounds showing just such a Hizbullah position right next to a UN building. Solid evidence also surfaced that UNIFIL members collaborated with Hizbullah to enable the kidnapping of Israeli troops from inside Israel proper—the move that started that war in the first place.[161]

Ahhh, the United Nations. Nice to know where hundreds of millions of American tax dollars have been going, isn't it?

Turning the clock back again, from 1948 to 1956, Israel was attacked repeatedly by Arabs using Egyptian and Jordanian territories as their bases. In 1956, when Egypt blockaded it at the Strait of Tiran, Israel struck back hard. France and Great Britain were peeved at Egypt's Nasser as well for nationalizing the Suez Canal, so the time was ripe.

In a lightening assault, Israel soon found itself on the banks of the Suez Canal.

Before Western pressure forced it to withdraw—note the inaction of the UN to stop Arab attacks on Israel and so forth, which provoked the Sinai Campaign (sound familiar? 1948 all over again)—Israel's David Ben-Gurion received assurances that if Egypt ever played the same blockade game again, it would be recognized as a *casus belli*. This would become very important, once again, in the not-too-distant future.[162] A United Nations emergency force was also set up in Gaza and at the Strait of Tiran to supposedly prevent such happenings again.

So, tell me please, as has been noted before, what good is a fireman who, at the first smell of smoke, disappears from sight?

In spring 1967, Egypt's President Nasser must have been all sugared up once again. Pharaoh amassed one hundred thousand troops, but instead of chariots, he positioned planes, tanks, artillery, and so forth on Israel's border, reinstated the blockade, and ordered the UN force out of Gaza so his tank divisions would have an open door.

Without a wink, the UN turned tail and ran—leaving Israel (say it with me) all on its own.

Nasser, meanwhile, got other Arab nations to jump aboard his own latter-day *Final Solution* bandwagon as well. While Syria was up to its eyeballs in this right from the start, others—like Jordan's young King Hussein—had to be lured into this a bit later.

Big mistake.

Well, as you probably know (although not you younger readers), things didn't quite turn out as Arabs planned. In six days in June 1967, Israel destroyed several Arab air forces, left hundreds of their tanks smoldering, took thousands of prisoners, and so forth. Remember Ben-Gurion's *casus belli* deal in 1956 regarding any renewal of blockade?

Oh, yes—I almost forgot. Israel also now found itself holding all of the Sinai Peninsula (in which it developed oil fields, established important air bases, and at last gained a little strategic depth) up to the Suez Canal; in control of the strait from which it had been repeatedly blockaded; on top of the Golan Heights, from which its farm villages and fishermen on the Sea of Galilee had been repeatedly attacked; in Gaza; and back in Judea and Samaria—the West Bank, from which all Jews were either previously slaughtered or later excluded from as a result of Transjordan's land grab in 1948. Places like Hebron—where the Hebrew patriarchs and some of the matriarchs are buried—and elsewhere once again saw Jews.

And in a rare moment (divine guidance?), something else next happened that proved not to be par for the UN's usual course. After much argument, and thanks to America and Great Britain—folks who also opposed Israel in the past—the final draft of the UN document, UNSC Resolution 242, which dealt with any future Israeli withdrawal, was worded in a precise way that called for the creation of secure and real borders to replace Israel's '49 Auschwitz lines. It also allowed for a necessary revision of those borders in order to undo—somewhat at least—the travesty of the '49 UN-imposed lines.

Let's take another look at these already footnoted quotes.

Here's Britain's Lord Caradon on 242: "It would have been wrong to demand that Israel return to its positions of June 4, 1967, because those positions were undesirable and artificial. After all, they were just the places where the soldiers of each side happened to be on the day the fighting stopped in 1948. They were just armistice lines. That's why we didn't demand that the Israelis return to them."

President Ronald Reagan said on, September 1, 1982, "In the pre-1967 borders, Israel was barely ten-miles wide. The bulk of Israel's population within artillery range of hostile armies. I am not about to ask Israel to live that way again."

Regardless of the renewed pressure already accompanying the new American administration, Israel must insist upon those territorial adjustments it was allowed in order to right a historical wrong. A fair compromise must be demanded by Israel's own new leaders, regardless of what President Obama may have in mind to appease his still-rejectionist Arab buddies.

The State Department opposed Israel's creation from the start and has been hostile ever since. Expect more of the same, if not worse, coming from the Foggy Folks with the Obama administration.

The Jews the new president appoints to work with him are mostly as reassuring on this matter as James Baker's stick-it-to-the-Jew-of-the-Nations "Jew Boys" were before—a good shield to deflect criticism later from Jews who really care (no matter how many Passover Seders he sets up and Holocaust speeches he makes for show). Sympathy for dead Jews needs to be replaced with a sense of fair play and empathy for live ones.

I truly hope I'm wrong here. I would love to have to apologize later on. But, recall that the new president had already sent his well-known, anti-Israel friend and special envoy, Robert Malley (raised in a family of anti-Zionists and communists who counted Yasir Arafat as a close friend), to Lebanon's slave master and Iran's best buddy, Syria, before he even took the oath of office.

Now, again, pray tell, what might that have been all about?

Decades ago, Israel had already offered a retreat from well over 90 percent of the Golan Heights to Syria in return for a true peace.

'Twasn't good enough for Iraq's Saddam Hussein's twin butchers in Damascus, the Assad boys—neither papa nor junior. So, guess who and what will be offered up to try to wean Syria away from Iran? The same folks whose arms are going to be twisted even more than they already were by Dr. Condoleezza Rice & Co. to believe that Mahmoud Abbas's latter-day Arafatian Fatahniks are really the good cops in the good cop/bad cop game set up to get Israel to swallow the medicine. After all, President Bush had already begun arming, training, funding, and otherwise supporting those alleged doves of peace. And now the new American leader has pushed this into high gear.

Trust me, Jew of the Nations, to such folks you should give away the store and bare the necks of your kids.

With a final return (for now) to the United Nations, let's just say that with Arab genocidal actions being/having been waged against millions of Kurds and black Africans, and Arab murder and subjugation being waged against millions of Copts, Jews, Imazighen/Berbers, and others, the only thing that the United Nations seems capable of doing is vilifying Israel for its determination and imperfect attempts to survive in an imperfect world and defend itself despite the United Nations' indifference. Indeed, most of all of the latter's official condemnations have been aimed solely at Israel.

Perhaps it is time for the Israeli people to seriously consider withdrawing from the United Nauseating Nations or, at the very least, make sure that they support their own newly-elected leaders, insisting that they stand their ground and demand the fair territorial compromises Israel is entitled to and must have, regardless of who is tightening the screws.

Chapter 33

THE SAUDI "PEACE" (OF THE GRAVE) PLAN: AN OFFER ISRAEL MUST REFUSE

ACCORDING TO A *Times of London* story on November 16, 2008, then-President-elect Obama stated that Israel would be crazy not to accept the resurrected Saudi "peace" plan. He since has repeated this and is moving toward increasing the pressure on Israel to accept this alleged Arab bargain. Earlier, President Bush and Secretary of State Rice were trying very hard to force this November Thanksgiving turkey down Israel's throat as well.

Earlier still, a stop along President Bush's Middle East trip—after again pressuring Jews to further accept his vision of Abbas's latter-day terrorist Arafatians as being the good cops—took President Bush to the sands of the Saudis and other Arabian Peninsula nations. A photo was published worldwide of the president wielding a sword along with Bahraini hosts, and President Bush brought along a New Year's present—tens of billions of dollars in military aid. *Hey, if we don't sell it to them, the Brits, Germans, French, and so forth certainly will,* or so goes the argument.

During that visit, Bush asked if perhaps the Arabs might reach out to Israel a bit more. Saudi King Abdullah responded that he didn't know what else he could do. After all, he came up with his own "peace" (of the grave) plan some time ago, the one President Obama now claims Israel would be nuts to reject. Here's the Saudi plan in a nutshell: if Israel (and not a Jewish Israel) "merely" agrees to return to its pre-'67, nine-mile-wide, '49 armistice line—not border—existence, and then consents to being swamped by millions of alleged "returning" jihadist refugees (many, if not most, of whom were newcomers to the Mandate themselves, and their descendants) created because the Arab attempt to nip a reborn Israel in the bud backfired, along with everything else that the Arabs demand for the Jewish state's suicide, then the Saudis and other Arabs might normalize relations with Israel.

Gosh. Such a deal! (Not!)

Again, the above is the plan that President Obama considers to be an offer that Israel simply cannot refuse and intends to force it to accept at the price of G_d only knows what, but I can guess. Of late, as we discussed earlier, Mr. Obama speaks about some possible modifications to the Saudi plan—but Arabs have repeatedly said they would have nothing to do with such changes, and the president knows this quite well. Let's see. I'd love to be able to say I worried over nothing.

Of course, American leaders would accept such a plan for America given similar circumstances (yeah, right). What's even more sickening is that they get stuck-in-the-ghetto-minded Uncle Abe (instead of Uncle Tom) Jews like Ehud Olmert and Shimon Peres (and too many of their American brethren) to sing praises to it as well.

The Desert Kingdom has long gotten away with a virtual free pass from America and most of the rest of the world. The same folks—including academics and others who should know better—who routinely scrutinize Israel and the actions it is forced to take merely to survive act deaf, dumb, and blind when it comes to the Saudis and too many other Arabs controlling much of the world's oil and influencing many other petrodollar-connected, multi-national corporations as well as foreign policy and academia in the process. Together, this power and influence—via their many tentacles and manifestations—make the much spoken about "Zionist lobby" look less than pitiful.

Years back, when I was a card-carrying member of the London-based Anti-Slavery Society, persistent reports spoke of slavery throughout Arab lands, in the oil fields, and other places as well. It was still "above ground" on the Arabian Peninsula up until the latter part of the twentieth century.[163] But it was all treated as though it did not exist. Have you ever noticed the many black Saudis and other Arabs? Guess who and what their mothers mostly were? The Sudan, as just one example, is, to this day, a ready source of black slaves courtesy of the Arab/Arabized north.

What else can the Saudis do to reach out to the Jews? Here are some suggestions. On President Bush's trip, he pledged some twenty billion dollars in state-of-the-art aircraft, missiles, bombs, and so forth to the Saudis, supposedly to bolster them against the Iranian bogeyman.

The problem is, despite all of those Arabs prancing around with their swords, each time they were threatened—by fellow Arabs like Saddam or the Iranians—America had to save them with our own blood and money anyway, despite billions of dollars in military aid given previously. Not to mention the Saudis' gift to America of most of the suicide/homicide bombers of 9/11.

Previous sophisticated weaponry and aircraft that the Saudis pledged to place to face the Iranian threat were stationed a stone's throw from Israel instead. Indeed, they have been expanding the King Faisal Air Base at Tabuk. Prior to Bush's new holiday gift, the base contained about fifty advanced F-15 fighter-jets, which were sent to the northwestern facility on the eve of the U.S.-led war against Iraq in March 2003. Other promises related to those sales later proved to be worthless as well.[164]

So much for past and future similar Arab guarantees. What else could the Saudis do for Israel? How about honoring the pledges above, for starters?

The Protocols of the Learned Elders of Zion is perhaps one of the most flagrantly anti-Semitic doctrines ever written. Guess who was one of the latter-day leaders in endorsing and spreading it around?

While the Saudis aren't the only Arabs still doing this sort of hate-spreading stuff ("peaceful" Egypt still freely indulges), ending such practices is another suggestion for *what else*, as is ending dehumanizing *kilab yahud*—Jew dogs—even further by routinely also calling them sons of apes and pigs. Extend this further by revising the textbooks of Arab children, hatred in the media, sermons, and so forth that routinely demonize Jews and Israel, and an Arab "peace" plan might become more believable.[165]

Since America is poised to force a *Pax Saudia* on Israel, are you ready for more?

Israel was squeezed by President Clinton at Camp David and Taba to cave in to Arafat and abandon its right to defensible "secure and recognized" borders instead of pre-'67 Auschwitz/armistice lines à la resolution 242. While Arafat rejected the plan, it became the new starting point for President Bush's subsequent Annapolis travesty. With numerous anti-Israel friends and advisors, and given his own predilections, it is now President Obama's as well.

During the era of Clinton's "Oslo Peace" in the 1990s, following that forced handshake between Arafat and Israel's Yitzhak Rabin, the more Israel tangibly conceded to Arabs, the more it bled.[166]

Guess who was paying Arab families tens of thousands of dollars each for having a *shahid* member blow up Jewish kids in teen night clubs, buses, pizzerias, and so forth during the intifada (conducted under Arafat and Abbas's Fatah good cops' watch—not that of Hamas's bad cops)? Maybe Saudi despots, who condemn women victims of rape to hundreds of lashes and humiliation, could revise their policy here also.

The Saudis, like other Arabs, are always quick to claim the whole region as solely Arab land. Hence their additional concern about Iranians and others who call that body of water in the north the Persian Gulf instead of the Arabian Gulf. More than just words are involved here.

Since Arabs claim all that they acquired after Muhammad and successor Caliphal armies burst out of the Arabian Peninsula in the seventh century c.e., conquering and forcibly Arabized millions of non-Arab peoples and their lands, and then rejected the rights of Jews (one half in Israel who were refugees from "Arab"/Muslim lands), Kurds, Imazhigen/Berbers, black Africans, and so forth in a later age of nationalism to some resurrected political rights of their own, perhaps the Saudis need to be reminded of another time period in what is now their own country.

As I have written elsewhere, when Muhammad, the prophet of Islam, fled enemies in Mecca to Medina in 622 C.E. (the Hijrah), the inhabitants welcomed him. Medina had been developed centuries earlier as a thriving date palm oasis by Jews fleeing the Roman assault on Judaea (the banu-Qurayzah and banu-al-Nadir tribes, and so forth). Medina's mixed population of Jews and pagan Arabs opened their doors to the future prophet of Islam.

Muhammad learned much from the Jews. During his long sojourn with the Jews of Medina, his followers were instructed to pray toward Jerusalem. Early prominent Arab historians such as Jalaluddin came right out and openly stated that this was done as an attempt to win support among influential Jewish tribes (the "People of the Book") for Muhammad's religio-political claims. Contemporary scholars concur.[167]

It is from the Temple Mount in Jerusalem (which Arabs claim Jews have no connection to—including President Obama's good buddy, Mahmoud Abbas) that Muslims believe Muhammad ascended to heaven on his winged horse. A mosque, the Dome of the Rock, would later be erected on this Jewish holy site after the Arab imperialist Caliphal conquest of the land in the seventh century C.E.

Arab imperialism? *Shhh.*

Only nasty Zionists and Crusader Westerners do that stuff—don'tcha know? Just ask your all-too-typical Middle East Studies Association (MESA) professor of history, Middle Eastern studies, or political science these days. Or don't—if you intend to pursue an academic career.

There is no doubt that Jews had an enormous impact on both Muhammad and his new religion. The holy sites for Muslims in Jerusalem (i.e. the mosques erected on the Temple Mount of the Jews) are now deemed "holy" precisely because of the critical years Muhammad spent after the Hijrah with the Jews.

As politically incorrect as it might sound, the Temple Mount of the Jews simply had no prior meaning to pagan Arabs.

While there was some early Christian influence, intense scholarship has shown that the holy Law (Halakha) and holy Scriptures of the Jews had a tremendous influence on the Quran, Islamic holy law (Shari'a), and so forth.

Muhammad's Jerusalem connection was most likely not established until after his extended stay with his Jewish hosts. This was no mere coincidence.

When the Jews refused to recognize Muhammad as the chief political and religious honcho, he turned on them with a bloody vengeance. Before long, with the exception of Yemen, there were virtually no Jews left on the Arabian

Peninsula. And the direction of prayer was changed away from Jerusalem and toward the Kaaba in Mecca instead.

Now, imagine, since Arabs claim all of Israel because of their previous conquests, that descendants of Arabian Jews staked their own claims as well? How about declaring Medina as a Jewish city?

Certainly, when demands by Arabs for compensation and the like regarding Arab refugees come to the front burner, Jewish refugees from "Arab" lands—who number more and who left behind far more property and financial assets than their Arab counterparts did due to a war that Arabs themselves started—need to put forth their own demands and need to be backed by an Israeli government that will state unambiguously that there will be no fulfillment of the one claim without the other.

What else can the Saudis and other Arabs do to convince Jews that the alleged Saudi "peace" plan now being promoted is indeed not simply a Trojan horse peace of the grave?

As I've pointed out often before, the solution to the Arab/Israeli mess is not as complicated as many others have claimed.

When enemies make peace, they truly negotiate so that a real compromise, meeting the needs of both parties, is at least somewhat achieved. One party doesn't simply just offer a take-it-or-leave-it ultimatum like Abbas & Co. are now doing.

The Arab game plan is, in reality, simply a ploy to force Israel to yield in "diplomacy" what hundreds of millions of Arabs have not been able to achieve on the battlefield.

Seen as a starting point for further negotiations, not a take it or leave it gimmick, the Saudi plan might actually have some value.

Getting rid of the plan's stipulation requiring Jews to allow their sole state to be swamped by allegedly returning Arab jihadis raised on Jew-hatred is a must, as just one example. Keep in mind that more Jews fled Arab/Muslim lands as refugees in a war Arabs started than Arabs who fled in the opposite direction.

As is deliberately re-emphasized in this book, if Arabs really want to reach out to Jews and others in the region (which they don't), all they have to do is grant them a tiny portion of the same rights they demand for themselves.

The day Arabs can, at long last, get themselves to do this, they will find an Israel bending over backwards, sideways, and forwards to be a good neighbor—and to the entire region's benefit as well.

Chapter 34

AHMADINEJAD—LIAR, HYPOCRITE, OR JUST ISLAMIST IRANIAN STOOGE?

As we have already read, upon the death of Islam's Prophet, Muhammad, in the early seventh century c.e., the armies of his Caliphal successors burst out of the Arabian Peninsula and spread out in all directions.

Over the next centuries—and continuing to this very day—Arab colonialism and imperial jihadi conquests would either directly or indirectly forcibly Arabize millions of native non-Arab peoples.

As just a few examples of this lingering ordeal, in Syria, Kurdish children are currently forced to sing praises to their "Arab" identity while not being allowed to even speak their own native tongue; millions of black Africans (not only Sudanese) have been killed, enslaved, and so forth in the name of the Arab nation; prominent Copts in Egypt have advised Israel to consent to the same Arabization they have been forced to undergo in order to "be accepted;" Imazhigen/Berbers have been slaughtered for asserting their own identity; and so forth. All of this has been noted already.

And, again, you'll hear none of the above in your typical college classroom taught by your MESA "expert" who will be too busy condemning Israel's security fence and checkpoints for inconveniencing Arabs who want to blow Jewish kids apart instead.

Get the picture?

But before we leave this thought, keep one other key example in mind.

Iran's president, Mahmoud Ahmadinejad, has repeatedly called on Europe to make a place for Israel's Jews. He, like Arab and other Iranian leaders, calls for Israel's destruction and actively participates—via supplying arms and support to Arab terror organizations and states—in trying to accomplish this even before Iran becomes a nuclear power.

It seems that the Iranians—who at least partially jumped on the Arab bandwagon centuries ago—have also bought into the Arab delusion, at least when it fits their own needs.

So, Ahmadinejad simply ignores one-half of Israel's six million Jews who know nothing of "Europe" as a home. They are from Jewish refugee families who fled what Arabs refer to as "purely Arab patrimony," where, despite Arab claims of tolerance, they were commonly known as *kilab yahud*—Jew dogs—

and treated as such. An additional million or more of these Jews who fled Arab murder and subjugation live in France, the Americas, and elsewhere.

Iran itself, Muslim but not Arab (like points east through Pakistan into India and beyond—courtesy of earlier Arab jihads), was the home of more than six thousand Jews who now live just in New York. Hundreds of thousands of other Iranian Jews now live elsewhere, many in Hollywood, California.

Iran's Jewish community dates back over 2,500 years—at least since the days when Cyrus liberated them from Babylonian captivity. The Jewish holiday of Purim, recorded in the Bible's Book of Esther, is about Ahmadinejad's alleged "European" Jewish community.

Iran supported Judaea's fight for independence against Rome some two thousand years ago, and on the eve of the Arab conquest itself in the seventh century C.E., an army of tens of thousands of Jews was recorded to have allied themselves to Persian armies fighting the hated Byzantines.[168]

Today, with Jews intimidated, tried as spies for Israel, and the like, there are fewer than twenty thousand Jews remaining in Iran itself.

Lots more could be elaborated upon here on this subject. Suffice it to say that Ahmadinejad and Iran have simply used the Arab (and others') ploy of denial to further their own national interests.

So, he sees no Jews native to the region in his midst. They're all simply European transplants. The Tunisian Jewish professor, Albert Memmi, is an important source for all of this. His book *Jews and Arabs* is still must reading for anyone wanting to get a sense of balance here. But I've jumped ahead a bit, so let's return now to how this lie has been perpetuated.

In the wake of their own imperial conquests and colonization of the region, the very definition of *Arab* appears to have been deliberately muddied so to allow for the Arabs to claim the whole region for themselves.

Thus, the children of Arab fathers, all Arabic speakers, and any who simply wish for convenience's sake—i.e., among other things, to escape taxation and subjugation—to identify themselves as such are declared to be as "Arab" as the Arabs who conquered and colonized them in the first place from the Arabian Peninsula.

Take a good look at the "Arab" militias committing atrocities against blacks in the Sudan. See if you notice any racial differences between victim and victimizer. Yet, to the true Arab, black skin is enough for you to be regarded as *'abd*—slave—whatever delusions you may have about your own identity.

Indeed, in a televised interview (courtesy of the highly respected Middle East Media Research Institute) with Abd Al-Bari 'Atwan, editor-in-chief of the London daily, *Al-Quds Al-Arabi*, which aired on BBC Arabic TV on November

7, 2008, the latter stated that in any Arab country, the new American president would be called a slave.[169]

We currently speak of twenty-one "Arab" states—where Arab identity is professed in constitutions and so forth—allowing Arabs to live their deliberate, subjugating lie. The twenty-second expects to be born soon, and on the ashes of the Jews' sole, microscopic state—not as its long-term neighbor—regardless of what the Arabs' so-called *'abd* American president says.

Before the age of nationalism, where one empire after the other (including the Arabs' own Caliphal varieties) absorbed numerous different peoples, this had an imperfect unifying effect.

So, with Islam as its main unifying and driving force, Arabs could get non-Arabs like the great Kurdish leader Salah al-Din (Saladin) to jump on their bandwagon in furthering the Dar ul-Islam. Recall that these are the people whom Arabs would later massacre, gas, culturally subjugate, and so forth—fellow Muslims, mind you—for daring to assert their own identities and demand rights as such. Before Saddam's gassings in "Arab" Iraq, the Kurdish nationalist, Ismet Cherif Vanly wrote *The Syrian (Arab) "Mein Kampf" Against the Kurds*. The title of the book says it all—and it is going on today as well.

With the nineteenth-century reawakening of dormant ethnic/national identities accompanying the beginning of the collapse of major empires, Arabs saw themselves as sole heirs to most of a region ruled largely by the Turks for the previous five centuries. While diplomats would soon speak of Arabia for the Arabians, Judea for the Jews, Armenia for Armenians, and Kurdistan for Kurds, in Arab eyes, there could be no division of "their" pie. For most Arabs, there was no justice in the region other than Arab. And in relation to our discussion about Iran and Israel, it had all started this way.

The Arabian general Khaled ibn al-Walid conquered the land of Israel in 634 C.E. from the Byzantines, and not long afterwards, Abu Musa al-Ash'ari led the invasion of Iran from Basra via its current, oil-rich, southwestern Khuzestan province.

By Roman times, the land of Israel had been renamed Judaea. After the second revolt in 133–135 C.E., Hadrian got fed up with the Jews' persistence (and heavy Roman losses) and tried to stamp out their hopes for freedom once and for all. He renamed the land itself after the Jews' historic enemies, the Aegean sea people, the non-Semitic Philistines—*Syria Palaestina*. Prior to that time, the Greeks used that Philistine designation to denote the geographical coastal strip, not a country or people.

Like vultures wanting their share of the kill, some neighboring Arabs joined the Romans in their assault on the Jews.

Arabs like to claim that they were the aboriginals in the land. In reality, while the coastal region was indeed sometimes identified by the Greeks with Philistine invaders, there—again—was no country nor nation known as "Palestine," ever.

As we have also seen earlier, the land was known as Judaea, and its inhabitants were Judaeans, Jews. The Romans knew the difference between Arabs and Jews as well. Recall those earlier quotes from Rome's ancient hostorians.

So much for Arab "aboriginals." And remember that it was Ahmadinejad's own Muslim, but non-Arab, Iran that was the chief ally of the Jews in their fight for freedom against Rome.

Back to the future.

As we have seen, along with the Arab colonialization of Judaea/"Palestine" (along with many other places), Arabs spread into Iran as well.

While Khuzestan traded back and forth, it became basically linked to Iran despite repeated Arab invasions over the centuries from southern Iraq. But, despite this link, Khuzestan, according to the *Encyclopedia Iranica*, became "extensively Arabized" to the point that in Safavid times the province was known as Arabistan.

The Arabs have long remembered this, and Iraqi Arabs under Saddam Hussein's banner launched the long Iran-Iraq war in the 1980s, which was largely fought over this oil-rich and strategically important area.

Earlier, to deal with this problem, Iran ruthlessly suppressed any manifestations of Arab nationalism. By the early twentieth century, a proposal had been put forward to even outlaw the Arabic language.

Now think about this a minute. Like in Iran, Arabs entered the land of Israel/Judaea/Palestine as settlers, imperial conquerors, and colonizers. While this fact of life is true for other conquerors as well, Arabs only see in others what they themselves have truly perfected as they waged repeated murderous jihads and forcibly Arabized more than six million square miles of mostly other, non-Arab peoples' lands. That's why this point must be emphasized.

Recall that so many Arabs were recent arrivals themselves into the Palestinian Mandate that the UNRWA had to adjust the very definition of *refugee* from its prior meaning of persons normally and traditionally resident to those who lived in the Mandate for a minimum of only two years prior to 1948.

Recall earlier solid evidence provided for substantial Arab immigration into the Palestine Mandate.

Arab settlers and colonizers.

Now, we're all familiar with the Arab take on this, but how do Iranians like Ahmadinejad see the picture? Well, at any hint of unrest in Khuzestan/

Arabistan, Iran is quick to act in its own national interests—as it should. So, for example, when Khuzestani Arabs of the *Nahda* (renaissance) movement bombed Iranian targets in Ahwaz and elsewhere, Iran arrested thousands of Arabs and set out to "fix" the problem by any means necessary.[170]

While this is still going on as I write, keep in mind that Iranians are doing likewise to Kurds, Baluchis, and others as well who dare to assert their own political rights. Thousands have been killed as a result over the years in the name of Iranian nationalism.

So, this all begs the question, Why, in Ahmadinejad's eyes, is Israel supposed to consent to national suicide so Arab settlers and colonizers can have their twenty-second state and second one in Palestine at the expense of the Jews' lone one, but his own Arabistan and its six to eight million oppressed Arabs should not gain independence from Iran as well?

Moving on to another related issue, with Iran's continuously blatant threats to Israel's very existence with its advancing nuclear program and long range missile tests, the reality is that Iran is indeed playing with fire in its baiting of the Jews. Ahmadinejad and the mullahs may calculate that Iran can absorb what might be coming and for which they are indeed asking for by threatening Israel this way. But all peoples must take such threats seriously. And, in light of frequent past experiences over the millennia (Iran's and other Holocaust-deniers, such as President Obama's friend, Mahmoud Abbas, notwithstanding), especially Jews.

A few words of advice, however. If Israel is forced to act, this cannot be done halfway. Tit for tat will not work. The location of the Iranian nuclear facilities and its massive armed forces are just part of the problem.

Iran's Hizbullah proxies in southern Lebanon—armed to the teeth with tens of thousands of rockets and such courtesy of Iran and Syria—must be hit massively and simultaneously à la June 5th, 1967, when Israel took out multiple Arab air forces and such. The murderous, rejectionist leadership must be targeted there as well.

If this is not done, at the very least all of northern Israel will pay an unacceptable price. And Hizbullah has learned how to protect itself very well with concrete, underground bunkers, and the like, set up—of course—amid its human shield civilian population and such. None of this should be taken lightly, and it isn't, I'm sure. One could hope that saner minds in Iran will take control of the situation.

Not that long ago, after all, during the days of the late Shah, Jews had it much better. This was true for much of Iran's history after the spread of Islam; ups and downs often according to whether the mullahs or the shahs were calling the shots.

While Israel's close relationship with the Pahlavis may have complicated matters—and why shouldn't Israel have sought friends in the region, since the Shah, with all of his imperfections, was no more despotic than anything the Arabs or Iran's own mullahs have to offer?—there still might be hope for a better tomorrow, considering the Jews' millennial relationship with the Iranian people.

Yet Israel can't simply wait for hope to materialize into something better. In the meantime, while Ahmadinejad and others try to cover their own rejectionist hatred with lame excuses, please remember them for the liars, hypocrites, and/or Arab Islamic stooges they are. As advised earlier in this book, when you hear Iranians complain about "Palestine," be sure to answer them with *Arabistan*.

Chapter 35

RIGHT CONCEPT, FLAWED
ANALOGY, DONE PURPOSELY

SPEAKING BEFORE A special session of Israel's Parliament in honor of the sixtieth anniversary of the resurrection of the Jewish state in 2008, President George W. Bush stressed the idea that appeasement does not work.

He used the example of Hitler's attack on Poland in 1939, which ushered in World War II in Europe, and the words of an American senator who expressed that if he'd only had the chance to chat with Hitler, things might have been different.

Another time, another place, perhaps Bush's words would have sounded more sincere and had more meaning.

Iran, North Korea, Syria, and other aggressive dictatorships must indeed be confronted unabashedly—much better than the world is doing right now. Witness the pitiful response to what is still happening to those who truly sought independence for Lebanon from its Syrian slave masters.

But this was the wrong analogy for the president to bring up before the Knesset.

You don't have to be the best student of history to know what the appropriate analogy was/is regarding Israel and those who would see her destroyed. Many of us have written about it, and the president had undoubtedly seen or heard of this more accurate comparison one way or another himself. So, why bring up the subject—appeasement—at all if you choose to ignore your own advice?

Judea (land of the Jews) and Samaria are roughly Israel's current version of 1938 Czechoslovakia's Sudetenland. They have thousands of years of Jewish history and presence connected to them—including in modern times, until the Arab massacres.

Forced expulsions, forced conversions, horrendous wars, repeated conquests, and such took their tolls, but until the 1920s and 1930s—and after 1948, when Transjordan created itself in 1922 from the lions' share of the original 1920 Palestine Mandate on the east bank, grabbed Judea and Samaria (the "West Bank") and made it *Judenrein*—the Jews never renounced their claims.

The Arabs themselves ruled, colonized, and settled the land earlier after their own imperial armies burst out of the Arabian Peninsula in the seventh century C.E. and spread in all directions, conquering and forcibly Arabizing (going on to this very day) millions of non-Arab peoples and spreading the Dar ul-Islam as well. Those who did not consent were slaughtered.

The two Arab Caliphal empires based in Damascus and Baghdad had replaced the Byzantine Empire, which had succeeded that of the Romans. And there were others later on in between as well. The last of Israel's imperial conquerors were Turks, who ruled for over four centuries prior to the Brits' victory in World War I.

The land was thus conquered by a series of imperial powers upon the fall of Israel/Judea to Rome.

Towns such as Bethlehem, Hebron, Bethel, Shechem, Jericho, Gilboa, and so forth should ring a bell.

So, given all of the above, here's the real analogy both the past and the current American president and State Department deliberately ignore. After World War I, the Austro-Hungarian Empire was defeated and fell apart. Among the various peoples yearning to gain political freedom were Czechs and Slovaks, bringing about a very imperfect—but necessary—union (until relatively recently) for the good of both. Czechoslovakia was thus created in 1918. While other peoples also lived in various parts of the new country, those other folks (especially Germans and Poles) already had ethnic national homelands of their own.

But the fact that many ethnic Germans had earlier spread elsewhere within the Austro-Hungarian Empire would come back to haunt the new nation. Much of its Bohemian and Moravian border regions—the Sudetenland in German—was populated by ethnic Germans. Furthermore, much of the area's important industry was controlled by them as well.

Indeed, Czechoslovakia was constantly plagued by problems involving its large number of Sudeten Germans who had "other plans." After Hitler annexed Austria in 1938 in the *Anschluss*, he turned to other "German" areas as well.

As is well known, by threatening war in September 1938, Hitler cowed Czechoslovakia's "friends" to force it to agree to give up its rich and strategically important Sudetenland to the Nazis—with Britain's prime minister, Neville Chamberlain, claiming in Munich that he had thus gained "peace for our time." Czechs were expelled from the border regions in their own country. The irony is that the Czechs had a good army, and, backed by the Allies, could have put up a good fight. They were shafted instead.

Now, *that*, friends, is appeasement.

Before long, Hitler grabbed what was left of Czechoslovakia, bombed Poland, and the world was at war again anyway. So, once more, why did President Bush, while addressing the Knesset—with the whole world watching—skip over this and begin his lesson with Poland instead? Why? Because the real analogy President Bush should have referred to in the Knesset stinks to high heaven. Just substitute Judea and Samaria (the West Bank) for the Sudetenland, and you have another Munich sellout in the making. The parallels are breathtaking.

Yet, from the get-go, a hostile State Department—which rejected Israel's rebirth in the first place—has sought to force Israel to accept armistice lines artificially imposed upon it in 1949, which turned the nation of the Jews into a nine-mile wide rump state. As we have seen, those lines merely represented the points at which the combined Arab assault from about a half-dozen different countries was halted. They were mostly never meant to be Israel's political borders.

The State Department routinely employs hypocritical double standards, along with an absurd moral equivalency, and routinely acts in ways that endanger Israel's very existence. Unfortunately, America now has a new president who is evidently gung ho regarding the Foggy Folks' plans for Israel.

After Israel was once again forced to fight for its life in 1967, the Arab goal of annihilation backfired big time, and Israel ridded itself of those '49 Auschwitz lines. The only thing the latter temptation had achieved was to constantly invite yet more Arab aggression.

Remember, this conflict has never been about how big Israel is, but that Israel *is*.

Recall the comments of Lord Caradon, Under Secretary of State Eugene Rostow, and other architects of the final draft of UNSC Resolution 242 after the 1967 war explaining why Israel was not expected to return to the indefensible armistice lines of 1949 and was entitled to secure and real borders instead. Yet that is what the Obama administration evidently now is demanding.

So, the real reason President Bush left out that far more accurate model of appeasement—the '38 Munich travesty, the sacrifice of Czechoslovakia by its "friends"—at his Knesset presentation was because it is much too close to what America (Israel's best friend) has recently (and under President Obama, increasingly) been pressuring Israel to do unto itself.

As Hitler had designs far beyond a Czechoslovakian (but heavily ethnic German) Sudetenland in the past, if one currently believes that all the Arabs want is Gaza and the West Bank, I have not one but ten bridges to sell you. As the president was delivering his Knesset speech in Israel, Arabs were blasting Jews who were shopping in a mall in Ashkelon. A bit earlier, another Arab was massacring students in a yeshiva with weapons Secretary of State Rice insisted that the Jews provide for Abbas's "moderates" themselves.

Knowing full well that southern Israel got nothing but thousands of mortar and rocket attacks launched from Gaza in exchange for its full withdrawal, Secretary of State Rice & Co. (with Bush on again, off again) insisted, as does the new Obama team as well, that the same thing next happen to Tel Aviv, Jerusalem, and elsewhere in Israel's narrow waist (adjacent to Judea and Samaria), where most of its population lives. That, indeed, is the far-more-than-likely scenario if Israel caves in to what its "friends" have been pressuring it to do regarding the heavily Arab-populated West Bank—especially President Obama himself of late.

Any observer of this conflict with functioning neurons knows the post-'67 Arab destruction-in-stages game plan for Israel. They also know—by even the alleged Arab good cop's own words—that their *hudnas* (ceasefires) are only designed to gain strength and time in order to deliver the final blow later on down the road. Arafat called this tactic the "Peace of the Quraysh," copying what Muhammad did to his Meccan enemies some fourteen centuries ago. Abbas's Fatahniks are sweet-talking Arafatians in suits and have stated the same thing. Abbas, the moderate, ran on a platform for Israel's destruction—but by more "acceptable" means. Please recall—blown buses bring bad press.

Think about what Iran and Syria have done to Lebanon via supporting and arming Hizbullah and you'll get a glimpse at what's in store for a West Bank in which Israel has not been granted a meaningful territorial compromise, à la 242.

Israel's great air force won't do it any good when it has to bomb itself because there was no adequate buffer preventing a massive Arab invasion (as occurred in 1948 and was attempted later as well). And would America or any other sane nation permit enemies sworn to their destruction to set up missile bases and such within a stone's throw of their own borders and main population centers?

Who will stop Iran from doing this, as they've supplied Hizbullah and Hamas already?

Keep in mind that thirty-eight Israels fit into just President Bush's home state of Texas—not to mention a comparison to all of America. And while the president was indeed correct about appeasement, Israel must demand a more honest assessment from its best friend.

Chapter 36

PROCLAIM LIBERTY THROUGHOUT THE LAND—THE ISRAEL AID ISSUE

Proclaim liberty throughout all the land unto all the inhabitants thereof.

—*LEVITICUS 25:10, HEBREW BIBLE*

I AM A PROUD, fourth-generation Philadelphia boy. In the earlier portion of the last quarter of the nineteenth century, my great grandfather, Benjamin, eloped with his fourteen-year-old bride, Esther, married in Elkton, Maryland, and proceeded to sire my grandfather and more than a dozen of my grand uncles and aunts—Philly's famous (besides the steak sandwiches) Esther and Benjamin Honigman Family Circle.

My grandfather served in World War I and my dad in World War II. Dad later put in almost three decades with the Philadelphia Police Department, retiring as a lieutenant.

Now, let's begin.

I often hear folks complaining about all that aid we give to those Jews "over there." True, Israel has received two to three billion dollars in aid each year from us for some time now, about the same that Egypt receives. Not to mention the other Arab states. That aid is much appreciated, is largely returned to us via purchases in America, and comes with a big downside as well. Lately this has been manifested in the suicidal concessions recent American presidents (including the new one) and the State Department expect Israel to make to Mahmoud Abbas's alleged "good cops," who still refuse to recognize the Jewish state.

Please take a good look at the opening quote above from the Hebrew Bible, aka "Old Testament." That is also the inscription on the symbol of America's Revolution, the Liberty Bell, which sits within almost a stone's throw of where I was born in Philly.

There are no people who share—indeed, gave—the values Americans so cherish more than the Jews. Indeed, when Europeans arrived here, they saw America as the "New Zion." The all-American holiday, Thanksgiving, was modeled after the Hebrews' fall harvest festival, the holiday of Sukkot, the Feast of the Tabernacles.

Israel—the resurrected Jew of the Nations, as the Hebrew prophets foretold—is still a shining "light unto the nations" (as G_d wanted it to be, the definition of its choseness), with all of its human imperfections.

Compare it, for starters, using the same lenses of moral scrutiny to what's in its neighborhood (that leaves out the typical university classroom), and Israel truly shines. There are Arabs serving in Israel's parliament who openly side with other non-Israeli Arabs who call for Israel's literal extinction. Find the Arab or other Muslim country with freedom like that. "Arab" Syria's Kurds and "Arab" North Africa's Berbers are prevented from such things as speaking their own, non-Arab languages or naming their children non-Arab/Islamic names.

America helps Israel because it is in its own interests to do so—despite all the petrodollar connections, including those in the State Department and at the highest levels of government.

President George H. W. Bush and his appointed fellow petrodollar best buddy, James Baker III, supported Saddam Hussein in Iraq until the latter made his moves on that giant oil well known as Kuwait. Killing, gassing, and maiming hundreds of thousands of Kurds and dispatching others as well *made no nevermind* no nevermind prior to this. And yet, some proclaimed we went to war with Iraq to save the Jews. Again.

I am sure Israel felt this way when it was told by Bush I that it had to keep its hands tied behind its back while Saddam sucker punched it with about forty missiles aimed at Jewish civilian populations. Did anyone know then whether or not Saddam would have those warheads topped with biological or chemical materials he possessed? Had Israel responded back then, there likely would have been no need for Bush II's Iraq II.

And remember Bush and Baker's ire over Israel's taking out Saddam's nuclear reactor at Osirak in Operation Opera?

Decades earlier, like-minded bigots claimed that America fought World War II to "save the Jews."

Reality check.

Germany declared war on the United States on December 11, 1941, not vice-versa. We fought the war to save Europe—not Jews—and very likely ourselves afterwards. American bombers were given orders not to bomb Nazi Final Solution facilities or railway tracks leading to Auschwitz, while flying over them to get to the area's industrial targets. Jews fleeing Nazis were denied entry into America, while Nazi butchers like Dr. Mengele were aided by us to escape to South America and elsewhere, including to the United States.

The Jews' virtual "saint," President Franklin Delano Roosevelt, gave orders that had the United States send the German ocean liner, the *S.S. Saint Louis,* away from Florida. It was loaded with prominent German Jews trying to escape the Holocaust. Many, if not most, wound up dying in gas chambers and such. A movie, *The Voyage of the Damned*, would later be made about this.

So, let's cut the manure about America fighting to save Jews. Let's return to the aid issue.

The war in Iraq—whether you support it or not—costs America more, for the sake of Arabs, in one week than Israel gets in foreign assistance in one year. And we have been fighting in Iraq for years now.

America has already spent about seven hundred billion dollars for Iraq, with much more set to come. It would take Israel centuries to get this from America. And Israel does not ask for American blood, body parts, and souls to be shed on its behalf or to be bribed to display America's own values and democratic inclinations. How long will the latter last among Arabs after America's exit from Iraq?

Ironically, the one people in Iraq who better share those values—the Kurds—are the folks the James Baker types in the State Department are determined to shaft (again) on behalf of their Arab friends who want to be sure oil fields in Kurdish lands remain part of the "purely Arab patrimony."

Baker's law firm represents Saudi Arab interests in the United States—including defending them in a lawsuit filed by America's 9/11 victims.[171] Baker's law partner has been America's ambassador to Riyadh, and Bush II's Secretary of State Rice had an oil tanker named after her, and so forth. Egypt gets almost the same amount of aid as Israel, and many of the other overtly or covertly mostly despotic, anti-democratic Arab countries get bundles as well. Mind you, this does not count places like non-Arab, but Muslim, Afghanistan or Pakistan.

Together, Iraq and Afghanistan cost Americans about eight hundred billion dollars by the end of 2008. And what about the trillions of dollars America has given to Europe over the years? Why do the same folks who complain about America saving Jews not mention any of the above?

Having stated this, I believe that before even one cent in aid is given to anywhere else in the world, no American should be going to bed hungry, homeless, or worrying about their family going bankrupt due to health problems. We do need to take care of the homefront first—especially if we have this kind of money to spread around, including to those who hate us.

But, as with other topics discussed in this book, when the issue of American aid to Israel arises, fairness indeed demands that it be judged in the broader perspective.

Chapter 37

IF JEWS HAD ANY BRAINS, THEY'D BE CHRISTIANS.

Now, Don't Be Offended

ANN COULTER APPEARED on Donny Deutsch's CNBC television program, *The Big Idea*, in October 2007. While discussing her book, *If Democrats Had Any Brains, They'd Be Republicans*, she lectured her Jewish host that Jews needed to be "perfected." Explaining why Jews should just convert, Coulter responded to Deutsch's inquiry about her potential no Jews allowed position with, "No, we think we just want Jews to be perfected, as they say."[172]

Perfected...You know, like Ann and her fellow Christians.

Honest Ann—I commend her for stating age-old, traditional beliefs lifted right out of Christian Scripture—next was surprised that Donny seemed offended. I mean, after all, why can't those Jews see all the good Christian "love" brought them over the centuries—inquisitions, crusades, expulsions, blood libels, pogroms, forced ghettoization, humiliation, and a pattern of massacre.

Those Jews must be blind!

Precisely!

Coulter would not write the book hinted at above, *If Jews Had Brains, They Would Be Christians*, but best believe Ann thinks Jews are indeed stubborn and blind—things her own faith has taught for millennia. See Mel Gibson's movie if you're a doubter, where an androgynous devil incarnate runs amid "his children" crying for Jesus's blood. Once you dehumanize a people, anything done to them becomes acceptable.

Churches in Europe still have statues and pictures commemorating such things as Jews stabbing the Host of the Eucharist to allegedly "kill Jesus" again; a fallen Jewish princess with blinders over her eyes; Jews poisoning wells to cause plague; and so forth. Geoffrey Chaucer gives a fourteenth-century "account" of one of many infamous blood libels against Jews in "The Prioress' Tale" (Hugh of Lincoln) in his *Canterbury Tales*.[173] The first picture of a Jew in England is entitled, "Aaron, son of the Devil." And even the enlightened Michelangelo's sculpture of Moses has what most viewers will see as devil's horns coming from his head, regardless of alleged rays of light explanations.

Back to loving Ann. Coulter elaborated about how Judaism is just a religion of laws and how Jesus relieved the world of this burden. I guess she never heard, as just a few examples, of these paraphrases from the Hebrew Bible, aka the Old Testament:

- Offer Me not your vain sacrifices if you do not justice for the widow and the orphan;
- What does the Lord require of thee but to do justice, love mercy, and walk humbly with thy G_d
- Love thy neighbor as thyself
- Or the Hebraic demand that a portion of the field be set aside for the needy.

Since Ann rejects Hebraic laws, she must not like the Ten Commandments either. Yeah, Ann, there are laws. And there is Christianity's Canon Law and such, too. But the essence of Judaism is the G_d-inspired ethical faith exemplified in the above paraphrases. Jews must show love of G_d by how they act (*mitzvot*), not by just what they say or believe.

While the Coulter types typically talk of Judaism's "exclusivity" complex, in reality, it is just the opposite. It is Christianity that historically has claimed that it possessed the sole key to heaven, not Judaism.

I had mixed feelings about Coulter up until that show. There are things she says which I agree with. Some said that those disturbing comments were just more of Coulter's shtick. I cannot accept that. Ann is bright, and the offense that she dismissed outright or merely makes light of has a particularly bloody and tragic history behind it.

While Donny was baffled by Coulter's honesty, he was also pathetic in how he handled it. I cringed watching. But, perhaps by necessity. In medieval days, Christians put Jews and their religion on public display for ridicule. These were known as disputations, and Jewish leaders were summoned to defend some aspect of their religion.

As Ann lives in a country of more than three hundred million people, more than 90 percent self-described as Christians, and about five million Jews (maybe half of whom give a hoot), when she does such things as taking Deutsch to task on television, it rings an all-too-familiar tone, something Jews have heard and had to survive for centuries.

As the Jewish "defender" of his people and faith walked a delicate line in how he responded during disputations (his minority people could be damned if he "won" and damned if he "lost"), so Donny needed to keep his ratings up and not offend the offender—or his bosses and audience.

Many Jews know Christian theology well. I certainly do. But do Christians like Coulter ever ask themselves why Jews are "stubborn" or "blind" to the formers' attempts to force their "love"?

Perhaps a well-known ancient Roman historian can explain it for them. You see, when Rome persecuted Christians, it was largely because the only thing they knew about the latter was that their leader was crucified as a Jewish patriot against Roman oppression.

Remember the crown of thorns and "King of the Jews" mockery the Romans placed above Jesus' head on the cross, and so forth? Christians were seen as just another sect of Jews—those same folks who took on the mighty Roman Empire for more than a century for their freedom and independence.

Visit the Arch of Titus, standing tall in Rome to this very day, to see how Rome felt about its victory over the Jews. Jesus lived amidst all of this turmoil. In modern times, think of the Soviet conquest of Latvia, Hungary, and Lithuania, or the Nazi conquest of Poland, France, and so forth for an analogy. Should these conquered peoples not have yearned for worldly freedom? If so, then why have Jews been criticized for wanting the same thing over the millennia?

I suggest that Coulter & Co. take a look below to see one of the main reasons why Jews must reject Christianity's version of divine "truth." Once again, here is the Roman historian, Tacitus (Volume II, Book V), writing after Judaea, the tiny nation of the Jews, took on mighty Rome:

> The Jews acknowledge one God only, and conceive of him by the mind alone, condemning, as impious, all who, with perishable materials, wrought into the human shape, form representations of the Deity. That Being, they say, is above all, and everlasting, neither susceptible of likeness nor subject to decay. In consequence, they allow no resemblance of Him in their city, much less in their temples. In this way they do not flatter their kings, nor show their respect for their Caesars.[174]

You see, while other ancient peoples deified their great leaders, Jews bent over backward to show the gulf between man and G_d, the ethical G_d of history, who, by the way, they introduced to the world. In any other ancient society, Moses and David would have been turned into gods. The Jews recorded them as sinners instead. No accident.

What I have written above would have gotten me killed over the centuries, and my people likely would have been rounded up and burned in the local synagogue as well. I may lose some friends as a result. Regardless, the truth cries out to be heard.

Like Ann, I must be honest, and must refuse to play the ghetto Jew (Uncle Abe instead of Uncle Tom) role.

I have dear Christian friends who probably were as sickened by Coulter's remarks almost as much as I was. But, there is a hard fact they must face up to and reflect upon—Coulter was simply telling it as she has been taught, like it or not.

Chapter 38

GANDHI, MUMBAI, AND BEYOND

THE ATROCITIES COMMITTED in Mumbai, India, in the name of the ongoing jihadi quest for the spread of the Arab and Arabizeds' Dar ul-Islam in late 2008 were but a continuation of a war waged by Muhammad's followers for about fourteen centuries now against the Dar al-Harb, the realm of war (i.e. all peoples and lands not yet conquered either in the name of what Arab pipedreams proclaim to be "purely Arab patrimony" and/or the faith of the Arabs' *Seal of the Prophets*.)

As Arab armies burst out of the Arabian Peninsula around mid-seventh century C.E., lands native to other Semitic but non-Arab peoples (despite the wishful thinking of those who espouse the Winkler-Caetani Theory—Jews, Assyrians, Phoenicians/Lebanese) as well as those of Copts, Imazhigen/Berbers, Kurds, Persians and other Aryan peoples, Turks, black Africans, Indians, and others fell one after another to Arab and Arabized imperial conquests. Numerous millions of people were slaughtered in this process—continuing to this very day.[175] Others willingly jumped on the Arab bandwagon to gain shares of the conquests.

Muhammad of Gaur first spread the Dar ul-Islam into India in the twelfth century C.E., and the highlight of these conquests came with the Moghul Empire several centuries later.

The results were lasting, and the partition of the Indian subcontinent into a Muslim Pakistan and largely Hindu India in 1947 (and later, a Muslim Bangladesh as well) reflected this. During that same year, Arabs would reject a similar partition plan for what was left of the original 1920 Mandate of Palestine after Arab Transjordan was created from nearly 80 percent of it in 1922.

There are, indeed, similarities between what Israel faces in Judea and Samaria today and what India faces in Kashmir and elsewhere. The one big difference, of course, is that there are about one billion Indians (who were never earlier subjected to a forced diaspora like the Jews were after taking on Rome) facing their jihadi enemies instead of some six million Jews facing similar threats from hundreds of millions of Arabs and/or Arabized.

Over the years, more and more Indians themselves have begun to notice this. As they do, they see the linkage between Arabs blowing up Jews on buses and restaurants, and Arabs or Arabized Pakistanis blowing up and massacring Hindus and others in Parliament and in hotels in Mumbai.

Before moving on, something else must be said about those partitions of the Mandate of Palestine and the Indian subcontinent mentioned earlier. While working for the liberation of India from British imperial occupation, Mohandas Gandhi opposed the partition of the Indian subcontinent into a Hindu India and a Muslim Pakistan. He believed that people of all religious faiths should be able to get along in the same nation. He was assassinated by a Hindu nationalist.

So much for getting along. Some places it works. Some places it is laughable. The Mahatma did not understand the nature of the enemy he was facing, an enemy who sees justice only in terms of its own ilk.

Gandhi opposed Zionism—the national liberation movement of the Jews—to the very end; his major statement circulated as an editorial in the *Harijan* of November 11, 1938. Among other things, while first professing his supposed "sympathies" for perennially persecuted Jews, he next claimed that, "Palestine of the biblical conception is not a geographical tract."[176]

Actually, he did get that one right. "Palestine" wasn't. It represented a vague, coastal geographical area according to the ancient Greeks.

Recall that the name itself was bestowed on Iudaea /Judaea—the defined land of the Jews—by Hadrian, after the Jews' second major war (133–135 C.E.) for their independence against Rome. To squash their hopes once and for all, he renamed the land itself after Israel's historic enemies, the Philistines (Syria Palaestina), a non-Semitic Greek people from the area around Crete.

But Israel and Judaea were well-known nations/kingdoms peopled by Israelites/Hebrews/Jews.

Gandhi saw the religious claims of Jews as their main, if not only, leg to stand on in this conflict—which he rejected.

However, the differences which separated Jews from Arabs were not simply theological. While Gandhi has plenty of company here in his booboo (including academics), this doesn't excuse it. What made matters worse, if you don't really know, you shouldn't really say. Especially if you see yourself, or are seen by others, as a major voice for justice and morality in this world.

With all due respect to a man whom in some ways I otherwise admire, Gandhi knew about as much about Jews and their history as most Jews know about the various Indian peoples. The difference, however, is that Jews would never have told the latter to remain forever victimized and at the potential receiving end of those with a long history of bloody conquest and persecution.

While it would be nice if we all just really "got along," and there was no need for nationalism, national borders, and such, the reality is that this belief is too often fiction—and especially when it comes to the millennial Jewish experience, something Gandhi acknowledged himself when admitting "his sympathies."

So, what else is new?

In a post-Auschwitz age, people may grudgingly cry crocodile tears for dead Jews (à la Holocaust and such), but too often have no room for empathy for live ones. They expect perfection of the Jew of the Nations while excusing or ignoring the much worse sins of those who aim to destroy it.

Check out Gandhi again, "However, my sympathy does not blind me to the requirements of justice. Why should they (Jews) not, like other peoples, make that country their home where they are born?"[177]

I guess he had not heard of the Dreyfus Affair in "enlightened" France; or had not seen pictures of Jews waving their medals from World War I in front of the Nazis; or had not heard of Grant's General Order No. 11 calling for the expulsion of the Jews of the South during America's Civil War; or of the Damascus Blood Libel in nineteenth century Arab Syria, etc.

Again, what you don't really know, you really shouldn't comment on.

Imagine, for one moment, that India—as massive as it is—underwent the experiences that the Jews in their tiny state did in their fight for freedom and independence against an imperial power like Rome, culminating in much of the population massacred and most of the rest forcibly exiled in that great Diaspora already mentioned.

Next, imagine that those hypothetical Indians (like those real Jews) in almost everywhere that they eventually landed—the Muslim East as well as the Christian West—never knew what the morrow would bring—massacres, forced conversions, expulsions, ghettoization (the mellah in the "Arab" world), demonization, and such culminating in a holocaust which wiped out one third of all Indian people.

Would Jews insist that Indians remain forever at someone else's mercy and give up on a resurrected national existence needed simply to survive?

I think not. Yet that's what Gandhi expected of Jews.

Einstein—a Zionist who, like most other Jewish nationalists, heeded closely Rabbi Hillel's advice about caring for the "others" (in this case, Arabs) while seeking a better tomorrow for themselves, disagreed with Gandhi on these issues. So I'm in good company.[178] After Gandhi's assassination, Einstein had an exchange of letters with India's replacement candidate for Prime Minister, Jawaharlal Nehru, on the same topic.[179]

Unlike Indians, Jews were literally forced into those above-mentioned positions and had earlier tried desperately to follow Gandhi's advice to be "accepted," but to no avail. As nasty as some aspects of the British Raj were, they do not compare to those millennial experiences of stateless Jews.

Should Jews have not wanted something better for their children? Should they have continued to put their trust only in those who declared them to be G_d-killers, children of the devil, killers of Prophets, sons of apes and pigs, dogs, and such with periodic and predictable consequences?

Sadly, the otherwise wise Gandhi thought so.

Let's take another look below at how the ancient historians saw this identity issue.

As you have surely noticed—and as is spelled out in the Introduction to this book—I deliberately weave in repetition of key points into many chapters' main themes. So, here's yet another relevant look at my oft-used, favorite quotes from Vol. II, Book V, *The Works of Tacitus*, which discussed the Jews' first major revolt in 66–73 C.E. for their freedom and independence against the Soviet Union (or British Empire, Mr. Gandhi)—of its day, Rome. There were others (Dio Cassius, Josephus) who wrote about such things as well, "It inflamed Vespasian's resentment that the Jews were the only nation who had not yet submitted. Titus was appointed by his father to complete the subjugation of Judaea. He commanded three legions in Judaea itself. To these he added the twelfth from Syria and the third and twenty-second from Alexandria. Amongst his allies were a band of Arabs, formidable in themselves and harboring toward the Jews the bitter animosity usually subsisting between neighboring nations."

No, Rome was not just referring to the Jews' "religious identity," which Gandhi spoke of, but to a distinct nation and people. If Indians can have a homeland, and Arabs almost two dozen created mostly via conquest of non-Arab peoples' lands, then why single out and deny Jews their sole, miniscule, resurrected one that you need a magnifying glass to find on a world map?

Toward the end of the movie *Gandhi* starring Ben Kingsley, there is a telling scene. Numerous people are seen walking in opposite directions, depicting the population exchange involving many millions of people going on after the Indian subcontinent's first partition.

The same thing happened after the Arabs' attack on a reborn Israel in 1948.

For every Arab refugee created as a result of this, there was a Jewish refugee fleeing Arab/Muslim lands—where they were commonly known as *kilab yahud*, Jew dogs. Unlike Arabs, however, the Jews didn't have almost two dozen other states (again, most conquered from non-Arab peoples) to choose from. And, unlike Arabs, Jews didn't herd their own refugees into camps for use as political pawns.

Finally, those in India and elsewhere who still demand that Israel agree to suicide so that Arabs can have yet another state must also take the following into consideration.

How about allowing the creation of yet another Muslim state on Gandhi's own Indian subcontinent—besides Pakistan and Bangladesh? Guess which nation has the largest population of Muslims in the world? I'll give you a hint, it starts with an "I" and it is not Israel nor Italy, and not even Indonesia—it's number two.

Not that I agree with this (I don't), but there are still Indians today making the same arguments that Gandhi made earlier in terms of Israel and Zionism. And there are, after all, about two hundred million Muslims in India.

With each new Arab or Arabized atrocity against India, those anti-Israel voices become fewer and fewer, but the ignorance leading up to those earlier political positions must nonetheless be confronted head on.

The wars of the Dar ul-Islam and/or Arabism target any and all who dare stand in their murderous, subjugating way—be they in Kosovo, Darfur, Kurdistan, Israel, Lebanon, Egypt, the Philippines, Thailand, North Africa, and elsewhere including India.

As we have seen, the war against what Arabs call "their" Jew dogs has never been about how big Israel is—but that Israel is.

Jews were murdered along with Hindus and others in Mumbai in November 2008. Reports from Indian officials stated that the Jews were singled out for special torture; a rabbi and his pregnant wife included. The couple's bloodied two-year-old son had been clinging to his mother's body and was saved by his Indian nanny.

I have, at last, one final thought (for now, at least) on these matters. I'm hoping that, in death, this tragedy, committed in the name of the Dar ul-Islam, will bring closer together both India and the Jew of the Nations—Israel—to confront a common enemy which refuses to grant any justice whatsoever to any but its own.

Chapter 39

WHY IS THIS SO HARD TO UNDERSTAND?

TALK ABOUT CLOSE! The Israelis were rivaling America's Bush–Gore race of 2000 in their own early 2009 election. As this analysis was being drafted, either Tzipora Livni or Benjamin Netanyahu could have wound up becoming the next Israeli prime minister.[180] Both sought the support of an important third party to form a viable government, that of Avigdor Lieberman's Yisrael Beiteinu. Lieberman's party surged and won a substantial number of seats in Israel's Parliament, the Knesset. Lieberman and his growing no-nonsense, head-out-of-the-sand popularity continues to give heart palpitations to many, so that's what this chapter is largely all about. News articles and other commentary have highlighted Israeli Arabs' fear of Lieberman.

While focusing on their fears, I've found—in none of those analyses—any attempt to seriously explain Netanyahu or Leiberman's positions—which we'll get to shortly. National Public Radio has also displayed its usual one-sided, "anti-Israel liberal" slant against that mean Israeli Goliath manhandling poor innocent "Palestinians." For NPR and its ilk, Lieberman is that Goliath personified. Eric Westervelt interviewed Arabs regarding Lieberman's popularity, but decided to totally ignore finding out why this is so, leaving his listeners with same impression most of the rest of the mainstream media is dishing out. So much for NPR, BBC, *The New York Times* and so forth as far as "balance" is concerned.[181]

OK, now let's begin. *Webster's Collegiate Dictionary* defines *treason* as "the violation of the allegiance owed to one's sovereign or state; betrayal of one's country and, specifically in the United States, consisting only in levying war against the U.S. or in giving aid and comfort to its enemies."

A few years back, Arab students attending Hebrew University demonstrated against the visit of Prime Minister Ariel Sharon, screaming—among other things—"We are all Ahmed Yassins." Pictures of Israeli Arabs appeared in newspapers all over the world holding up Yassin's portrait in protest marches. Yassin was the Israeli dispatched-to-Paradise leader of Hamas, the organization which openly calls for (and acts upon) Israel's destruction which Israel recently was forced to go after again.

Increasingly, Israeli Arabs—who number some 20 percent of Israel's population with one of the highest birth rates in the world—have attacked fellow Jewish citizens simply because they are Jews. It has become commonplace for them to hold demonstrations in their towns similar to what we've seen above at Hebrew University. Not only do Jews have to fear Arabs outside of their borders, they now have to increasingly fear those within.

Israeli Arab Knesset members openly side with those who deliberately disembowel Jews. Too many Israeli Arabs have cheered when Jews have been targeted and terrorized by either bad cop Hamas or good cop Fatah terrorists. Israel was partially resurrected so that there would be at least one place in the entire world where this sort of thing would not happen. So such Arab actions are totally unacceptable.

Totally.

In reality, however, this is nothing new. Rabbi Meir Kahane warned of such things decades ago and was branded a racist for coming to the same logical conclusions which Lieberman and others have come to, and for which they too are now being portrayed as unreasonable racists, fascists, and the like. Listening to NPR—supported by many Jewish donors—that's certainly the message one receives. So, what makes Israeli Arabs shudder about Lieberman? He demands that the freest Arabs anywhere in the Middle East—Israel's—show loyalty to the state in which they live or be denied citizenship. And he expects that Israeli Arabs will not terrorize or intimidate Israeli Jews. Racist? Unreasonable? Fascist? What other nation would put up with such outright treason against both the state and its citizens?

Please look at *Webster's* definition above again—especially how America itself regards such things. Imagine the fate of anyone in any Arab country plotting against the state, its leaders, or its people. We don't have to imagine; the graveyards are filled with such folks—if their bodies weren't donated to the vultures instead. Let's make sure that this point is so clear that even NPR's crew, the BBC, and *The New York Times* can understand it. We're not talking about American students at Kent State University protesting American policies or the war in Viet Nam. What we're talking about, again, is the freest Arabs to be found anywhere in the Middle East (those in Israel, whose language has been made the second official language of the Jewish state, while Kurdish kids in "Arab" Syria and Imazighen/Berber children in parts of "Arab" North Africa are not even allowed to speak their own native languages) supporting terror, murder, and the destruction of the very nation in which they live and the murder of their fellow citizens.[182] If the above isn't treason, then once again I'm the Passover Bunny.

In any Arab country, anyone engaging in such activity against the state would not long be of this world. For sure. Indeed, in any other nation—including America—jail would likely be the minimum fate. So, someone with clout and the nerve to once again say in Israel what must be said has once again surfaced—Lieberman, thank G_d!

As Lieberman and a growing number of others tired of the one-sided destruction-in-stages games Arabs have been playing have increasingly come to learn the hard way, it is long past time for Israel to act in its own crucial interests the way all other nations would act.

The typical mainstream media story portrays a victory for Netanyahu, Lieberman, and their allies as a setback for peace with Arabs. But these are the same folks who never bother to press Arabs on what they really mean themselves regarding that alleged "peace." I don't believe that this is an accident either. And the new American president, unfortunately, falls into this same category as well.

Take a look at a typical Netanyahu "extremist position." In preparation for his upcoming meeting with President Obama in Spring 2009, Bibi needed to prepare a long overdue and firm response to the Arabs' refusal to recognize Israel as a Jewish state while demanding a twenty-second nation for themselves. According to a report in *Haaretz.com* on April 25, 2009, "Netanyahu will tell Obama that he will not recognize a nation-state providing Palestinian self-determination if the Palestinians don't recognize Israel as the nation-state of the Jewish people. From the standpoint of the Israeli prime minister, the requirement that the Palestinians recognize Israel as the nation-state of the Jewish people is a fundamental demand in any negotiations on a final settlement. It is not a precondition to conducting negotiations, but rather necessary to progress toward an agreement."

So, there is a dose of Jewish extremism for you, same as Hamas blowing up buses and blasting civilian homes with rockets, correct? Now, I'm not sure what Lieberman's particulars are regarding the rest of the above loyalty issue that he's branded a racist for, but here are mine as I spelled out years ago in my own previously published articles.

Those Arabs who display such treachery as described above must, preferably, be expelled from the country. Jail time only costs Israeli taxpayers money that there's much less of in Israel these days due to Arab rejectionist actions and attitudes—on both sides of the Green Line (the '49 armistice lines). Indeed, some Israeli Arabs have been actively involved in terrorism themselves. Jailing such folks only winds up with Israel getting blackmailed later—trading numerous, live Arab butchers and wannabes for the bones of a few dead Jews.

As we have seen, in the broader perspective of the problem, Arabs could have had their twenty-second state long ago—if that's all that they wanted. Unlike Einstein's concern for Rabbi Hillel's "others," the Arabs have showed no such concern. Any objective assessment of the facts would show this. There's no need to rehash all the proposals for compromise yet again. I've certainly done that enough here. The reality is that Arabs still want their second state in mandatory Palestine to exist in place of—not alongside of—Israel. And that goes for Mahmoud Abbas's alleged Fatah "moderates" as well.

So, at the very least, Israel needs to kick those who articulate and exhibit such behaviors out of the country. I'd include treasonous, self-destructive Jews as well.

Trade them for those Jews still trapped and living in fear in "Arab" and/or other Muslim countries. Enact a death penalty and take fewer live prisoners who commit crimes aiming to murder and terrorize. Absurd. Spending money to keep them alive while their innocent victims are no more. And then tell the multitudes of protesting hypocrites all over the world that Israel, like all nations, must have its lines in the sand which cannot be crossed in terms of acceptable behavior by those wishing to live within its borders.

Chapter 40

JESUS'S BONES: SO, MY FRIENDS, HOW DOES IT FEEL

... to at least partially walk in another man's shoes?

BEFORE I BEGIN, let me first state that I don't want to ruffle the feathers of my Christian friends—but it would be nice if they treated others this same way. You'll see what I mean shortly. An AP story on February 27, 2007, announced that the Discovery Channel would air *The Lost Tomb of Jesus* on March 4. The program dealt with two ancient stone boxes from Roman-occupied Judaea (not "Palestine") that Oscar-winning director, James Cameron, and some researchers claim holds the bones of the Christian Messiah, Son of G_d, G_d incarnate—Jesus of Nazareth—and His human family. Of course, Cameron's mere assertion brings into question sacred Christian doctrine of the divinity of Jesus and His all-essential Resurrection. Without the latter, He was basically just another dead Jew—one of many thousands crucified by Rome in its conquest of Judaea.

As expected, many Christians were quite upset, and some were trying to pressure the Discovery Channel from airing the program. I, as a Jew who grew up with Christians knocking at my door telling me I was going to hell because I did not believe as they do, can understand their feelings quite well; actually, far better than they themselves do. While the odds of these ossuaries actually holding the remains of Jesus and Mary Magdalene are very slim, there was/is still much good history that such a program potentially offers to its viewers.

Arabs, for example, and as we have seen earlier, love to proclaim that Jesus and His followers were "Palestinians," not Jews. The program's harshest critics argued that Mary and Jesus were very common names of Jews—not Arabs—found on many other ossuaries and in other places as well during this time period. While this is really not "news," in this day and age—with Israel constantly vilified—such a reminder was/is timely and worthwhile.

While some contest the translation of the Hebrew names found at the site, if they are indeed correct—which they may very well be—then we do have, at the least, an interesting find placing a Jesus, a Mariamene, a Judah son of Jesus, and so forth in the same family grave. Did the producers and such make money from this? Of course—like everyone else does with projects of interest. So, this all begged the question, why should the Discovery Channel's program have been axed because it might have offended some Christians, but not the hundreds of television and radio programs broadcast constantly all across America and elsewhere dedicated to converting Jews and proclaiming that the latter's faith is lacking and deficient? You know, à la Ann Coulter, whom we read about earlier. Are those not offensive to Jews? Not to mention the forced conversions Jews were constantly subjected to by Christians over the ages before television existed?

Perhaps these paraphrases can help explain, "Ye do not get to the Father except through the Son;" "Why do you not hear the words I tell thee? It is because you [Jews—not "just" Pharisees] are of your father, the devil, and you do your father's deeds;" and so forth—taken right out of the Christian New Testament.

One of the first pictures of a Jew that we know of in Europe was later entitled, "Aaron, son of the devil." Michelangelo placed devil-looking horns on his famous statue of Moses. While some claim that they represented rays of light, imagine how the masses interpreted/interpret them. Not that long ago, a prominent Southern Baptist leader, Reverend Bailey Smith, proclaimed, "G_d almighty doesn't hear the prayer of a Jew." His views are still shared by millions today.[183] While many Christians protest abuses and intolerance within Islam, they really do need to reflect upon their own history, current beliefs, and actions as well. As many good Christian scholars have come to acknowledge, the road to Auschwitz was carefully paved over the millennia by such "sacred" beliefs.

As I frequently like to point out, a reading of the Roman historians, who wrote right around the time of Jesus, is very useful to see the Jews' problem with what Christians made of Joshua—Jesus—of Nazareth. So, here's Tacitus yet again (Volume II, Book V, *The Works of Tacitus*), writing after the Jews took on the mighty Roman Empire for their freedom and independence, and noted several times before, "The Jews acknowledge one God only, and conceive of Him by the mind alone, condemning, as impious, all who, with perishable materials, wrought into the human shape, form representations of the Deity. That Being, they say, is above all, and everlasting, neither susceptible of likeness nor subject to decay. In consequence, they allow no resemblance of Him in their city, much less in their temples. In this way they do not flatter their kings, nor show their respect for their Caesars." Please read the above very carefully, my dear Christian friends, for it sums up the main reason for the break between our two faith communities.

For the Jew, as we have seen, no human—no matter how great—could be equated in any way with G_d. That is something pagans all around the Jews did—not Jews. In fact, Jews bent over backwards to show the imperfections of even their greatest leaders—Moses and David—to avoid any semblance of deification just as Tacitus pointed out. In any of their surrounding neighbors' lands, both men would have been turned into gods and worshiped. It is no accident that Paul, a Jew raised in the Hellenistic world of the Greeks, had to sell his own special ideas (Jesus as the Greek Logos, and so forth) about Jesus to a predominantly non-Jewish audience outside of Judaea that was used to such ideas.

Many a television program has been devoted to the historicity of stories associated with the Hebrew Bible—Old Testament to Christians. They have been aired without demands by Jews to squash or alter the message. In the end, at least some channels ran this fascinating program. Whether one chose to watch or not to watch it, love it, hate it, critique it, or whatever. It was, among many other things, an important lesson in teaching Christians to learn to walk in their Jewish brothers' shoes.

Chapter 41

REPORTS FROM THE INSIDE: THE REAL PROBLEM WITH PRESIDENT OBAMA'S KHALIDI

IT WAS THE weekend when Americans set clocks back an hour for Daylight Savings Time, a few months before the 2008 presidential election. Thus, I guess it was only fitting that, given all the then current fuss about the *Los Angeles Times's* refusal to make public even a transcript, let alone the existing video tape, of then Senator Obama's love fest with Professor Rashid Khalidi and his ilk (no doubt, like-minded anti-Israel Jews included), I'll turn the clock back now here as well but by almost three decades.[184]

You see, Fox News meant well, and while most of the mainstream media in general was either ignoring the story or downplaying it, Fox—and even Senator McCain's people themselves—missed the real problem while at least bringing the disturbing story up.

It is not that President Obama indeed has far too many friends, advisors, admirers, and so forth who are blatant anti-Semites let alone anti-Zionists (not that there's really a difference—one deliberately targets Jews for "special treatment," the other, in a post-Holocaust world, carefully revises the target to the Jew of the Nations), it is that those folks demand that all others see justice only through their own eyes.

So, let's turn the clock back once again to the period of my graduate school days, decades ago to when this problem was already well under way. Having to be employed full time for financial reasons while doing my earlier, nicely progressing doctoral work at the Kevorkian Center for Near Eastern Studies, issues involving my bread and butter day job later required an upward move to the Midwest. As hindsight is always the best sight, I realized later how huge a mistake that was.

Part of my new professional consulting position involved guest lecturing at dozens of universities and colleges across a multi-state region to try to at least minimally balance resident, anti-Israel professors. The Middle East Studies Association (MESA) was already being hijacked by an anti-Israel clique, and the only Jews that got/get ahead were/are most often those who out-Arab the Arabs in their vilification of Israel. In an age when budgets were tightening, many also remembered who buttered their own bread as well and this undoubtedly—despite protestations to the contrary—affected what was and wasn't presented to students in the classroom. Mucho bucks and other support and research opportunities have been provided to such programs—at all levels—via the Arab petro-spigot and other foreign players in the Middle East.[185]

To simply get a somewhat fair—not "pro-Zionist"—hearing about Israel, students are usually forced to take courses offered by the separate Jewish Studies Department, yet another way too many MESA academics can virtually ostracize Israel from the official Middle East Studies program.

While some Jewish professors like the idea (including a well-known scholar of the Dead Sea Scrolls with whom I studied and have had fairly recent correspondence with on this subject), there is definitely a rotten fish to be smelled in this development. Nevertheless—and as should be the case (but in stark contrast to what will be described below)—those same above students will get an honest appraisal of the imperfectly human quest of a resurrected Jewish nationalism in their Jewish Studies courses.

Please recall, again, what I had to say about the book's chapter structure in the Introduction and allow me reiterate just a few of my own many personal examples.

Having been invited to be one of several presenters at a mega-event in Columbus, before hundreds of people, covering American foreign policy considerations in the region back in the late seventies, I prepared accordingly. As I was slated to be the last to present, I listened carefully to the others, but when I heard a local university professor switch gears to lecture about nasty Zionists stealing poor Arabs' land (one of President Obama's close academic friend's exact same lines) I had no choice. I tore up my presentation, threw it into the air, and unleashed both barrels in response.

After the presentation, I was approached by another professor who introduced himself as a representative of the university's Middle Eastern Studies program. After a chat about where I did my earlier studies, he asked me if I'd consider resurrecting my doctoral work. I laughed and asked him if he had heard what I heard coming out of the mouth of his colleague. Why would I put my fate into such an academic program's one-sided hands?

I was assured that there were others who could serve as my PhD dissertation advisor. On that note, while still working full time, I reentered academia.

Not wanting to drag this painful tale of woe out, let me just say that my initial gut reaction proved to be all-too-correct.

The tenured chief honcho who covered the modern Middle East was definitely a pea (if a bit more subtle) in the same pod as his colleague with whom I shared a stage a few years earlier. And into his hands only—I was much later informed—I would have to be placed. Had I known this from the start, I would have not wasted my time and money.

While teaching an advanced class, for example, on the Palestine Mandate period, he never once mentioned such things as Britain's Colonial Secretary Winston Churchill's crucial Cairo Conference of 1921. It was that Conference, which led to the gift of almost 80 percent of the original 1920 territory of the Mandate of Palestine to Arab nationalism in 1922 with the creation of what would later be renamed Jordan. And the latter fact was never mentioned as well! This in a doctoral seminar on the Palestine Mandate. An accident? I think not, for doing so might lead students to question the preferred lesson that usurping Jews stole all of Palestine from Arabs.

Again, while also—but a bit more subtly than the more extreme Columbia-types—promoting the theme of nasty Zionists and the need to create Arab state #22 (second, not first, in Palestine), that same academic never once mentioned the plight of over thirty-five million Kurds who remain stateless to date; who have been gassed and/or otherwise subjugated and slaughtered by Arabs, Turks, and Iranians; who had their language and culture periodically outlawed; and who had their one best chance at statehood aborted by a collusion of British petroleum politics and Arab nationalism. My work on this subject—in part to fill such sickening, hypocritical omissions—can be found on the recommended reference list of Paris's acclaimed Institut d'Ètudes Politiques—Sciences Po. It was written while I was still a doctoral student.

But, please pardon me. I am mistaken. Recall that said professor did mention Kurds once—when he mocked their continuing subjugation. I'll never forget the smirk on his face when he mentioned this as he was reminiscing about his travels through southeastern Turkey, "Kurdistan."

Recall, that—to his credit—the other professor (for whom I was a T.A.) invited me to do a one-day presentation to students on the Kurds. Notice, however, that he too wouldn't touch this subject himself with a ten-foot pole. Afterwards, the Arabs in class caused such a commotion that I was chastised for merely presenting the plight of another non-Arab people—besides Jews—who were also seeking a tiny slice of justice in a region proclaimed by Arabs to be solely their own. Arab genocide against blacks in the Sudan, subjugation and murder of Copts, Assyrians, Imazighen, and so forth were going on back then as well and, again, only rarely a peep out of the MESA hypocrites over any of this.

As just one last personal example of the problem a now President Obama's Khalidi-type friends and advisors present, let me return to that professor's graduate seminars.

I'll never forget one Greek Orthodox woman who I'm sure has a great position at some university today. I can't think of her name, but I do remember her well.

Her idol was Hajj Amin al-Husseini, the Grand Mufti of Jerusalem, who spent World War II in Berlin at Hitler's side and organized a division of Muslim Nazis, "the Hanzar." He also played a first-hand role in instigating the genocide of Europe's Jews, Serbs and Gypsies. After World War II, he actively recruited Nazi officers into Arab governments of the Middle East.

When she presented her research on the Mufti at our doctoral seminar, all the above was ignored altogether and said professor, of course—her mentor and featured guest at her wedding—sat through it all approvingly. I watched him very closely. Where were the probing questions and critique about such a violent and controversial figure? He certainly had/has plenty to say regarding Israel and the Arabs—sorry, *Palestinians*.

Now, contrast this with my own research about Ze'ev Vladimir Jabotinsky, the man most responsible in the early Mandate era for Jewish defense against Arab slaughter, father of the modern Likud Party in Israel. Said professor had no problem emphasizing his alleged "fascist connections" in his remarks to me.

When it came time for me to prepare for the last leg of my doctoral work, guess who was denied a dissertation advisor? So much for that earlier assurance that not all teachers were of the same "persuasion" as the one whom I shared a stage with that night in Columbus. Wasted time, thousands of dollars, and left hanging in the wind, my growing family moved to Florida not long afterward.

The above is even more often the story on campus these days as well. A little bit of good news is that now there are at least some watchdog organizations and endeavors like Professor Daniel Pipes's Campus Watch and David Horowitz's Academic Bill of Rights. Still, academia largely proceeds full speed ahead, intimidating all who dare to disagree and dismissing critics simply as right-wing fanatics.

Israel continues to thus be placed under that high power lens of moral scrutiny by academic practitioners of the double standard, and woe unto all who beg to differ.

So, the above is the real problem with President Obama's Khalidi-type friends and associates.

Being "pro-Arab" is not the concern—as Fox News, meaning well, had nevertheless presented the case. At least they made an issue of this.

The problem has always been that for Arabs and their spokesmen and promoters, anyone who claims that scores of millions of non-Arabs (whom Arabs once conquered during their own imperialist expansions) also deserve a slice of the justice pie in the region is, by definition—for Arabs—anti-Arab.

There is no justice other than Arab justice. To be pro-Arab one must demonize and deny any others any justice at all.

Whether then Senator Obama's alleged statement about Israel's "genocide" against Palestinians (Arabs by another name—most of whom came from elsewhere) and other gems reported to be on that unreleased *Los Angeles Times* video tape were true or not, his admiration, association, and so forth of, by, or with the anti-Semitic and/or anti-Zionist likes of Farrakhan, Rezko, Khalidi, Jeremiah Wright, Jessie "Hymietown" Jackson, Brzezinski, Jimmy "Apartheid Israel" Carter, Chas Freeman, Robert Malley, George Soros, General McPeak, Samantha Power, or Khalid Al Mansour and so forth have to be beyond coincidental.

And this should be the real cause of concern—even for those all-too-many let's jump onto the cattle cars for relocation again fellow tribal members of mine.

Chapter 42

WHO WON'T BE MAKING JOKES ABOUT WMD

THE FRONT PAGE Associated Press article in the March 29, 2004, *Daytona Beach* (Florida) *News–Journal* was entitled "Report Faults Israeli Intelligence on Iraq." Ah, I should have known. The Jews were to blame after all. What else is new?

The Bush Administration had been coming under increasing fire due to its inability to find weapons of mass destruction in Iraq, one of the main reasons it gave in launching its attack in the first place. It turns out that Israel intelligence may have been less than perfect in these regards as well.

As an educator who also has an extensive background in the ecological and environmental sciences (one of only fifty teachers in the entire state who was asked by the Department of Education to help write the educational guidelines for those subjects in Florida), let me state right from the start that there's much about Republican positions regarding air, water, pollution, energy policies, and the ecological interrelationships which support life itself that bother me. Having said that, let me next state that I believe that the Bush Administration was being unfairly targeted on the weapons of mass destruction (WMD) issue.

While Jay Leno & Co. (and later, even the president himself) cracked jokes, and AP writers such as Matthew Fordahl also made light of the subject in papers such as *The Herald* in Rock Hill, South Carolina, where I was visiting on July 16, 2003 ("For Today's Giggle, Try Asking Google to Find Weapons of Mass Destruction"), there is one group of people who surely will never be joining in that laughter. And they were not the only ones for whom the subject is deadly serious—literally.

"The Kurds have no friends but the mountain" is a piece of aging Kurdish wisdom. And while the confirmed mass gassings and other repeated slaughters of this people over the decades have too often been treated as "yesterday's news," all the hype about whether or not Adolph—er Saddam—Hussein had weapons of mass destruction in Iraq brought their tragic story back onto center stage, or at least should have. During this same time period, Syrian Arabs renewed their still continuing assault on "their" Kurds as well.

Thirty-five million truly stateless (no almost two dozen states—as Arabs already have) Kurds are the native, non-Arab, non-Turkic, non-Semitic people who were promised independence in Mesopotamia—the ancient heartland of

Kurdistan—after the Ottoman Turkish Empire collapsed in the wake of World War I. They were the Hurrians of the Bible and the Medes of Persian history. Saladin, the mighty medieval Muslim warrior, was a Kurd. Unfortunately, after World War I, Kurds soon saw earlier promises of independence sacrificed on the altar of British petroleum politics and Arab nationalism. Arab Iraq was born instead.

Its imperial navy having recently switched from coal to oil power, Great Britain did not want to anger the strategically important "Arab" world, possessing its own extensive oil wealth, by agreeing to support a Kurdish nationalism which was viewed by Arabs with the same disdain as they display toward the nationalist movement of Israel's Jews (one half of whom descended from refugees from the "Arab"/Muslim world) or any other of the subjugated peoples who dared to assert their own identities and demanded political rights.

As we have seen already, many Imazighen/Berbers are having their culture virtually erased and have been told that they must name their children with Arab/Islamic names—not those from their own culture—with similar things being done in Syria to Kurds. Has anyone read about this in their own local newspaper or in *The New York Times* or heard of it on CNN?

Imagine if the Jews were doing such stuff to Arabs in Israel? Front page news, more UN special sessions blasting "racist Zionists," more ammunition for the anti-Israel chorus in academia, and so forth.

Despite their own various internal differences, by 1970 Kurds from all over the region had largely put their hopes and dreams into the creation of one independent Kurdish state as the major Talebani and Barzani factions merged in common cause, not unlike similar situations involving Greeks, Armenians, and Jews in their own respective earlier diasporas.[186] The frustration arising from the abortion of the earlier Mesopotamian dream (a cause supported by such personalities as President Woodrow Wilson, Sir Mark Sykes, and others) lead to decades of revolts and problems in Syria, Turkey, Iraq, and Iran as well.

In a post-imperial age when other dormant nations were reawakening, the Kurds were repeatedly told that they were unworthy of such desires—by so-called "friends" and foes alike.

The Foggy Folks still have no "roadmap" planned for them, academics won't mention them, and so forth. Perhaps blowing up civilian buses, restaurants, and teen nightclubs, or decapitating victims and playing with their body parts on television—like Arabs have done—might get them a bit more attention. Not that I wish any of this, but such tactics seems to be working for Arabs in their demand for state number twenty-two, their second, not first, Arab one in the original April 25, 1920, borders of the Palestine Mandate.

That brings us back to current times.

While repeated partitions were planned for the geographic area of "Palestine," none have been allowed for a much larger Mesopotamia. Only Arabs have been allowed to have their nationalist desires sanctioned in a land in which millions of Kurds, Jews, Assyrians, and others as well have lived long before the Arab conquests in the seventh century C.E. and the continuing forced Arabization process ever since.

In their frustration, Kurds have subsequently been caught up in numerous regional and global rivalries, being used and abused by all Syrian and Iraqi Arabs, Turks, Iranians, Soviets, Brits, Russians, Americans, and others as well. Israel's record here could likewise be better, but one could argue that Israeli support would be, under past and current circumstances, a kiss of death.

Post-World War I Iraq was largely divided between two major factions: Arab nationalists, who saw Iraq simply as one part of the overall greater Arab patrimony, and Iraqi nationalists. The latter—some Kurds, Assyrians, Turkmens, a few Arabs, and so forth (with few exceptions, Iraq's two hundred thousand Jews basically watched carefully from the sidelines)—deluded themselves into believing that Arabs would allow a true equality to emerge within the country.[187] Yet earlier Iraqi history should have taught another lesson.

The Arab Caliphate of the Umayyads, based in Damascus, had been replaced in the eighth century during the Abbasid Revolution. The latter established its imperial base farther east in Baghdad and was supported largely by non-Arab converts to Islam, the Mawali, who demanded an equality that Arabs back then had also refused to give.

Short of another major Abbasid-like revolution, and with the decline and fall of the Ottoman Turkish Empire, Iraq's Arabs (Shi'a or Sunni)—having once again regained their position of dominance—were not likely to give it up. Sure enough, subsequent massacres of non-Arab populations and the continued forced Arabization of their cultures and lands helped squash most of the modern "Iraqi" nationalist delusions. While, in theory, this would be a nice, American-styled democratic solution, centuries of reality regarding actual Arab practices and subjugating attitudes tell quite a different story.

In the 1970s, after promoting Kurdish military support for the Shah of Iran against Iraq, America pulled the rug out from under the Kurdish leader, Mullah Mustafa Barzani, when the Shah made his temporary peace with Iraq. Tens of thousands of Kurds were subsequently slaughtered as a result. A repeat performance came in 1991, when, as we've seen, President George H. W. Bush called for the Kurds and the Shi'a to revolt in order to topple Saddam from within. When they heeded his call, he then stood by and watched as Kurdish men, women, and children were massacred by the thousands. Just a bit earlier, thousands more had been gassed to death—five thousand in Halabja alone—and all of this with the might of the U.S. military within a stone's throw of the action. The pathetic excuse meekly offered later on was that America had been "tricked" by Iraq in agreements regarding terms of the ceasefire. This will forever be a stain on America's honor, despite after-the-fact "no fly" zones subsequently set up by the Allies.

Besides the thousands of Kurds and Shi'a Arabs who were immediately killed, tens of thousands of others subsequently died due to the lingering effects of poison gas—most definitely a WMD. Remember all of this the next time someone offers up a chuckle about Saddam's weapons of mass destruction or pursues the blame game on this subject.

Adding insult to injury, at a time when much of the world—including America—is now demanding that the sole, miniscule, resurrected state of the Jews accept the probability that a terrorist twenty-second Arab state—and second Arab one in Palestine—be created right in its very backyard, these same alleged voices of ethical enlightenment still insist that there will be no "roadmap" for the creation of an independent Kurdistan. Even earlier talk of a federal solution, whereby Kurds would at least gain effective local autonomy within a united Iraq, now seems to be losing out to the majority Shia's other plans for dominance after America's exit.

While other murderous megalomaniacs do indeed exist elsewhere, and America cannot simply assume the roles of world policeman, judge, and jury, there were and still are very good reasons to bring about the end of Saddam Hussein's regime—whether we're ever able to locate his other types of WMD or not. Just ask those Kurdish parents who bore witness to mass graves holding hundreds of their children being unearthed—a scene right out of the Holocaust. Hundreds of thousands of Kurds have been killed by Arabs over the past century.

This subsequently brings up another issue. Just how do we define weapons of mass destruction?

Thanks to Israel's surgical strike removing the immediate nuclear threat almost three decades ago (for which it was universally condemned—with George H. W. Bush and James Baker III leading the pack), Iraq's nuclear option suffered a severe setback. But ample evidence suggests that he didn't give up on this endeavor, and Iranians (and probably others as well) were also gassed by Saddam—so no one doubts his possession and willingness to use this latter type of WMD.

It is not too difficult to hide poison gas—or even its delivery systems—in a country as large as Iraq, especially since weapons inspectors had been out of the country for a long time. And we now know that Syria had been in collaboration with Iraq regarding all kinds of things. Convoys of trucks had been seen passing from Iraq into Syria, and the latter has its own huge stock-piles of such weaponry. So it would be easy to hide Iraqi WMD this way.[188]

Additionally, Saddam had plenty of time to learn the lesson of the 1967 Arab–Israeli war that it wasn't a good idea to leave your weapons easily exposed. No one ever claimed that the Iraqis are stupid, even if some of Saddam's actions antagonizing America (and giving it little choice but to act) in recent decades might suggest otherwise.

So what was all the fuss about WMD really all about?

Could it have been just plain old domestic politics being played out by opponents of George W. Bush (I voted for the "other guy" the first time around) during election time in 2004 and/or another example of the hypocrisy and double standards of the rest of the world which place Israel under a high-power lens in judging its struggle to survive while ignoring the literally scores of millions of non-Arab peoples who have been massacred, seen their cultures and languages "outlawed," and the like for simply daring to assert their own identities and resisting forced Arabization?

Is it that the murder of hundreds of thousands of Kurds by Arabs over the decades simply doesn't matter?

It hasn't mattered, after all, in places like the Sudan, where Arabs have waged a genocidal war against non-Muslim and Muslim black Africans—killing, maiming, and enslaving millions. Until relatively recently, there wasn't even voiced outrage by the United Nations or European Union, nor trial in Geneva either. And, if it really did matter, would it make a difference whether we could or could not locate the hidden WMD that we already knew Saddam had and used against people?

The concern and ongoing debate should therefore not be about locating Saddam's WMD, but providing the long term justice the victims of his WMD deserve.

What will happen once America packs up and leaves the country and the taxpayers, Turks, and so forth get tired of the "no fly" zones? Unless we work out an arrangement for our own long-term presence (possible bases in relatively stable and friendly Iraqi Kurdistan?), the tanks and planes Iraq's Arabs mostly kept leashed in confronting America will very likely once again wreak vengeance against America's strangely loyal Kurdish friends, even with the Shi'a now at the helm.

Recall that the Sunni Arab, Abu Musab al-Zarqawi, of al-Qaida fame and the probable butcher who the CIA believes beheaded the American Jew,

Nicholas Berg, on camera, wrote a letter that was intercepted by U.S. allied (Kurdish) forces in Iraq. He was also the guy who is believed responsible for the slaughter of Shi'a in Baghdad and Karbala. In the letter he listed four enemies. America, of course, was No. 1. No. 2 was the Kurds. Here's what he says about them: "They are a lump in the throat and a thorn whose time to be clipped has yet to come."[189]

A mounting American death toll and other costs brought ever more pressure for an American retreat, right or wrong, and it will soon largely be carried out under President Obama's watch.

While the dream of an American-style democratic Iraq is honorable, the odds of Arabs of any stripe—Shi'a or Sunni—granting non-Arabs any real political equality (unless they are totally "Arabized" first) are next to nil. The Shi'a have simply used the Kurds up until now as a counterweight to the Sunnis who have been blowing them up.

As one of several analogies to this, the original Egyptians—the Copts—have largely been Arabized, but they still have many serious problems, such as murders, burned down churches, and other forms of intimidation. Yet, Arabs continue to lecture the world about "racist Zionists" and largely get away with it.

Despite all of this, America has insisted that—at the most—a modified federal version of a failed "Iraqi" nationalism will be all that Kurds might be offered in a post-Saddam Iraq—as if Saddam alone was the problem or created those subjugating Arab attitudes toward non-Arabs all by himself. Back in 2004, and today as well, even this possibility seems to have vanished as Kurdish interests were and are, once again, pushed onto the back burner.

It is more than doubtful that a post-Saddam Iraq will view "political equality" any differently than when Saddam was forcibly removing Kurds from their oil-rich lands around Mosul and Kirkuk and replacing those he didn't murder with Arabs.

The American occupation, despite much good that it has brought to the land, has increasingly been resented. And those who aligned themselves most with America—the Kurds in particular—will once again be sought out for revenge when it is all over. Yet, without a prolonged, guided, and powerful American occupation, there is but a slim chance for an inclusive Iraqi nationalism to emerge. Even with America's presence, this had only a slight chance for success. There are simply too many powerful forces working against it.

While America has been playing a delicate balancing act trying to soothe Turkey's fears regarding its own large Kurdish population and not angering the Arab oil sheikhs and autocrats with the prospect of the loss of what they see as "purely Arab patrimony" to the Kurds, it must begin to reassess this overall policy.

Certainly if Arabs, most of whom still deny Israel's right to exist, are deemed deserving of some two dozen states, some thirty-five million stateless Kurds living in varying degrees of danger and subjugation are, at long last, deserving of one. This should be the issue being debated now, not Saddam's weapons of mass destruction.

Chapter 43

ATTENTION AP AND ALL YOU MAINSTREAM MEDIA FOLKS

I HAVE A FAVOR to ask of the Associated Press, Reuters, the BBC, *New York Times*, and the rest of you mainstream media folks. While the examples below date back a few years, they're as relevant today as they were then, so let's take a look.

In reports published during the week of May 7, 2007, articles dealing with the possible finding of King Herod's tomb became news. They spoke of the Judean Desert, Judea, the Jews' revolt for freedom, and so forth.

But, here's the problem. Don't you know that these were/are all merely Zionist concoctions?

Indeed, you showed that you were aware of this since you identified Herodium, at the beginning of those articles, as being on the West Bank (as you did likewise for Hebron), not Judea. By negating the former designation, you proved that you indeed knew how to put those Jews in their place! Michael "Israel among the top three evils in the world" Moore and Jimmy "Apartheid Israel" Carter must have been proud.

To avoid confusion and misleading your readers, however, from now on please be more consistent in your opposition to those fabricating Jews.

Additionally, the other correct designations you should have used, therefore, would have been the West Bank (not Judean) Hills, the West Bank (not Judean) Desert, and so forth. The New Testament made the same mistake—so you're in good company, I guess.

Matthew 2:1 claims that Jesus was born in Bethlehem of Judea, instead of Palestine.

Ugh! Those Zionists have indeed been up to their misleading tricks for quite some time.

In the future, please don't Judaize those places; that's just what those conniving Hebrews want! Just ask the new president's good friend, Columbia University's Professor Rashid Khalidi and his ilk.

Also, please refrain from reporting about the Jewish temple and Temple Mount in Jerusalem as well. As the Arabs will surely tell you, the Jews never had a temple there. Mere pipedreams.

Even the moderate Mahmoud Abbas and his latter day Fatah Arafatians—

not to mention Islamic Jihad and the Hamasniks—will be glad to supply you with its true name, Buraq's Mount.

They'll let you know that it was really named for Muhammad's winged horse with the head of a woman, which took him there from the Arabian Peninsula to ascend to heaven after he learned of the Temple (of Solomon) Mount itself in the first place from the Jews, founders of the date palm oasis at Medina.

The Jews, many of whom fled to Arabia after the Roman wars mentioned above, gave Muhammad refuge in Medina during his Hijra (flight) from Mecca in the seventh century C.E. He would later repay them with mass slaughter, rape, and enslavement for not accepting his religio-political leadership.

The Muslim Prophet says he spoke to the angel Gabriel to learn of the temple and other such things.

Nice, but he also spent a long time in Medina with Jewish teachers (and met Christians elsewhere, whose religion was an offshoot of that of the Jews) who introduced him to G_d, Abraham, ethical monotheism, and so forth in the first place.

While in Medina, in the words of ancient Arab historians themselves, like Jalaluddin, he even had his followers turn toward Jerusalem while praying for a while to win the Jews' important support for his claims. And, by the way, it is the Book of the Jews that mentions Gabriel and so forth in the first place. Certainly nothing of such matters was to be found in sources of Muhammad's earlier fellow pagan Arabs themselves.

Gabriel's chat with Muhammad, the latter's Jewish tutors.

A coincidence? Something more?

Nah, just more of that same Zionist propaganda!

Next.

Don't dare listen to those who will explain that the land was known as Judea—land of the Judaeans (Jews)—and Samaria for almost three thousand years until British imperialism divided the land in the early twentieth century after defeating the Ottoman Turks in World War I (who ruled it for more than four centuries) into a west bank and an east bank (of the Jordan River). The Brits' original Mandate of Palestine was granted to them on April 25, 1920, and covered both banks clear up to the border with modern Iraq.

Recall that those same Hebrew fabricators will next claim that in 1922 British imperialism rewarded its Hashemite Arab allies from the Arabian Peninsula (remember the movie *Lawrence of Arabia*?) with the entire east bank—so, right from the getgo, Arab nationalism was granted almost 80 percent of all of "Palestine." The Brits' East Bank rep back then, Sir Alec Kirkbride, wrote about this in his book, *A Crackle of Thorns*. So did Transjordan's Emir Abdullah in his memoirs. Later, when Transjordan attacked a nascent Israel in 1948 and seized non-apportioned land on the other (west) side of the Jordan River, the West Bank designation for Judea and Samaria took further hold. And you read about all of these lies earlier.

So, on behalf of Roman, British, and Arab imperialism and expansionism, you media folks are obviously correct in renaming Israel, Judea, and Samaria from their prior three thousand-year-old designations to the newer ones. Remember, regardless of what the Gospel of Matthew says, Jesus was born in Bethlehem of the West Bank, not Judea!

Those treacherous Zionists will also tell you that after their ancestors desperately fought for freedom and independence against both their Roman oppressors and Herod—whom your own reports and articles stated was seen by most Jews as a Roman stooge—no other people, besides the Jews, ever had an independent nation there. The land was subsequently conquered by one imperial power after another—including the Arab Caliphates, which ruled it for several centuries from either Damascus or Baghdad.

Those Jews will next claim that the vast majority of Arabs arrived in the wake of those above seventh century c.e. Arab imperial conquests when they burst out of the Arabian Peninsula and spread in all directions, massacring and conquering millions of native non-Arab peoples and forcibly Arabizing their lands. They'll also say that most Arabs didn't settle themselves in "Palestine" until after the late nineteenth century. Furthermore, they will have the nerve to cite the Minutes of The Permanent Mandates Commission of the League of Nations and numerous other sources to make their point.

Everyone knows how deceitful Jews can be.

Remember, this is all Zionist propaganda, as is the Jews' claim that the Emperor Hadrian, after they dared to revolt a second major time against Roman rule in 132–135 c.e., decided to end their hopes once and for all by renaming the land itself after their historic enemies, the Philistines—a non-Semitic sea people from the Aegean area around Crete. Judaea was thus renamed Syria Palaestina.

So, those deceitful Zionists hold that the very name "Palestine" itself represents the imperial conquest of the Jews and the tragic consequences that followed.

Now, if all the above is not enough, there's something else that adds even more to the confusion. Most of you mainstream media folks supposedly don't like nasty imperialism and the bitter fruits of it. I don't either. So, I can't understand why you insist on using names like "Palestine" and the "West Bank," born of imperial conquest and massacres of Jews in their quest for freedom in their own land, in your articles instead of the names by which those places were known for thousands of years before.

OK, it is time to end this little mind game. As I'm sure my intelligent readers have guessed by now, none of the above are mere figments of Hebrew imagination or Zionist propaganda. They all represent solid fact and history.

My real confusion, thus, is why the Associated Press, the BBC, *The New York Times*, National Public Radio, and most of the rest of the mainstream media treat such things as if they were.

Chapter 44

KURDS, JEWS, AND SHI'A SHOES

ON A LATE 2008 visit to Iraq, President Bush had to duck when a Shi'a Arab journalist threw shoes at him in protest of American policies in Iraq. During a news conference, Muntadhar al-Zaidi yelled out, "This is a gift from the Iraqis, a farewell kiss, you dog," and fired away. Dogs are about as low as you go in the Arab world. Forget about *Marley and Me*, *Rin Tin Tin*, or *Old Yeller*.

I wish I could say that I was shocked by this disrespect usually reserved for such folks as those tolerant Arabs' *kilab yahud*—Jew dogs. I was not.

Polls show that most Arab Iraqis—especially Shi'a—supported al-Zaidi. While he was roughed up by those with a stake in the current regime, those later reports reveal the pulse of the nation. While the Sunni have no love for America either, they now fear what's in store for themselves later on.

While estimates of the dead vary (hundreds of thousands), the 60 percent of Iraq who are Shi'a had their own aspirations suppressed only via the iron fist of the Sunni Arabs' Saddam Hussein. He employed the same murderous tactics against them as he did with non-Arab Kurds in the north. Similar bloody actions against others in neighboring Iran by the majority non-Arab, Persian Shi'a are probably not a bad model for what to expect after America leaves a Shi'a-dominated Iraq as well. Payback time, so to speak. And don't expect America's new President Obama to move back in.

Unfortunately, Kurds will also be caught up in this murderous, age-old Arab feud. The one thing both Shi'a and Sunni Arabs agree on (just like with Israel, the black African Sudan, Berber North Africa, and elsewhere) is that Kurds should have no claims on alleged "purely Arab patrimony."

Having supported America's move against Saddam, decades of intense study, publication about, and professional involvement with the region still made me very wary.

While the Arabs owed Great Britain a huge debt for the very creation of a united, Arab-ruled Iraq out of the post-World War I Mandate of Mesopotamia, this didn't stop them, not long afterwards, from rising up against what they only saw as British imperialism.

No giving the devil his due here. Use him, then lose him.

I can understand that. Too bad Arabs can't grant this same understanding to others though.

As I like to point out, imperialism is only nasty when it is not Arabs dishing it out. How do you think the region became "purely Arab patrimony" in too many an Arab mind in the first place?

Without the Brits' involvement, the Turkish phoenix rising under Ataturk from the ruins of the centuries' old Ottoman Empire would have surely grabbed the oil-rich region around Mosul (which it formerly ruled) and probably would have extended its claim to the black gold of age-old Kurdish Kirkuk as well.[190]

To make the new prospective Arab state viable (the British navy had recently switched from coal to oil and was the main arm of the British Empire), the Brits had to attach the oil of the Kurdish north to the Sunni Arab center and Shi'a Arab oil of the south.[191]

In the process of siring the Middle East's version of Yugoslavia, London thus shafted Kurds out of the best chance they ever had at regaining their independence—something the Brits had promised them earlier as well.

After having their very country created and handed to them by the Brits (who also supplied aircraft and such to fight the Kurds), the Arabs soon revolted to try to drive them out.

Granted, imperialism has its nasty side, and the Brits created an Arab Iraq for their own reasons, yet still...

So, the point here is that America should have known not to expect any gratitude from most Iraqi Arabs either. Hence the thrown shoes, the thrower now a national hero, and so forth.

There's yet another angle to this.

Think of all the American blood, lives, money, and other aid that have been spent for the sake of Arabs in Iraq, giving them new freedoms which they have never had.

Trillions of American dollars will be spent before it is over, billions each month. Visit a local Veterans Administration (VA) hospital to see just some of the other tragic, lasting costs. That shoe-thrower who called President Bush a dog would have literally been fed to the dogs if he had tried that trick with the man America freed him from.

The innocents who died in Iraq whom the shoe thrower complained about mostly died because of the same cowardly Arab trick Israel deals with daily. Arabs routinely use their non-combatants as human shields and then call the international press corps in to view the damage, all against the Geneva Conventions, and so forth. They shoot and then run behind the skirts of their women and toys of their kids.

Was/is America hoping to get something positive for itself as a result of its Iraq expenditures? Sure. But does that erase the above truisms?

Think about those anti-Israel voices quick to protest about two billion dollars in aid sent to Israel each year, an investment whose return comes back to us positively in many ways.

The war in Iraq costs America more in one week than Israel gets in foreign assistance in one year. And, in exchange for that assistance, the State Department and, evidently the new American president, feel that they have the right to pressure Jews into suicidal concessions to Arabs who will never grant them any real peace—except that of the grave.

America has already spent almost a trillion dollars for Iraq, with much more set to come. And after Iraq, ditto for Afghanistan and Pakistan, additional Muslim countries.

Recall, it would take Israel centuries to get this much aid from America. And Israel doesn't ask for American blood to be shed on its behalf or to be bribed to display America's own values and democratic inclinations. How long will the latter last among Arabs after America's exit from Iraq?

Ironically, the one people in Iraq who had better share our values—the Kurds—are the folks whom the Arabist James Baker III-types in the State Department are determined to shaft yet again on behalf of Arabs who want to be sure that oil in Kurdish lands remains part of the "purely Arab patrimony."

Sound familiar?

Same shafting game you read above, just different recipients.

While I did not vote for the Obama-Biden ticket largely because of the long list of known anti-Semitic and/or anti-Israel friends and advisors President Obama has long associated and aligned himself with (including the rabid anti-Semite whose church Mr. Obama sat in for over two decades), Senator Joe Biden—despite his other problems—seems to have a better grasp of the Yugoslavian nature of Iraqi demographics than most politicians.

I'm hoping, against the odds, that Biden will pull more weight than the shaft the Jews and the Kurds Arabist types which are all-too-common in the State Department and among the President's key foreign policy advisors.

Chapter 45

THE LITMUS TEST—NPR AND ISRAEL

To my Jewish brothers. To my Arab brothers. So that we can all be free men at last.

IN HONOR OF Holocaust Memorial Day back in 2007, National Public Radio ran a program focusing on Israel's nominating a deceased man from Tunisia, Khaled Abdulwahab, as its first Arab Righteous Gentile—one of the non-Jews who risked their own lives to save Jews during the Holocaust.

It was a great program and interviewed family members from both sides, including a Tunisian Jewess and her new friend and Arab counterpart.

Having given NPR its due, this all begs the question, Why the silence over all the years about the nasty other side of this story?

Hajj Amin al-Husseini—the Grand Mufti of Jerusalem in the era of World War II—was Hitler's great friend and ally. Among other things, he personally recruited the Bosnian Muslim Hanjar (Saber) Division of the Waffen SS. And there were not a few other examples of Arab/Muslim collaboration with Nazis as well.

The normal Arab response has often been that in their war against the Jews, the enemy of my enemy is my friend. And, "after all," everyone knows that Jew hatred and the Holocaust were just a "Western" problem.

Nice try, and the often all-too-willingly gullible—like NPR—buy into it.

Were politics involved in the Arab decisions to join the Nazis?

Sure—for Arabs, politics mixed with religion are always involved.

During that very same NPR program, the subject of Darfur and the Sudan came up—another genocide against another people.

Yet—surprise (not)—while the hero of the Holocaust's ethnic identity, Arab, was highlighted (while ignoring Arab collaboration with the Nazis), no mention was given to the identity of the perpetrators of the decades old massacres, rapes, expulsions, enslavement, and so forth of some two million not-sufficiently Arabized black African Sudanese—Arabs and willingly-Arabized blacks.

A little comparison, please.

Imagine the unimaginable—Jews raiding innocent Arab villages and doing the above to millions of Arab civilians, posing no threat, harboring no terrorists, or committing no aggression against them.

Would the world have stood by for decades and not stopped this? Would the identity of the perpetrators have been ignored or, at best, placed in the umpteenth paragraph of the news article where it could be very likely missed altogether? Would it have taken NPR decades to do a program about this?

Would the MESA academics ignore this in their classrooms?

Do I even need to ask those above questions?

You see, there is, unfortunately, a good analogy here. Arabs opposed the rebirth of Israel because of religio-political reasons. But religion and politics are virtually always intimately intertwined in Islam.

Once a land is conquered in the name of Islam, it can never revert back to its non-Islamic identity—the age-old Dar ul-Islam vs. the Dar al-Harb thing.

The rebirth of Israel—half of whose Jews are from refugee families from Arab/Muslim lands—was thus opposed on Muslim religious grounds.

But the other, political side of this coin is that, as has been repeatedly seen, upon the collapse of the Ottoman Turkish Empire (which ruled most of the region for over four centuries), Arabs declared virtually the whole area to be solely theirs. And woe unto those who didn't play ball.

Scores of millions of non-Arabs were caught up in this racist Arab game, including fellow non-Arab, not Arabized enough, Muslims.

That's what Darfur is about today, Arab genocide against black African fellow Muslims.

But one would have never known this listening to that NPR program discussing Darfur while praising Abdulwahab. Decades earlier, the main Arab targets in the Sudan were non-Muslim blacks in the south whose crime was wanting freedom from the oppression of the Arab north.

A similar story can be told about Arab actions and attitudes toward Kurds, Assyrians, Copts, native Jews, Imazighen/Berbers, and so forth—massacres, gassings, subjugation, outlawing of native cultures and languages, and so forth. And, as in Darfur, the Kurds and Imazhigen are, for the most part, also Muslims. In other words, Arab racism—pure and simple—by the very folks who place that label on Jews.

As I frequently point out, how dare others demand a sliver of the justice Arabs so forcefully demand for themselves?

Now, please revisit the opening quote at the very beginning of this chapter.

It is the beginning of Professor Albert Memmi's very important book, *Jews and Arabs*.[192]

Memmi—like the Jewish family saved by Khaled Abdulwahab—is a Tunisian Jew. Despite having actively fought for independence against the French, Memmi and the vast majority of Tunisia's Jews felt unable to stay in the country many lived in prior to the seventh century C.E. Arab conquest upon the creation of the new Muslim state. Most went to Israel or France and became part of the other side of that famous refugee coin—Jews fleeing the "Arab" world—created after the attack by a half-dozen Arab nations on a miniscule, resurrected Israel in 1948—that few ever talk about.

As for the Arab line—too often repeated by the ignorant abroad—that Jewish suffering was solely a Western Christian problem, "so why should Arabs be 'victimized' for it?" Please listen to how Memmi, the Tunisian Jew who fought for Tunisian independence and whose ancestors very likely predated the Arab conquest of Amazigh/Berber Tunisia, answers this: "The truth is that we lived in the Arab countries amidst fear and humiliation. I will not take the time here to recite another litany, that of the massacres that *preceded* (Memmi's own emphasis) Zionism, but I can make it available to you whenever you wish. The truth is that these young Jews from the Arab countries were Zionists before Auschwitz. The state of Israel is not the result of Auschwitz, but of the Jewish condition everywhere, including the Arab countries."[193]

Indeed.

Now, NPR travels the world to conduct interviews for its programs. Much too often those programs are slanted against Israel.

Professor Memmi has been a world-famous academic and author for decades—and, by the way, very much a "left-winger" as well—should be right up NPR's alley, not so?

The litmus test for fairness and objectivity when it comes to the study of any conflict should be whether the same lenses of moral scrutiny are used when critiquing all parties involved.

So, to answer my own question about that proposed NPR Memmi interview, I expect that to happen when the majority of academics follow that same standard when comparing Israel to other players in the Middle East.

In other words, don't hold your breath.

Chapter 46

TALL SHIPS, NETANYAHU, AND AMERICA

BY EARLY 2009, President Barack Obama was now at the helm in Washington, and his administration's successful and unsuccessful foreign policy-related appointees and moves vis-à-vis the Middle East were fast confirming some of the worst fears that at least a few of us had before his election regarding the Middle East. At least 78 percent of American Jews deliberately turned a blind eye to the more-than-obvious handwriting on the wall regarding this.

While President Obama was settling in, Israel was trying to form a new government on its own.

Sickened by the previous crew led by Prime Minister Ehud Olmert, the Israeli public turned once again to folks whom they felt would best keep the nation's crucial interests closest to their hearts.

With an old/new leadership under Benjamin Netanyahu reemerging, my mind drifted to another era.

It was a moment in time never to be forgotten—July 4, 1976.

And there I was, alongside the bay in Brooklyn, watching those spectacular tall sailing ships from numerous countries passing under the Verrazano-Narrows Bridge in salute to America's two hundredth birthday. Tears of pride were in many of our eyes that day—including my own. My own father and grandfather, of blessed memories, were American naval veterans of the two world wars themselves.

I was there with my closest friend, Arie, whom I met four years earlier while fishing under that same bridge. Arie is from Israel, and something else was unfolding back then—at almost the very same moment that those tall ships were gloriously sailing by in full regalia—which would psychologically link Israel and America together in many a mind thereafter.

In the night before and during the early morning hours of July 4, 1976, Israel launched Operation Thunderball, aka Operation Thunderbolt...

Aka, Operation Entebbe.

On June 27, Air France Flight 139 was hijacked by Palestinian Arabs and some European soulmates. The plane was taken to Idi Amin's Uganda, where the hijackers were met with open arms.

As had happened a generation earlier, the passengers were soon asked to form two lines—one for Jews, the other for Gentiles. Most of the latter were freed, the Jews became Idi Amin's "guests." Amin's buddies next announced that the Jews would be killed if their demands were not met.

I won't prolong this now. It is an amazingly true story which sired several movies and so forth. Look it up on the Internet, rent one of the movies, or whatever. But, what you need to know, is that on July 4, 1976, Israel raided Uganda's Entebbe Airport, freed the hostages, and showed the world that it was possible to defeat terror if the will to do so was there—a lesson some still need to learn today. It was a wonderful present commemorating America's own liberty as well.

There was one Israeli combat fatality. Lieutenant Colonel Yonatan Netanyahu, of Israel's elite Sayeret Matkal, commanded the ground strike force. He was killed by a Ugandan soldier and was buried on Jerusalem's Mt. Herzl soon afterward. Yoni was an intellectual, a Dean's List Harvard scholar who returned to Israel to resume his earlier combat officer role during the stressful years leading up to the 1973 Yom Kippur War. He was a truly remarkable human being—both a man of the world as well as a true son of Zion reborn.

When my own son was born (G_d bless), we named him Jonathan in honor of King Saul's son, Prince Yonatan—King David's closest friend—and Yoni Netanyahu.

Today, the mainstream media would, no doubt, portray Yoni as a right-wing extremist. Take a look at how it has constantly dealt with Israelis going after the non-stop terror machine and its willing supporters in Gaza and elsewhere. Indeed, any Jew who refuses to stick his head in the sand regarding what the Arabs' true intentions are regarding the acceptance of a Jewish Israel is branded this way.

So, that brings me back to the 2009 Israeli elections and another Netanyahu, Binyamin (there's no "J" in Hebrew). Bibi, like his older brother Yoni (of blessed memory), and his younger brother, Iddo, also served in the Sayeret Matkal. And, unlike too many other Israeli leaders who feel that they have to prostrate themselves and resume a ghetto Jew stance while begging the Gentile world just to be able to survive, this Netanyahu also refuses to fit into that pathetic mold.

While I am not naïve regarding Prime Minister Netanyahu's own real and/or potential flaws (he certainly has them), I nevertheless support him as the best all-around choice Israel currently has.

His main opponent, Olmert's Foreign Minister Tzipora (Tzipi) Livni, was too comfortable with ex-Secretary of State Condoleezza Rice. The latter's non-stop, one-sided, suicidal demands (which her boss also had to approve) placed upon Israel right up until the very moment President Bush's team left office were an abomination and travesty in light of what Israel really faces regarding either Fatah's Abbas or Islamic Jihad and Hamas. The latter are merely more honest in their murderous intent.

Netanyahu knows this.

And I believe he'll have the strength to resist the even more painful turns of the screw which have already begun in the Obama administration.

Attempting to form a coalition in order to resume his earlier role as Prime Minister, Netanyahu unabashedly promised a renewal of both the Jewish and Zionist spirit—something all too lacking in Israeli leadership during the recent past.

Of course, such "attitude" from Jews always scares folks like *The New York Times*, National Public Radio, CNN, NBC, BBC, the European Union, the Foggy Folks, and so forth.

He's a right wing, nationalist hardliner because he refuses to bare the necks of Jewish kids to either the State Department's alleged Fatah good cop or Hamas bad cop terrorists—neither of which show Israel on a map or in their own Arab kids' textbooks. Or because he refuses to have Israel return to its '49 armistice line—not border—nine-mile wide, sub-rump state status. I travel almost three times that distance, just one way, to go to work.

Arabs claim twenty-one states to date in their Arab League, on over six million square miles of territory, conquered and forcibly Arabized from mostly non-Arab peoples (with Abbas's PLO having observer status as the twenty-second in waiting), but how dare Jews claim a sole, miniscule, resurrected one of their own—about the size of New Jersey.

On July 4, 1976, Yonatan Netanyahu re-sent both America and the entire world a message that Jews have been delivering for thousands of years.

Rabbi Hillel, who lived during the Roman occupation of Judaea, restated by then already ancient Jewish teachings when he proclaimed, "If I am not for myself, who will be for me? [But] If I am not for others, what am I?"

Israel has tried very hard to come to an honest accommodation with Rabbi Hillel's current "others" who see the entire region as merely their own. Justice, through Arab eyes only.

Israel has tried to reach more than fair compromises with its Arab others—certainly light years beyond what Arabs have offered to the scores of millions of non-Arabs with whom they have clashed and competed with themselves.

But, as we have repeatedly noted, nothing will really change until the above Arab mind-set changes.

As some of us have pointed out many a time, it is not the size of Israel that bothers Arabs. It is that Israel *is* which is their problem.

Again, try to find Israel on a map of the world or on a globe without a magnifying glass.

President Obama and his new secretary of state, Hillary Rodham Clinton, can pick up the traditional State Department rant against Israel all they want, but this basic Arab rejectionist fact still remains the same. Nothing changes until Arab leaders will say in Arabic to their people that they accept a permanent Jewish Israel in the neighborhood. And the "settlements" America complains about are on just that small buffer, non-apportioned territory of the Mandate that Israel is entitled to by UNSC Resolution 242 to give it the relatively "secure "borders instead of the '49 Auschwitz/armistice lines it had prior to 1967.

Until that overall Arab mind-set changes to allow others a share of the justice pie, Israel must concentrate on that first half of Rabbi Hillel's famous quote.

It is long overdue for Israel to once again have a leader who will place Israel's own crucial national interests first before consenting to any new deals (likely not worth the paper they may or may not be written on) with Arabs which will only endanger it further down the road. The Arabs have openly bragged about their well-known destruction-in-phases scenario.

The West's alleged "moderate" sweet-talking Arafatians in suits, Mahmoud Abbas & Co., still refuse to recognize a Jewish Israel and demand that the latter consent to being swamped by millions of so-called "returning" Arab refugees. Recall that half of Israel's Jews fled so-called "Arab"/Muslim lands due to that same war that Arabs started in 1948. The refugees hardly anyone (besides Jews) ever talks about.

Given this reality check, Prime Minister Benjamin Netanyahu must send the same message to the world his late brother, Lt. Colonel Yonatan Netanyahu, did over three decades ago—a message I've often written about and espouse as well.

Bibi must demand—not beg—empathy for live Jews, not crocodile tears of sympathy for dead ones.

What would over three hundred million Americans in a three thousand mile wide America do given the true—not State Department pipedream—nature of the beast Israel faces?

If I am not for myself, who will be for me?

Chapter 47

IF IT'S BIKE WEEK, IT MUST BE KRISTOF

(Juan Cole vs. Daniel Pipes)

WHILE *The New York Times*'s Nicholas Kristof is no stranger to such positions throughout the entire year, he frequently comes out with his gems of Middle East wisdom right around Bike Week here in Daytona Beach, Florida, when tens of thousands of Harley enthusiasts arrive to also spread hot air around town. This year ('09) Nick was a bit late.

Like others of his ilk—Thomas Friedman (better of late), David Ignatius, Richard and Roger Cohen, just to name a few, who are also obsessed with creating that twenty-second Arab state (second, not first, Arab one within the original April 25, 1920, borders of the Mandate of Palestine)—Kristof loves to lecture Israel about the need to bare the necks of its kids so that Arabs, who conquered over six million square miles of territory from mostly non-Arab peoples, can have that additional state as well.

Remember Jabotinsky's 1937 speech about appetite vs. starvation? Kristof's syndicated op-ed, published in the *Daytona Beach News-Journal* on March 20, 2009 ("Like Minds Cluster When Grazing From the Daily Me"), compared academics Juan Cole and Daniel Pipes as sources of information regarding the Middle East.[194] Kristof prefers Juan Cole. Shocking. (Not!) I have never met Cole, but I had studied under a number of his academic twins in my own masters and doctoral program days.

Recall that while also—but a bit more subtly than President Obama's dear friend, Rashid Khalidi—promoting the themes of nasty Zionists and the need to create Arab state #22, one particular academic specialist on the Turks (so, he couldn't claim ignorance) almost never mentioned the plight of some fifteen million Kurds in Turkey (of some thirty-five million total) who remain stateless to date and who have been subjugated, massacred, and oppressed by Arabs, Turks, and Iranians alike. Again, the only time this professor ever mentioned Kurds at all in his graduate seminars was when he mocked their plight while speaking of his travels in Turkey. I will never forget the hypocritical smirk on his face.

The Turks have tried to erase the Kurds' identity, renaming them "Mountain Turks," outlawing their language and culture, and so forth. All ignored by such academics above—for whatever their obnoxious reasons (perhaps not to anger the Turkish government, which often sponsors and supports their research and other work, and so forth). Such treatment led to frustration, periodic violent explosions, and the formation of the Kurdistan Workers' Party, the PKK.

Keep in mind when comparing the formation of violent, analogous Arab organizations—like Fatah, Islamic Jihad, Hamas, the PLO, Hizbullah, and so forth—that, unlike almost two dozen nations that Arabs already claim as their own, tens of millions of Kurds remain truly stateless to date—and frequently at all others' mercy.

As we have seen, Kurds had been gassed and otherwise slaughtered by Arabs repeatedly and had their one best chance at statehood aborted by a collusion of British petroleum politics and Arab nationalism after World War I.

In Juan Cole's *Informed Comment* blog of February 11, 2009, he proclaimed Israel's new incoming government as being prone to racism ("racialist"), apartheid, and so forth.[195] This is nothing new; these are his positions from the get-go. That has been how one typically gets ahead in Middle Eastern Studies for quite some time now. As we've seen, Israel is routinely investigated to the nth degree, while a blind eye is turned to literally millions of victims of Arab massacres, gassings, genocide, enslavement, dhimmitude, subjugation, and so forth. And woe unto the student who dares to question such duplicity. Again, been there, done that…unfortunately.

I wonder what the typical (there are some very rare exceptions—who may risk their own positions by so indulging) MESA specialist is discussing in his or her classroom related to such things as the amazing exchange between Amazigh/Berber and Arab spokesmen captured on video courtesy of the Middle East Media Research Institute (MEMRI) regarding Arab subjugation of both Jews and Imazhigen, who lived peacefully together in "Arab" North Africa for millennia before the Arab conquest?[196] (Please see the source for footnote #196.) Recall also the latest news that Berbers are increasingly not even allowed to name their children with Amazigh names and have to use Arabized Islamic ones instead.[197] Similarly, Kurds have been told in Syrian Kurdish villages that they can't use their own language.[198]

Anyone willing to place a bet about what the nauseating answer will be to that above question?

The stench of hypocrisy too often coming out of the alleged Ivory Tower is appalling, and those folks, in turn, often have the power to squelch a true exchange of ideas, suppress legitimate debate and dissent, and decide who gets to join them later in academia—as this author witnessed and fell prey to firsthand. "Academic freedom" too often works only for those who occupy their respective bully pulpits.

With the ascendancy of Benjamin Netanyahu and Avigdor Lieberman, the assorted hypocrites and practitioners of the double standard now bemoan the end of the so-called peace process because—finally—at least most Israeli Jews have woken up to the reality that the end game for both the West's alleged Fatah good cops of Abbas and the bad cops of Hamas is really the same regarding Israel. The façade of a difference is largely about who will gain access to and control the billions of dollars in foreign aid and military assistance that is and will be pouring in—especially from Uncle Sam. Recall that Arafat stashed numerous millions of dollars or more in foreign bank accounts. And how does his wife (Arafat was gay and his romps with young boys are legendary) afford that expensive pad in Paris?[199]

Of Abbas and Hamas, Hamas is simply more honest.

The Foggy Folks need alleged good cops if they are to convince Israel to bare its collective neck even further to rejectionist Arabs—regardless of what organization they belong to.

Now, in contrast to the plethora of Juan Coles in academia, Daniel Pipes has long approached the Middle East with a far more realistic and objective appraisal of the facts at hand. He refuses to change lenses when studying Arabs and Jews, for example, and has been virtually prophetic regarding such things as 9/11, militant Islam, and so forth.[200] And he is disliked by not a few colleagues for just this reason.

As we have seen, the Juan Coles of the Ivory Tower have focused primarily on Israel and America as the region's culprits. The fact that the vast majority of conflicts today, for example, involves militant Islam and/or real Arab racism is of no concern to them. What does the fight in the Philippines have to do with Israel and "Palestine"? Thailand? Kashmir? Kosovo/Kosova in the Balkans? What do the murder and subjugation of Egyptian Copts, North African Imazighen/Berbers, Assyrians, those Kurds mentioned above, or Arab genocide in black Africa's Sudan have to do with a virtually microscopic Israel?

The truth is that Israel is on the front lines of the age-old war the Arabs and willingly-Arabized have waged for more than thirteen centuries now, the conflict of the Dar ul-Islam versus the Dar al-Harb.

Once again, here are just a few examples of the real problem. Arab and other hypocritical, duplicitous academics won't touch these with a ten-foot pole.

Recall Sudan's ex-president Gaafar Muhammad al-Nimeiry's statement during the earlier slaughter of nearly a million blacks (and over a million more since): "the Sudan is the basis of the Arab thrust into black Africa, the Arab-civilizing mission."[201]

While Kristof's Juan Cole-type sources of enlightenment are passionate about such things as Rudyard Kipling's nineteenth-century poem "The White

Man's Burden," supposedly typifying continued Western colonialist and imperialist attitudes toward the Third World, why are such blatantly Arab racist, colonialist, and imperialist attitudes and mind-set most often ignored?

Is it that the Arab man's burden is kosher, but the white man's isn't? In the typical university course, that's surely the apparent answer. Recall Cole's recently noted worries about alleged Israeli "racialism."

Let's also reconsider this other earlier quote from the Syrian Arab Ba'th Constitution—something, I'm sure, the Rashid Khalidi or Juan Cole clones' students never hear a peep about. Certainly, none of the many academics I ever studied with brought it up.

"The Arab fatherland belongs to the Arabs. They alone have the right to direct its destinies. The Arab fatherland is that part of the globe inhabited by the Arab nation that stretches from the Taurus Mountains, the Pacht-i-Kouh Mountains, the Gulf of Basra, the Arab Ocean, the Ethiopian Mountains, the Sahara, the Atlantic Ocean, and the Mediterranean Sea."[202]

Purely Arab patrimony hogwash, and I'll repeat my earlier question: are any Eskimos included in this ongoing Arab plan of conquest?

The typical "scholarly" reaction if it involves Arabs is: hear no evil, see no evil, speak no evil. After all, don't forget that these are Arabs we're talking about—not Jews. Besides, it is all probably just made up racist, fascist Zionist propaganda anyway.

As you have deliberately and constantly been reminded, Arabs have habitually claimed virtually the entire region solely for themselves: the Arab-Israeli, Arab-Kurd, Arab-black African, Arab-Amazigh/Berber, and other such conflicts in a nutshell.

Until this subjugating, murderous Arab insanity is solved, it makes no difference how many concessions Israel offers up. And the new American president is attempting to tighten the vise daily.

Arabs will willingly take all that the West pressures the Jews to give, as it plays nicely into the "destruction-in-phases" scenario.

Israel must resist becoming the West's sacrificial lamb for cheaper Arab/Iranian oil prices and enhanced business relations with over one billion Arabs and other Muslims.

And so, summing it up, here's a good rule of thumb to follow for those truly interested in a realistic and objective analysis of what's really going on over there: when it comes to sources such as Juan Cole or Daniel Pipes, whatever Kristof and his ilk tell you, definitely choose the opposite.

Chapter 48

THE POT CALLING THE KETTLE BLACK— MEMORIES OF OLD ATHENS

*O*HIO, THAT IS.

There is an expression, "The pot calling the kettle black." It refers to someone claiming a sin in others that is at least as prevalent, if not more so, in the accuser than it is in the accused. Hypocrisy is the name of the game.

Turn the clock back about three decades.

Some things change, others never will—such as the acceptance of anyone else's political rights in a multi-ethnic region that most Arabs see exclusively as their own. As we've seen, that's the Arab-Israeli conflict in twenty words or less.

To be accepted, and not literally exterminated, one must do what perhaps Egypt's most successful Copt did—consent to this age-old forced subjugation and Arabization. Dr. Boutros Boutros Ghali became a top official in President Anwar Sadat's government and went on to become Secretary General of the United Nations..."Uncle Butros" instead of "Uncle Tom."

Recall that he also instructed that for it to be accepted, Israel, as an entire country, had to also consent to being Arabized—like tens of millions of Kurds and Imazighen who are now told that they cannot even speak their own non-Arabic languages.

Back in the 1970s, when I was a specialist consultant for a major organization while trying to finish my own doctoral work, one of my main jobs involved being brought in by dozens of major colleges and universities across a three-state region in the near Midwest to balance and/or debate anti-Israel spokesmen on campus: Ohio State University, Oberlin College, Wittenberg University, The College of Wooster, Ohio Wesleyan, Denison, Wright State University, University of Akron, Cleveland State, University of Cincinnati, Kent State, and others as well.

One such visit was to Ohio University in Athens, near some of my small-mouth bass fishing grounds in the Hocking River. OU was famous for its English language program for foreign students, so there were numerous folks there from all over the Arab and African worlds.

Those were the days of the United Nations' infamous Zionism Equals Racism resolution. As we have seen, Arab and pro-Arab professors were already hijacking the campus scene, including at OU. Some folks thus arranged for me to come to deliver a lecture to balance one given previously by the other side.

The assorted anti-Israel crew was "loaded for game" when they heard of my invitation—but so was I.

Recall that I was a member of the Anti-Slavery Society, and persistent reports were coming through of slavery (and worse) still being practiced in Arab lands, the lands of some of the same folks screaming about alleged "Zionist racists." I prepared a small booklet called *Look Who's Calling the Kettle Black*, which consisted of about a dozen short articles dealing with the hypocrisy of the Arab position. I had numerous copies prepared for distribution.

I had some of my host students in the audience ready for action. They were in the company of hundreds who packed the lecture hall, including college officials, professors, and so forth. Unlike some of the Hillel organizations elsewhere, the director at OU was on the ball when it came to these issues. My cadre consisted largely of Hillel members.

After my presentation, I had my usual question-and-answer session. That was when the proverbial manure hit the fan. I was anticipating a Zionism-equals-racism question from the audience and, sure enough, I was blessed with one.

I calmly replied, "Since you are so concerned about such issues, I believe you'll be interested in the packet of information you are about to receive." I then had my cadre pass out the booklets.

After the commotion and dust settled, and it was time to leave for my hotel, several carloads of Arab and other anti-Israel students followed me. Along with alerting the local law enforcement, some members of my group decided it was best to keep me company that night. Think of the Danish cartoons and the Pope's comment incidents today. The Arab idea of free speech is the same now as it was back then, and as it has always been.

The next day, before returning to my office about two hours away, I decided to visit the nearby famous boot factory in Nelsonville. What I'm going to relate next may sound a bit melodramatic, but it was for real.

I was on one of the top floors of the factory outlet looking at brand-name dress boots. There was hardly anyone else there, so I was sort of isolated.

All of a sudden, I spotted a half dozen tall, black men down the aisle from me. One of them then called out, "Mr. Hooonigmannn!" After my experience the night before, I figured that my time on Earth was just about up. There were definitely folks at OU who wanted to kill me that night. I nervously stood my ground as they ran up to me.

And if you offered me a million dollars, I would not have traded it for the subsequent experience.

As they grabbed my hands, they said, "Thank you so much for last night. We had never heard or seen what you shared with us before."

Should I be ashamed to tell you of the tears in my eyes at that moment?

These were not just any folks. These were students, sent by their countries, who would later go on to become some of their nations' future professionals and leaders.

As I did on dozens of other campuses, through scores of other platforms, and in dozens of op-eds for leading newspapers all over the region, I tried my best to help change some minds—one at a time.

The struggle is as hard, if not harder, today. But those of us who care have no other choice but to continue in this ever-growing uphill battle for a bit of justice for the Jew of the Nations.

Chapter 49

HUGO'S PEACE PLAN

I HAD CALLED IT quite a while back in my "It's So Bad It's Good" and my "Watch Out for the Set Up" print and Web editorials. While President George W. Bush and his secretary of state, Dr. Condoleezza Rice, really weren't given much choice other than to publicly express disappointment with the results of the Arabs' Saudi-hosted Mecca Accord, which brought Hamas and Abbas together but blatantly rejected anything at all to do with coming to a peaceful resolution of the conflict with their Jewish neighbor, I had predicted that the Foggy Folks' position would very shortly revert back to normalcy—squeeze the Jews, no matter what.[203]

Sure enough, the ink had just about dried on that good cop/bad cop Arab accord when State resurrected the earlier alleged Saudi peace (of the grave) plan, the plan that President Obama now claims Israel would be crazy to reject.

In case you forgot, here's a summary of that plan: Israel, surrounded by almost two dozen Arab states carved out of over six million square miles of territory that Arabs conquered mostly from non-Arab peoples, first agrees to return to its 1949 armistice lines, not borders, which make it virtually invisible on a world map. Next, after becoming once again a sub-rump state, Israel must consent to being inundated by millions of alleged "returning" Arab refugees.

Now, hold onto your seats. There's more recent news regarding all of this.

Amid all of these developments, I bet you missed the latest coming out of that additional source of ethical enlightenment from Venezuela.

Iran's President Ahmadinejad's good buddy, Venezuelan President Hugo Chavez, has evidently tired of his spat with Washington and has offered to bury the hatchet. Wait until you read this breaking news!

Here's Hugo's peace plan for America: first, to show good faith, the United States must pay billions of dollars in reparations for its capitalist exploitation over the past two centuries of Latin America—its people and its resources. This has sired deep resentment in the Latin Street. Next, Washington must then rescind its Monroe Doctrine. After all, what right does one sovereign nation have to tell another sovereign nation whom it can or can't have relations with and what the extent of those relations must be? Third, the United States must agree to give back California, Texas, New Mexico, and the entire southwest lands conquered and forcibly gringoized from Latin Americans. President George W. Bush must return his ranch to Mexico as well. And, finally, Washington must agree to an unlimited return of tens of millions of the descendants of those Latins who were displaced during America's drive for its Manifest Destiny. Any border fences or walls must also be taken down as well to help facilitate this. Forget about such terms as "illegal immigrants;" for example, they can all really show you their "original" family deeds in Los Angeles, San Antonio, Phoenix, and so forth.

Now, if Washington will just agree to all of the above, President Chavez will then recognize America's right to exist in its new constricted borders despite the obvious problem involving native Americans. Since Latin America has that same "Indian" problem south of the border, El Presidente has decided not to make a point of this.

For the sake of justice and peace for all—or at least our—time, Washington must consent to Chavez's offer, or it will continue to be seen as being merely the imperialist, exploitative, capitalist, expansionist, war-mongering nation that many already accuse it of being.

So how do you like them apples? What a breakthrough for peace and better relations, right? Well, I guess you know by now that Hugo didn't really come up with this plan.

But think about it a minute—and then think about what the current and past few American administrations are setting Israel up for.

The only real difference is that Jews have lived continuously—despite ups and downs—in the land of Israel for well more than three thousand years. Their presence and wars for freedom and independence are well documented by the Moabites, Assyrians, Iranians, Egyptians, Romans, Byzantines, Arabs, Turks, and others themselves.

Check out these paraphrased excerpts from Wikipedia. The original sources can be found in the article as well.

The Mesha Stele (popularized in the nineteenth century as the "Moabite Stone") is a black basalt stone, bearing an inscription by the ninth-century B.C.E. Moabite king King Mesha, discovered in 1868 at Dhiban (biblical "Dibon," capital of Moab), now in Jordan. The stele is notable because it is thought to be the earliest known reference to the sacred Hebrew name of God, YHWH (Jehovah, in English). It is also notable as the most extensive inscription ever recovered that refers to ancient Israel, and French scholar Andre Lemaire reported that line 31 of the stele bears the phrase "the house of David."[204] The inscription of thirty-four lines is written in the Moabite Language. It was set up by Mesha, about 850 B.C.E., as a record and memorial of his victories in his revolt against the Kingdom of Israel during the reign of King Ahaziah after the death of Israel's King Ahab.[205]

Can ex-President Bush say that about his ranch in Texas? How about fellow Texan, James Baker?[206]

The most recent Obama Administration position is that the Saudi peace (of the grave) plan will be a "basis for negotiations," and—as we noted previously— he is now talking also about an American plan. Yet, I still say, horsefeathers! What's to negotiate? Let's see. "OK, Arabs, we'll meet you halfway. We'll 'only' agree to have half as many alleged millions of jihadi refugees, raised from the cradle to the nursing home on murderous Jew-hatred, as you insist upon, shoved down our throats, and that's after we're forced to become a nine-mile wide speck of a state again."

I don't think so.

As many of us have been pointing out, the stench of Munich '38 is indeed again in the air. Peace for all, or at least our time—with Israel, instead of the Czechs, as the sacrificial offering. And what makes matters even worse, the Czechs themselves are now joining the European Union chorus in demanding that Israel expose its collective neck this way.

What a shame.

With a new Israeli government now at the helm, Benjamin Netanyahu as Prime Minister and Avigdor Lieberman as Foreign Minister, let's hope that Israel regains its formerly virtually lost sovereignty and dignity. This is the time to hold ground and insist on reasonable peace terms for a miniscule Israel that a three thousand-mile wide America itself would insist upon.

Hamas and the Palestinian Authority's Abbas's Fatah leadership (latter day Arafatians in suits) both deny Israel's right to exist as a Jewish state no matter what their many assorted whitewashers say.

Despite the mounting pressure from the world's assorted hypocrites and Arab oil junkies, Israel's new leaders must offer Arabs peace for peace, recognition for recognition, and negotiate a compromise over disputed—not "purely Arab"—territories.

Period.

There is much that both Arabs and Jews (and many others as well) can gain from each other in a peaceful Middle East.

But the Arabs still have not come up with an honest plan for this to occur. To date, they're simply applying that old piece of wisdom—diplomacy as war by other means.

While it may be easier to turn the screws on six million Israeli Jews than to demand a sliver of justice for scores of millions of other non-Arab peoples in the region from hundreds of millions of rejectionist Arabs and other Muslim supporters, is this really something that America wants to be a party to? That's, unfortunately, what has been increasingly happening.

If you are concerned about this grossly unfair treatment of Israel, now is the time is to let the powers that be know this.

And it wouldn't hurt for those who disagree to take another look at and rethink Hugo's "peace plan" above when considering Israel's ongoing fight for survival and its quest for justice.

Chapter 50

YA MUSTAPHA: WRAPPING IT UP (FOR NOW)...*ET TU, CZECHS?*

BACK IN THE early seventies when I was at the Kevorkian Center for Near Eastern Studies, a group of us used to go, after late classes, to the nearby Cafe Feenjon on MacDougal Street in Greenwich Village. I remember one night in particular, not only because of the belly dancer doing her thing right next to my seat at the table. It was not long after Israel was forced to fight for its life again—attacked on Yom Kippur, the holiest day on the Hebrew calendar—in 1973. The Jews in our group were arguing over how much territory Israel should give up for peace with the Arabs. I happened to notice that the Arab students were having a grand time watching the Jews arguing among themselves.

I just couldn't resist. I walked over to their table and took a seat. Their laughter soon turned to stone faces. I smiled and said, "Hey, don't stop enjoying what you see over there for my sake. I find it hysterical, too—but keep this in mind: some of us have your number on all of this stuff."

I continued, "We know that it is not the size of Israel that is the real issue for you guys. It is that Israel *is* that will always be your problem. Now, while you're amused at some of those Jews over there, you're going to have to deal with at least some others of us who have eyes wide open with our heads out of the sand."

Hushhhh.

Even with the rhythmic song, *Ya Mustapha*, playing in the background, you could have heard a pin drop. I then got up and went back to my original table.[207]

Among its other goals, this book has largely been an attempt to present a sense of the injustice that has been perpetrated against the admittedly imperfect, resurrected state of the Jews by those who should know better. Some things change. Others don't. It was the response of the intelligentsia, not so much the rabble, during the Dreyfus Affair in "enlightened," late nineteenth century France and in Russia which did more to prompt two very assimilated Jews, Theodor Herzl, the father of modern political Zionism, and Dr. Leo Pinsker to write, respectively, *Der Judenstat* in 1896 and the haunting *Auto-Emancipation* in 1882.[208]

This book has also not been an attempt to excuse Israel from any of its real human sins committed in an attempt to survive amid a sea of Muslim enemies—Arab and non-Arab—sworn to its destruction. I have not focused on any of those real or alleged lapses—for they were indeed overwhelmingly that—lapses, neither official or unofficial policy.

No Jews dance in the street when innocent Arab children are killed. No Jews play with Arab visceral entrails and show off their bloody hands to the cameras. No Jews stop pregnant Arab mothers in their cars and shoot both them and their kids dead at point blank range. No museum is erected to display mementos of dead Arabs' body parts, and so forth.

It is not uncommon for Arabs to do such things and much more when the situation is reversed.[209] And when Arab kids die, it is most often because they are deliberately used as human shields by their own heroes. They are not deliberately targeted as Jews are—despite the Arabs' Jenin and Gaza-like earlier lies about Deir Yasin.

The latter was one of three strategically located villages where Arab "militants," involved in blocking the resupply of Jewish Jerusalem, took refuge, ambushed relief convoys, and fired at irregular Jewish fighters of the Irgun and Stern Gangs upon their entrance into the village.

In the heat of the ensuing battle, many lives were tragically lost. While, in retrospect, it was probably carnage that could have been avoided, the irregular Jewish fighters were desperate to break the Arab blockade of Jerusalem. Among other things, Deir Yasin was but an early example of the same old Arab human shield game again. Some Arab fighters were even found dressed as women to avoid capture or worse. After the intense fighting was over—in which the Jews suffered many casualties themselves, Arab leaders—using *taqiyyah* (legitimate Arab lying for the cause) tactics—played the "massacre" for all that it was worth.[210]

To find such allegedly objective books focusing on Israeli sins, which either covertly or overtly demonize Israel, look no further than those written by too many of the MESA-type academics discussed earlier. Remember? Those who insinuate or openly proclaim that Israel is racist, imperialist, fascist, has no right to exist, and so forth—the same ones who either ignore or whitewash the real murderous racism, genocide, and imperialism committed by Arabs against scores of millions of non-Arab peoples in the region.

Scrutiny of Israel is not the problem; it never has been—despite the claims and complaints of the assorted anti-Zionist crew.

I had and have no problem with professors or others scrutinizing Israel—as long as it is done fairly and in proper perspective, given the realities which Israel has been faced with daily from its rebirth.

The problem has always been that far too often—such as with my own experiences—that alleged scholarly quest for truth and objectivity totally disappears when it comes to doing likewise with the so-called "Arab" and/or Muslim world which surrounds the Jewish state. And then those in control over others' careers have say over who does and doesn't join them in academia. That's what denying a doctoral student a dissertation advisor translates to.

I don't blame that duplicitous professor mentioned earlier, nor his ilk, for not wanting me to join them in the ivory tower.

From their own narrow perspectives, I'm sure they knew what they'd have to deal with had I arrived there—no more free passes for the abuses of the Turks or teaching about the Palestine Mandate period and leaving out Colonial Secretary Churchill's separation of Transjordan (almost 80 percent of the total area) and handing it over to Arab nationalism, or ignoring Arab abuse, intimidation, and subjugation of scores of millions of non-Arabs in the region—for starters.

I don't blame them, for that's apparently the nature of their own perceived sense of balance and fairness—as sickening as it is.

Yet, these folks are intelligent—so they know the sins of both commission and omission that they are indulging in, which makes what they deliberately choose to do so much worse.

No, I don't blame them, but what does this all say about universities which allow such biased academics to conduct themselves in such a way—especially since classes at the university are supposed to model diversity of opinion and open debate? The truth is that too often students who dare question the anti-Israel slant they are frequently confronted with do so most definitely at the risk of their academic futures in far too many Middle East and other related programs.

OK, enough of my own past story for now. Let's fast forward to the present.

In early 2009, President Obama's personal choice to head the National Intelligence Council, former Ambassador to Saudi Arabia, Charles (Chas) Freeman, repeated the calumny that it was his mere scrutiny and criticism of Israel which forced him to withdraw his name for that nomination.

To repeat, scrutiny is not the problem. But unfair scrutiny—done out of context of what Israel has constantly been faced with since its rebirth—is. But Chas had too many other things (ethical issues involving ties to China, Saudi Arabia, and so forth) he wasn't mentioning which were causes of concern as well.[211] But hey—blame the Jews.

Hopefully, the various subtopics analyzed in my own endeavor will stimulate further interest and follow-up by my readers.

Faced with non-stop violence and hostility from its rebirth from those who claim virtually the entire region solely for themselves and massacre those who disagree, Israel has, nonetheless, tried very hard to seek a truly just and balanced peace with its neighbors, not the peace of the grave offered up to it by them. The latter includes the Arabs' latest endeavor—the alleged Saudi peace plan. Any truly objective analysis would come to this conclusion.

I will end this account (for now) with news coming out of Europe and from the Obama Administration in America as of May 2009.

As we discussed earlier, Israel had finally reopened its collective eyes and, once again, elected leaders who at least appear willing to assert Israel's sovereignty and to act accordingly. The last Israeli leadership under Ehud Olmert virtually relinquished Israel's sovereignty to the wishes and bullying tactics of an American State Department that fought against Israel's rebirth and has been mostly hostile.

The first duty of any sovereign nation—whether an America which stretches three thousand miles from coast to coast with two giant oceans as buffers, Great Britain, France, Russia, Germany, China, India, Saudi Arabia, or a miniscule Israel—must be the safety of its people. In other words, the security and survival of the sole Jewish state should not be placed in jeopardy so that Arabs can have their twenty-second. There are now plans to make Israel virtually non-contiguous for the sake of the contiguity of proposed Arab state #22.

See what happens to Israel when you link Gaza with the West Bank on the map on page 255, regardless of one's ingenuity of creation.

Should I state what the proper response of Israel's leaders to such plans should be? I had better not, so just use your imagination.

While this should all be a no-brainer, these are, after all, Jews we're talking about here, and that still too often gets in the way of otherwise rational non-Jews' thought processes. At least some Christian teaching, after all, still proclaims that Jews were/are doomed to be eternal wanderers for their rejection of Christian theology. And we already know what Arabs think about their exclusive Dar ul-Islam and purely Arab patrimony.

With the exception of Israel in those nations mentioned several paragraphs above, all others have travelled thousands of miles away from home to fight wars over perceived national interests and security. Additionally, all—including America—have conquered and acquired lands belonging to others in the name of their own respective manifest destinies and such. Think about what the Arabs did and continue to do in these regards.

Recall that the ascendancy of Benjamin Netanyahu as prime minister and his appointment of Avigdor Lieberman as foreign minister caused massive outcries among those who prefer their Jews ghetto-style instead—begging to just be allowed to exist.

Again—Bibi and Lieberman's alleged crimes?

They demand that Arabs show true accountability and commitment to real peace before agreeing to any further territorial concessions and have the alleged audacity to demand loyalty from all of Israel's citizens—Arabs included. Heavens!

Whereas Bibi's predecessor, Ehud Olmert, acted blindly toward Israeli Arab intimidation, terrorism, and repeated acts of treason within Israel proper (Arab Knesset members openly siding with Hamas and such), perpetrated by the freest Arabs living anywhere in the region (Israel), Lieberman has said that such acts will finally be handled the same way any other sane nation would do in order to survive.

For this, Israel's new foreign minister has been branded a racist extremist by the same folks who have watched Arabs enslave, gas, murder, subjugate, wage genocide against, and forcibly Arabize millions of non-Arabs in the region. A region where Syrian Kurdish kids are forced to sing songs praising their "Arab" identities, and where the use of the Kurdish language has been outlawed; where the existence of the majority Imazighen/Berber population of North Africa is virtually negated in the Moroccan constitution; where black Africans are massacred en mass by the Arabs and willingly Arabized in the north.[212]

During a meeting of foreign ministers of the European Union, they discussed how they would deal with the new, non-groveling Jews. All were determined to force Israel to agree to disregard sanity, the facts, and its vital national security interests. While all—including America's new president—demand that the Netanyahu government announce its acceptance of the alleged "two-state" solution, none have confronted the alleged Arab moderates about their own open, continuous rejection of Israel as a Jewish state—the same Arab rejection which has prevented peace between Arab and Jew right from the get-go.

President Obama and the EU's moderate buddy, Mahmoud Abbas, have demanded that Israel allow itself to be swamped by millions of alleged Arab refugees—after its forced retreat to the sub-rump state status of the '49 armistice lines. As we've seen, then Senator Obama claimed that Israel would be crazy to reject such a "peace" (the Saudi plan) that would essentially turn Israel into yet another de facto Arab state.[213] Hence the "moderate" Arab rejection of the word *Jewish* in front of Israel. The Hamas "bad cops" don't even indulge in such word games, to their credit.

That twenty-one nations covering over six million square miles of territory— with scores of millions of non-Arabs living in them—are declared to be Arab, members of the Arab League (the PLO having observer status as the twenty-second state in waiting), and press the claim that virtually the entire region is solely theirs, none of this is of interest to those who met in Spring 2009 in

Prague in the former Czechoslovakia, now the Czech Republic, to complain about Israel's new, "anti-peace" government.

Now add to this another fact that some of us insist on repeating since Arabs and their supporters constantly pretend otherwise.

What the European Union, America, and most of the rest of the world are really calling for is not a two-state solution, but a three-state solution. They are demanding that a second Arab state—not first—emerge within the original 1920 borders of Mandatory Palestine.

As we come to the book's close, recall—yes, yet again—that the modern state of Jordan was carved out of almost 80 percent of the original April 25, 1920, Mandate and was handed over, by Colonial Secretary Winston Churchill, to Arab nationalism in 1922. This point is crucial and indeed relevant to the portioning out of justice—however imperfect—to both Arab and Jewish nationalism (Zionism) alike. As we've seen, it was also recognized as such by the British and King Abdullah, the Arab Emir of Transjordan himself. So that proposed new state—created after forcing Israel back to its suicidal, 1949 armistice lines, not borders—will be indeed be the Arabs' second, not first in "Palestine"—a point that, for obvious reasons, they and their assorted mouthpieces choose to ignore or deny.

Regarding these developments, Britain's Middle East envoy, former Prime Minister Tony Blair, repeatedly told folks, "We need a combination of strong political negotiations toward a two-state solution."[214] Translate this as meaning tightening the screws, yet again, on the Jews regardless of the fact that what Israel got after its earlier total withdrawal from Gaza—non-stop Arab terror, death, and destruction from thousands of Arab mortars, rockets, and so forth launched into Israel proper—will be the likely scenario after its forced withdrawal from virtually all of the "West Bank," once again making Judea *Judenrein*. But this time, courtesy of its "friends" (a lesson the Czechs should know all-too-well), a nine-to-fifteen-mile-wide Israel will have its capital, main airport, main port, key population and industrial centers, and such exposed as the main targets.

Blair, like many of his American political counterparts who also move through the revolving doors of business and government is likely also to be learning to milk the Arab petrodollar cow for all that he can.

While lots could be said about the hypocrisy of other European sycophants to the medieval Arab potentate petrodollar, let's just stick with the Brits for now and only deal with just a few of the many aspects to their hypocrisy. The other nation I will focus upon (and which should be even more shamed of itself) will continue to emerge as we proceed.

That Blair is allegedly concerned about peace should be a good thing, correct? Now, who could complain about that? Or does Tony believe that Netanyahu actually enjoys having Israel's kids and other innocents constantly targeted by his Arab pals? In a gesture to President Obama, Israel had recently caved, removed some road blocks to make Arab travel easier—and soon had a teenager axed to death and another one seriously wounded as a result—a repetition of past experiences as well.

The problem, of course, is what we mean by "peace."

You see, Bibi and Lieberman appeared to be finally calling for the Arabs to clearly define this—and that was deemed to be too much to ask of Arabs by their assorted supporters.

One of Blair's British predecessors, after all, had promised the former Czechoslovakia and the rest of the world "peace" over a half century ago at Munich. Hitler claimed he only wanted the Sudetenland, that part of Czechoslovakia that had millions of ethnic Germans in it.

So, the Czechs and Slovaks (who had a respectable army) were sold out to Hitler in 1938 by their so-called "friends," Britain's Neville Chamberlain & Co. The world was soon at war anyway after the Nazi invasion of Poland.

Blair and Britain's Foreign Minister, David Miliband, who earlier called for the recognition of Hamas (an organization totally dedicated to Israel's destruction), know full well that even their darling Abbas's latter-day Arafatian "moderates" call all dealings with Israel merely a "Trojan horse" that is used to win diplomatically what could not be won on the battlefield—advancing the Arabs' well-known, decades' old destruction-in-phases strategy for Israel's demise.

To reiterate, there is no difference between Hamas and Abbas vis-à-vis Israel in the long term.

As we have seen, Abbas is simply willing to play the game to gain huge amounts of Western cash and support against his rivals. Recall that he is also Arafat's (of Swiss bank account fame) handpicked Fatah successor.

The Brits are no dummies when it comes to the Middle East. They have been meddling in it for centuries. Among numerous other results of this, some thirty-five million Kurds remain stateless to date because of their earlier shenanigans.

Who amongst the EU Foreign Ministers called for a two-state solution in Iraq—the former Mandate of Mesopotamia—where Kurds were indeed promised independence after World War I? And was anyone—especially the French, the former colonial rulers—calling for a state for tens of millions of long-oppressed, murdered, and subjugated Imazighen/Berbers in "Arab" North Africa? Are any of those MESA hypocrites in academia doing so?

The one-sided venom is saved for Israel.

Read carefully this excerpt from a televised debate noted earlier between an Amazigh/Berber spokesman, Ahmed Adghrini, Secretary-General of the Moroccan Amazigh Democratic Party, and an Arab spokesman regarding North Africa:

> With regard to what Yahya said, let me point out, first of all, that he is defending Arab identity, which is of no interest to the Amazigh people. Arab identity is something particular to the Arabs, and does not concern the Amazigh, or North Africans of other identities.
>
> Arab identity is specific to the Arabian Peninsula and to the countries concerned with this, but not to the Amazigh or the non-Arab residents of North Africa. That's one thing.
>
> With regard to the Jews, I don't have to tell you that their history in our region goes back to 1,000 B.C.E. The history of the Amazigh in North Africa goes back 2,957 years. In forty years or so, we will have three thousand years of history behind us, throughout which the Jews lived together with us.
>
> For the Jews too, Arab identity is of no concern, just as it is of no concern to the aboriginal residents of North Africa.[215]

Where were the foreign ministers in Prague who threatened "Arab" Sudan with action if did not stop its racist, genocidal policies against its black population, or deal with what we have seen other Arabs engaged in above?

Better yet, if there must be another two-state solution involving Arabs, why aren't the EU, the State Department, the media, academia, and President Obama demanding it in the master hypocrite Ahmadinejad's own nation?

Recall that Iran's oil-rich western province of Khuzestan has been known as Arabistan for centuries due to its primarily Arab population. Iranians have violently suppressed the latter in the name of their own national interests, all the while demanding that Israel commit national suicide to achieve some other Arabs' aspirations.

What makes matters even worse is that the Brits also know the difference firsthand between a *hudna*—the most that even those Arab "moderates" offer to Israel—and real peace.

The former, modeled after what the Prophet Muhammad offered up to his enemies until he could muster the strength to deliver the final blow (the Peace of the Quraysh), is but a temporary respite from hostilities. One does not give away the store nor bare the necks of one's innocents—the Arabs' deliberate targets of choice—for such a "deal."

Moving to the other side of the world, several decades ago, the Brits were engaged thousands of miles away from home, just a few hundred miles off the coast of Argentina.

The Falklands War was fought in the name of Great Britain's national interests and sovereignty. Now think about this long and hard when you hear the Brits pretend that Israel has no right to be concerned over the violent happenings on its very doorstep and in its very backyard and the need for those secure borders—not armistice lines—promised to it after the 1967 War by the final draft of UNSC Resolution 242 (of which Britain's own Lord Caradon was one of the chief architects).

Closer to Tony Blair's home, does anyone recall what the movie, Mel Gibson's *Braveheart,* was all about? Have a chat with the Scots, Irish, and so forth about was done in the name of the Brits' royal majesty's realm.

OK, the stench of the world's hypocrisy and double standards regarding Israel could fill volumes—so I'll end the discussion of it for now.

But what was even more astounding and unbelievable in that recent springtime in Prague was that the legendary twentieth-century victim of all victims of British machinations and appeasement—the very nation hand-delivered to Hitler at Munich by its earlier British "friends"—then also demanded that Israel consent to a replay of this travesty in the twenty-first century.

Foreign Minister Karel Schwarzenberg of the Czech Republic, whose country was the current EU president, joined the anti-Netanyahu/Lieberman chorus—knowing full well that the claim that all that Arabs want is Judea and Samaria (the West Bank) has about the same amount of truth in it as Chamberlain's promises did in Munich 1938.

Shame on them all.

As Prime Minister Benjamin Netanyahu readied for his first visit with the new American president during the second week of May, 2009, check out some excerpts from Caroline Glick's "Column One" article in the May 8 *Jerusalem Post*: "Arctic winds are blowing into Jerusalem from Washington these days. As Prime Minister Binyamin Netanyahu's May 18 visit to Washington fast approaches, the Obama administration is ratcheting up its anti-Israel rhetoric and working feverishly to force Israel into a corner.

"Using the annual AIPAC conference as a backdrop, this week the Obama administration launched its harshest onslaught against Israel to date. It began with media reports that National Security Adviser James Jones told a European foreign minister that the US is planning to build an anti-Israel coalition with the Arabs and Europe to compel Israel to surrender Judea, Samaria and Jerusalem to the Palestinians.

> According to *Haaretz*, Jones [General James L. Jones, President Obama's hand-picked National Security Advisor[was quoted in a classified foreign ministry cable as having told his European interlocutor, "The new administration will convince Israel to compromise on the Palestinian question.

We will not push Israel under the wheels of a bus, but we will be more forceful toward Israel than we have been under Bush."

He then explained that the US, the EU and the moderate Arab states must determine together what "a satisfactory endgame solution," will be. As far as Jones is concerned, Israel should be left out of those discussions and simply presented with a fait accompli that it will be compelled to accept."[216]

No further comment—except to say that I hope the 78 percent of Jews who voted for all of the above are satisfied with what they got. They cannot say that the proverbial handwriting on the wall was not crystal clear regarding this, nor that they were not warned. Some of us tried.

Not long ago, my friend and veteran author, Diane Wolff, sent me the following quote, "However absorbed a commander may be in the elaboration of his own thoughts, it is sometimes necessary to take the enemy into consideration."[217]

Guess what? This goes for Jews, too—especially for them, for millennia the world's preeminent victim and scapegoat par excellence.

And as this book comes to its conclusion, let's pray that Prime Minister Netanyahu and Foreign Minister Lieberman will have what it takes to resist what will likely follow in the months ahead. And, unfortunately, from America's new leader, as well.

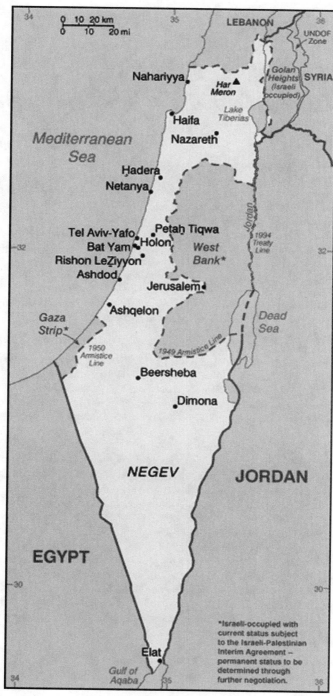

Israel and the Middle East.

NOTES

1: NAKBA: THE TRAGEDY THAT DIDN'T HAVE TO BE

1. Vladimir (Ze'ev) Jabotinsky, *Evidence Submitted to the Palestine Royal Commission* (London: The New Zionist Press, 1937). See also *Microfiche Records of British Colonial Office Palestine Original Correspondence, 1927–1934* (1927: C.O.733/134/44134 and 44154; 1928: C.O.733/150/57134, C.O.158/57410, C.O.186/77086; 1930: C.O.733/192/77282; C.O.200/87086; 1931: C.O.733/209/87353; 1932: C.O.733/218/97086; 1934: C.O.733/258/37376; C.O.262/37437-8).

2. Leo Pinsker, "Auto-Emancipation: An Appeal to His People by a Russian Jew (1882)," *The Zionist Idea*, ed. Arthur Hertzberg (New York City: Atheneum, 1959), 179–198.

3. Theodor Herzl, "Der Judenstat (The Jewish State, 1896)," in *The Zionist Idea*, ed. Arthur Hertzberg (New York City: Atheneum, 1959), 201–226.

4. *Evidence Submitted to the Palestine Royal Commission.*

5. Albert Memmi, *Jews and Arabs* (Chicago: J. Philip O'Hara, Inc., 1975). See also Norman Stillman, *The Jews of Arab Lands* (Philadelphia: Jewish Publication Society of America, 1979); and Joseph Wahed, "Jews Are Our Dogs," *The New York Sun*, August 22, 2006.

6. Philip K. Hitti, *History of the Arabs* (London: MacMillan St. Martin's Press, 1970), 755–757. See also summary comments of Drs. Rashid Khalidi, Benny Morris, James Gelvin, Bernard Lewis, and others in "Palestinian Nationalism," Wikipedia, en.wikipedia.org/wiki/Palestinian_nationalism; and Thomas Kiernan, *Arafat—The Man and the Myth* (New York City: W. W. Norton and Co., Inc., 1976), 22–24.

7. 'Abdallah Ibn Husain, *Memoirs of King Abdullah of Transjordan*, ed. Peter Graves (London: Jonathan Cape, 1950). See also Howard M. Sachar, *The Emergence of the Middle East, 1914–1924* (New York City: A. Knopf, 1969), 404; and Sir Alec Kirkbride, *A Crackle of Thorns: Experiences in the Middle East* (London: John Murray Publishers Ltd., 1956), 27.

8. "Dennis Ross on Fox News Sunday," transcript excerpts of Brit Hume interview with Dennis Ross on Fox News, April 21, 2002, www.foxnews.com/story/0,2933,50830,00.html.

9. Joseph Farah, "Arab Leaders Caused Refugee Problem," *Mid-East Realities*, July 28, 2008, www.middleeast.org/forum/fb-public/1/5007.shtml.

10. "Sheikh Izz ad Din al-Qassam." Encyclopedia of the Middle East, www.mideastweb.org/Middle-East-Encyclopedia/sheikh_izz_ad-din_al-qassam.htm. Some accounts give Latakia as his birthplace; others give Jableh. Both are in Syria.

11. Tacitus, *The Works of Tacitus*, Oxford Translation, vol. II (New York City: Harper and Brothers, 1898), Bk. II 67–73, Bk. V 264–276.

12. "UN Security Council Resolution 242—Definition," WordIQ.com, www.wordiq.com/definition/UN_Security_Council_Resolution_242.

13. Ibid. See also Eugene Rostow, *Peace in the Balance—The Future of U.S. Foreign Policy* (New York City: Simon and Schuster, 1972), 264–273; and Eugene Rostow, "Resolved: Are the Settlements Legal? Israeli West Bank Policies," *The New Republic*, October 21, 1991.

14. Pierre Rehov, producer, *The Trojan Horse*, 1992. See also "Faisal's Trojan Horse," trans. Memri.org, Aish.com, July 2, 2001, www.aish.com/jewishissues/middleeast/Faisals_Trojan_Horse.asp.

15. Ibid.

16. *Evidence Submitted to the Palestine Royal Commission.*

17. See Mahmoud Abbas quote in "A Collection of Historical Quotations Relating to Arab Refugees," EretzYisroel.Org, http://www.eretzyisroel.org/~jkatz/quotes.html.

2: À LA ALAA

18. Malkah Fleisher, "Mahmoud Abbas: I Don't Accept Israel as a Jewish State," Israel National News, April 27, 2009, www.israelnationalnews.com/News/News.aspx/131055.

19. Dio Cassius, *Dio's Roman History*, trans. Earnest Cary (Cambridge, MA: Harvard University Press), Epitomes Bk. LXIII 173, Bk. LXIV 233–235, Bk. LXV 259–271, Bk. LXIX 447–451. See also Tacitus, Bk. II 67–73, Bk. V 264–276.

20. Ibid.

21. Tacitus, Bk. V 269–273.

22. "Habiru," Wikipedia, en.wikipedia.org/wiki/Apiru. See also "Ancient Hebrews—the Habiru?" What Is Matter? August 9, 2006, www.whatismatter.org.

23. Tacitus, Bk. V 274.

24. Hitti, 240. See also William R. Polk, *The Arab World* (Cambridge, MA: Harvard University Press, 1980), 4.

3: WHAT WOULD IBN KHALDUN SAY?

25. 'Abd-ar-Rahman Ibn Khaldun, *The Muqaddimah—an Introduction to History*, ed. N. J. Dawood, trans. Franz Rosenthal (Princeton, NJ: Princeton University Press, 1967), 14, 29, 30–31, 130–131.

26. Ibid., 11–14, 31, 102–103, 106, 110, 131, 183–186.

27. Ibid., 425.

28. Ibid., 102–103, 110.

29. Ibid.

4: ARAFAT'S JESUS

30. Tacitus, 264.

31. Dio Cassius, Epitome, Bk. LXIX 451.

32. Bernard Lewis, "The Palestinians and the PLO," *Commentary Magazine*, January 1975, 32, www.commentarymagazine.com/viewarticle.cfm/the-palestinians-and-the-plo-5467.

33. "Sheikh Izz ad Din al-Qassam."

5: ATTACK OF THE AMNESIACS

34. Pierre Tristam, "Barbarism Beneath Israel's Boot," *Daytona Beach News-Journal*, April 9, 2002, www.pierretristam.com/Bobst/Archives/C040902.htm.

35. "Yasser Arafat," NobelPrize.org, nobelprize.org/nobel_prizes/peace/laureates/1994/arafat-bio.html.

36. Minutes of the Permanent Mandates Commission of the League of Nations, domino .un.org/UNISPAL.NSF/a47250072a3dd7950525672400783bde/ea08ec2300e1e17c052565e f006425ba!OpenDocument. See also Joan Peters, *From Time Immemorial* (New York City: Harper and Row, 1984), 226, 230–233, 296–308.

37. *From Time Immemorial*, 395. See also Fred Gottheil, "The Smoking Gun: Arab Immigration Into Palestine, 1922–1931," *Middle East Quarterly* vol. X, no. 1 (Winter 2003); Moshe Aumann, "Land Ownership in Palestine—1880–1948," in Michael Curtis, ed., *The Palestinians—People, History, Politics* (New Brunswick, NJ: Transaction Books, 1975).

38. "UN Security Council Resolution 242—Definition." See also Simons; *Peace in the Balance*, 269–279; and "Resolved."

39. "Resolved."

40. "Dennis Ross on Fox News Sunday."

41. "Faisal's Trojan Horse" and Rehov. Pierre Rehov's documentary *The Trojan Horse* shows Arafat and his various spokespersons stating that peace negotiations with Israel are part of a strategy leading ultimately to the destruction of the Jewish State.

6: IN DEFENSE OF BANTUSTAN

42. Ismet Cherif Vanly, *The Syrian "Mein Kampf" Against the Kurds: The Kurdish Problem in Syria: Plans for the Genocide of a National Minority* (Amsterdam, 1968). See also "Syria," U.S. Department of State (February 18, 2005), www.state.gov/g/drl/rls/hrrpt/2004/41732.htm; "Syria: Language Research," U.S. English Foundation Research, www.usefoundation.org/view/841; Rebwar Fatah, "The Legal Status of Kurds and Other Non-Arab Ethno-Religious Groups in Syria," London: On Line Presentation/School of Oriental and African Studies, February 19, 2009; Human Rights Watch. "Genocide in Iraq—The Anfal Campaign Against The Kurds" (July 1993), http://www.hrw.org/legacy/reports/1993/iraqanfal/; Chris Kutschera, "Mad Dreams of Independence: The Kurds of Turkey and the PKK," Middle East Report, July–August 1994; "Kurds Being Arabized," Israel and Palestine, January–February 1976, 9–10; United States Institute of Peace, "The Kurds in Syria," Special Report, no. 220, April 2009, www.hks.harvard.edu/cchrp/pdf/RadwanZiadeh_KurdsNSyria.pdf; Edip Yuksel, "Yes, I Am a Kurd," Yuksel.org, Fall 1998, www.yuksel.org/e/law/kurd.htm; "New Legislation Consolidates Discrimination Against Syrian Kurds," Kurdish Human Rights Project, October 24, 2008, www.khrp.org/content/view/412/41/; "Kurds in Syria," Wikipedia, en.wikipedia.org/wiki/Kurds_in_Syria; Arnon Groiss, trans., ed., *The West, Christians and Jews in Saudi Arabian Schoolbooks* (New York City: Center for Monitoring the Impact of Peace, American Jewish Committee, 2003); History of the Copts, www.copts.net/history.asp; E. Hess, ed., "Hatred Is Sacred" Says Syrian Minister of Education, Suleyman Al-Khash (May 1968): Extracts from Arab School Texts (Jerusalem: Ministry for Foreign Affairs, 1968); Arnon Groiss, trans., ed., *Jews, Christians, War and Peace in Egyptian School Textbooks* (New York City: Center for Monitoring the Impact of Peace, American Jewish Committee, 2004); "Assyrians: A Historical Summary," Assyrian Information Management, aim.atour.com/; Maurice Roumani, *The Case of the Jews from Arab Countries: A Neglected Issue* (Tel Aviv: World Organization of Jews from Arab Countries, 1978); Walid Phares, "The Oppression of Middle East Christians: A Forgotten Tragedy," Arabic Bible Outreach, www.arabicbible.com (June 17, 2009).

7: RESOLUTION TO KILL THE RESOLUTION

43. Margaret Tutwiler, "State Department Briefing No. 5," U.S. Department of State Electronic Research Collections, January 9, 1992, dosfan.lib.uic.edu/ERC/briefing/daily_briefings/1992/9201/005.html.

44. Nicholas Burns, "U.S. Department of State Daily Press Briefing no. 79," May 21, 1997, http://www.hri.org/news/usa/std/1997/97-05-21.std.html.

45. "ADC Rejects Rumsfeld's Remarks on Israeli Occupation and Settlement Activities," American-Arab Anti-Discrimination Committee (ADC), August 8, 2002, www.adc.org/index.php?id=487. See also "Occupied Palestinian, Arab Land Is Real Estate Won: Rumsfeld," IslamOnline.net, www.islamonline.net/English/news/2002-08/08/article13.shtml.

46. Dore Gold, "Defensible Borders for Israel," *Jerusalem Letter*/Viewpoints, no. 500, June 15–July 1, 2003, www.jcpa.org/jl/vp500.htm.

47. Ibid.

48. Ibid.

49. Ibid.

50. "Under Fire Palestinian Leader Gets Obama's First Call," ABS-CBN News, January 22, 2009, www.abs-cbnnews.com/world/01/21/09/under-fire-palestinian-leader-gets-obamas-first-call. See also Fleisher.

51. Joseph Lerner, "Secretary of State James A. Baker III, Israel and Saddam Hussein." Independent Media Review Analysis (January 2, 2004), www.imra.org.il/story.php3?id=19323. See also Anne E. Kornblut, "The Bush Family and the Jews," Slate, April 17, 2002, www.slate.com/id/2064424/; Garance Franke-Ruta, "Jews in Play?" The American Prospect, April

30, 2003, www.prospect.org/cs/articles?article=jews_in_play; Anshel Pfeffer, "Jerusalem and Babylon: Courting the Jewish Vote—In the Open," Haaretz.com, 2009, www.haaretz.com/hasen/spages/1037268.html (June 17, 2009).

8: MISSING: ONE ARAB ALTALENA

52. "The War of the Zionist Right Against Sari Nusseibeh," MidEast Web (January 6, 2008), www.mideastweb.org/log/archives/00000665.htm.

53. "What Led to the 1993 Oslo Peace Negotiations?" Palestine Facts, 2009, www.palestinefacts.org/pf_1991to_now_oslo_background.php. See also James Phillips, "The Floundering Oslo Peace Process," The Heritage Foundation, May 28, 1998, www.heritage.org/Research/MiddleEast/EM528.cfm.

9: THINKING JERUSALEM

54. Albert Hourani, *A History of the Arab Peoples* (New York City: MJF Books, 1991), 17–18. See also Abraham Katsh, *Judaism and the Koran* (New York City: A. S. Barnes and Co., Inc., 1954), 110; and Sam Shamoun, "Muhammad's Changing of the Qibla," Answering Islam, www.answering-islam.org/Shamoun/qiblah.htm.

55. Desecration. Jerusalem: Ministry of Foreign Affairs.

10: CHUTZPAH: ARAB STYLE

56. Polk, 428–429.

57. 'Abdallah Ibn Husain, *My Memoirs Completed*, trans. by H. Glidden (Washington, D.C.: American Council of Learned Societies, 1954), 91–92. See also Sachar, 404.

58. Kirkbride, 27.

59. Benjamin Netanyahu, *A Durable Peace: Israel and Its Place Among the Nations* (New York: Warner Books, Inc., 1993), 143–145.

60. Moshe Dayan, *Story of My Life* (New York City: Wm. Morrow and Co., 1976), 366.

61. "UN Security Council Resolution 242—Definition." See also Dr. Chaim Simons, "Israel's Title to and the Legality of Jewish Settlement in Hebron," The Collected Writings of Rabbi Dr. Chaim Simons (June 2007), www.geocities.com/chaimsimons/hebronlegality.html.

11: BEWARE OF GREEKS—ER, ARABS—BEARING GIFTS

62. Rehov. See also "Faisal's Trojan Horse."

12: TOO PREDICTABLE

63. "Protocol Additional to the Geneva Conventions of 12 August 1949, and relating to the Protection of Victims of International Armed Conflicts (Protocol I), 8 June 1977," International Committee of the Red Cross, International Humanitarian Law–Treaties and Documents, http://www.icrc.org/ihl.nsf/COM/470-750046?OpenDocument. See also "The Geneva Conventions, Law of Armed Conflict," Brookside Associates Medical Education Division, www.brooksidepress.org/Products/OperationalMedicine/DATA/operationalmed/Manuals/SeaBee/Fieldcombatopssection/LOACGenevaConventions.pdf.

64. "President George W. Bush: Remarks in Birmingham, Ala., Nov. 3, 2003," Defend America, www.defendamerica.mil/iraq/nov2003/usviews110303.html. See also "Vice President Cheney Delivers Remarks to the Republican Governors Association," The White House (October 25, 2001), georgewbush-whitehouse.archives.gov/vicepresident/news-speeches/speeches/vp20011025.html.

65. Ibid. See also "The Geneva Conventions, Law of Armed Conflict."

66. Charles Krauthammer, "What Happened to the Powell Doctrine?" *The Washington Post*, April 20, 2001. See also Colin Powell, "Excerpts from Colin Powell, 'US Forces: The Challenges Ahead,' Foreign Affairs, Winter 1992," Brooklyn College, academic.brooklyn.cuny.edu/history/johnson/powell.htm.

13: A Lesson from Kosovars and Palestinians for Atlasians

67. Hugh Fitzgerald, "Fitzgerald: Taqiyya: A Quiz," Jihad Watch, http://www.jihadwatch .org/archives/019919.php. See also Hitti, 755–757; and "Zuheir Mohsen," Wikipedia, en.wikiquote.org/wiki/Zuheir_Mohsen.

68. Tacitus, Bk. V 264.

69. "Annals of Euthychius I," *Twenty Centuries of Jewish Life in the Holy Land*, ed. Dan Bahat (Jerusalem: The Israel Economist, 1975), 23.

70. Arlene Kushner, "Links to Terrorism," The Center for Near East Policy Research, October, 2004, canadiancoalition.com/unrwa/UNRWA_TerrorReport.html#_Toc86488077. See also "United Nations Relief and Works Agency for Palestine Refugees in the Near East," Wikipedia, en.wikipedia.org/wiki/UNRWA.

71. Gottheil.

72. Middle East Media Research Institute, "Debate About New Berber-Jewish Friendship Association in Morocco on Iranian Al-Alam TV," *Special Dispatch* 1695, (August 24, 2007), http://www.memritv.org/report/en/2640.htm. See also "Thousands of Algerian Berbers Protest New Language Law," North-of-Africa.com, July 25, 1998; "The Moroccan Constitution Negates the Existence of the Amazigh People and Its Identity," North-of-africa.com, March 24, 2009, north-of-africa.com/article.php3?id_article=571; Zighen Aym, "Cultural Apartheid in North Africa," *The Amazigh Voice*, December 1995–March 1995, www.ece.umd.edu/~sellami/ DEC95/review2.html; and "Arabist Repression Against Amazigh Students," North-of-Africa .com, Jan. 15, 2008, http://www.north-of-africa.com/article.php3?id_article=462.

73. Carter Vaughn Findley, *The Turks in World History* (New York City: Oxford University Press, 2005), 214–215. See also Kutschera.

74. Vanly, 4. See also Fatah; Human Rights Watch; "Kurds Being Arabized;" United States Institute of Peace; Yuksel; and "Kurds in Syria."

14: Qassam/Kassam—So, What's In a Name?

75. Minutes of the Permanent Mandates Commission of the League of Nations. See also *From Time Immemorial*, 230–235, 265, 270–271, 275–277.

15: Evolution of the Suicide/Homicide Bomber

76. *The Koran*, trans. by N.J. Dawood (Middlesex: Penguin Books, 1959). See also Sayyed Muhammed Hussein Fadlallah, "Al-Isra' (Isra', The Night Journey, Children of Israel)," Bayynat, english.bayynat.org.lb/Quran/al_isra11.htm; "The Koran and the Jews," FrontPage Magazine, June 3, 2004, www.frontpagemag.com/readArticle.aspx?ARTID=12825; and Shaykh Prof. Abdul Hadi Palazzi, "What the Qur'an Really Says," The Temple Mount in Jerusalem, www.templemount.org/quranland.html.

77. Sa'ad Jawad, *Iraq and the Kurdish Question: 1958–1970* (London: Ithaca Press, 1981), 41, 120, 128.

78. "Using the Civilian Population in the Gaza Strip as Human Shields." Intelligence and Terrorism Information Center at the Israel Intelligence Heritage and Commemoration Center (January 21, 2008), www.terrorism-info.org.il/malam_multimedia/English/eng_n/pdf/ hamas_e049.pdf. See also James Phillips, "End Hamas Hostage Strategy to Bring Peace to Gaza," The Heritage Foundation, January 6, 2009, www.heritage.org/Research/MiddleEast/ wm2188.cfm.

79. Farah. See also "A Collection of Historical Quotations Relating to Arab Refugees."

80. Nonie Darwish, "The Gaza Prison Camp," *The Huffington Post*, April 13, 2009. See also "Israel's Peace Initiative, May 14, 1989," usembassy-israel.org.il/publish/peace/may89.htm.

81. "Dennis Ross on Fox News Sunday."

82. Rehor. See also "Faisal's Trojan Horse."

16: Hunting Quail and Sitting Ducks

83. "UN Security Council Resolution 242—Definition." See also Simons; *Peace in the Balance*, 264–273; and "Resolved."

84. Franke-Ruta. See also Pfeffer.

85. Alex Safian, "The Robert Malley-Arafat Connection," Committee for Accuracy in Middle East Reporting in America, February 2, 2008, www.camera.org/index.asp?x_print=1&x_context=8&x_nameinnews=88&x_article=1437. See also "Robert Malley," Discoverthenetworks.org, www.discoverthenetworks.org/individualProfile.asp?indid=2310; and Mark Hemingway, "Robert Malley Surfaces Again," National Review Online, November 11, 2008, corner.nationalreview.com/post/?q=YjdkOGI1OWQwMGI2ZTBkMjI1YTA0YmVkODg3YTgyMjA=.

17: Appetite Versus Starvation

86. Tacitus, 264.

87. Cassius, Epitome Bk. LXIX, 451.

88. "The Palestinians and the PLO," 32.

89. Cassius, 447. See also "The Palestinians and the PLO," 32.

90. Minutes of the Permanent Mandates Commission of the League of Nations. See also From Time Immemorial and Gottheil.

91. *Evidence Submitted to the Palestine Royal Commission,* 12–13. See also Arthur Hertzberg, *The Zionist Idea* (New York City: Atheneum, 1959), 557–570.

92. Fitzgerald. See also Hitti, 755–757; "Zuheir Mohsen;" and "Palestinian Nationalism."

93. Thomas Bois, *The Kurds* (Beirut: Khayat Publishing Co., 1966), 135. See also Who Are the Kurds? *PBS Online NewsHour*, www.pbs.org/wgbh/pages/frontline/shows/saddam/kurds/.

94. Fitzgerald. See also Hitti, 755–757; and "Palestinian Nationalism."

18: Mind-Boggling: the Hypocrisy and Double Standards

95. David Brooks, "All Hail Moore," *The New York Times*, June 26, 2004.

96. George Lenczowski, *The Middle East in World Affairs* (Ithaca, NY: Cornell University Press, 1962), 131.

97. "Full Text of Al-Zarqawi Letter," International Institute for Counter-Terrorism (February 12, 2004), http://212.150.54.123/documents/documentdet.cfm?docid=62. See also Primary Document: National Review Online, February 12, 2004. See also Abu Musab al-Zarqawi, "Zarqawi's Cry," National Review Online, www.nationalreview.com/document/zarkawi200402121818.asp.

98. Larry Everest, "How the U.S. Used Iraq's Kurds: A History of Betrayal," www.cbpa.drake.edu/hossein-zadeh/papers/KurdsBIDOM.htm. See also Barry Lando, "History of Complicity," Salon.com, November 19, 2004, dir.salon.com/story/news/feature/2004/11/19/saddam_chemical_weapons/print.html; Human Rights Watch; Aaron Latham, "What Kissinger Was Afraid of in the Pike Papers," New York, October 4, 1976; Jonathan Rauch, "Why Bush (Senior) Didn't Blow It in the Gulf War," ReasonOnline, October 27, 2001, www.reason.com/news/show/34590.html (June 17, 2009); and "1991: The South Iraq and Kurdistan Uprisings," Libcom.org, September 9, 2006, libcom.org/history/articles/iraq-south-kurdistan-uprisings-1991.

99. Richard Cottam, Nationalism in Iran (Pittsburgh: University of Pittsburgh Press, 1964), 3, 6, 268–274, 284.

19: April Magic

100. Rehov. See also "Faisal's Trojan Horse."

20: Al Chait Shechatanu, We Have Sinned Against You

101. "Dennis Ross on Fox News Sunday."

102. "Under Fire Palestinian Leader Gets Obama's First Call." See also Karen Laub, "Obama Envoy: Two State Solution Is the Only Solution," Yahoo News, April 17, 2009, news.yahoo.com/

s/ap/20090417/ap_on_re_mi_ea/ml_mideast_us;_ylt=AqoqBpfMhdGDD9Rj4fpp9zVvaA8F; "Farrakhan on Obama: 'The Messiah Is Absolutely Speaking,'" World Net Daily (October 9, 2008), http://www.worldnetdaily.com/?pageId=77539; "Obama's Pro-Hamas Church," *Investor's Business Daily*, March 25, 2008, www.ibdeditorials.com/IBDArticles.aspx?id=291335140632942; Ed Lasky, "Samantha Power Uncut," American Thinker, October 5, 2008, www.americanthinker.com/blog/2008/10/samantha_power_uncut.html; and William Mehlman, "The Company He Keeps," Mideast Outpost, April 25, 2009, mideastoutpost.com/archives/000557.html.

103. "President George W. Bush: Remarks in Birmingham, Ala., Nov. 3, 2003." See also "Vice President Cheney Delivers Remarks to the Republican Governors Association."

104. Adam Kredo, "Samir Kuntar's Bloody Deeds," *Jerusalem Post*, May 28, 2008, www.jpost.com/servlet/Satellite?cid=1211872831853&pagename=JPost percent2FJPArticle percent2Fprinter. See also "Samir Kuntar," Wikipedia, en.wikipedia.org/wiki/Samir_Kuntar; and Tali Hatuel, "Pregnant Mum Gunned Down," *The Sydney Morning Herald*, May 3, 2004.

21: UNCLE BOUTROS AND UNCLE TOM—A LESSON IN ARAB TOLERANCE

105. Julius Wellhausen, *The Arab Kingdom and Its Fall*, trans. M. G. Weir (Calcutta: University of Calcutta Press, 1927), 278–311.

106. Amos Elon, *Flight into Egypt* (New York City: Pinnacle Books, 1980), 90, 80–92.

107. Memmi, v.

22: LONG LIVE ARABISTAN!

108. British Ahwazi Friendship Society, "Human Rights and the Ahwazi Arabs," July 2007, www.hlrn.org/img/violation/dossier.pdf. See also British Ahwazi Friendship Society, "Israel Condemns Sweden for Supporting 'Separatism,'" December 9, 2008, www.ahwaz.org.uk/2008/12/iran-condemns-sweden-for-supporting.html; and Gregory Noll, "Khuzestan: Oil, Ethnicity, and Conflict in Iran," ICE Case Studies no. 178, April 2006, www1.american.edu/ted/ice/khuzestan.htm.

109. Cottam, 114, 110–117.

110. "Human Rights and the Ahwazi Arabs." See also "Israel Condemns Sweden for Supporting 'Separatism.'"

111. "War and Peace—and Deceit—in Islam."

23: PANTSIL, DARFUR, AND THE ARAB MAN'S BURDEN

112. Wadhams, Nick. "ICC Presents Evidence of Mass Deaths in Sudan." IOL News (June 15, 2006), www.iol.co.za/index.php?set_id=1&click_id=68&art_id=qw1150357860174B252.

113. Aguda, 177–178. See also "Grass Curtain;" "International Criminal Court Prosecutor Tells Security Council Entire Darfur Region Is a 'Crime Scene,'" United Nations Security Council, SC/9349/June 5, 2008; Opoku Agyeman, "Pan-Africanism vs. Pan-Arabism: A Dual Asymmetrical Model of Political Relations," Middle East Review (MER), Summer 1984, American Academic Association for Peace in the Middle East.

114. "Video: Islamic Jihad's Insight into Pallywood." Honest Reporting (March 17, 2008), www.honestreporting.com/articles/45884734/critiques/new/Video_Islamic_Jihads_Insight_into_Pallywood.asp.

115. Aguda, 177–178.

116. The Baath Arab Socialist Party National Leadership, "The Constitution of the Baath Arab Socialist Party," www.baath-party.org/eng/constitution2.htm.

24: PARTNERS: THE ULTIMATE TROJAN HORSE

117. "Incitement, Anti-Semitism, and Hatred of Israel in Palestinian School Textbooks," Jewish Virtual Library, November 2001, www.jewishvirtuallibrary.org/jsource/Peace/patext1.html. See also "Hamas Covenant 1988: The Covenant of the Islamic Resistance Movement, August 18, 1988," The Avalon Project, Yale Law School, avalon.law.yale.edu/20th_century/hamas.asp.

118. Fleisher.

25: SETTLERS, NOW THINK ABOUT THIS LONG AND HARD

119. Kushner. See also "United Nations Relief and Works Agency for Palestine Refugees in the Near East."

120. Minutes of the Permanent Mandates Commission of the League of Nations. See also Gottheil and *From Time Immemorial*.

121. "Sheikh Izz ad Din al-Qassam."

122. "Under Fire Palestinian Leader Gets Obama's First Call."

123. "UN Security Council Resolution 242—Definition." See also Simons.

124. Ibid.

26: CHANUKAH CORROBORATIONS

125. Cyrus the Great, "Kurash (Cyrus) the Great: The Decree of Return for the Jews, 539 B.C.E.," *Ancient History Sourcebook*, www.fordham.edu/halsall/ancient/539cyrus1.html.

126. Hebrew Bible, Ezra 1:1–8.

127. Dio Cassius, 447–451.

128. F. E. Peters, *The Harvest of Hellenism* (New York City: Simon and Schuster, 1970), 232, 281–308.

129. Tacitus, Bk. V 269.

27: FOCUS ON THE HERE AND NOW

130. "Farrakhan on Obama: 'The Messiah Is Absolutely Speaking.'" See also "Obama's Pro-Hamas Church."

131. Khaled Abu Toameh, "PA officials 'surprised' by US Middle East plan," *The Jerusalem Post*, May 21, 2009. See also Robert Satloff, "The Mecca Accord: The Victory of Unity Over Progress," *Policy Watch*, no. 1195, February 12, 2007, The Washington Institute for Near East Policy; "Blair Says Two-State Solution to Israel-Palestinian Conflict Is Top Priority," *Voice of America News*, June 27, 2007; and "Leadall: Two-State Solution Hammered Home to Netanyahu," *Earth Times*, April 1, 2009.

28: SAMIR KUNTAR AND OTHER LESSONS FOR THE DIASPORA

132. Kredo. See also "Samir Kuntar."

133. Hatuel.

134. Safian. See also "Robert Malley" and Hemingway.

29: ISRAEL OWES GAZA NOTHING—EXCEPT AN ULTIMATUM

135. "Blair Says Two-State Solution to Israel-Palestinian Conflict is Top Priority." See also "Leadall: Two-State Solution hammered home to Netanyahu;" Barry Schweid, "Tony Blair Holds Out Hope for Two-State Solution," *The Washington Post*, May 14, 2009, www.washingtonpost.com/wp-dyn/content/article/2009/05/14/AR2009051403723.html; and "Blair Urges U.S. to Pressure Israel," CBNNews.com, December 5, 2008, www.cbn.com/CBNnews/495382.aspx.

136. Israel Ministry of Foreign Affairs, "The Armistice Agreements, Vol. 1–2: 1947–1974" (January 12, 1949), www.mfa.gov.il/MFA/Foreign+Relations/Israels+Foreign+Relations+since+1947/1947-1974/THE+ARMISTICE+AGREEMENTS.htm.

137. Gabriel Schoenfeld, *The Return of Anti-Semitism* (New York City: Encounter Books, 2004).

138. Krauthammer. See also Powell and "Powell Doctrine," Wikipedia, en.wikipedia.org/wiki/Powell_Doctrine.

139. Alan Dershowitz, "The Real Jimmy Carter," FrontPageMagazine.com, April 30, 2007. See also Michelle Malkin, "The Cintons' Foreign Funders," December 18, 2008, michellemalkin.com/2008/12/18/the-clintons-foreign-funders/; and Naomi Klein, "James Baker's Double Life," *The Nation*, October 12, 2004.

140. "Barack Obama links Israel peace plan to 1967 borders deal," [London] *Sunday Times*, November 16, 2008. See also Laub.

141. Gold.

30: No, Mr. Jihadi, Gaza Isn't Warsaw

142. "Video: Gaza Is an Israeli Concentration Camp," Patrick Buchanan: Right from the Beginning (January 16, 2009), buchanan.org/blog/video-buchanan-gaza-is-an-israeli-concentration-camp-1355.

143. "Yellow Badge," Boston University Theology Library Archives, sthweb.bu.edu/archives/index.php?option=com_awiki&view=mediawiki&article=Yellow_badge. See also "Yellow Badge," Wikipedia, en.wikipedia.org/wiki/Yellow_badge.

144. Middle East Media Research Institute. "Palestinian Leader: Number of Jewish Victims in the Holocaust Might Be 'Even Less Than a Million...' Zionist Movement Collaborated with Nazis to 'Expand the Mass Extermination' of the Jews." Inquiry and Analysis 95 (May 30, 2002), www.memri.org/bin/articles.cgi?Area=ia&ID=IA9502.

145. "Protocol Additional to the Geneva Conventions of 12 August 1949, and relating to the Protection of Victims of International Armed Conflicts (Protocol I), 8 June 1977." See also "The Geneva Conventions, Law of Armed Conflict."

31: Between Ankara and Jerusalem

146. Ibid.

147. Lenczowski, 131. See also "British Petroleum Politics, Arab Nationalism, and the Kurds," 34.

148. "British Petroleum Politics, Arab Nationalism, and the Kurds," 35.

149. Jawad, 128. See also Peter Sluglett, *Britain in Iraq: 1914–1932* (London: Ithaca Press, 1976).

150. Omran Feili and Arlene Fromchuck, "The Kurdish Struggle for Independence," *Middle East Review* vol. IX, Fall 1976, 51. See also The Baath Arab Socialist Party National Leadership and 'Abd Al Rahman al-Bazzaz, "This Is Our Nationalism," *Man, State, and Society in the Contemporary Middle East*, ed. Jacob Landau (New York City: Praeger Publighing, 1972).

151. Sluglett, 10–11.

152. "Report: Arab Funding of Important Subjects in UK Universities: A Degree of Influence," Islamization Watch, islamizationwatch.blogspot.com/2009/03/arab-funding-of-important-subjects-in.html. See also Stanley Kurtz, "Saudi in the Classroom," National Review Online, July 25, 2007, article.nationalreview.com/?q=YjRhZjYwMjU4MGY5ODJmM2MzN GNhNzljMzk4ZDFiYmQ=; Richard Kerbaj, "Uni Draws More Fire Over Saudi Cash," The Australian, April 25, 2008, http://www.theaustralian.news.com.au/story/0,25197,23595469-5013404,00.html; Erick Stakelbeck, "Saudis Multi-Million Dollar PR Machine," Campus Watch, March 10, 2008, http://www.campus-watch.org/article/id/4891; Erick Stakelbeck, "Public Schools Teach the ABCs of Islam," CBNNews.com, http://www.cbn.com/cbnnews/460652.aspx; John R. MacArthur, "The Vast Power of the Saudi Lobby," Harper's Magazine, April 17, 2007, www.harpers.org/archive/2007/04/jrm-pubnote-20070417; Jonathan Shanzer, "Follow the Money Behind Anti-Israel Invective on Campus," CAMERA On Campus, Spring 2009; and Lee Kaplan, "The Saudi Fifth Column on Our Nation's Campuses," FrontPage Magazine, April 05, 2004.

153. Findley, 214–215.

154. Zachary Lockman, "February 13, 2007," Committee on Academic Freedom Letters, Middle East Studies Association, www.mesa.arizona.edu/about/cafmenaletters.htm#Feb1307. See also "Letters on Turkey: May 27, 2008," Middle East Studies Association, www.mesa.arizona.edu/caf/letters_turkey.htmln.

155. Jawad, 124.

32: Hamas, Gaza, and the UNN (United Nauseating Nations)

156. Honigman, 34–36.

157. Elon, 84–92.

158. Desecration. Jerusalem: Ministry of Foreign Affairs.

159. "Harper Doubts UN Post Deliberately Targeted," CBC News (July 2006), www.cbc.ca/news/viewpoint/yourspace/un_lebanon.html. See also "United Nations Relief and Works Agency for Palestine Refugees in the Near East."

160. Ibid.

161. "United Nations an Accomplice in Hezbollah Kidnapping," The Volokh Conspiracy (July 21, 2006), volokh.com/posts/1153523571.shtml.

162. Blockade of Israel…recognized as *Casus belli* after 1956 Sinai Campaign, B.L. Slantchev, March 4, 2004 dss.ucsd.edu/~bslantch/courses/nss/lectures/23-Arab–Israeli-conflict.pdf.

33: The Saudi "Peace" (of the grave) Plan: an Offer Israel Must Refuse

163. Ellen Knickmeyer, "Darfur Slaughter Rooted in Arab-African Slavery," *The Seattle Times,* July 2, 2004. See also "Abd Al-Bari Atwan, Editor-in-Chief of Al-Quds Al-Arabi Calls on Obama to Impose the American Model on Arab Countries: In an Arab Country, Obama Would Be Called a Slave; Arabs Are the Epitome of Racism," MEMRItv.org, Interview aired on BBC Arabic TV (November 7, 2008), www.memritv.org/clip/en/1906.htm; "Slavery," Encyclopedia Britannica's Guide to Black History, www.britannica.com/blackhistory/article-24160; Adrea Rosenberg, "The Middle East Slave Trade," *Middle East Review,* Winter 1976–1977, 60–62.

164. "King Faisal Air Base," GlobalSecurity.org, www.globalsecurity.org/military/world/gulf/tabuk.htm.

165. *The West, Christians and Jews in Saudi Arabian Schoolbooks.* See also Hess; *Jews, Christians, War and Peace in Egyptian School Textbooks*; "Incitement, Anti-Semitism, and Hatred of Israel in Palestinian School Textbooks."

166. "What Led to the 1993 Oslo Peace Negotiations?" See also "The Floundering Oslo Peace Process."

167. W. Montgomery Watt, Muhammad—Prophet and Statesman (London: Oxford University Press, 1961), 98–99, 112–118.

34: Ahmadinejad: Liar, Hypocrite, or Just Islamist Iranian Stooge?

168. "Annals of Euthychius I," 23.

169. Knickmeyer. See also "Abd Al-Bari Atwan, Editor-in-Chief of Al-Quds Al-Arabi Calls on Obama to Impose the American Model on Arab Countries: In an Arab Country, Obama Would Be Called a Slave; Arabs Are the Epitome of Racism;" and "Slavery."

170. "Human Rights and the Ahwazi Arabs." See also "Israel Condemns Sweden for Supporting 'Separatism;'" "UNPO Resolution in Support of Indigenous Ahwazi Arabs in Iran," Unrepresented Nations and Peoples Organization (June 27, 2005), www.unpo.org/content/view/2697/236/.

36: Proclaim Liberty Throughout the Land: the Israel Aid Issue

171. Lerner.

37: If Jews Had Any Brains, They'd Be Cristians (Now, Don't Be Offended)

172. "Anne Coulter: Jews Should Be Perfected (Video)," RightPundits.com (October 11, 2007), www.rightpundits.com/?p=948.

173. Geoffrey Chaucer, "The Prioress' Tale," *The Canterbury Tales,* www.readprint.com/chapter-1772/Geoffrey-Chaucer.

174. Tacitus, Bk.V 269.

38: GANDHI, MUMBAI, AND BEYOND

175. *The Legacy of Jihad: Islamic Holy War and the Fate of Non-Muslims.* See also Andrew Bostom, C–SPAN Video Library Interview, Heritage Foundation Seminar, May 9, 2006.

176. Rasoul Sorkhabi, "Einstein and the Indian Minds: Tagore, Ghandi and Nehru," *Current Science* vol. 88, no.7, April 10, 2005, 1187–1191, http://www.ias.ac.in/currsci/apr102005/1187.pdf.

177. Ibid.

178. Ibid. See also Walter Laqueur, *A History of Zionism* (New York City: Schocken Books, 1976), 156, 468.

179. Benny Morris, "Einstein's Other Theory," *The Guardian*, February 16, 2005, www.guardian.co.uk/world/2005/feb/16/israel.india.

39: WHY IS THIS SO HARD TO UNDERSTAND?

180. "Israeli Elections Too Close to Call," NPR.org, February 10, 2009.

181. Eric Westervelt, "Israeli Nationalist Expected to Gain in Election," National Public Radio, February 9, 2009, www.npr.org/templates/transcript/transcript.php?storyId=100436058.

182. "Arabist Repression Against Amazigh Students." See also "Thousands of Algerian Berbers Protest New Language Law;" "The Moroccan Constitution Negates the Existence of the Amazigh People and Its Identity;" Aym; "Kurds Being Arabized;" "Syria;" "Syria: Language Research;" United States Institute of Peace; Yuksel; "Kurds in Syria;" "New Legislation Consolidates Discrimination Against Syrian Kurds;" and Vanly.

40: JESUS' BONES: SO, MY FRIENDS, HOW DOES IT FEEL?

183. John W. Kennedy, "The Ultimate Kibitzer," *Christianity Today*, February2009, www.christianitytoday.com/ct/2009/february/27.32.html.

41: REPORTS FROM THE INSIDE: THE REAL PROBLEM WITH PRESIDENT OBAMA'S KHALIDI

184. "McCain Slams Obama over Foreign Policy Exposure," CBNNews.com, October 29, 2008, http://www.cbc.ca/world/usvotes/story/2008/10/29/mccain-latimes.html?ref%3Drss.

185. "Report: Arab Funding of Important Subjects in UK Universities: A Degree of Influence." See also Kurtz; Kerbaj; "Saudis Multi-Million Dollar PR Machine;" "Public Schools Teach the ABCs of Islam;" MacArthur; and Herb Denenberg, "The Anti-American Fifth Column Is Based in Leading Colleges, Universities," The Bulletin, January 29, 2009, http://thebulletin.us/articles/2009/01/29/herb_denenberg/doc49814b9d2cc2f701435825.txt.

42: WHO WON'T BE MAKING JOKES ABOUT WMD

186. Martin Van Bruinessen, *Agha, Shaikh, and State: On the Social and Political Organization of Kurdistan* (Rijswijk: Netherlands Organization For The Advancement of Pure Research, 1978), 36.

187. Jawad, 120, 41.

188. Jamie Glazov, "Interview (with Ryan Mauro): Iraqi WMD Mystery Solved," *Global Politician*, March 3, 2006.

189. "Full Text of Al-Zarqawi Letter."

44: KURDS, JEWS, AND SHI'A SHOES

190. Arshak Safrastian, *Kurds and Kurdistan* (London: The Harvill Press LTD, 1948), 6.

191. Sluglett, 110–111, 130.

45: THE LITMUS TEST (NATIONAL PUBLIC RADIO AND ISRAEL)

192. Memmi, V.

193. Ibid, 34.

47: IF IT'S BIKE WEEK, IT MUST BE KRISTOF (JUAN COLE VS. DANIEL PIPES)
194. Nicholas Kristof, "Like Minds Cluster When Grazing from the Daily Me," *Daytona Beach News-Journal*, March 20, 2009.
195. Juan Cole, "Right Wing Sweeps Israel: Racialist Avigdor Lieberman Kingmaker Two State Solution Dead, Challenge to Obama," *Informed Comment* (February 11, 2009), http://www.juancole.com/2009/02/right-wing-sweeps-israel-racialist.html (accessed June 30, 2009).
196. "Debate About New Berber-Jewish Friendship Association in Morocco on Iranian Al-Alam TV." See also "The Problems with Darfur's Muslims Is."
197. "Arabist Repression Against Amazigh Students." See also "Thousands of Algerian Berbers Protest New Language Law;" and "The Moroccan Constitution Negates the Existence of the Amazigh People and Its Identity."
198. The United States Institute of Peace, "The Kurds in Syria," *Special Report*, no. 220, April 2009, www.hks.harvard.edu/cchrp/pdf/RadwanZiadeh_KurdsNSyria.pdf (accessed June 30, 2009). See also Yuksel and "Kurds in Syria."
199. "Arafat died of AIDS, Confirms Palestinian Leader," *Israel Today* (July 12, 2007), www.israeltoday.co.il/default.aspx?tabid=178&nid=13412 (accessed June 29, 2009). See also "Suspicions Grow that Arafat Died of AIDS," Forums of Pravda.ru (November 6, 2004), posted November 7, 2004, http://engforum.pravda.ru/archive/index.php/t-104335.html (accessed June 29, 2009).
200. Daniel Pipes, *Militant Islam Reaches America* (New York: W.W. Norton & Co., 2002).
201. O. Olowadare Aguda, "Arabism and Pan-Arabism In Sudanese Politics," *Journal of Modern African Studies* vol. II, no. 2, 1973, 177–178.
202. "The Constitution of the Baath Arab Socialist Party," Article 7. See also Al-Bazzaz.

49: HUGO'S PEACE PLAN
203. Satloff.
204. *Biblical Archaeology Review*, May/June 1994, 30–37.
205. "The Mesha Stele," *Wikipedia*, en.wikipedia.org/wiki/Mesha_Stele (accessed June 30, 2009). See also The Qur'an: Sura 5:20–21; Sura 17:104; and Fadlallah.
206. Lerner. See also Kornblut and Klein.

50: YA MUSTAPHA: WRAPPING IT UP (FOR NOW)...*ET TU, CZECHS?*
207. Ya Mustapha on YouTube! www.youtube.com/watch?v=DGdcCLyPC_U.
208. Hertzberg. See also Theodor Herzl, *The Jewish State (Der Judenstat)* (Mineola, NY: Dover Publications, 1989), 207–223.
209. Hatuel. See also Gabriel Schoenfeld, *The Return of Anti-Semitism* (New York City: Encounter Books, 2004); and "Incitement, Anti-Semitism, and Hatred of Israel in Palestinian School Textbooks."
210. Deir Yasin Myth Debunked, radio interviews of surviving Arabs: http://cc.msnscache.com/cache.aspx?q=israeli+accounts+of+deir+yasin&d=76035719501419&mkt=en-US&setlang=en-US&w=3188cde1,37c070ae. See also "Lying (Taqiyya and Kitman)," *TheReligionofPeace.com Guide to Understanding Islam*, www.thereligionofpeace.com/Quran/011-taqiyya.htm (accessed June 30, 2009); Gerald A. Honigman, "Taqqiyah...Or, What's Implicit About Implicit," *American Daily*, June 27, 2006, www.americandaily.com/article/14266 (accessed June 30, 2009); and Mitchell Bard, *A Guide to the Arab-Israeli Conflict* (Chevy Chase, MD: American-Israeli Cooperative Enterprise, 2002), 132–135.
211. Charles Freeman, "Blame The Lobby," *The Washington Post*, March 12, 2009; Sammy Benoit, "The Chas Freeman Controversy," *American Thinker*, March 6, 2009.
212. Cole. See also Vanly; "Syria;" and "Syria: Language Research."
213. "Barack Obama links Israel peace plan to 1967 borders deal."

214. "Blair Says Two-State Solution to Israel-Palestinian Conflict Is Top Priority." See also "Leadall: Two-State Solution Hammered Home to Netanyahu;" Schweid; and "Blair Urges U.S. to Pressure Israel."

215. "Debate About New Berber-Jewish Friendship Association in Morocco on Iranian Al-Alam TV."

216. Caroline Glick, "Column One," *The Jerusalem Post*, May 8, 2009.

217. Web site: http://www.rand.org/pubs/monograph_reports/2007/MR1287.pdf.

BIBLIOGRAPHY

"1991: The South Iraq and Kurdistan Uprisings." Libcom.org (September 9, 2006), libcom.org/history/articles/iraq-south-kurdistan-uprisings-1991.

"Abd Al-Bari Atwan, Editor-in-Chief of Al-Quds Al-Arabi Calls on Obama to Impose the American Model on Arab Countries: In an Arab Country, Obama Would Be Called a Slave; Arabs Are the Epitome of Racism." MEMRItv.org. Interview aired on BBC Arabic TV (November 7, 2008), www.memritv.org/clip/en/1906.htm.

"ADC Rejects Rumsfeld's Remarks on Israeli Occupation and Settlement Activities." American-Arab Anti-Discrimination Committee (ADC; August 8, 2002), www.adc.org/index.php?id=487.

Aguda, O. Olowadare. "Arabism and Pan-Arabism in Sudanese Politics." Journal of Modern African Studies vol. II, no. 2 (1973): 177–178.

Agyeman, Opoku. "Pan-Africanism vs. Pan-Arabism: A Dual Asymmetrical Model of Political Relations," Middle East Review (MER) (Summer 1984), American Academic Association for Peace in the Middle East (AAAPME).

al-Zarqawi, Abu Musab. "Zarqawi's Cry." National Review Online, www.nationalreview.com/document/zarkawi200402121818.asp.

Ali, Sheikh. "Holier Than Thou: The Iran-Iraq War." Middle East Review 17: 50–57.

"Ancient Hebrews—the Habiru?" What Is Matter? (August 9, 2006), www.whatismatter.org.

"Annals of Euthychius I." Twenty Centuries of Jewish Life in the Holy Land. Edited by Dan Bahat. Jerusalem: The Israel Economist, 1975.

"Anne Coulter: Jews Should Be Perfected (Video)," RightPundits.com (October 11, 2007), www.rightpundits.com/?p=948.

"Arabist Repression Against Amazigh Students," North-of-Africa.com (January 15, 2008), http://www.north-of-africa.com/article.php3?id_article=462.

"Arafat died of AIDS, confirms Palestinian leader." Israel Today (July 12, 2007), www.israeltoday.co.il/default.aspx?tabid=178&nid=13412.

"Assyrians: A Historical Summary." Assyrian Information Management, aim.atour.com/.

Aym, Zighen. "Cultural Apartheid in North Africa." The Amazigh Voice (December 1995–March 1995), www.ece.umd.edu/~sellami/DEC95/review2.html.

The Baath Arab Socialist Party National Leadership. "The Constitution of the Baath Arab Socialist Party," www.baath-party.org/eng/constitution2.htm.

"Barack Obama links Israel peace plan to 1967 borders deal," [London] Sunday Times (November 16, 2008).

Bard, Mitchell. Myths and Facts—A Guide to the Arab–Israeli Conflict. Chevy Chase, MD: American-Israeli Cooperative Enterprise (AICE), 2002.

Begin, Menachem. The Revolt (New York City: Dell Publishing Co., 1978).

Benn, Aluf and Barak Ravid. "Netanyahu to Offer U.S. 3-Part Plan for Peace Talks." Haaretz.com (April 25, 2009).

Benoit, Sammy. "The Chas Freeman Controversy." American Thinker (March 6, 2009).

"Blair Says Two-State Solution to Israel-Palestinian Conflict Is Top Priority," Voice of America News (June 27, 2007).

"Blair Urges U.S. to Pressure Israel." CBNNews.com (December 5, 2008), www.cbn.com/CBN-news/495382.aspx.

"Blame the Lobby." The Washington Post (March 12, 2009), www.washingtonpost.com/wp-dyn/content/article/2009/03/11/AR2009031103384.html.

Bois, Thomas. *The Kurds* (Beirut: Khayat Publishing Co., 1966).

Bostom, Andrew. C–SPAN Video Library Interview. Heritage Foundation Seminar, May 9, 2006.

———. *The Legacy of Jihad: Islamic Holy War and the Fate of Non-Muslims.* New York City: Prometheus, 2005.

British Ahwazi Friendship Society. "Human Rights and the Ahwazi Arabs" (July 2007), www .hlrn.org/img/violation/dossier.pdf.

———. "Israel Condemns Sweden for Supporting 'Separatism,'" (December 9, 2008), www .ahwaz.org.uk/2008/12/iran-condemns-sweden-for-supporting.html.

British Colonial Office Palestine Original Correspondence (Mandate, Jabotinsky, Separation of Transjordan etc.), 1927–1934.

Brockelmann, Carl. *History of the Islamic Peoples.* New York City: Capricorn Books, 1960.

Brooks, David. "All Hail Moore." *The New York Times* (June 26, 2004).

Burns, Nicholas. "U.S. Department of State Daily Press Briefing no. 79" (May 21, 1997), http:// www.hri.org/news/usa/std/1997/97-05-21.std.html.

Cassius, Dio. *Dio's Roman History*, translated by Earnest Cary. Cambridge, MA: Harvard University Press, n.d.

Chaucer, Geoffrey. "The Prioress' Tale." The Canterbury Tales, www.readprint.com/chapter-1772/ Geoffrey-Chaucer.

Cole, Juan. "Right Wing Sweeps Israel: Racialist Avigdor Lieberman Kingmaker Two State Solution Dead, Challenge to Obama." Informed Comment (February 11, 2009), http:// www.juancole.com/2009/02/right-wing-sweeps-israel-racialist.html.

"A Collection of Historical Quotations Relating to Arab Refugees," EretzYisroel.Org, http://www .eretzyisroel.org/~jkatz/quotes.html.

Cottam, Richard. Nationalism in Iran. Pittsburgh: University of Pittsburgh Press, 1964.

Curtis, Michael, ed. *Religion and Politics in the Middle East.* Boulder, CO: Westview Press, 1981.

———. *The Palestinians—People, History, Politics.* New Brunswick, NJ: Transaction Books, 1975.

Cyrus the Great. "Kurash (Cyrus) the Great: The Decree of Return for the Jews, 539 B.C.E." Ancient History Sourcebook, www.fordham.edu/halsall/ancient/539cyrus1.html.

Darwish, Nonie. "The Gaza Prison Camp." *The Huffington Post* (April 13, 2009).

Dayan, Moshe. *Story of My Life.* New York City: Wm. Morrow and Co., 1976.

De Atkine, Norvell B. and Daniel Pipes. "Middle Eastern Studies: What Went Wrong?" Academic Questions (Winter 1995–1996), at Daniel Pipes.org, www.danielpipes.org/392/ middle-eastern-studies-what-went-wrong.

Denenberg, Herb. "The Anti-American Fifth Column Is Based In Leading Colleges, Universities," The Bulletin (Philadelphia; January 29, 2009), http://thebulletin.us/articles/2009/01/29/ herb_denenberg/doc49814b9d2cc2f701435825.txt.

"Dennis Ross on Fox News Sunday." Transcript excerpts of Brit Hume interview with Dennis Ross on Fox News (April 21, 2002), www.foxnews.com/story/0,2933,50830,00.html.

Dershowitz, Alan. "The Real Jimmy Carter." FrontPageMagazine.com (April 30, 2007).

The Dhimmis: To Be a Jew in Arab Lands, documentary movie, Ergo Media, Inc., 1987.

Domke, D. Michelle. "Civil War in the Sudan: Resources or Religion." ICE Case Studies, no. 3, http://www1.american.edu/ted/ice/sudan.htm.

Dunlop, D. M. *Arab Civilization to A.D. 1500.* New York City: Praeger Publishers, 1971.

El Sayyad, Abdul Sattar. "The Jews in the Quran." Proceedings of the Fourth Conference of the Academy of Islamic Research. Cairo: Al Azhar, 1970. In Arab Theologians on Jews and Israel, edited by D. F. Green, 1976.

Elon, Amos. *Flight into Egypt.* New York City: Pinnacle Books, 1980.

el-Sadat, Anwar. *In Search of Identity.* New York City: Harper Colophon Books, 1977.

Everest, Larry. "How the U.S. Used Iraq's Kurds: A History of Betrayal," www.cbpa.drake.edu/ hossein-zadeh/papers/KurdsBIDOM.htm.

Fadlallah, Sayyed Muhammed Hussein. "Al-Isra'(Isra', The Night Journey, Children of Israel)." Bayynat, english.bayynat.org.lb/Quran/al_isra11.htm.

"Faisal's Trojan Horse," trans. Memri.org, Aish.com (July 2, 2001), www.aish.com/jewishissues/middleeast/Faisals_Trojan_Horse.asp.

Farah, Joseph. "Arab Leaders Caused Refugee Problem." Mid-East Realities (July 28, 2008), www.middleeast.org/forum/fb-public/1/5007.shtml.

"Farrakhan on Obama: 'The Messiah Is Absolutely Speaking.'" World Net Daily (October 9, 2008), http://www.worldnetdaily.com/?pageId=77539.

"Fatah Website Calls for Israel's Destruction." Federation of American Scientists (August 10, 1998), www.fas.org/irp/news/1998/08/980810-fatah.htm.

Fatah, Rebwar. "The Legal Status of Kurds and Other Non-Arab Ethno-Religious Groups in Syria." London: On Line Presentation/School of Oriental and African Studies (February 19, 2009).

Feili, Omran and Arlene Fromchuck. "The Kurdish Struggle for Independence." Middle East Review vol. IX (Fall 1976).

Findley, Carter Vaughn. *The Turks in World History.* New York, NY: Oxford University Press, 2005.

Fitzgerald, Hugh. "Fitzgerald: Taqiyya: A Quiz." Jihad Watch, http://www.jihadwatch.org/archives/019919.php.

Fleisher, Malkah. "Mahmoud Abbas: I Don't Accept Israel as a Jewish State." Israel National News (April 27, 2009), www.israelnationalnews.com/News/News.aspx/131055.

Franke-Ruta, Garance. "Jews in Play?" The American Prospect (April 30, 2003), www.prospect.org/cs/articles?article=jews_in_play.

"Full Text of Al-Zarqawi Letter," International Institute for Counter-Terrorism (February 12, 2004), 212.150.54.123/documents/documentdet.cfm?docid=62.

Gabriel, Brigitte, "Interview With Brigitte Gabriel," video, www.thepromiseofhome.com/Media/Interviews/BrigitteGabriel/tabid/71/Default.aspx

Gemayel, Bashir. "The Liberation of Lebanon," *Middle East Review* (Fall 1982).

"The Geneva Conventions, Law of Armed Conflict." Brookside Associates Medical Education Division, www.brooksidepress.org/Products/OperationalMedicine/DATA/operationalmed/Manuals/SeaBee/Fieldcombatopssection/LOACGenevaConventions.pdf.

Gilbert, Sir Martin. *The Jews of Arab lands: Their History in Maps.* London: Furnival Press, 1976.

Glazov, Jamie. "Interview with Ryan Mauro: Iraqi WMD Mystery Solved." Global Politician (March 3, 2006).

Glick, Caroline. "Column One." *The Jerusalem Post* (May 8, 2009).

Goitein, S. D. *Jews and Arabs: Their Contacts Through the Ages.* New York City: Schocken Books, 1955.

Golan, Matti. *The Secret Conversations of Henry Kissinger.* New York City: Quadrangle, The New York Times Book Co., 1976.

Gold, Dore. "Defensible Borders for Israel." Jerusalem Letter/Viewpoints, no. 500 (June 15–July 1, 2003), www.jcpa.org/jl/vp500.htm.

Goldschmidt Jr., Arthur. *A Concise History of the Middle East.* Boulder, CO: Westview Press, 2005.

Gottesman, Lois. "Middle East Studies in the U.S.—Combating Academic Anti-Semitism," Campus Watch (Fall 2004), www.campus-watch.org/article/id/1360.

Gottheil, Fred. "The Smoking Gun: Arab Immigration Into Palestine, 1922–1931." *Middle East Quarterly* vol. X, no. 1 (Winter 2003).

"Grass Curtain." International Institute of Social History, http://www.iisg.nl/collections/sudan1.php.

Groiss, Dr. Arnon, trans. and ed. *The West, Christians and Jews in Saudi Arabian Schoolbooks.* New York City: Center for Monitoring the Impact of Peace, American Jewish Committee, 2003.

———. *Jews, Christians, War and Peace in Egyptian School Textbooks.* Center for Monitoring

Peace and Cultural Tolerance in School Education, American Jewish Committee, 2004.
"Habiru," Wikipedia, en.wikipedia.org/wiki/Apiru.
"Hamas Covenant 1988: The Covenant of the Islamic Resistance Movement, August 18, 1988." The Avalon Project, Yale Law School, avalon.law.yale.edu/20th_century/hamas.asp.
"Harper Doubts UN Post Deliberately Targeted." CBC News (July 2006), www.cbc.ca/news/viewpoint/yourspace/un_lebanon.html.
The Hebrew Bible.
Hemingway, Mark. "Robert Malley Surfaces Again," National Review Online (November 11, 2008), www.corner.nationalreview.com/post/?q=YjdkOGI1OWQwMGI2ZTBkjI1YTA0YmVkODg3YTgyMjA=.
Hertzberg, Arthur. The Zionist Idea. New York City: Atheneum, 1959.
Herzl, Theodor. Old New Land (Altneuland). Translated by L. Levensohn. New York: Bloch Publishing Co., 1941.
Hess, E., ed. "Hatred Is Sacred" Says Syrian Minister of Education, Suleyman Al-Khash (May 1968): Extracts from Arab School Texts. Jerusalem: Ministry for Foreign Affairs, 1968.
"History of the Copts," www.copts.net/history.asp.
Hitti, Philip. History of the Arabs. London: MacMillan St. Martin's Press, 1970.
Hoge, Warren. "International War Crimes Prosecutor Gets List of 51 Sudanese Suspects." The New York Times (April 6, 2005).
Honigman, Gerald A. "The Problems with Darfur's Muslims Is . . . " North-of-Africa.com (December 10, 2007), north-of-africa.com/article.php3?id_article=455.
———. "British Petroleum Politics, Arab Nationalism, and the Kurds." Middle East Review (Fall 1982).
———. "Taqqiyah . . . Or, What's Implicit About Implicit." American Daily (June 27, 2006), www.americandaily.com/article/14266.
"Hospital concealment strengthens suspicion: Arafat died of AIDS." Israel Insider (November 11, 2004), http://web.israelinsider.com/Articles/Diplomacy/4348.htm.
Hourani, Albert. A History of the Arab Peoples. New York City: MJF Books, 1991.
Human Rights Watch. "Genocide in Iraq—The Anfal Campaign Against the Kurds" (July 1993), http://www.hrw.org/legacy/reports/1993/iraqanfal/.
Ibn Husain, 'Abdallah. Memoirs of King Abdullah of Transjordan. Edited by Peter Graves. London: Jonathan Cape, 1950.
———. My Memoirs Completed. Translated by H. Glidden. Washington, D.C.: American Council of Learned Societies, 1954.
Ibn Khaldun, 'Abd-ar-Rahman. The Muqaddimah—an Introduction to History. Edited by N. J. Dawood. Translated by Franz Rosenthal. Princeton, NJ: Princeton University Press, 1967.
"Incitement, Anti-Semitism, and Hatred of Israel in Palestinian School Textbooks." Jewish Virtual Library (November 2001), www.jewishvirtuallibrary.org/jsource/Peace/patext1.html.
"International Criminal Court Prosecutor Tells Security Council Entire Darfur Region 'Crime Scene,' Sudan Not Cooperating on Arrest of Two Indictees." United Nations Security Council, SC/9349 (June 5, 2008).
Ireland, Philip. Iraq: A Study of Political Development. London: Jonathan Cape LTD, 1937.
Israel Ministry of Foreign Affairs. "The Armistice Agreements, Vol. 1–2: 1947–1974" (January 12, 1949), www.mfa.gov.il/MFA/Foreign+Relations/Israels+Foreign+Relations+since+1947/1947-1974/THE+ARMISTICE+AGREEMENTS.htm.
"Israel's Peace Initiative, May 14, 1989," usembassy-israel.org.il/publish/peace/may89.htm.
"Israeli Elections Too Close to Call." NPR.org (February 10, 2009).
Jabotinsky, Vladimir (Ze'ev). Evidence Submitted to the Palestine Royal Commission. London: The New Zionist Press, 1937.
———. Samson the Nazirite. London: Martin Secker, 1930.

———. *The War and the Jew.* New York City: The Dial Press, 1942.

———. *Turkey and the War.* London: T. Fisher Unwin, Ltd., 1917.

Jawad, Sa'ad. *Iraq and the Kurdish Question: 1958–1970.* London: Ithaca Press, 1981.

Josephus, Flavius. *The Life and Works of Flavius Josephus.* Translated by William Whiston. New York City: Holt, Rinehart, and Winston, n.d.

Kaplan, Lee. "The Saudi Fifth Column on Our Nation's Campuses." FrontPage Magazine (April 05, 2004), http://www.frontpagemag.com/readArticle.aspx?ARTID=13551.

Katsh, Abraham. *Judaism and the Koran.* New York City: A. S. Barnes and Co., Inc., 1954.

Katz, Samuel. *Battleground—Fact and Fantasy in Palestine.* New York City: Bantam Books, 1973.

Keddie, Nikki. *The Roots of Revolution.* New Haven, CT: Yale University Press, 1981.

Kennedy, John W. "The Ultimate Kibitzer." Christianity Today (February 2009), www.christianitytoday.com/ct/2009/february/27.32.html.

Kerbaj, Richard. "Uni Draws More Fire Over Saudi Cash." The Australian (April 25, 2008), http://www.theaustralian.news.com.au/story/0,25197,23595469-5013404,00.html.

Khouri, Fred. *The Arab–Israel Dilemma.* Syracuse, NY: Syracuse University Press.

Kiernan, Thomas. *Arafat—The Man and the Myth.* New York City: W. W.Norton and Co., Inc., 1976.

"King Faisal Air Base." GlobalSecurity.org, www.globalsecurity.org/military/world/gulf/tabuk.htm.

Kirkbride, Sir Alec. *A Crackle of Thorns: Experiences in the Middle East.* London: John Murray Publishers Ltd., 1956.

Klein, Naomi. "James Baker's Double Life." *The Nation* (October 12, 2004).

Klieman, Aaron. "The Resolution of Conflicts Through Territorial Partition: The Palestine Experience." Comparative Studies in Society and History vol. 22, no. 2 (1980): 280–290.

———. *Foundations of British Policy in the Middle East: The Cairo Conference of 1921.* Baltimore, MD: The Johns Hopkins Press, 1970.

Knickmeyer, Ellen. "Darfur Slaughter Rooted In Arab-African Slavery." *The Seattle Times* (July 2, 2004).

The Koran. Translated by N. J. Dawood. Middlesex: Penguin Books, 1959.

"The Koran and the Jews." FrontPage Magazine (June 3, 2004), www.frontpagemag.com/readArticle.aspx?ARTID=12825.

Kornblut, Anne E. "The Bush Family and the Jews." Slate (April 17, 2002), www.slate.com/id/2064424/.

Kramer, Martin. *Ivory Towers on Sand: The Failure of Middle Eastern Studies in America.* Washington, D.C.: Washington Institute for Near-East Policy, 2001.

Krauthammer, Charles. "What Happened to the Powell Doctrine." *The Washington Post* (April 20, 2001).

Kredo, Adam. "Samir Kuntar's Bloody Deeds." Jerusalem Post (May 28, 2008), www.jpost.com/servlet/Satellite?cid=1211872831853&pagename=JPostpercent2FJPArticle percent2Fprinter.

Kristof, Nicholas. "Like Minds Cluster When Grazing From the Daily Me." *Daytona Beach News-Journal* (March 20, 2009).

"Kurds Being Arabized." *Israel and Palestine* (January–February, 1976): 9–10.

"Kurds in Syria." Wikipedia, en.wikipedia.org/wiki/Kurds_in_Syria.

Kurtz, Stanley. "Saudi in the Classroom." National Review Online (July 25, 2007), article.nationalreview.com/?q=YjRhZjYwMjU4MGY5ODJmM2MzNGNhNzljMzk4ZDFiYmQ=.

Kushner, Arlene. "Links to Terrorism." The Center for Near East Policy Research (October, 2004), canadiancoalition.com/unrwa/UNRWA_TerrorReport.html#_Toc86488077.

Kutschera, Chris. "Mad Dreams of Independence: The Kurds of Turkey and the PKK." Middle East Report (July–August 1994).

Landau, Jacob, ed. *Man, State, and Society in the Contemporary Middle East.* New York City: Praeger Publishers, 1972.

Lando, Barry. "History of Complicity." Salon.com (November 19, 2004), dir.salon.com/story/
    news/feature/2004/11/19/saddam_chemical_weapons/print.html.
Laqueur, Walter. *A History of Zionism*. New York City: Schocken Books, 1976.
Lasky, Ed. "Samantha Power Uncut." American Thinker (October 5, 2008), www.americanthinker
    .com/blog/2008/10/samantha_power_uncut.html.
Latham, Aaron. "What Kissinger Was Afraid of in the Pike Papers." *New York* (October 4, 1976).
Laub, Karen. "Obama Envoy: Two State Solution Is the Only Solution." Yahoo News (April 17,
    2009), news.yahoo.com/s/ap/20090417/ap_on_re_mi_ea/ml_mideast_us;_ylt=AqoqB
    pfMhdGDD9Rj4fpp9zVvaA8F.
"Leadall: Two-State Solution Hammered Home to Netanyahu," *Earth Times* (April 1, 2009).
Lenczowski, George. *The Middle East in World Affairs*. Ithaca, NY: Cornell University Press, 1962.
Lerner, Dr. Joseph. "Secretary of State James A. Baker III, Israel and Saddam Hussein." Indepen-
    dent Media Review Analysis (January 2, 2004), www.imra.org.il/story.php3?id=19323.
Lesch, Anne. *Arab Politics in Palestine, 1917–1939: The Frustration of a National Movement*.
    Ithaca, NY: Cornell University Press, 1979.
"Letters on Turkey: May 27, 2008." Middle East Studies Association, www.mesa.arizona.edu/caf/
    letters_turkey.html.
Lewis, Bernard. "The Palestinians and the PLO." Commentary Magazine (January 1975), www
    .commentarymagazine.com/viewarticle.cfm/the-palestinians-and-the-plo-5467.
Lewis, Jonathan Eric. "Iraq's Christians—Saddam Persecutes Them Too." *Wall Street Journal*
    (December 22, 2002).
Lockman, Zachary. "Behind the Battles over US Middle East Studies." Middle East Report On-
    line (January 2004).
———. "February 13, 2007." Committee on Academic Freedom Letters. Middle East Studies
    Association, www.mesa.arizona.edu/about/cafmenaletters.htm#Feb1307.
Loftus, John, and Mark Aarons. *The Secret War Against the Jews*. New York City: St. Martins
    Griffin, 1994.
"Lying (Taqiyya and Kitman)." TheReligionofPeace.com Guide to Understanding Islam, www
    .thereligionofpeace.com/Quran/011-taqiyya.htm.
MacArthur, John R. "The Vast Power of the Saudi Lobby." Harper's Magazine (April 17, 2007),
    www.harpers.org/archive/2007/04/jrm-pubnote-20070417.
Malkin, Michelle. "The Clintons' Foreign Funders." MichelleMalkin.com (Dec. 18, 2008),
    michellemalkin.com/2008/12/18/the-clintons-foreign-funders/.
Mansfield, Peter. *The British in Egypt*. New York City: Holt, Rinehart, and Winston, 1971.
"McCain Slams Obama over Foreign Policy Exposure." CBNNews.com (October 29, 2008),
    http://www.cbc.ca/world/usvotes/story/2008/10/29/mccain-latimes.html?ref%3Drss.
Mehlman, William. "The Company He Keeps." Mideast Outpost (April 25, 2009), mideastoutpost
    .com/archives/000557.html.
Meinertzhagen, Col. Richard. *Middle East Diary, 1917–1956*. London: The Cresset Press, 1959.
Meir-Levi, David. "Yasser Arafat." www.DiscoverTheNetwork.org, www.discoverthenetworks
    .org/printindividualProfile.asp?indid=650.
Memmi, Albert. *Jews and Arabs*. Chicago: J. Philip O'Hara, Inc., 1975.
"The Mesha Stele." Wikipedia, en.wikipedia.org/wiki/Mesha_Stele.
Middle East Media Research Institute. "Debate About New Berber-Jewish Friendship Associa-
    tion in Morocco on Iranian Al-Alam TV," Special Dispatch 1695, (August 24, 2007),
    http://www.memritv.org/report/en/2640.htm.
———. "Palestinian Leader: Number of Jewish Victims in the Holocaust Might Be 'Even Less
    Than a Million…' Zionist Movement Collaborated with Nazis to 'Expand the Mass
    Extermination' of the Jews." Inquiry and Analysis 95 (May 30, 2002), www.memri
    .org/bin/articles.cgi?Area=ia&ID=IA9502.

Minutes of the Permanent Mandates Commission of the League of Nations, www.domino.un
.org/UNISPAL.NSF/a47250072a3dd7950525672400783bde/ea08ec2300e1e17c0525
65ef006425ba!OpenDocument.

"Mohandas Karmachand Ghandi." Wikipedia, en.wikipedia.org/wiki/Ghandi.

"The Moroccan Constitution Negates the Existence of the Amazigh People and Its Identity." North
-of-Africa.com (March 24, 2009), north-of-africa.com/article.php3?id_article=571.

Morris, Benny. "Einstein's Other Theory." The Guardian (February 16, 2005), www.guardian.co
.uk/world/2005/feb/16/israel.india.

Moutafakis, George. "The Role of Minorities in the Modern Middle East Societies." Middle East
Review (Winter 1976).

Netanyahu, Benjamin. *A Durable Peace: Israel and Its Place Among the Nations.* New York:
Warner Books, Inc., 1993.

"New Legislation Consolidates Discrimination Against Syrian Kurds." Kurdish Human Rights
Project (October 24, 2008), www.khrp.org/content/view/412/41/.

Nicola, Nasser. "Indian-Israeli Ties Could Neutralize Delhi's Palestinian Policy." CounterCurrents
.org (April 2, 2009), www.countercurrents.org/palestine.htm.

Noll, Gregory. "Khuzestan: Oil, Ethnicity, and Conflict in Iran." ICE Case Studies no. 178 (April
2006), www1.american.edu/ted/ice/khuzestan.htm.

"Notes on Muhammadanism," Wikipedia, en.wikisource.org/wiki/Notes_on_Muhammadanism.

"Obama's Pro-Hamas Church." Investor's Business Daily (March 25, 2008), www.ibdeditorials
.com/IBDArticles.aspx?id=291335140632942.

"Occupied Palestinian, Arab Land Is Real Estate Won: Rumsfeld." IslamOnline.net, www
.islamonline.net/English/news/2002-08/08/article13.shtml.

Oded, Arye. "The Islamic Factor in Afro-Arab Relations." *Middle East Review* (Fall 1974).

Oren, Michael. *Six Days of War.* Oxford: Oxford University Press, 2002.

Palazzi, Shaykh Prof. Abdul Hadi. "What the Qur'an Really Says." The Temple Mount in Jerusalem, www.templemount.org/quranland.html.

"Palestinian Nationalism." Wikipedia, en.wikipedia.org/wiki/Palestinian_nationalism.

Parks, James. *A History of Palestine From 135 A.D. to Modern Times.* New York City: Oxford
University Press, 1949.

Peters, F. E. *The Harvest of Hellenism.* New York City: Simon & Schuster, 1970.

Peters, Joan. *From Time Immemorial.* New York City: Harper & Row, 1984.

Pfeffer, Anshel. "Jerusalem and Babylon: Courting the Jewish Vote—In the Open." Haaretz.com
(2009), www.haaretz.com/hasen/spages/1037268.html.

Phares, Walid. "The Oppression of Middle East Christians: A Forgotten Tragedy." Arabic Bible
Outreach, www.arabicbible.com.

Phillips, James. "End Hamas Hostage Strategy to Bring Peace to Gaza." The Heritage Foundation
(January 6, 2009), www.heritage.org/Research/MiddleEast/wm2188.cfm.

———. "The Floundering Oslo Peace Process." The Heritage Foundation (May 28, 1998), www
.heritage.org/Research/MiddleEast/EM528.cfm.

Pipes, Daniel. "The Muslim Claim to Jerusalem." Middle East Quarterly (September 2001),
www.danielpipes.org/84/the-muslim-claim-to-jerusalem.

———. "The Refugee Curse." New York Post (August 19, 2003), DanielPipes.org, www
.danielpipes.org/1206/unrwa-the-refugee-curse.

———. *Militant Islam Reaches America.* New York: W. W. Norton and Co., 2002.

Polk, William R. *The Arab World.* Cambridge, MA: Harvard University Press, 1980.

Porath, Yehoshua. *The Emergence of the Palestinian-Arab National Movement, 1918–1929.*
London: Frank Cass, 1974.

"Powell Doctrine." Wikipedia, en.wikipedia.org/wiki/Powell_Doctrine.

Powell, Colin. "Excerpts from Colin Powell, 'US Forces: The Challenges Ahead,' Foreign Affairs,

Winter 1992." Brooklyn College, academic.brooklyn.cuny.edu/history/johnson/powell.htm.

"Pregnant Mum (Tali Hatuel) Gunned Down." *The Sydney Morning Herald* (May 3, 2004).

"President George W. Bush: Remarks in Birmingham, Ala., Nov. 3, 2003." Defend America, www.defendamerica.mil/iraq/nov2003/usviews110303.html.

"Protocol Additional to the Geneva Conventions of 12 August 1949, and relating to the Protection of Victims of International Armed Conflicts (Protocol I), 8 June 1977." International Committee of the Red Cross, International Humanitarian Law–Treaties and Documents, http://www.icrc.org/ihl.nsf/COM/470-750046?OpenDocument.

"Rabat Forbids Berber Names." North-of-Africa.com (February 23, 2009), north-of-africa.com/article.php3?id_article=563.

Rabinowitz, Beila. "Hamas in Ascendance as the 'Mother of All Turf Wars' Begins in Gaza." MilitantIslamMonitor.org (January 27, 2006), www.militantislammonitor.org/article/id/1589.

Rauch, Jonathan. "Why Bush (Senior) Didn't Blow It in the Gulf War." ReasonOnline (October 27, 2001), www.reason.com/news/show/34590.html.

Raymond, Ibrahim. "The Coptic Conundrum." *The American Thinker* (October 26, 2008).

———. "War and Peace—and Deceit—in Islam." Middle East Forum/Pajamas Media (February 12, 2009), www.meforum.org/2066/war-and-peace-and-deceit-in-islam.

Rehov, Pierre (Producer). *The Trojan Horse*, 1992. Produced in France with English subtitles, http://www.pierrerehov.com/trojanhorse.htm.

"Report: Arab Funding of Important Subjects in UK Universities: A Degree of Influence." Islamization Watch (March 31, 2009), islamizationwatch.blogspot.com/2009/03/arab-funding-of-important-subjects-in.html.

"Robert Malley." Discoverthenetworks.org, www.discoverthenetworks.org/individualProfile.asp?indid=2310.

Rosenberg, Adrea. "The Middle East Slave Trade." *Middle East Review* (Winter 1976–1977): 60–62.

Rostow, Eugene. "Resolved: Are the Settlements Legal? Israeli West Bank Policies." *The New Republic* (October 21, 1991).

———. *Peace in the Balance—The Future of U.S. Foreign Policy*. New York City: Simon and Schuster, 1972.

Rotberg, Robert I. "Sudan and the War in Darfur." Foreign Policy Association, Great Decisions, 2005.

Roumani, Maurice. *The Case of the Jews from Arab Countries: A Neglected Issue*. Tel Aviv: World Organization of Jews from Arab Countries, 1978.

Rubin, Barry. "The Terror and the Pity." *Middle East Review of International Affairs* vol. 6, no. 1 (March 2002).

Sachar, Howard. *The Emergence of the Middle East*, 1914–1924. New York City: A. Knopf, 1969.

Safian, Alex. "The Robert Malley-Arafat Connection." Committee for Accuracy in Middle East Reporting in America (CAMERA; February 2, 2008).

Safrastian, Arshak. *Kurds and Kurdistan*. London: The Harvill Press, Ltd., 1948.

Salibi, Kamal. "The Lebanese Identity." *Middle East Review* (Fall/Winter 1982–1983).

"Samir Kuntar." Wikipedia, en.wikipedia.org/wiki/Samir_Kuntar.

Sassani, Jaff. "Kurdish Nation Political Histories Are Full of Failed Struggles to Achieve Independence for Kurds." The Sassanian Kurd Defense Committee (SKDC), jaff-sassanie.com/ShowContent.aspx?id=155&language=E.

Satloff, Robert. "The Mecca Accord: The Victory of Unity Over Progress." The Washington Institute for Near East Policy. Policy Watch, no. 1195 (February 12, 2007).

Schoenfeld, Gabriel. *The Return of Anti-Semitism*. New York City: Encounter Books, 2004.

Schweid, Barry. "Tony Blair Holds Out Hope for Two-State Solution." The Washington Post (May 14, 2009) www.washingtonpost.com/wp-dyn/content/article/2009/05/14/AR2009051403723.html.

"Seven Principles of Media Objectivity." Honest Reporting, www.honestreporting.com/a/media_objectivity.asp.

Shamoun, Sam. "Muhammad's Changing of the Qiblah." Answering Islam, www.answering-islam.org/Shamoun/qiblah.htm.

Shanzer, Jonathan. "Follow the Money Behind Anti-Israel Invective on Campus." CAMERA On Campus (Spring 2009).

Shapiro, Simona. "Iraq War Pushes Little-Known Assyrians to Fore." *The Jewish Daily Forward* (April 4, 2003).

Shaw, Stanford. *History of the Ottoman Empire and Modern Turkey*, vol. I. Cambridge, MA: Cambridge University Press, 1976.

Shechtman, Joseph. *Fighter and Prophet—The Last Years*. New York City: T. Yoseloff, 1961.

———. *The Vladimir Jabotinsky Story: Rebel and Statesman—The Early Years*. New York City: T. Yoseloff, 1956.

"Sheikh Izz ad Din al-Qassam." Encyclopedia of the Middle East, www.mideastweb.org/Middle-East-Encyclopedia/sheikh_izz_ad-din_al-qassam.htm.

Simons, Dr. Chaim. "Israel's Title to and the Legality of Jewish Settlement in Hebron." The Collected Writings of Rabbi Dr. Chaim Simons (June 2007), www.geocities.com/chaimsimons/hebronlegality.html.

Sinai, Anne and Allen Pollack, eds. *The Syrian Arab Republic*. New York City: AAAPME, 1976.

———. *The Hashemite Kingdom of Jordan and the West Bank*. New York City: AAAPME, 1977.

Sinai, Anne, ed. "Ethnic and Religious Minorities in the Middle East." *Middle East Review* (Spring 1977).

———. "The Positions of the Palestinian Organizations." *Middle East Review* (Fall 1974).

"Slavery." Encyclopedia Britannica's Guide to Black History, www.britannica.com/blackhistory/article-24160.

Sluglett, Peter. *Britain in Iraq: 1914–1932*. London: Ithaca Press, 1976.

Sorkhabi, Rasoul. "Einstein and the Indian Minds: Tagore, Ghandi and Nehru." Current Science vol. 88, no.7 (April 10, 2005): 1187–1191, http://www.ias.ac.in/currsci/apr102005/1187.pdf.

Stakelbeck, Erick. "Public Schools Teach the ABCs of Islam," CBNNews.com (January 9, 2009), http://www.cbn.com/cbnnews/460652.aspx.

———. "Saudis Multi-Million Dollar PR Machine," Campus Watch (March 10, 2008), http://www.campus-watch.org/article/id/4891.

Stillman, Norman. *The Jews of Arab Lands*. Philadelphia, PA: Jewish Publication Society of America, 1979.

"Syria." U.S. Department of State (February 18, 2005), www.state.gov/g/drl/rls/hrrpt/2004/41732.htm.

"Syria: Language Research." U.S. English Foundation Research, www.usefoundation.org/view/841.

Tacitus. *The Works of Tacitus*, Oxford Translation, vol. II. New York City: Harper and Brothers Publishers, 1898.

"Thousands of Algerian Berbers Protest New Language Law." North-of-Africa.com (July 25, 1998).

Toameh, Khaled Abu. "PA officials 'surprised' by US Middle East plan." *The Jerusalem Post* (May 21, 2009).

Tristam, Pierre. "Barbarism Beneath Israel's Boot." *Daytona Beach News-Journal* (April 9, 2002). Found at Candide's Notebooks, www.pierretristam.com/Bobst/Archives/C040902.htm.

Tutwiler, Margaret. "State Department Briefing No. 5." U.S. Department of State Electronic Research Collections (January 9, 1992), dosfan.lib.uic.edu/ERC/briefing/daily_briefings/1992/9201/005.html.

"U.S. Copts Association, www.copts.com.

"UN Security Council Resolution 242—Definition." WordIQ.com, www.wordiq.com/definition/UN_Security_Council_Resolution_242.

"Under Fire Palestinian Leader Gets Obama's First Call." ABS-CBN News (January 22, 2009), www.abs-cbnnews.com/world/01/21/09/under-fire-palestinian-leader-gets-obamas-first-call.

"United Nations an Accomplice in Hezbollah Kidnapping." The Volokh Conspiracy (July 21, 2006), volokh.com/posts/1153523571.shtml.

"United Nations Relief and Works Agency for Palestine Refugees in the Near East." Wikipedia, en.wikipedia.org/wiki/UNRWA.

"United Nations Security Council Resolution 242." Wikipedia, en.wikipedia.org/wiki/UN_Security_Council_Resolution_242.

The United States Institute of Peace. "The Kurds in Syria." Special Report, no. 220 (April 2009), www.hks.harvard.edu/cchrp/pdf/RadwanZiadeh_KurdsNSyria.pdf.

"UNPO Resolution in Support of Indigenous Ahwazi Arabs in Iran," Unrepresented Nations and Peoples Organization (June 27, 2005), www.unpo.org/content/view/2697/236/.

"Using the Civilian Population in the Gaza Strip as Human Shields." Intelligence and Terrorism Information Center at the Israel Intelligence Heritage and Commemoration Center (January 21, 2008), www.terrorism-info.org.il/malam_multimedia/English/eng_n/pdf/hamas_e049.pdf.

Uslu, Emrullah. "Ankara Considering PKK's Proposals on Dialog." Eurasia Daily Monitor volume 6, issue 88.

Vali, Ferenc. The Turkish Straits and NATO. Stanford: The Hoover Institution Press, 1972.

Van Bruinessen, Martin. Agha, Shaikh, and State: On the Social and Political Organization of Kurdistan. Rijswijk: Netherlands Organization for the Advancement of Pure Research, 1978.

Vanly, Ismet Cherif. The Syrian "Mein Kampf" Against the Kurds: The Kurdish Problem in Syria: Plans for the Genocide of a National Minority. Amsterdam, 1968.

"Vice President Cheney Delivers Remarks to the Republican Governors Association." The White House (October 25, 2001), georgewbush-whitehouse.archives.gov/vicepresident/news-speeches/speeches/vp20011025.html.

"Video: Gaza Is an Israeli Concentration Camp." Patrick Buchanan: Right from the Beginning (January 16, 2009), buchanan.org/blog/video-buchanan-gaza-is-an-israeli-concentration-camp-1355.

"Video: Islamic Jihad's Insight into Pallywood." Honest Reporting (March 17, 2008), www.honestreporting.com/articles/45884734/critiques/new/Video_Islamic_Jihads_Insight_into_Pallywood.asp.

Von Grunebaum, G. E. Modern Islam—The Search for Cultural Identity. New York: Random House/Vintage Books, 1964.

Wadhams, Nick. "ICC Presents Evidence of Mass Deaths in Sudan." IOL News (June 15, 2006), www.iol.co.za/index.php?set_id=1&click_id=68&art_id=qw1150357860174B252.

Wahed, Joseph. "Jews Are Our Dogs." The New York Sun (August 22, 2006).

"What did the Arabs do about Jordan's annexation of the parts of Palestine they captured?" Palestine Facts, www.palestinefacts.org/pf_1948to1967_jordan_annex.php.

"The War of the Zionist Right Against Sari Nusseibeh." MidEast Web (January 6, 2008), www.mideastweb.org/log/archives/00000665.htm.

Watanabe, Teresa. "Church Plans Divestment Vote Over Israel Issues." Los Angeles Times (April 30, 2005).

Watt, W. Montgomery. *Muhammad—Prophet and Statesman*. London: Oxford University Press, 1961.

Wellhausen, Julius. *The Arab Kingdom and Its Fall*. Translated by M. G. Weir. Calcutta: University of Calcutta Press, 1927.

Westervelt, Eric. "Israeli Nationalist Expected to Gain in Election." National Public Radio (February 9, 2009), www.npr.org/templates/transcript/transcript.php?storyId=100436058.

"What Led to the 1993 Oslo Peace Negotiations?" Palestine Facts (2009), www.palestinefacts.org/pf_1991to_now_oslo_background.php.

"Who Are the Kurds?" PBS Online NewsHour (September 6, 1996), www.pbs.org/wgbh/pages/frontline/shows/saddam/kurds/.

"Yasser Arafat." NobelPrize.org, nobelprize.org/nobel_prizes/peace/laureates/1994/arafat-bio.html.

Ye'or, Bat. *The Dhimmi: Jews and Christians Under Islam*. Madison, NJ: Fairleigh Dickinson University Press/Association of University Presses Consortium, 1985.

"Yellow Badge." Boston University Theology Library Archives, sthweb.bu.edu/archives/index.php?option=com_awiki&view=mediawiki&article=Yellow_badge.

"Yellow Badge." Wikipedia, en.wikipedia.org/wiki/Yellow_badge.

Yuksel, Edip. "Yes, I Am a Kurd." Yuksel.org (Fall 1998), www.yuksel.org/e/law/kurd.htm.

"Zuheir Mohsen," Wikiquote, en.wikiquote.org/wiki/Zuheir_Mohsen.

To Contact the Author

Honigman6@msn.com